THE
LANDSCAPE
OF
Praise

A Liturgical Conference Book

The Liturgical Conference
8750 Georgia Avenue, Suite 123
Silver Spring, MD 20910-3621

THE
LANDSCAPE

OF

Praise

Readings in
Liturgical Renewal

EDITED BY

Blair Gilmer Meeks

TRINITY PRESS INTERNATIONAL
Valley Forge, Pennsylvania

Trinity Press International, P.O. Box 851, Valley Forge, PA 19482-0851

Library of Congress Cataloging-in-Publication Data

The landscape of praise : readings in liturgical renewal / edited by
    Blair Gilmer Meeks.
        p. cm.
    A collection of essays that appeared in the periodical, Liturgy,
the journal of the Liturgical Conference.
    Includes bibliographical references and index.
    ISBN 1-56338-155-9 (alk. paper)
    1. Liturgics. 2. Church renewal. I. Meeks, Blair Gilmer.
BV170.L36 1996
264 – dc20   96-33873
                                                                CIP

Printed in the United States of America

96   97   98   99   00   01   10   9   8   7   6   5   4   3   2   1

To Virginia Sloyan
Strong voice for justice and renewal

Contents

Part II
The Languages of the Liturgy

Part III
The Proclamations of the Liturgy

Part IV
There Is No East or West

Preface

How good to thank you, Lord,
to praise your name, Most High,
to sing your love at dawn,
your faithfulness at dusk....
For your work brings delight,
your deeds invite song.
(Ps. 92:2–3, 5)*

Our delight is in praising God. Whatever else divides us, we are united in that delight. This book is for students of praise, for all who will hear its diverse voices and join their delight in the praise of God. It seeks to serve all those who study liturgy as the discipline of freeing praise for exalting God, whether they are found in seminaries and university graduate programs of religious studies, in denominational and ecumenical gatherings, or in parishes and congregations where liturgy as the people's response to the redeeming God is taken seriously.

In this age of expanding access to information, we hold concurrently the impression that we are in control of our own lives and the dread that we are alone in a time and space dominated by technology. Our praise of God, as the psalmist knew, is what breaks the hold of our preoccupations and reveals a space in which God's grace may recreate us and the world. In the liturgy of praise, giving up the pride of our self-construction precedes the Spirit's making us disciples of Jesus Christ. Praise creates space and time for a landscape of freedom and joy in which we may breathe.

We learn to praise from the voices of others. The Liturgical Conference's two publications, *Liturgy* and *Homily Service,* have expressed its commitment to the renewal of worship in local assemblies and its encouragement of the movement toward Christian unity. From this memory comes accountability to the next generation. In *Landscape of Praise* the voices echo from two generations.

Landscape of Praise is an ensemble work. Its contributions were first written at the invitation of two successive *Liturgy* editors and were collected here on the advice of sixteen consultants, all teachers and liturgical practitioners at places as various as Aquinas Institute, the Washington National Cathedral and Sing Sing

---

*Psalm Text, ICEL translation from the Liturgical Psalter (copyright 1994 International Commission on English in the Liturgy, Inc. All rights reserved.)

Correctional Facility. The contributing writers — there are forty-four of them — represent a wide span of traditions and experience.

My profound thanks go to my colleagues at The Liturgical Conference for their involvement in the project. Executive director Ralph R. Van Loon, now retired, negotiated its inception. Editors Virginia Sloyan and Hilary Hayden, OSB, compiled the responses of the consultants. At all stages, Viginia's inestimable advice and perceptive eye for what is appropriate made the project viable. Thanks go also to our art consultant and intern from Wesley Theological Seminary, V. Patrick Ellis, especially for his work on the index and for finding Sr. Mary Grace Thul's drawings to accompany each section. And finally thanks to our Board of Directors and our faithful readers whose regular requests to see these articles made available for classroom and parish study led to the book's publication.

BLAIR GILMER MEEKS
editor, *Liturgy*

Contributors

WILLIAM SETH ADAMS, professor of liturgics and Anglican Studies, the Episcopal Theological Seminary of the Southwest, Austin, Texas

MARY BARBARA AGNEW, C.PP.S., assistant professor, Department of Theology and Religious Studies, Villanova University, Villanova, Pennsylvania

HORACE T. ALLEN, JR., professor of worship, Boston University School of Theology, Boston, Massachusetts; cochair, English Language Liturgical Consultation

RICHARD ALLEN BOWER, dean and rector, St. Paul's Cathedral, Syracuse, New York

WALTER BRUEGGEMANN, professor of Old Testament, Columbia Theological Seminary, Decatur, Georgia

DAVID G. BUTTRICK, professor of homiletics and liturgics, Vanderbilt University Divinity School, Nashville, Tennessee

MELVA COSTEN, professor, the Interdenominational Theological Center, Atlanta, Georgia

JOHN T. FESPERMAN, curator, Division of Musical History, National Museum of American History, Smithsonian Institution, Washington, D.C.

CATHERINE GUNSALUS GONZÁLEZ, professor of church history, Columbia Theological Seminary, Decatur, Georgia

RONALD L. GRIMES, professor of religion and culture, Wilfrid Laurier University, Waterloo, Ontario, Canada

TAD GUZIE, assistant dean, Department of Graduate Division of Educational Research, University of Calgary, Alberta, Canada

PAUL W. F. HARMS, professor emeritus of preaching, Trinity Lutheran Seminary, Columbus, Ohio

JOHN S. HASCALL, O.F.M. CAP., pastor, Holy Name of Jesus Church, Assinnins (Baraga), Michigan

J. FRANK HENDERSON, professor emeritus of bio-chemistry, University of Alberta, editor, *National Bulletin on Liturgy*, adjunct professor of liturgy, Edmonton, Alberta, Canada

ROBERT W. HOVDA, Liturgical Conference editor, 1965–78; author, "The Amen Corner," *Worship*, 1983–92; died February 5, 1992

WALTER HUFFMAN, dean of chapel and professor of worship, Trinity Lutheran Seminary, Columbus, Ohio

IRENE V. JACKSON-BROWN, independent scholar; 1993–94 scholar in residence, Schomburg Center for Research in Black Culture (New York Public Library); former research fellow, Institute for Sacred Music, Worship and the Arts, Yale University; lives in Washington, D.C.

MARGARET MARY KELLEHER, O.S.U., associate professor, Department of Religion and Religious Education, the Catholic University of America, Washington, D.C.

NATHAN R. KOLLAR, professor of religious studies, St. John Fisher College, Rochester, New York

GORDON LATHROP, professor of liturgy and worship, Lutheran Theological Seminary, Philadelphia, Pennsylvania

PAUL V. MARSHALL, associate professor of worship and pastoral theology, Yale University Divinity School, New Haven, Connecticut

JAMES NOTEBAART, director, Office of Catholic Indian Ministry, Minneapolis, Minnesota

IRENE NOWELL, O.S.B., director of community formation, Mt. St. Scholastica, Atchison, Kansas

BARBARA O'DEA, D.W., superior general, Daughters of Wisdom; lives in Rome, Italy

ELAINE J. RAMSHAW, associate professor of pastoral care, Luther Seminary in Saint Paul, Minnesota

GAIL RAMSHAW, associate professor, LaSalle University, Philadelphia, Pennsylvania

RACHEL REEDER, editor, Washington, D.C.

DON E. SALIERS, professor of theology and liturgics and Director of the Masters of Sacred Music Program, Emory University, Atlanta, Georgia

MARK SEARLE, associate professor of liturgy, the University of Notre Dame; editor of *Assembly*, Notre Dame Center for Pastoral Liturgy (1978–83); died, August 1992

FRANK C. SENN, pastor, Immanuel Lutheran Church, Evanston, Illinois; president, the Liturgical Conference

GERARD S. SLOYAN, professor emeritus of religion at Temple University; currently teaching at the Catholic University of America, Washington, D.C.

S. ANITA STAUFFER, study secretary for worship, Department for Theology and Studies, Lutheran World Federation, Geneva, Switzerland

DANIEL B. STEVICK, professor emeritus of liturgics and homiletics, Episcopal Divinity School, Cambridge, Massachusetts; lives in Swarthmore, Pennsylvania

LAURENCE HULL STOOKEY, the Hugh Latimer Elderdice Professor of Preaching and Worship, Wesley Theological Seminary, Washington, D.C.

THOMAS J. TALLEY, professor emeritus, the General Theological Seminary, New York City

SAMUEL TORVEND, editor of liturgical resources, Augsburg Fortress, Minneapolis, Minnesota

HAROLD DEAN TRULEAR, dean of first professional programs, professor of church and society, New York Theological Seminary, New York City

ANTHONY UGOLNIK, Kresge Professor of English, Franklin and Marshall College, Lancaster, Pennsylvania; priest, Saints Constantine and Helen Russian Orthodox Church, Reading, Pennsylvania

CATHERINE VINCIE, R.S.H.M., assistant professor of liturgical and sacramental theology, Aquinas Institute, St. Louis, Missouri

WYATT TEE WALKER, pastor, Canaan Baptist Church, New York City

MICHAEL WARREN, professor, Department of Theology, St. John's University, Jamaica, New York

JAMES F. WHITE, professor of liturgical studies, Department of Theology, University of Notre Dame, Notre Dame, Indiana

SUSAN J. WHITE, assistant professor of worship and spirituality, Brite Divinity School, Fort Worth, Texas

DOMINGA ZAPATA, S.H., Hispanic American consultant, Ethnic Ministries Office, Archdiocese of Chicago, Chicago, Illinois

Consultants

WILLIAM SETH ADAMS, professor of liturgics and Anglican studies, The Episcopal Theological Seminary of the Southwest Austin, Texas

HORACE T. ALLEN, JR., professor of worship at Boston University School of Theology, Boston, Massachusetts

MARK BANGERT, professor of liturgy and music, the Lutheran School of Theology at Chicago

S. MARIAN BOHEN, O.S.U., faculty, Sing Sing Correctional Facility (Ossining, New York) in New York Theological Seminary program and in Mercy College program

ANDREW D. CIFERNI, vice-president for academic affairs and academic dean, Washington Theological Union, Silver Spring, Maryland

MARY FROHLICH, assistant professor, Catholic Theological Union, Chicago, Illinois

WALTER HUFFMAN, dean of chapel and associate professor of worship, Trinity Lutheran Seminary, Columbus, Ohio

BRUCE JENNEKER, canon precentor at Washington National Cathedral, Mount St. Alban, Washington, D.C.

THERESA F. KOERNKE, I.H.M., assistant professor, Word and Worship Department, Washington Theological Union, Silver Spring, Maryland

GORDON LATHROP, professor of liturgy and worship, Lutheran Theological Seminary, Philadelphia, Pennsylvania

MARK W. OLDENBURG, associate professor of liturgics and chaplain, Lutheran Theological Seminary at Gettysburg, Gettysburg, Pennsylvania

ELAINE J. RAMSHAW, associate professor of pastoral care at Luther Seminary in Saint Paul, Minnesota

GAIL RAMSHAW, associate professor, LaSalle University, Philadelphia, Pennsylvania

LAURENCE HULL STOOKEY, the Hugh Latimer Elderdice Professor of preaching and worship, Wesley Theological Seminary, Washington, D.C.

GORDON E. TRUITT, editor of *Pastoral Music* and *Music Educator*, the National Association of Pastoral Musicians, Washington, D.C.

CATHERINE VINCIE, R.S.H.M., assistant professor of liturgical and sacramental theology, Aquinas Institute, St. Louis, Missouri

INTRODUCTION

Surveying the Landscape

FRANK C. SENN

The Landscape of Praise is a collection of essays by a number of authors representing a wide ecumenical spectrum. What is the glue that holds these pieces together? First, they all appeared in one periodical, *Liturgy*, the journal of The Liturgical Conference; and second, the authors all share broadly in the programmatic goals of the modern liturgical movement.

The Liturgical Conference has existed for more than fifty years as an organization dedicated to liturgical reform and renewal. In its early days it was a Roman Catholic organization, having been founded by Benedictines. The Conference was a product of and contributed to the modern liturgical movement that had an agenda which included the revision of liturgical rites to expose their primitive shape and content, the communitarian spirit of the liturgy, the role of the general priesthood of the baptized in the liturgy, agitation for the vernacular and the connection between worship and daily life. After the implementation of the liturgical reforms promulgated by the Second Vatican Ecumenical Council, The Liturgical Conference moved in two simultaneous directions: toward the realization of the reforms in local assemblies and toward an ecumenical approach to liturgical renewal. These two directions require further comment.

First, The Liturgical Conference has always had a pastoral base; it is not an academic society. It has been concerned with actual liturgical celebrations in real liturgical assemblies. These assemblies are primarily local. That is to say, the body of Christ that is spread throughout the world assumes concrete expression in the local community of faith, congregation or parish. The membership of The Liturgical Conference has consisted primarily of lay people and clergy who have drawn on the work of scholars.

Secondly, the ecumenical tenor of The Liturgical Conference has had two directions. First, there was an early realization that the separate churches were drawing on a common liturgical heritage (e.g., the shape of the liturgy) and facing common pastoral issues (e.g., the relationship of liturgy and culture). Issues such as lectionary reform or liturgy and justice could be more effectively grappled with together than separately. Increasingly the national Liturgical Weeks

1

sponsored by the Conference between 1940 and 1969 were attended by non-Roman Catholics, and since 1979 The Liturgical Conference has been explicitly ecumenical. The second intention of the Conference's ecumenical agenda since then has been to actively promote the unity of the churches through liturgical renewal. To the extent that prayer informs belief and that practice influences profession, similar liturgical rites and ceremonies can promote a convergence in faith and order on the local level as well as on the global level.

These two directions of the Conference — local and ecumenical — are reflected in this collection of essays. First, the articles, taken as a whole, are written by persons who are concerned with the performance of specific liturgical acts in the worship of the local assembly — but liturgical acts grounded in sound liturgical theory. Second, they are written by an ecumenical array of scholars and worship planners, representing especially the churches committed to the Western liturgical tradition. Within and across these predominantly European-American traditions are concerns also for the religiocultural traditions of African- , Asian- and Latino-Americans.

The essays are grouped into four sections which are arranged in a certain logical progression that can provide a comprehensive introduction to the theory and practice of Christian worship. The first section is foundational, dealing with the Spirit, shape and content of the liturgy as "the work of God's people." The second section deals with the "Languages of the Liturgy;" "languages" is intentionally plural because ritual action, symbol and environment serve as "visible words" that communicate the grace of God. Language serves the task of "proclamation" (section 3), forms of which include preaching, art, readings, music, ritual action and symbols. Proclamation of the word of God in these various forms is a corporate action that includes the ministries of ordained leaders of the community of faith and other liturgical leaders of the assembly. The assembly is constituted to participate in the mission of God in the world. In the fourth and last section "There Is No East or West," inculturation and intertraditional worship are explored.

Finally, this introduction inquires into the question of where we are going liturgically. The official worship books have been painstakingly compiled and implemented. Nevertheless, renewal by the churches and church renewal through the liturgy have been uneven. In some instances the vision of the liturgical assembly or the practice of liturgical actions projected in the worship books has not been understood or implemented. So, for example, the liturgical assembly is not engaged in performing its corporate and public work; the people are a captive audience on whom are inflicted the opinions and tastes of the worship leaders. Also, substantive preaching and the celebration of the eucharist on the Lord's day are still goals to be met so that the full menu of word and sacrament may be offered to God's people. In other instances superb denominational resources are ignored in the conviction that they are a hurdle in reaching the unchurched. Have the goals of the liturgical movement been accomplished, so that we must now move on to deal with other issues?

In this writer's opinion, the liturgical movement is passé only if the worship of the contemporary, local assembly does not need to connect with the worship of God's people in Christ Jesus from other times and places; if the church's liturgy can be performed by leaders only rather than enacted by the priesthood of believers; if the liturgy does not lead to believers; if vernacularization does not lead to concern for inculturation; and if inculturation does not lead to special solicitude for the culturally oppressed. I hope this book will succeed in persuading a new generation of worship leaders that the goals of the liturgical movement are still worth pursuing.

Part I

The Spirit of the Liturgy

"In baptism we move from death to new birth, from burial to resurrection, from darkness to light, from the stain of sin to the cleansing power of grace, from ourselves into the family of God. We are never the same again because the chaos and self-centeredness of our lives are washed away, and we are joined to Jesus Christ. The waters that drown us are also the waters that give us life."

— S. Anita Stauffer in *Liturgy: Dressing the Church*

Liturgy is the form of faith which both reflects and sustains the communal faith of the church; when liturgy is forgotten or malformed the consequent impact is the loss of the faith/strength of the church.

I

Liturgy as the Form of Faith

HORACE T. ALLEN, JR.

This brief article is written as its author is engaged with Reformed and Presbyterian pastors, laity and liturgical scholars, in an evaluation and definition of the renewal of worship in that family of churches. The meeting is being held, appropriately enough, at the John Knox International Reformed Centre in Geneva, Switzerland. One note of self-criticism that has constantly recurred is the danger in our tradition of liturgy's becoming highly didactic, especially when it includes children and youth who presumably must be "instructed" as to the meaning of action, language and sequence.

Worse, when we spent one evening viewing video tapes of eucharistic sequences in various European settings we were appalled to *see* just what poor and confusing "lessons" we were teaching, in terms of clerical presidential style, visual appointments, the role of music (classical and folk), deadly silences or grim speech, useless gestures and book dependence. This rather confessional preface is meant to alert the reader to problems of liturgical celebration that may extend beyond the bounds of the Reformed or Calvinist tradition. Indeed, the publication by the Holy See of the new *Catechism of the Catholic church* could itself become a pressure point by which didactic tendencies will make themselves felt in a new way in Roman Catholic circles and celebrations. Perhaps the problem we all face could be summed up by affirming as a basic principle that *the purpose of liturgy is not to instruct the community about something else.* One of my Genevan colleagues described this danger as an "instrumental" view of worship. Not only is this view inherently destructive of good worship, he observed, but it borders on the idolatrous. For Calvinists, that is strong language.

Thus the thesis of this essay is: liturgy is the form of faith. This can be ✓ expounded by asking two questions: What is faith? and What is liturgical form?

From *Liturgy: Worship That Forms Faith* 12, no. 1.

What is faith?

For the purposes of this essay one might speak of faith as *communal commitment*. However personal and private the life of faith is, especially in times of
trial, temptation and torment, at bottom faith is an experience of commitment that is received from a community, nurtured in community and finally
tested there, by word and sacrament. Opting out of that community is in
fact, therefore, the renunciation of faith (just as in another context, leaving
the community is called "excommunication"). So Calvin observes that "revolt
from the Church is denial of God and Christ."[1] This of course is the meaning of his classic dictum that "to those to whom he [God] is a Father the
Church must also be a mother."[2] However problematic these gender-specific
references may seem for some, they must be dealt with in order fully to
grasp the direction of Calvin's ecclesiology. The most obvious point is that
the locus of faith is not in the pious individual soul but in a social setting
that can only be described by the most universal corporate human reality —
which we share with much of the sentient created order — the family. So
also contends another Swiss theologian, Karl Barth: "It is not the Christian
individual as such but the community which, in its individual members and
through their reciprocal ministry, is edified, and lets itself be edified, and edifies
itself."[3]

Further, Calvin's use of this familial image of the church does need, in an
inescapable way, its gender-specific language, for it links the earthly church with
the (trinitarian?) life of the Deity in a relationship of obvious intimacy. There
is a vital sense in which the "begetting" roles of mother and father are essential
to describe the way in which individual human beings become faithful children.
And without entering into the technical, linguistic discussion of the word "father," one can at least echo biblical scholar Raymond Brown, who points out
that in the Lukan writings (the birth narratives and Acts), the images of the
church are heavily feminine (see Mary, Anna, Hannah).[4] Just so in the Pauline
corpus the images are "house," "planting" (of seed in the ground) or "bride/body
of Christ."[5]

So, as stated above, the Christian understanding of faith — and certainly that
of our Jewish "mother" — is profoundly a matter of some kind of communal,
familial experience. This is surely a concrete foundation of the church's somewhat surprising decision early in its life to baptize infants, so long as they have
been born into a family that may in some fashion and with some honesty be
defined as "Christian." The baptismal liturgy in the Presbyterian Church (USA)
is so clear on this point that it deliberately does *not* ask the questions of faith
"on behalf of" the infant being baptized, nor does it ordinarily allow for the
participation of "sponsors" or "godparents" but rather unequivocally asks those
questions of the parent(s) and the congregation present. It is of course precisely this emphasis that the creative and reforming Rite of Christian Initiation
for Adults (RCIA) of the Roman Church has recovered in Catholic contexts.

Faith is therefore, in its origins, sustenance and regular expression, a communal experience of commitment.

As a child, regularly on the Lord's Day morning, I would raise the hazardous question with my parents, "Do we *have* to go to Sunday school/church today?" knowing full well that, short of illness or domestic emergency, there actually was no question. And on the last occasion when we three worshiped together of a Christmas Eve, at the singing of the opening hymn, "O Come, All Ye Faithful," the faith consciousness struck with astonishing force: "No wonder I love this hymn: I've been singing it between these two persons for well over fifty years."

This personal anecdote raises the second thesis of the essay concerning liturgy as the particular and essential *form* of faith, personally or corporately conceived.

What is liturgical form?

It is not only in architecture that "faith takes form," though inevitably it does — for good or ill as my travels aptly demonstrated. Liturgical experiences in Geneva varied with the spaces: St. Pierre's, Calvin's *Auditoire* and then a small chapel at the John Knox Centre for a eucharist with myself as celebrant and many others from Europe, Africa, Asia and the Pacific seated on the floor around a small, low table. After Geneva there were the vast, hugely impersonal cathedrals of Florence and Berlin, the focused space of Florence's Baptistery and the wonderfully sounding spaces of the *Thomaskirche* in Bach's Leipzig, as well as his *Nicholaikirche* (which functioned in the last days of the East German state as the place of revolutionary gatherings). On the way home there was the equally resonant Gothic chapel of King's College, Cambridge, England.

Faith does "take" architectural form, but more importantly it "takes" liturgical shape, which in turn will inevitably shape that faith. However varied the liturgical experience of the universal church through its twenty centuries, there are actually only a few basic forms or structures of worship, and they have to do with sequence, setting and sensory participation. These might simply be listed as calendars (daily, weekly, annual, civil and human), Bible services, sacramental services, pastoral offices, prayer/praise/devotional rites and occasions of very personal meditation or confession. All of these forms are essential to a well-formed communal faithfulness, and *all* also require some level of mutual participation and meeting. Even where in corporate worship people seem to pay very little direct attention to one another, most, if not all, would affirm the essential importance of the presence of all the others. Nor dare we forget the seriousness with which the early church orders such as the *Apology* and the *Didache* speak of the necessity to include absent members in eucharistic participation.

Losing connections

This raises the final and perhaps most critical point (in a frankly negative sense) of this essay. As confessed in its opening paragraphs, vast and historic traditions of Christian worship have, by reason of didacticism, formalism, clericalism, loss of historical memory and triumphalism, actually destroyed the forms they inherited, including the vital relationships among those forms. Thus, for instance, "Easter" has in one tradition or another lost its connection with baptism, eucharist or the *Pascha*. And thus "Sunday" has lost its connection with Resurrection Day or eucharist or serious, thoughtful and participated proclamation. (In both of these instances the thoughtless adoption of pagan nomenclature is probably a large part of the problem.) Thus also, morning and evening meals have lost their connection with prayer, Psalter and scripture. Thus also, weddings and funerals in many Protestant contexts have largely ceased to be occasions of prayer, praise and proclamation in word and sacrament. And finally, worst of all, that classic norm of word and sacrament itself has hardly ever succeeded in being a lively, perceived unity of form. For centuries and for many traditions, either the sacrament has seemed an occasional and unnecessary "addition" to the sermon service or the sacramental service seemed not truly to need a sermon.

Small wonder therefore that in our day, when society is becoming a violent shambles and a mere skeleton of community, our forgetful churches, whose historic forms were given us to secure and form faith, are now losing out to secularism, cynicism and individualistically oriented spiritualities, charismatically preoccupied assemblies with their collapse of intentional form into mindless repetition or that final indignity to the assembled, committed local community, the living-room presence of neither word, sacrament, prayer or praise but the domination of demanding religious, even "evangelistic," entertainers.

Perhaps this essay should have carried the subtitle, "Shape Up for Faith's Sake."

Notes

1. John Calvin, *Institutes of the Christian Religion* trans. Henry Beveridge (Grand Rapids, Mich.: Wm. B. Eerdmans, 1953), 2:290.

2. Calvin (1953), 281.

3. Karl Barth, *Church Dogmatics*, IV, 2, trans. G. W. Bromiley (Edinburgh: T. & T. Clark, 1958), 627.

4. Raymond E. Brown, *The Birth of the Messiah* (Garden City, N.Y.: Doubleday, 1977), 457.

5. Barth (1958), 644.

2

Art of Our Own Making

Rachel Reeder

Usually when we experience visual, verbal or dramatic talent, we are standing before someone else's art, enjoying its beauty and truth to be sure but blessedly isolated from its creation in human struggle and pain. The liturgy, however, is art of our own making; we will not, cannot, do it well unless we are engaged in the world as wholeheartedly as God is, whose self-giving in Jesus the Christ is the archetype for every liturgical act. I hope we do not come to the liturgy as spectators, nor for entertainment or even refreshment, though on occasion it will no doubt provide us amply with both. Rather should liturgy be the simple and powerful effort of people in the midst of life to keep festival in their abundance and to make memorial in their loss, ever striving to make life better and to push its meaning to the furthest reaches of human experience.

If so, then liturgy is an art that can only get better with talent and practice. The liturgical talent belongs to everyone, though not everyone polishes it to its brightest shining; it is our responsibility for one another, our being together in God, that graces us with the ability to see and feel life complete through all its complications and contradictions. The liturgy is more than a fascinating story; it is participation in the story, the ability to listen closely to others in our neighborhoods and the world, to suffer for them and to trust them with the thread of our life's meaning, to accept them, the poor and the rich, the gifted, the not-so-gifted, the powerful and the powerless, as characters in the story. The liturgical talent is an insistent, hurting vision of the church; it is the knowledge that we can turn our backs on no one because everyone is part of our living and dying. In the liturgy we imitate the life of Christ and all that great company who, filled with God's spirit, never let go of the basic elements of earth until they win a blessing. For the most part, people who are involved in crafting the liturgy do not lack materials. Mud, blood and breath; water, bread and kinship; the moon, earth and sky belong to everyone; the art and poetry of liturgical celebration is a universal and practical affair.

From *Liturgy: The Art of Celebration* 8, no. 3.

Good liturgical expression is equivalent to care for these earthly things — for themselves, not for their usefulness to us — and respect for their part in the drama that is culture. If we let them, they may be bearers of the spirit for us, but their freedom holds the key to inculturation and its importance. Wherever the church is, or the synagogue or other worship space, there is the center of the world, the point at which all these things are distinct from human control but where, if we but cherish them, they are also malleable to human striving and becoming.

How we should do the liturgy, then, is also how we should live, but the first (liturgy) is not reducible to the second (life). Liturgy is ritual prayer, God and humankind conversing in and for and with the whole world; it must be capable of moving us to encourage one another and build one another up (1 Thess 5:10–11). Above all, the liturgy must be understood as the deed of one actor, the assembly, which is one body, though each of its members "has been given a special gift, a particular share in the bounty of Christ" (Eph 4:7). The dynamic of liturgical celebration is the same one that emerges in the life of families and community. In a spirit of love, in the liturgy as in other forms of relationship, we grow fully into Christ on whom the whole body depends: "bonded and held together by every constituent joint, the whole frame grows by the proper functioning of each part, and builds itself up in love" (Eph 4:16).

The forms of the liturgy must be replete with this truth; mutuality and intimacy of this depth must find expression in our public prayer. The handshake and the casual greeting before and during our prayer must be intentional; we must be taught again if we do not already know that our gestures, posture and movement give or withhold our presence to one another. What in our sophisticated, informal and permissive age does dressing up or down, or standing one way or another say about our presence to one another? The way we hold our hands and whether or not we make eye contact over the bread and cup — these simple actions reveal our relationship to the environment and our attitude toward one another. To forget this is to forget the plain fact of our embodiment, which makes doing the liturgy very awkward. In the same way, greeters, acolytes, readers and presider must first be members of the assembly and present to one another in love.

The art of celebration is therefore carefully prepared by our involvement in this life and by our regular immersion in some form of contemplation. The first of these, our participation in the world's redemption, was the burden of the Pauline letter reminding the citizens of Thessalonika that they were not to sit idly by ("minding everybody's business but their own," 2 Thess 3:11) while waiting for the day of the Lord. It doesn't bear thinking how its author would admonish us. Can the mayor of a major city be arrested for alleged drug abuse and not be prayed for by name in the city's churches? I have seen it happen. Can we really celebrate freedom in South Africa or Eastern Europe and not publicly mourn the children of war and poverty, the little sheep of God's pasture, who barely survive in the midst of our plenty? I have seen it happen. The news on

Sunday morning propels us into church, but when the service begins, we are on another planet.

The other side of liturgical preparedness, our immersion in some form of contemplation, also has to do with being at home in the play. We can put it this way: as liturgy is related to justice, so it requires our devotion; that is, we can stake our lives on the significance of the action. But for that we must bring whole selves to the assembly — not whole in the sense of having nothing broken — but whole in the sense that everything we are and everyone we know comes with us to the part.

"God makes a way for us," some of us will say, "which is midway between struggle and repose"; "when I enter into myself, there God is," others will say; still others may not seek to articulate their own piety — perhaps they will follow a twelve-step program or an ancient or modern monastic rule or the institutes of some religious house. But all humankind, including the very active, perhaps even the very secular, can and must live as much attuned to the imagination as to the cognitive acts of the mind. The contradiction is too great otherwise, for to love the world as God loves the world is to embrace it as it is and run with it, straining toward salvation.

3

The Spirit of the Liturgy, A Wonderland Revisited

Frank C. Senn

Romano Guardini wrote his now famous essay on "the spirit of the liturgy," in 1935.[1] Is it possible for Christians living today to speak of this spirit with anything like the confidence and comprehensiveness that Guardini achieved? At first glance the answer seems to be no. In 1935, the liturgy, especially among Roman Catholics, was experienced as an enduring, objective reality that was impervious to change. Although Guardini was an early advocate of renewal, he wrote about the liturgy as something objective — as something that stood over against people and to which people responded more or less objectively. This perception has changed drastically since Vatican II. Now the liturgy is experienced as an activity or "work of the people," and its spirit has developed in ways that Guardini never imagined.

Recent liturgical renewal

To the ancient Greeks, *leitourgia* was a political activity, not an objective reality. Its formal aspects evolved gradually, as local communities became more self-aware. The modern liturgical movement has sought to recover this adaptability to changing circumstances. Indeed, we who have served on commissions charged with the task of liturgical revision know firsthand how a political decision or a vote here or there altered the outcome of texts and rubrics. Moreover, we built a fair number of permissive rubrics into our liturgical orders. Even with this flexibility, however, some presiding ministers take liberties with the words and actions of the liturgy in order to make the experience more relevant to or inclusive of people in the liturgical assembly. On both counts we experience

---

From *Liturgy: In Spirit and Truth* 5, no. 3.

the liturgy not as an objective reality but as the changing self-expression of a community concerned to renew its life and revitalize its mission. In Roman, reformed and free-church traditions, the liturgy must be an authentic expression of the assembly.

Nevertheless, once a community adopts expressions of its identity, they tend to become objective standards — the community's rule and norm. The "memoirs of the apostles" that were read in Christian liturgical assemblies during the second century became authoritative through liturgical use even before they became canonical scripture. The Bible is the church's book, but once canonized it stands in judgment over the church. The same is true of creeds and liturgies. The acts of confessing and praying in the spirit of Christ become our *lex credendi, lex orandi*. The worship books adopted in the 1970s become the liturgical norms of the 1980s.

In addition to liturgical adaptability, the modern liturgical movement has sought a recovery and adaptation of tradition that enables the local liturgical assembly to be conscious of living in unity not only with other contemporary assemblies but also with confessing and praying Christians of other times and places.

This recovery of the church as a "communion of saints" goes hand in hand with a recovery of the eschatological consciousness of early Christianity. In turn, this tradition makes us aware of the transcendental or eternal dimensions of Christian community and liturgy. We offer the sacrifice of praise and thanksgiving "with the church on earth and the hosts of heaven."

Liturgical renewal has expanded our consciousness of who the church is. Though we don't meet in the same kinds of buildings, speak the same languages or sing the same tunes as Christians of other times and places, we know we are still engaging in the same kinds of ritual activities. Down through the centuries, from one continent to another, Christians have assembled on the Lord's day to hear the word of God, celebrate the sacraments of Christ, confess their sins, profess their faith, praise the Holy Trinity and pray for the world. Comparative studies have demonstrated how remarkably similar the "shape of the liturgy" is in various ecclesial traditions.[2]

It is clear, therefore, that the essential elements of Christian liturgy have not changed that greatly since 1935, and we may indeed speak with confidence about the spirit of the liturgy.

Sacrament of encounter

Liturgy is not a book; it is an encounter between God and Christians, and between Christians and the world. Guardini began his essay by speaking of "the prayer of the liturgy," but the liturgy is not simply prayer. Liturgy is first and foremost rite.[3] It is a pattern of action that comprehends both what the church does when it confesses and prays, and also what God does through the proclamation of the word and the administration of the sacraments. The "public work" that is done when the assembly for word and sacrament convenes is not only the work of the people but the work of God as well — the divine service.[4]

The communication that takes place in the liturgical event is more than the transmission of propositions. Relationships are formed and reformed and life is affirmed. This happens not just with words but by words joined to a bath, a laying on of hands, a sharing of bread and cup. In these and other ritual actions, God's speaking becomes "visible." God is as embodied in the divine word as we are in human speech. There is no escaping this visible, palpable reality unless we eschew both God and ritual. Christianity is incarnational; it can never dispense with sacramental and sacrificial acts. Even when Christians meditate apart from ritual, they do so not to be absorbed into an eternal void but to be filled with the word of the God who not only claims us for God's own but also gives God's self to us in perfect love.

Objective and subjective

In a balanced psychology of the liturgy, a realm of numinous reality becomes an "objective" phenomenon through "visible words," and this phenomenon is experienced subjectively by the worshiper. In this view, we are not as hesitant as Guardini to regard liturgy as an emotional experience. We take for granted that it will have some kind of emotional impact on the worshipers. If we know enough about the sociological and psychological situation of the congregation and how they experience the relationship between worship and daily life, we can even plan and perform liturgy to elicit a certain emotional response. The question that needs to be asked is whether liturgy should be designed to have a particular emotional impact on people. Do we really know the point at which the word of God must address the individual? Can we really assume that we know the directions in which the Holy Spirit wills to lead the church?

There is a growing emphasis on the subjectivity of liturgy today. This emphasis is no doubt a well-intentioned effort to make liturgy relevant to personal and social life, and it affects especially the use of certain kinds of music, ranging from gospel songs to Christian "popular" tunes. Yet to understand subjectivity properly and to correct certain aberrations, it is time to reconsider Guardini's words on "the spirit of the liturgy." Prayers should be voiced with feeling, but they should also be informed by theology. We believe that liturgy should be expressive of the life and mission of the church; it should also be conducted with the kind of reserve that gets worship leaders out of the way of God's word. We are rightly concerned that liturgy reflect the indigenous culture of the people whose public work it is, but does not the Christian calling to live "in but not of" the world require a transcultural exposure that also preserves a sense of the church's catholicity and its eschatological character?

Guardini taught that the liturgy should be characterized by theological thought, a reserved style and transcultural expressions because it is the public work of the whole people of God. As he put it, "The liturgy is not celebrated by the individual but by the body of the faithful."[5] Each individual must be able to participate in such a way that the whole church should be edified. The spirit of the liturgy resists individualism.

To be sure, each Christian has a unique relationship with God, an obligation to apply the word of God to life and to pray. But the liturgy is the public proclamation of the word of God, the celebration of the sacraments and the sacrificial response of the church to the grace of God. Because of its public character it is presided over by officially called ministers who have been authorized to fill this role. As the self-expression of the church, liturgy has a communitarian character and it forms a corporate spirituality.[6] That is to say, the individual is incorporated into the Christian community by God's sacramental action, and this incorporation into the community determines one's identity, vocation and destiny.

Discerning the spirits

"To each is given the manifestation of the Spirit for the common good" (1 Cor 12:7). Paul could not imagine a Christian community in which some members were without a gift to contribute to the whole. And just as individuals were ungrateful to the Spirit if they withheld their gifts, so was the community ungrateful if it failed to find a use for all gifts. But discovering the gifts of the members also means testing the spirits.

All who perform a liturgical role must be recruited, trained and tested. The possible contributions of all members of the congregation must be sought out, evaluated and recognized just as carefully as we seek candidates for ordination. Some people may put themselves forward for questionable motives, or they may not have the necessary gift for a liturgical ministry. As those who cannot effectively preach or teach or preside should not be ordained to the ministry of word and sacraments, so those who cannot read in public should not serve as lectors; those who cannot be gracious hosts should not serve as ushers; those who cannot carry a tune should not sing in the choir. It may be painful to have to search for other ways in which individuals can serve the church, but the ideals of participatory democracy and fair play must be carefully balanced with the charismatic constitution of the church.

Artists especially should realize that they serve the whole community. Musicians, poets, visualgraphic and handicraft artists exercise a diaconal role in their liturgical ministry. They must develop two skills, the ability to work with committees and to accept constructive criticism. Conversely, the community must learn to recognize the artists' gifts and to accept the challenge of their insights. As the spirit of the liturgy abhors spiritual isolation, so it also requires self-sacrifice. C. S. Lewis's words about church music can be applied to all the liturgical arts. A blessing rests on the musician who gives people humbler fare than he or she might want and on the people who listen to music they cannot fully appreciate. "To both church music will have been a means of grace; not the music they have liked but the music they have disliked."[7]

The style of liturgy

If liturgy is the "public work of the whole people of God" and if each member of the church contributes to this effort according to the gift received, then the style of liturgy will be determined, to some extent, by the gifts available to a particular liturgical assembly, some of which are the gifts of social groups expressed through their culture.

Christian liturgy retains traces of the various cultures through which it has passed and to which it has been adapted. We chant a Hebrew "Amen," sing Greek canticles, pray the rhythms of Latin rhetoric, assemble in Gothic buildings, listen to German chorale preludes and extend an American handshake at the greeting of peace. In recent times the liturgy has been translated into new modes so that it may better express and reflect developments in various cultures. In America, the religious experience of black and Hispanic cultures is increasingly recognized in the liturgy, and the adaptation of cultural idioms in Africa and Asia provide other fascinating examples of indigenization. So how is it still possible for the liturgy to be, as Guardini said, "accessible to people of every condition, time and place"?[8]

The enculturation of the liturgy was not a question for Guardini, who simply assumed the endurance of the Greco-Latin spirit as the underlying cultural style of the liturgy. That cannot be assumed even of Roman liturgy today, and it does not take into account the ecumenical contributions of the reformed and free churches of northern Europe and North America. Yet this does not mean that Guardini's principle should be ignored.

What we can say is that liturgy must be accessible to all who comprise a particular assembly in all of its various manifestations: local congregation, regional diocese or synod, national convention or ecumenical council. Since liturgy is a public statement of the church's identity, it requires the distinctive contribution of each group of people within the church. At the same time the spirit of self-sacrifice requires each group to realize that they are not the totality of the church. Thus, some modes of expression in the liturgy will speak more to one group than to others, but there must be room for all the groups to make their contributions. The repertory of even a small community may range from Latin plainsong to German chorales, and from English part-songs to gospel songs and Hispanic folk music. Even if the local assembly does not actually reflect such cultural diversity, these varied styles remind it that it is part of the church catholic. Catholic liturgy cannot be otherwise than inclusive and pluralistic; it draws on the past as well as the present.

Symbols

The use of natural symbols is another way that the spirit of the liturgy survives as a universal in the midst of great cultural particularity. Guardini wrote that

> a genuine symbol is occasioned by the spontaneous expression of an actual and particular spiritual condition. But at the same time, like works of art, it must rise above the purely individual plane.... Consequently when a symbol has been created, it often enjoys widespread currency and becomes universally comprehensible and significant.[9]

Cultural studies show that the meanings of symbols are conditioned by social experience. There is not only the bread of nourishment but the bread of affliction. Symbols arise from social experience and speak to social need. For this reason symbols abound in multiple meanings, even though a particular culture may relate to only one special interpretation of a natural action such as bathing or dining. Still, multiple meanings are developed as the ritual action or material is carried into new times and places.

Recently there has been an effort to strip down the layers of interpretation to let the basic natural meanings of symbols emerge. Eucharistic theology, for example, has concentrated less on memorial and sacrifice and more on meal and fellowship. But as David Power has warned, "Any attempt to reduce the significance of liturgical symbols and speech to a single or preconceived meaning thwarts their efficacy."[10]

At play before the Lord

Guardini was one of the first to see that liturgy is a form of play:

> The liturgy wishes to teach but not by means of an artificial system of aim-conscious educational influences; it simply creates an entire spiritual world in which the soul can live according to the requirements of its nature.
>
> The liturgy is to purposeful spiritual exercises as play in the open fields is related to the gymnasium in which every game aims at a calculated effect.[11]

The spirit of the liturgy resists utilitarianism. As Gabriel Braso put it,

> The liturgy is not so much interested in immediate, easily controllable results as in a normal life flowing along regularly and without disturbance. The liturgy requires a disinterested, generous spirit, capable of wide horizons which are not always compatible with the concrete, tangible interests of a religious pragmatism.[12]

Liturgy opposes an ethos of practical usefulness and the programmatic interests of the institutional church. This ethos distorts liturgy by using it in the service of education, evangelism, stewardship and other functions of church life. It is not that liturgy does not teach or proclaim the gospel or provide opportunities for individuals to use their time, talents and treasures; but this is not what liturgy is for. Liturgy is the encounter between God and people, and what happens in this encounter or what results from it cannot be managed or predicted.

The spirit of the liturgy also resists aestheticism. Utilitarianism uses liturgy as the means to an end; aestheticism views liturgy as an end in itself. The value of liturgy is determined by the canons of beauty — good music, attractive furnishings, dignified vestments. Guardini was alert to the danger that "the liturgy will first be the subject of general eulogy, then gradually its various treasures will be estimated at their aesthetic value, until finally the sacred beauty of the house of God comes to provide a delicate morsel for the connoisseur."[13]

The German poet M. Hausmann criticized aestheticism when he voiced misgivings to T. S. Eliot about the suitability of Bach's *St. Matthew Passion* as a liturgical form. Used in this way, he contended, Bach's music is like being pleasantly told that one's brother has been killed in a concentration camp under terrible circumstances.[14] There's no doubt that Bach's passion music sheds profound spiritual and theological light on the passion narratives, but the reality of Good Friday is so stark that for centuries the church has not celebrated eucharist on this day and has preferred that no instruments be used to accompany singing at this liturgy. Sometimes the liturgy may prefer ugliness to beauty as a more appropriate expression of the divine and human encounter. The holy is *tremendum* as well as *fascinans;* it repels as well as attracts.

In, but not of, the world

Just as Guardini insisted that in liturgy truth is more important than beauty, so he insisted that truth is more important than ethics or moral order. He expressed this as "the primacy of the logos over the ethos."[15] Liturgy does not tell us how to live (ethos), but it gives us a vision of life (logos) which makes us uneasy with any ethos that is less than what God intended.

We are concerned about life in this world, of course. If our worship has any integrity, if it is done in spirit and truth, it will articulate our experience of the world and human history. As David Power has asked, "Can we in truth celebrate eucharist after the Nazi Holocaust and in the face of an imminent nuclear holocaust, and in a world half-populated by refugees, in the same way as we did before the occurrence of such horrors?"[16] We cannot, and so liturgy will change to express contrition as well as celebration, lament as well as praise. Always our liturgy will communicate our sorrow for the world as it is, our lament for the human situation, our vision of the end of all things.

The eschatological symbols that express our vision, our logos, are irrelevant to life in our secularized society: angels and archangels and all the company of heaven, the victory song to the lamb upon the throne, the maranatha. Such symbols appear, at least, to be esoteric and exclusive. Because the word whose life is fateful for all human life is revealed on its own terms and because those who have come to know the word have a special vision of human destiny, Christian liturgy must be esoteric and exclusive as far as "this world" is concerned. The liturgy of the eschatological community is relevant to the vocation and need of Christians to live "in, but not of, the world." The spirit of the liturgy is ultimately an eschatological spirit. The disciples of the risen Lord gather for this work on the Lord's day precisely because it is "the last and great day." In the spirit of the liturgy, they are disengaged from the world in order to begin the world all over again.

Notes

1. Romano Guardini, *The Church and the Catholic and the Spirit of the Liturgy*, trans. Ada Lane (New York: Sheed and Ward, 1953), 119–211.

2. Cf. Frank C. Senn, *Christian Worship and Its Cultural Setting* (Philadelphia: Fortress, 1983), 20–30.

3. Cf. Aidan Kavanagh, *On Liturgical Theology* (New York: Pueblo, 1984), 100ff.

4. Cf. Peter Brunner, *Worship in the Name of Jesus*, trans. Martin H. Bertram (St. Louis: Concordia Publishing House, 1968).

5. Guardini, "The Spirit of the Liturgy," 141.

6. Cf. Gabriel M. Braso, *Liturgy and Spirituality*, 2nd ed., trans. Leonard J. Doyle (Collegeville, Minn.: Liturgical Press, 1971), 99ff.

7. Cf. C. S. Lewis, *Christian Reflections*, ed. Walter Hooper (Grand Rapids: Wm. B. Eerdmans, 1967), 96–97.

8. Guardini, "The Spirit of the Liturgy," 159.

9. Ibid., 167.

10. David Power, *Unsearchable Riches: The Symbolic Nature of Liturgy* (New York: Pueblo, 1984), 67.

11. Guardini, *The Church*, 177.

12. Braso, *Liturgy and Spirituality*, xv.

13. Guardini, *The Church*, 196.

14. Cf. Paul W. Hoon, *The Integrity of Worship* (New York and Nashville: Abingdon, 1971), 69.

15. Guardini, *The Church*, 199.

16. David Power, "Liturgy, Memory and the Absence of God," *Worship* 57 (1983): 328.

4

The Bible and Christian Prayer

Gerard S. Sloyan

Augustine put the question to himself: "What is time?" He answered:

> If no one asks me, I know; if I want to explain it to someone who asks me, I do not know. Yet I state confidently that I know this: if nothing were passing away there would be no past time, and if nothing were coming, there would be no future time, and if nothing existed, there would be no present time.... If the present, so as to be time, must be so constituted that it passes into the past, how can we say that it is, since the cause of its being is the fact that it will cease to be? Does it not follow that we can truly say it is time, only because it tends to non-being?[1]

For page after page of that well-known eleventh chapter, the ingenious philosopher bishop put questions of this sort to himself and attempted answers that neither the Jews of the Bible nor the early Christian writers could have understood. They thought profoundly about time, but they did so in nothing like the neo-Platonist way that characterized this church father.

Time as a cultural obsession

Our modern situation is that we do not reflect on time in the manner of either Greco-Roman philosophers or biblical Jews. Consequently, turning to one or the other as a source of enlightenment on forms of Christian prayer as they relate to time may not be very helpful. But our culture is obsessed with time. We count it very valuable, measure our lives by it, reckon all sorts of things by time. (An Indian visitor remarked to me once in exasperation that no one had any idea of *distances* in America. "If you ask how far it is to Cleveland or Baltimore, you get an answer in hours! The people here have never heard of miles!") We time ourselves when trying an alternate route. We will do almost anything to save time. Avoiding things that are "a waste of time" is primary with most of us.

To explain time and its seasons in our biblical roots can be an archaic exercise unless we first have a few things straight. One is that most of us do not have

From *Liturgy: The Calendar* 1, no. 2.

the time to look into the historical origins of anything. When we learn a fact out of the past we tend to say, "Interesting," in a tone of voice that indicates the very opposite. What interests us is how to spend our time well, and we are the arbiters of what "well" means. Learning how the people of our biblical past viewed time is something very few of us have the time for.

"The Sunday service was too long this morning." That means it went beyond the psychological limit we had set for it. It was already too long before it began. Going to church every Sunday? Who can fit it into a crowded weekend, especially when it is scheduled during prime sleeping time? The fifteen-minute sermon can be intolerably long, yet the "shared prayer" of an hour not nearly long enough. In the first instance someone else is speaking, in the second we have a say of our own. Time speeds on wings in a three-hour Eastern liturgy for those who need this refreshment in a drab week. It moves on leaden feet for fifty minutes of brisk commerce with God in which no one except the functionaries have a real part to play. When it comes to prayer, time has no value of its own. It is an exponent of the store set on the activity itself, of the value assigned to praying in the company of others. The best test we have for determining satisfaction is how soon we want a thing to be over. A blessed eternity will consist in the total absence of the thought that it could or should be over.

Time as a biblical category

Much has been made of time as a biblical category in the last fifty years. The Jews thought in linear fashion, it is said, the Greeks in cyclic. For the ancient Hebrew, history, not myth, was the measure of God's activity. Biblical figures down through and including the Christian scriptures were governed by the before and after, the already and the not yet. This kind of thing appeared in print so often it almost could not be true. A contentious Scot named James Barr began to say in print in 1962 that it was not true, that it never had been true. It was always a scheme to classify what could not be comprehended so as to control it, a nineteenth-century apologetic technique to fight the charge that none of the biblical events really happened in history.

Barr has said, in a number of books and articles since then, that too much material in the Bible escaped history to be governed by it: the wisdom literature, notably the psalms; direct divine communication with individuals, viz., the oracles of seers; and the mythic telling of the creation, flood and exodus as contrasted with the historical destruction of Jerusalem by Nebuchadnezzar. While denying that history was the "supreme milieu" of God's revelation, Barr granted that the concept was a fair expression of a very important element in the Bible. A series of events through which the Lord of Israel was revealed is indeed a link between the so-called two testaments, but there were other equally pervasive and important axes, he maintained.

Lurking behind this discussion by Christians about the scriptures they took over from the Jews is their preempting of the haggadic element over the ha-lakhic. The desertion of the precepts of the law (*halakha*), in other words, was decisive in the choice of the other option, the storytelling tradition (*haggadah*). Thus, Stephen's speech in Acts 7 is an early tracing of promise and fulfillment in a community that has determined to continue to be Jewish under a historical aspect and not a legal one. It is important to recall the selectivity that marks any backward look to biblical patterns. Not only did the first Christians find the category of history congenial; they found the category of precepts of the law uncongenial. They made their choices accordingly.

"The long narrative corpus of the Old Testament," writes Barr, "seems to me, as a body of literature, to merit the title of story rather than history."[2] David Clines finds the literature of the Old Testament to be essentially story or poem. "Whether we take the historical books, wisdom, prophecy, or psalmody, it is only some genealogical lists, land allocations, prose sermons and laws (all of them set within a narrative framework) that escape the net of these two literary forms."[3] So much for the rabbis, whose option of the laws as central made every other literary form escape *their* net! Yet the rabbis would be quite at one with the Christians in acknowledging that there is in the biblical narrative an integrity, a whole history of God's activity with the people of God, that sheds light on each individual story. For the Christian, the story will always have been "addressed to another people, in a different country, from a past age," but it "can also become a direct word to us in our condition, calling for a fresh response of faith."[4]

Tales of another time and place

That last observation is of major importance to contemporaries for the simple reason that, however moving the biblical stories are, they are tales of an-other place and time; if you are not a Jew, of another people. This age in the West is impatient of narrative. Its agenda is this place and time. Tradi-tion is not only not compelling, it is even viewed as off-putting. The motive that made the Bultmann school go in an existential direction was the suspicion that post–World War I Europeans could no longer be engaged religiously by a mythic viewpoint, whether the correct name for it was history or story, saga or epic. That fabled creature "modern man" was thought to have only contem-porary, ahistorical and surely amythical concerns. Part of the vigorous response of Cullmann and others was that time was a salvageable category, that since the Bible itself had a historical framework no one claiming to be a Chris-tian could desert it. The truth was, both camps had right on their side. The Jewish spirit that produced both the Bible and the Christian scriptures was pro-foundly existential, finding in "history" basically a useful category to underscore the need for action now. As our forebears in the faith did, so must we do — or not do.

Told in this season

The Christian who sees in the corpus of scripture a record of the past mis-construes it. It was meant at all times to be a means for living Jewish, for living Christian, in this time and place. This consideration is paramount in the conduct of all Christian worship, religious education and ethical response. Appeals to the past as such, even the sacred past, are so much time lost. The mood must always be contemporary if it is to succeed as religion, even in the most traditional religious cultures. That does not mean that the mood should be vulgar or "pop," the charge usually brought against attempts at religious relevance. Relevance has to do with what applies properly to the matter at hand. The Aristotelian scheme of virtues called our relevance "prudence" (an alternative form of the word "providence"), meaning foresight or forethought: the wisdom shown in the exercise of a reasonable course of action. But an archaic approach to religion is unwise and scarcely reasonable. It characterizes the whole venture as finished, as over and done. *Pesach* for the Jew is deliverance now, fresh every spring, with new hope for final liberation. The Christian cycle of feasts, with Easter at its core, is rebirth from the death of sin and hope of resurrection in this city or town this season, not "in that Syrian garden, ages slain." The liturgy, the preaching that looks to yesterday and backward and not to today and forward, is archaeology: a symphony of dead forms.

Israel's break with the past

Having said so much about the uses of the past, it now seems safe to explore a bit of the past — but only in that spirit. The worship of Israel was "a composite creation whose roots lie in the pagan prehistory of that people" (Y. Kaufmann). But this statement could be misleading because of the gradual and organized evolution of religious forms in that part of the world. Biblical religion broke with the old religion by repudiating the worship of other gods than YHWH, forbidding the worship of the dead, spirits and animals. "All was reformed and brought into harmony with the new idea." Sacrifices in Israel bore no trace of the pagan conception in which the victim is conceived as the god or his enemy, or the rite is perceived to heighten the power of the god. There is no echo, either, in Israelite sacrifice of a struggle between good and evil. The mythical and magical elements of cognate pagan sacrifices are simply missing.

Israel's festivals were grounded in pagan concepts, but they were cut off from their pagan roots. Passover, Pentecost and Tabernacles, the three pilgrimage feasts, were all nature festivals in origin: the first a herdsman's and a farmer's combined, the second the end of the festival of the new grain (Passover the beginning of the reaping, Pentecost or Weeks the end), the third the ingathering of all produce. Gradually each of the three — none ever celebrating the life processes of the deity — was historicized. Passover came to commemorate the exodus (Exod 12–13; 23:15; 34:18; Deut 16:1–6), Pentecost the giving of the Law (this fell outside the biblical period), and Booths the Wandering in the Desert (Lev 23:42f.; Neh 8:13–18). Paganism grounded its festivals in the mythological history of the gods. Israel commemorated moments in the history of the people in which the wonders of yhwh manifested themselves. Put another way, when the seasons of agricultural life ceased to be uppermost, other events closer to the people's consciousness were chosen.

Ancient Israel seems to have celebrated the new year twice, once in spring (on the first of Nisan) and once in autumn (on the first of Tishri). The former was the priestly observance (Exod 12:2), the latter the popular one after the "end" of the year (Exod 23:16; 34:22). To the second was joined the Day of Atonement ten days later (Lev 23:27ff.; Num 29:7ff.). These together became the "days of awe" — the modern "high holy days" — with prayers for forgiveness and repentance, after the biblical period. The development that joined them as days of retribution thus came later.

The origins of the Sabbath are shrouded in mystery. It may be related to days of taboo in the Babylonian and Assyrian calendar, but by the time we first hear of it the day is associated with God's rest from creating (Gen 2:1–3). It is not innately sacred but is sanctified by the designation of God. The ethical reason is provided: the Sabbath is an occasion of rest for both laborer and beast (Deut 5:14; Exod 23:12).

The right time and season

The claim cannot be made for biblical religion that it first introduced religious observances according to the rhythm of people's lives. Among agricultural tribes, hunters and fishers, celebrations have always been tied to the seasons of the year, to great catches or the running of the game. Cessation from labor is always a reason to celebrate, hardship in life's struggle always a reason to impetrate. There is nothing peculiarly Israelite or Christian in that, only that the major feasts of Christians came to them fairly directly from Israel, where the feasts had already been transferred by the Jews away from their primitive agricultural significance. The investment of meaning centered on Jesus Christ and the Holy Spirit was the element that was new. But the rhythm of life in the regions of Christianity's rise was still agricultural. Hence the place of its major observances in two of those three times of the year made cultural sense: spring's first blooming and the early harvest before the heat of summer. The autumn harvest never made its way into the Christian calendar, not through the nativity of Mary (September 8) or the Holy Cross (September 14) or Michaelmas (September 29). Christian repentance appeared in early spring, not fall. The Epiphany came out of the Greek world as a countermeasure to the feast of Dionysus on January 6, the Nativity of Christ — the only major feast originating in the West — to counter the Saturnalian excesses of the winter solstice.

The claim has been made, and rightly, that the Jewish Sabbath changed human life in large segments of the globe. It led to the Christian observance of the first day of the week in the second century, doubtless as a way to be different from the Jews (although the phrase "on the Lord's day" appears in Rev 2:10). The Muslims in the seventh century chose the sixth day for rest and prayer. A weekly interruption of the ordinary thus characterized all three cultures. Two of them were to grow larger than the parent tradition and touch many peoples of the earth with the spread of Christian and Muslim empires.

The language of time

James F. White's *Introduction to Christian Worship* has a valuable chapter on "The Language of Time." He speaks of the biblical view of history, reviewed above, in these terms:

> Our present time is used to place us in contact with God's acts in time past and future. Salvation, as we experience it in worship, is a reality based on temporal events through which God is given to us. Our use of time enables us to commemorate and reexperience those very acts on which salvation is grounded. Time is a ... form of communication used in varying ways with different meanings in every culture. Time is a language that Christian worship also speaks fluently.[5]

From there he proceeds to the New Testament sense of time as *kairos*, the fitting season or movement; to remembering and anticipating, in the biblical protological and eschatological senses; then to Sunday and the church's week, followed by its calendar of seasons and feasts as testified to by the fathers and the councils. The raw materials are there for a Christian observance of time as prepared for by the world of the Bible.

The first lesson to be drawn is that biblical Jew and Christian alike employed tradition when it was useful and escaped its bonds when it no longer spoke to them. The principle was and is: "Tradition is not wearing your grandmother's hat. It is having a baby." When the mythical was found irrelevant, the agricultural less suitable, both were transcended. New experience of God in the Christian community brought new forms of worship, a new pattern in the week and year. That has always meant a search in Christian liturgies for those human experiences of God and human life that speak most forcefully to worshiping congregations. The four seasons prevail in this hemisphere and certain latitudes but not in all parts of the Christian world. The rhythms of the growth of crops prevail for some here but not for many.

It is the work season that is predominant everywhere. In a school-oriented culture like Europe's and ours, the reality of vacation, *Urlaub, villeggiatura,* also prevails. God help the liturgists who think that Whitsun means much besides "bank holiday" in England and *Ferragosto* anything remotely related to Mary's Assumption in Italy. The push is to be out of the cities and onto the beaches, not into the churches for barely remembered feast days. Easter remains a real remembrance of Christ because of the fact of spring, Christmas because of the darkness of early winter. Thanksgiving has its powerful reality in this country as a family day ("families" of all sorts). Memorial Day, the Fourth of July, Labor Day have not fared so well as the focus of liturgical celebrations.

But Mother's Day is not, however we may deplore the false sentimentality that often attends it. San Juan Bautista and Martin Luther King's birthday are terribly real in the places they are real, as is the Epiphany of the East in the midst of a sea of Western Christianity. The power of the Sabbath and the Sunday is still a strong pull. It is up to the Jew and the Christian to make the most of these realities that a secularized, union-organized culture has salvaged for them as protected days. One should give thanks to Caesar every once in a while — and Karl Marx. Without them, where would our world be as regards the things that are God's?

Celebrating naturally

All of this means that individual congregations and areas of the country must constantly be on the watch for times and a time when people naturally celebrate and implement well-planned worship at those times.

The beginning of a school year in fall — even for the great majority of people unrelated to schools — is more an American reality than the dying of summer. It is not an academic occasion for most. It is not even autumn in nature or football season for most. It is the resumption of real, unremitting working (or nonworking) life. The daily struggle has resumed. It should be fittingly marked. For the Christian, what better way is there to do it than with the feast of the Holy Cross (September 14), the sign of our redemption, our pain, our ultimate victory?

Something like this autumn reality marks the end of the school year, except that here life ends abruptly on a number of fronts rather than begins fairly evenly on one, the post–Labor Day week. There are graduations, weddings, first eucharists and confirmations galore. The earliest vacation plans begin to be realized and summer jobs begin for the young, accompanied by the awful realization that for many youth there is no work. It is a season of passage, a time that needs noting by a whole community of believers, not just by those who are making the passage.

Pentecost *may* be the feast indicated. Or if it falls too late or too early, another feast clearly related to the seasons in people's lives, not the one on their calendar. There is an element of risk here for it seems like the desertion of old and well-tried traditions in favor of that nonexistent unicorn, the "new tradition." It is not that. It is identifying traditions that are already meaningful in the culture and marking them in a Christ way or Holy Spirit way. The Christian church has traditionally never done anything but this. To continue in this path is to sanctify the seasons as people are able to, not as a ritual book that took its rise in another clime invites them to.

The basic requirement for any such ingenious approach to Christian life is that a few people everywhere, in every congregation and diocese and district, live a life alerted to the importance of time — not just to the passage or the ineluctability of time but to its rhythms, its human seasons, its potential to destroy and to save. No individual congregation can possibly be this ingenious on a regular basis. So thank God for the ritual books, even with their tombstones over dead observances. But Christian people are alive and well and living in Paris, Illinois — and Paris, France too. In both places they know the mood of their lives, what they wish to rejoice over and mourn and simply note the passage of. By all means, give them the opportunity. They have the time.

Notes

1. Augustine, *Confessions XI*, 14.
2. James Barr, *Journal of Religion* 56 (1977): 5.
3. David Clines, *Interpretation* 34 (1980): 117.
4. Brevard S. Childs, ibid.: 137.
5. James F. White, *Introduction To Christian Worship* (Nashville: Abingdon Press, 1980), 44–75.

5

Worshiping on the Lord's Day

Nathan R. Kollar

Sunday dawns, the first day of the week. Bells call the assembly to worship. Energetic and well-behaved young children grasp their parents' hands and walk the tree-lined sidewalks to the church. The town comes alive as families, older people, young couples and young single adults make their way to the church of their choice.

The sun may rise on such a Sunday, but it is also true that Sunday sidewalks can be very lonely places. Indeed an idyllic Sunday myth may cloud the reality of what we do, why we do it and what the consequences of our actions are. We will examine two aspects of Sunday — its myth and reality, and the people's role and power in the Lord's Day worship. First we will explore the reality of the event; and second, some suggestions for the reinterpretation of the myth.

The myth of Sunday shatters for many reasons: the actual reality of getting a family "to church" on their only day off combines with a deep-seated feeling that the service is empty and without relevance. The need to set an alarm clock and rise from sleep just to "get to church on time" can make Sunday's dawn oppressive. The community that finds its myth shattered in this way is probably no different from many other Christian communities who feel the same urge to celebrate Sunday in ways that are not described by the myth.

Whether our community steps into the idyllic or the shattered Sunday, it is rarely a mere frolic from bed to prayer bench. Sunday is a day of power strongly exercised, and its structures move us to action and thought. Fighting children, horrible sermons, inept ministers and narcissistic musicians do not advance the worshipfulness of the day; they do, however, help us to feel guilty for having failed to achieve the expected mythic Sunday. Such guilt is a compass; it points to Sunday as a most intense source of power. Our analysis of its power structures begins with a list of presuppositions.

From *Liturgy: The Power That Unites* 6, no. 2.

Conceptualizing Sunday

First, Jesus' incarnation is normative for understanding church and church life.[1] As Jesus was subject to the earth's physical, social and psychological laws, so the church is subject to the same laws. Thus we need to consult the social sciences as well as philosophy, history and theology in our attempt to understand Sunday and the Christian life. We may not want to admit that power and power relationships determine every level of life but they do. No human life is lived without power. To recognize and, if you will, baptize the relationship between power and Sunday is the goal of this article.[2]

Second, Sunday is a transformation of the Sabbath. As the seventh day of rest and liberation, the Sabbath looks to our imitation of God's creation-rest. Sunday, on the other hand, is the eighth day of creation; it looks to the present and future building of the kingdom, the continuation of creation and redemption in the Spirit. The Sabbath, the thankful rest that proclaims God's mighty deeds, is only part of the story.[3] When we concentrate on Sunday, we praise God's ongoing creative act that culminates in the kingdom. Power is active and important; we look at the world and wonder, "How can we help to build the kingdom?" Sunday reflects the power of creation as we pray, "your kingdom come."

Third, Sunday is the first day of the week; it begins at midnight. Sunday's dawn is not Saturday's sunset. Because time is such an important indicator of sacrality, the celebration of Sunday cannot be spread throughout the week. To make any or every day Sunday is to make no day Sunday. Sunday is primarily a time. That is why Sunday itself is powerful. It is the Lord's day, and people either do or do not share in its sacredness and power.

Fourth, symbolic events, such as Sunday or Sunday worship, are complex systems representing various symbols, but their complexity is only recognized by analysis. Usually, we perceive a symbolic event as a simple unity because we react to events as whole persons; our faith, emotions, thoughts and interpersonal relationships are integrated. This reaction is determined by the contexts that constitute every symbol and symbol system. Symbols without context are signs; they have one meaning, are primarily intellectual and can be easily manipulated. Symbols as symbols are always contextual; they have many meanings, appeal to the whole person and are constitutive of community. For our purposes we will accept Sunday worship as one important symbol in the web of relationships and symbols that we call Sunday.

The significant contexts of the Sunday event are the place of worship, the assembly and absent church members. Religious education classes, the various committees that shape this day's activities, Sunday newspapers and television shows, implicit and explicit cultural norms (freedom, democracy, competition and individualism) and the use of certain clothing, books or bodily gestures are also associated with Sunday. Each context is important for understanding and interpreting the Sunday event. Power is reflected in their configuration, though we usually react to it without reflection or analysis.

Fifth, Sunday is a day of and for people. In the history of the United States we can turn to descriptions of the frontier churches in order to understand this point. They were called "people's churches" because the laity were essential to their meaning, spread and development.[4] These were churches of, for and by the people. They reflected the American spirit of individualism, enterprise, plain gospel and equality. Sunday could be celebrated without an ordained minister. Anyone who felt called by God to preach stood in the midst of the assembly to do so, though there were as yet no women preachers. The same people who built the church prayed and sang in it. Ministers were from and for the community. Power resided in one's ability to repeat phrases from the Bible and to use ecclesial symbols, not in one's knowledge of the Bible's origins, church history or ceremony. This was the people's church, their religion, their Sunday. Sunday worship occurred on a day set aside for the Lord, and the attitude engendered by the worship service continued throughout the day.

These churches were and are inherently opposed to most contemporary traditions of the mainline churches; that is, they are against the elitist traditions now reigning in the mainline churches:

> In the history of clerical-lay relations, the mid-sixteenth century was a watershed.
> ...The Council of Trent etched the distinction between cleric and lay in a series of awesome decrees that affirmed transubstantiation, the objective power of the sacraments, the sacrificial character of the Mass....Confraternities, since the thirteenth century the primary agency of lay spirituality, were brought firmly under clerical supervision....The militant clergy of both faiths sought to impose on the masses what was essentially an elite pattern of religion, inaugurating an era of one-way religious pressure from the top down.[5]

Historically, neither Protestants nor Catholics have allowed the people's voice to be heard. Except for the left wing of the Reformation, a clerical elite has controlled the church and Sunday; especially in the Roman Catholic, Episcopal-Anglican, Lutheran and Reformed churches, Sunday has been the clergy's day to shine, whether in Protestant sermon or Catholic ritual.[6] In addition, because these were established religions, the clergy who controlled worship also controlled the secular law. The power of state and church were one.

If the churches want Sunday to become a people's day — want it to be truly a day for the assembly — then a realignment of power must occur in all the churches as it has already occurred in the secular realm. Certainly a people's Sunday will reflect our culture and the limited role we have in shaping a day that is already dominated by baseball, football, television and other leisure activities. This is the Sunday of the people, for the people and by the people.[7]

Sixth, "power" is difficult to understand. As Stanley Brenn comments, "The meanings of 'power,' 'influence,' 'control,' and 'domination' are uncertain, shifting and overlapping."[8] No matter how difficult the conceptualization, however, we recognize power when we experience its use: "To possess power or to be powerful is, then, to have a generalized potentiality for getting one's own way or for bringing about changes (at least some of which are intended) in other people's actions or conditions."[9]

Power in a liturgical context is subject to theological interpretation and intra-church conflicts concerning its exercise. Simply put, what kind of change occurs as a consequence of the exercise of power? Is it ontological, physical, social or psychological? Does the "power" of God or clergy or people change the person baptized, for example, or is the change effected by the power of all three? While this historical controversy is not under review here, we must realize that our interpretation of power will depend on these theological and denominational differences.

Power relationships can be schematized to help us discover how power is used or abused in the Sunday event. The following five models are adapted from Henry Mintzberg's *Power in and Around Organizations.*[10]

1. The presider may command power: "I command." In this model, only one person has power and only one goal is desired. If a powerful sermon is preached and many seek repentance, the goal is achieved; if the entire church receives communion, the goal is achieved; if a large collection occurs, the goal is achieved. Only the one in charge has power.

2. The second model, the "I'll listen, but I'm the one in command" model, varies from the first only slightly. The presider may listen to suggestions from other assembly members but is still in sole charge. Only if others gain the ear of the one in charge will they have some influence on the Sunday event. Worship goals will probably not reflect the listening process.

3. In the third model, the presider listens and accepts help, and then takes charge. This presider not only listens; he or she also realizes that the community's help is really needed to achieve a variety of goals. Here these others are permitted a helping role in worship, though they still do not share power.

4. The fourth model is a cooperative one. Here the presider recognizes that all worshipers must work toward achieving the goals of worship. The Sunday event demands a true coalition. Power can and will be bargained for as long as everyone remembers that the context extends beyond the liturgy to the rest of Sunday. A powerful liturgy presupposes a powerful life.

5. Finally, even anarchic power relationships can be schematized. The community may say, "Let us worship without worrying about the goals of our action." This model is not one of shared power; rather, as everyone works to achieve his or her own desires, worship becomes the narcissistic experience of individuals.

Sunday's power and might

Sunday is more than a celebration of the Lord's day. It is also a celebration of the power structures enlivened by God's almighty and reconciling Spirit. In examining the power structure of contemporary Christian churches we are faced with a common dilemma in liturgical studies: how to balance the designated texts for celebration with the actual celebration. I have chosen to review what is actually being done in the churches, using the institutional norms as references. We cannot presume that the liturgy of a specific church reflects institutional norms.

In this era, barriers between Christians established at the reformation are disappearing while new and different ones are taking shape. The churches that accept the symbolic methods of humanistic studies have more in common than those accepting the experience and methodologies of secular fundamentalism.[11] We must look to these new centers of belonging and meaning for our liturgical differences rather than to those derived from the Protestant reform.

Sunday: worship in the Spirit

From charismatic prayer groups to local house meetings, Christians gather in response to the Spirit's inner call.[12] Sometime during their adult life these worshipers experienced the Spirit, and they assemble now to recall and share that experience. As they often meet more than once a week, the appeal of their Sunday gathering must derive from something beyond the freshness of renewed acquaintance and habitual weekly ritual.

Their ritual looks something like this: when all have gathered in a circle, seated in chairs or on the floor, they sing a lengthy song, and someone reads from scripture. People respond to the reading with prayer, prophecy, witness and speaking or singing in tongues. Periods of silence alternate with readings and responses. After a final long period of silence a concluding song or prayer is offered, and refreshments follow. Even their ordinary talk is interspersed with further witnessing to Jesus' place in their lives.

At first glance this is certainly a Sunday in which the people present have total and full power in the assembly. A second glance, however, usually reveals one significant person that everyone looks to for guidance. The basis of membership is personal experience recognized and authenticated by the group but confirmed by the group leader. Others can come to the meeting but, unless they also experience the call of the Spirit, they will feel excluded. No special education is expected of the members or the leaders. Marks of power include a familiarity with biblical quotations, experience and external signs. This assembly may fit the first, second or fifth of the above power models.

Traditional Sunday worship

Sunday newspapers and glossy magazines describe the traditional places of worship: red-brick city churches and plain clapboard rural churches. Congregations are pictured praising God, openmouthed and hymnals in hand. Green-robed presiders raise high the consecrated bread, and icons appear shrouded in clouds of incense. "Traditional" worship is worship according to the pattern and instruments handed down from the previous generation. "The book," worship's central instrument, is the authoritative text or set of traditions that determines the pattern of worship. The traditional Sunday is inherited — from the pope, bishops, presbytery, parliament, congregational custom or doctrinal program.

The Roman Sacramentary and *The Book of Common Prayer* are instances of traditional worship. The membership requirements for worship in these traditions equal membership in the worldwide church. No demonstration of belonging is required. In large congregations anyone who wishes and has the inclination can participate, though the same cannot be said for the clergy who lead. In traditional celebrations, the presider needs the permission of the local bishop; no one can lead worship unless authorized to do so. The presider reads the book and directs the service. Continuity with the tradition is assured through the prayer leader's training and authorization. All other ministers act at the presider's command, which in turn reflects the command of "the book."

It may seem at first that the priest's domination of the service is only apparent, since the real power resides in the past. This is, however, the "I'll listen, but I'm still in charge" power relationship. The presider is required to listen to the past but, in fact, controls the service. Theology, polity and ritual look to the past to determine the present. Our forebears return again and again as norms for the present: the people of the Hebrew and Christian scriptures; Jesus in whose memory we act, and our parents, who taught us to act this way. The dominant instrument of power is the past as found in the church's normative texts and in their hierarchical interpretation in the sermon.

The worshipers enliven the past by their present celebration. Their word and action indicate that the fullness of worship requires a blend of the past and present, but the clergy are still the sacred keepers of the revelation. Ordination and education prepare them for their mission. They are supported by the people because there is no past without them, and there is no present church without the past. The clergy preach, preside over the eucharist, distribute communion, approve hymns and make announcements. At best the people are consulted; at worst, they are expected to pray, pay and obey.

The ritual itself has many instruments of people power, but usually they are not acknowledged. They include the procession bearing the scriptures, the presentation of the gifts, the money to be collected, the communion, the hymns, the great "Amen" and the dialogical responses. All are instruments of the people's power, but the context of clerical domination in many Protestant and Catholic churches results in a clerical Sunday that is only partially shared by the people.

Sunday: worship in time

A worship assembly should reflect the plurality and differences of its people. Christians must look not only to the past but also to the present and future because the church is in time and time flows. Many traditions now recognize the present concerns of people and the church's historicity. The pluralistic concerns of the entire communion of saints is recognized in the use and arrangement of the ecclesial symbolic events.

The lectionary or scripture, for instance, is recognized as normative, yet individual readers clearly articulate their understanding of the text. Leaders' whims and spontaneous repetitions are rejected; the words of the past are enlivened in the reading and projected to present and future through the homily.

The "Amen" is a congregational response of affirmation to prayer, eucharist, song and petition, and the litany reflects past categories and present needs. Freshly created each Sunday, the petitions reach into the depths of need and request. Here there is a place for silence and for spontaneous expressions of individual thanks, praise, petition and supplication.

Christians recognize fundamental aspects of their tradition in this "modern" celebration, but they may not feel completely at ease. Their uneasiness is the consequence of attempted balance between past forms and present-future necessities. The past forms prevent us from being overcome by contemporary crises, and the present initiatives allow us to acknowledge that the kingdom is not "pie in the sky by and by" but life here and now.

Just as the liturgical celebration recognizes what occurs outside it, so the format of the celebration is determined by those who prepare the Sunday liturgy. The various ministers, interacting with worship committees or with parish council subcommittees, shape the Sunday liturgy. Sometimes the people's voice overcomes academic or ministerial power. Finally, the liturgy reflects the recognition that we will assemble again next week. The liturgy of the word and the eucharist followed by the reading of announcements help us to recognize that we have much to do and that we must gather again to acknowledge in prayer the deeds and power of the coming of the kingdom.

In these churches ecclesial symbols enlivened by the people who celebrate them are the source of power. This is the fourth model of power: the presider and people recognize that the Sunday event has many different goals, and everyone is needed to bring the event to completion. For a moment on Sunday, the whole person living in a holistic community touches the kingdom.

Sunday: worship in sign

The pressures of the present and future have caused some to abandon Sunday and to choose another day for their celebration. This choice represents another attempt to adapt the Christian Sunday to the present culture. Some groups see the necessity of a special day, not as a symbol but as a sign. They seek one meaning for the Sunday event and the symbols that constitute it. Scripture may be replaced with contemporary literature, traditional ritual structure with a didactic atmosphere of instruction or consciousness raising and even the elements of bread and wine, if attended to, may be replaced with contemporary food and drink. Like the Unitarian mode of celebration, such worship emphasizes mind, philosophy and ethical behavior rather than the whole person.

Membership in one of these experimental groups is determined by experience and social role. Usually they are educated people who seem to want the warmth of the traditional Christian institutions without the binding traditional structures. Their own liturgical structures adhere to the present. They have little room for development, however, because their narrow interpretation of sign forbids the plurality of symbol from binding the past, present and future formation of the kingdom. As in the fifth power model, they assemble, conscious of the need to change the Christian way of life but unable to realize that Christianity is for everyday. Their structures are frozen in the present.

Postscript: unscientific and personal

The traditional division of Sunday worship into the liturgy of the word and the liturgy of the eucharist offers us an interesting dilemma. The power of the word is evident in both verbal and nonverbal expression. The word is conveyed through song, reading and homily. Something is given to which the congregation must respond. The power of the eucharist is also evident in the very nature of the prayer. We respond to the eucharist with awesome praise and thanksgiving because we have stood in the midst of the numinosity and *berakah* of power. Yet deep within the Gospel accounts and central to the eucharistic narration, we hear: he took bread, blessed it, broke it and said . . . Take and eat . . . my body and blood. . . .

His body was and is broken; his blood was and is spilt. He suffered and died. There is power in suffering and death, but that power is not what we expect it to be. The Sunday we celebrate looks to the kingdom and resurrection but at its core is suffering and death — the dialectical power that distinguishes the Christian life. If we are to baptize the power relationships inherent in Sunday, we must also face the suffering, death and resurrection of everyday life.

Notes

1. For a lengthy defense of this presupposition, see my "Church Membership: Some Dynamics of Belonging and Reconciliation," *Explorations* 2, no. 6 (July 1984): 5–20.

2. Reinhold Niebuhr's realistic approach to power relations admits the reality of love as well as sin. See especially his *Moral Man and Immoral Society* (New York: Scribner's Sons, 1932).

3. Eugene LaVerdiere, "The Origins of Sunday in the New Testament," in Mark Searle, ed., *Sunday Morning: A Time for Worship* (Collegeville, Minn.: Liturgical Press, 1982), 11–27. We cannot overlook Moltmann's challenge that forms the basis for my understanding of Sabbath. His comments might lead us to look toward some type of weekend or Sabbath-Sunday celebration rather than Sunday alone. See Jürgen Moltmann, *God in Creation: A New Theology of Creation and the Spirit of God* (San Francisco: Harper & Row, 1985).

4. Sydney Ahlstrom, *A Religious History of the American People* (New Haven, Conn.: Yale University Press, 1972), chapter 27.

5. Donald Weinstein and Rudolph Bell, *Saints and Society: The Two Worlds of Western Christendom, 1000–1700* (Chicago: University of Chicago Press, 1982).

6. William McCready, "The Role of Sunday in American Society: Has It Changed?" in *Sunday Morning*, 97–120.

7. For an extensive discussion of the various Christian traditions such as the magisterial, academic and folk, see my "Clash of Structures: American, Medieval, and Catholic," in *Explorations 5* (1987).

8. "Power," in *Encyclopedia of Philosophy* (New York: Collier Macmillan, 1967), VI: 424–27.

9. Ibid., VI:426.

10. Englewood Cliffs, N.J.: Prentice-Hall, 1983.

11. N. Kollar, "Secular Fundamentalism," *Explorations* no. 5 (May 1985): 5–18.

12. My indebtedness to Horton Davies must be recognized. What he says of England can be applied to the United States. See *Worship and Theology in England*, 5 vols. (Princeton, N.J.: Princeton University Press, 1961–70). Those familiar with his work will see his major presuppositions throughout this section.

6

The Little Easter and the Great Sunday

PAUL V. MARSHALL

Once in the recent past it was a mark of devotion to the liturgy to observe all available commemorations of saints on as many Sundays after Pentecost as possible. The result was that Sunday congregations almost never saw green vestments. Some of us even harbored a distaste for the seeming ordinariness of the "green Sundays," although such a distaste was obviously not shared by the translators of *dominicae per annum* as the "Sundays in Ordinary Time." Our desire was for some semblance of festivity in the Sunday liturgies after Pentecost, but the liturgists of several denominations, notwithstanding that they seemed to have changed the disciples' prayer from "teach us to pray" to "teach us to celebrate," began taking our red and white summer Sundays away from us with only the reminder that Sunday is, after all, *pasquetta*, a "little Easter."

That this tale of ancient woe meets with no sympathy from students of pastoral liturgy in their middle twenties is, of course, a testimony to the effectiveness of liturgical renewal. Today's Roman, Lutheran, Anglican and Presbyterian youth have no adolescent memories of any disquietude with green. For them Sunday has always been "little Easter."

This awareness of the importance of Sunday represents a great deal of progress; nevertheless, a word of caution is in order. Our collective liturgical consciousness is in error if it now assigns Sunday a place that has its liturgical identity only derivatively — if, that is, the "little Easter" is only understood in relation to the "real" Easter. We must not forget that canon 20 of the Council of Nicea, still occasionally cited as the reason that our liturgical demeanor during the fifty great days of Easter should be joyful, had as its first concern that no one should kneel "on the Lord's day."[1] Contemporary liturgical catechesis needs to continue to emphasize that Sunday, as a day that is essentially oriented to

---

From *Liturgy: The Calendar* 1, no. 2.

the future, stands in a complementary relation to the special commemorative aspects of the annual paschal observance. An examination of the development of Sunday and Easter will illustrate their special emphases.

Focus on the new creation

The primitive Christian liturgical cycle was not the year but the week. Early Christian writers were aware of Christian assemblies *"on* the first day of the week,"[2] and by the end of the first century the writer of the Apocalypse was using that day's new designation, "the Lord's day," without explanation.[3] By the turn of the century, "the Lord's day" had become the common name for the first day of the week among Christians. In the *Didache, for* example, this day is the Lord's day indeed; the first day is called "the Lord's day of the Lord."[4] *Kyriake hemera* by way of the Latin *dominica* survives in Romance languages as *domenica, domingo* and *dimanche.*

The first generations of Christians did not need to be reminded of the resurrection the way contemporary Christians sometimes do. Thus the first explanations of worship on the first day of the week were already theological rather than simply commemorative, although the event of Christ's rising was often cited as a warrant for its observance. The first of the reasons given in the *Epistle of Barnabas* for observing the Lord's day on the first day is not the event of the resurrection itself but the first day's new symbolism. Among Christians it was regarded as an eighth day of creation, a day beyond the Sabbath rest, "the beginning of another world."[5]

Ignatius of Antioch also drew a contrast between this day and the Sabbath, for on the first day Christians "came to new hope . . . living by the Lord's day, on which we came to new life."[6] The point is not merely that Christians rejoice to recall Christ's resurrection on the Lord's day but that they celebrate their entry into God's new order on that day. Thus, the Lord's day recalls the beginning of both the first and the new creation; it is a day of powerful beginnings, a day that surges up from the coming to rest on the Sabbath. The Lord's day became in time "the image of the age to come,"[7] and thus the Constitution on the Sacred Liturgy can identify it as "the original feast day."[8]

The special character of the Lord's day in the life of the early church is not to be found in the Sabbath; Sabbath observances were not transferred to the Lord's day, which was a work day for many Christians. But the Sabbath was honored on its own terms, and it shared with the Lord's day the distinction of having a name, *Sabbatum,* among the numbered days of the week in the liturgical calendar. At one time most Christians were not permitted to fast on that day, and many still may not. However, when the Sabbath was observed in Christian liturgical time, it was observed on Saturday, not Sunday.

Constantine's edict forbidding work on the Sun's day is traceable more to his longstanding devotion to the sun cults than to his reverence for the Christian day of worship, Eusebius's revision of the story notwithstanding.[9] Some Christians even greeted the imposition of rest on Sunday as an act sure to provide more idle hands for the devil's work.[10] Christian adoption of Sabbath observances on Sunday had to await the sixth century and the decision that the decalogue, reinterpreted along Christian lines, was normative for Christian life.[11]

The day of the Lord's supper

If we cannot look to transferred Sabbath observance or to the resurrection alone for the key to the character of the primitive Lord's day, then we must, as Willy Rordorf suggests, turn instead to the Lord's day celebration of the Lord's Supper. In the eucharist the church met the sacramentally present Christ, risen and bringing the new creation, risen and revealed to his disciples in the breaking of bread. Eschatologically the meal was a participation in the end time — a foretaste of the kingdom rather than an expectation of its coming. Historically, it was a meeting with the crucified and risen Christ now present with his church rather than a recollection of the events of his career.[12] Until the sixteenth century, we have no evidence of a significant Christian community that did not celebrate the eucharist on the Lord's day. But in the first and second centuries, we have no evidence that any commemoration of a particular event ever helped to shape a Lord's day celebration of the new creation. General commemorations of specific points in sacred history were not present until well into the fourth century. Until then and for a long time after, the Lord's day simply marked the presence with his church of the resurrected Christ.

If we understand the original observance of the Lord's day on Sunday as the weekly celebration of the presence of the resurrected Christ, whose coming was experienced by anticipation in the community's eucharist, then we may understand as well the annual Easter observance with its three-day historical commemoration of the Christian paschal mystery not as the model for Sunday but as a complement to it. The Easter celebration developed much later than the Lord's day; it arose as an annual celebration that interrupted the rhythm of the church's weekly worship cycle.

The commemoration of the paschal event

Historical commemoration in the church's liturgy may have developed as an expression of a lessened confidence in the imminence of the promised parousia; or perhaps it is better explained as an accommodation by the church to its new life as a civil institution of the Roman empire. Of late, however, both explanations have received close scrutiny.[13] Mircea Eliade's theory is not only simpler and easier to verify, it is also more convincing. He observes that societies sense their distance in time from the purity of foundational events and sense as well the *impurity* of lives lived in profane or common time; that is, they fear time. This "terror of time" drives them to suspend profane time and enter, through liturgical observance, the "great time" of their foundations.[14] Such observations are well-suited to account for Christian commemoration. In the developing Christian society, which was already separated in time from its constituting events, there were ever-increasing complexities: the increasing numbers of faithful, their geographical dispersion and the persecution they experienced from enemies within as well as from without. Those factors precipitated among Christians a perception of historical and moral separation from the events of the "great time" that had been witnessed by the apostles and first martyrs.

A ready model for a commemoration of the "great time" was present in Jewish celebrations of the Passover. As the paschal celebrations commemorated the people's passing from one state of life to another or from one identity to another, so the Christians commemorated the passing of Christ from suffering and death to his glorified state. The emphasis in the commemoration of his sufferings was later explained by wrongly linking the vocabulary of Passover with the Greek verb *paschein*, meaning "to suffer."

The Christian paschal observances were characterized by fasting, the reiteration of the history of the Passion and an all-night vigil, followed by a eucharist "of the resurrection." The length of these commemorative fasts was varied, and treated as a matter of indifference, but by the third century the standard fast lasted from Friday through Saturday night and ended in a eucharist.

It is generally understood that this practice originated in Ephesus, where Christians held their observance of the Passion on the day of the Preparations for the Passover, the day of its anniversary according to the chronology of John's gospel. When the fast concluded, a nocturnal celebration of the eucharist took the place of the Passover meal.[15]

As this paschal observance was held to coincide with the Jewish commemoration, it usually terminated, as did the Passover itself, on a day other than Sunday. Thus the church was faced with the celebration of the principal eucharist of the year on a day other than the Lord's day. The resulting "Quartodeciman controversy" need not detain us with its details, but several observations can be made about the relationship of the Lord's day and Easter by reference to it.

Although, as Thomas Talley has pointed out, it may have been known in other forms elsewhere, Easter was first heard of in Rome in its Quartodeciman form, and to the Romans of the late second century the displacement of the Lord's day—with its orientation to the future—by a weekday paschal feast whose emphasis was primarily historical-commemorative was unthinkable.[16] The "catholic solution" to the Easter controversy was, in the end, quite simple. It permitted the historicizing prepaschal fasts to continue, but it required their termination in a eucharist celebrated on the more eschatologically oriented Lord's day. Synods in many places agreed that "the mystery of the Lord's resurrection from the dead should never be celebrated on any other day but Sunday and that on this day only should we observe the end of the paschal fasts."[17] Christians were thus free to return to the events of their "great time," but always called back from that potentially sentimental emphasis on history by the Sunday eucharist and its celebration of the new age that awaits consummation.

The annual Easter celebration that we have inherited in this way transcends the limitations that Eliade finds in most liturgical observances in the history of religion. It does return worshipers to the "great time," where they can be purified of the stains of profane time. But, though they are plunged into Christ's death through baptism on the middle of the sacred three days, they are also drawn from that death to new life in the greater "great time" still not completely unfolded, the time for which Sunday is our chief symbol. For this reason Athanasius gives the best possible commentary on our "little Easter" mentality when he calls the whole of Easter's fifty days the "great Sunday."[18]

This discussion of the historical priority of Sunday, shows how the Lord's day's focus on the new creation serves as a control on the historical-commemorative aspects of our three-day paschal observance. The commemorative aspects of the paschal observance and of every eucharist preserve, on the other hand, our Christian hope. Thus, remembrance of the great time impels the church to hope for the right kind of future, that which began in Jesus Christ. Hope and memory, Sunday and Easter, serve each other.

Notes

1. Cf. *The Nicene and Post-Nicene Fathers*, 2nd Series, 19:100.

2. 1 Cor 16:1–3; Acts 20:7–12.

3. Rev 1:10.

4. *Didache*, 14:1.

5. *Ep. Barnabas* 15:8b–9.

6. Ignatius, *Ad Magnesios* 9:1.

7. Basil, *De Spiritu Sancto*, 27.

8. Constitution on the Sacred Liturgy, *The Documents of Vatican II*, ed. Walter M. Abbott, S.J. (New York: Herder and Herder, 1966), #106.

9. Eusebius, *Vita Const.*, 4.18.2.

10. Willy Rordorf, *Sunday* (London: Burns and Oates, 1968), 67ff.

11. Of the sixteenth-century reformers, Luther avoided the importation of Sabbath observance to Sunday, redirecting the Sabbath commandment in his *Small Catechism* to a veneration for "preaching and the Word" (*Die Bekenntnisschriften*, 508).

12. Rordorf, 245ff.; 275; and chapter 5 in general.

13. See, for example, the reexaminations of conventional Wisdom in Jaroslav Pelikan, *The Finality of Jesus Christ in an Age of Absolute History* (London: Lutterworth Press, 1965), and Thomas J. Talley, "History and Eschatology in the Primitive Pascha," *Worship* 47 (1973): 212–21.

14. Eliade's *Myth and Reality* (New York: Harper & Row, 1963), and *The Sacred and Profane* (New York: Harcourt, Brace and Jovanovich, 1959) provide an introduction to his thought on this subject.

15. I follow here the line taken in Talley; another view is that of Willy Rordorf, "Am Ursprung des Osterfestes am Sonntag," *Theologische Zeitschrift* 18 (1963), 167–89.

16. Talley, 219.

17. Eusebius, *Historia Ecclesiastica* 5:24.

18. Athanasius, *Ep. fest.*, 1.

7

Liturgy and Christian Social Action

Mary Barbara Agnew

At the root of the "unfinished agenda" of Christian worship[1] — its link with Christian social action — lie two neglected problems: the unremarked analogical use of the term "sacrifice" and a failure to take fully into account the effect of the church's new and open stance toward the world on the whole moral life of Christians. The results are a liturgical theology unable to contribute much to the agenda and a gap between Christian ethics and sacramental theology that adds nothing to the credibility of the claim that Christ's sacrifice is unique and possesses redemptive power for the whole world. These doctrinal assertions are frequently confessed in the liturgy; attention must be paid to them.

The meaning of sacrifice

Despite its alleged uniqueness, Christ's redemptive death, like all faith claims, depends on common terms for its explication. Sacrifice has been a major inter- pretative concept, one that has carried over into the theology of the eucharist: Christ's death is effectively remembered and presented in the eucharistic sac- rifice. But the term "sacrifice" is insufficiently probed and understood. The sacrifice of Christ is inadequately conceived as an act of self-denial (despite the agony of the passion); as an act of satisfaction (despite its legitimate use in theologies of redemption); or as a call to the Christian to be self-actualized (despite the transformative effects of living out the paschal mystery). What has not been sufficiently noted are the almost contradictory ethical and cultic mean- ings of sacrifice. And almost wholly undeveloped is an understanding of sacrifice as Christ's continual self-offering and intercession to God the Father, which is admittedly the only correct reading of the Epistle to the Hebrews.[2]

From *Liturgy: Ethics and Justice* 7, no. 4.

Common uses of the term "sacrifice" blur its theological clarity. A good part of the reformation quarrel concerned the way in which opposing communions understood the eucharist to be a sacrifice, but this term is also found on baseball scorecards. The "cross of sacrifice" is the major symbol for the tragically distant loss of Australia's military dead, yet the smallest children are urged to "make sacrifices" during Lent. At work in these instances is the character of sacrifice as a symbolic act; its meaning is not exhausted by its varied usages, most important of which are those having ethical (self-denying) and cultic (self-surrendering) connotations. The failure of theologians to advert to this makes them particularly vulnerable to polemics. For example, the ethical connotations of sacrifice are often invoked in considerations of Christ's passion and death, while the cultic referents appear when eucharistic worship is spoken of as sacrificial. But the cultic nuances conflict with the ethical when a theologian affirms that "the eucharist is the sacrifice of Christ," without recognizing that two contrary understandings are present in her or his work.[3]

With the introduction of the concept *memorial,* ecumenical discussions of the eucharist as sacrifice have made much headway, but these reflections still leave untouched the Catholic linkage between priesthood and sacrifice.[4]

At the level of worship itself, in the Catholic tradition, the meaning of sacrifice was thoroughly comprehended by the liturgy and the customs surrounding the "holy sacrifice of the mass:" it was almost entirely ethical in its connotations of penance and reparation for the punishment due to sin. Until Vatican II's reforms, the "holy sacrifice of the mass" was most frequently celebrated "for the souls of the faithful departed," namely, for the remission of the punishment merited by their sins.

The comprehensiveness of this symbolic world is rivaled only by the swiftness with which it has been replaced in the official liturgy. The reform of the calendar, the introduction of the vernacular and the abandonment of black as a liturgical color present the worshiper with an entirely new set of auditory and visual images. The appearance of white vestments at the burial rites, of the paschal candle being carried in the procession and of homilists giving praise and gratitude to God for "the gift of a Christian life to the deceased person" complete this major shift in the pattern. Even when it is offered for the deceased, the mass no longer suggests the self-denying, penitential aspects of sacrifice.

In general, the reforms provide for a community at table, with bread to eat and wine to drink; they summon the community each Sunday to remember Christ's resurrection and daily to rejoice in Christ's lordship, the seasons and saints. The historical and theological recovery of the primitive eucharist suggests the central symbolism of the meal. Christ's sacrifice has become sacramentalized, the sum of all that is symbolized in the gathering.

The link between liturgy and social action — or between liturgy and any earthly action — depends on one's perspective. Insofar as the world of the worshipers was comprised of the baptized in the era of Christendom and of Catholics in the ghetto church following Trent, the link was evident: one's primary relationship and responsibility was to the church in its three aspects. One prayed to the saints in the church triumphant, offered satisfaction for the church suffering in purgatory and kept the laws of the church militant, with special emphasis on "hearing" mass on Sundays and holy days of obligation. Today's demand that worship have a discernible effect on the behavior of the faithful in the larger world is analogous with this view, only the world is no longer limited to the church, the baptized faithful, whatever their state.

Ritual and ideology

An examination of the link between a ritual and its participants can also be made by employing, in Ricoeur's expanded sense, the concept of ideology. Insofar as Christian liturgy can be said to be the "social memory of a historical community" by which it is related to "some inaugural act which rounded it" and which is "repeated over time . . . to preserve a sense of social integration," liturgy can be treated as ideology.[5] As an integrating force, liturgy (as ideology) functions through a "communal set of images whereby [the group] can represent itself to itself and to others." But because liturgy (as ideology) functions at a prerational or preconscious level, it "is by its nature uncritical" and often functions in a "reactionary or at least socially conservative fashion"; that is, it can accommodate the new only in terms of the typical, as that which has been experienced before.[6] The "link" between Christian eucharistic liturgy and the community is, then, the images themselves: the ritual enactment of the paschal symbols and the "affective engagement" of community members precipitated by symbol.

The burden of liberation theology's critique of the liturgy is the potential of these symbols to become reactionary.[7] Not so clearly asserted is the fact that symbols also have eschatological power. On this point, Ricoeur suggests a "hermeneutics of affirmation," which tries to identify the emancipating modes of symbolization and their contribution to the "emergence of new meaning." This "hermeneutics of affirmation" finds in foundational myths and symbols a reference "that is not exhaustively or exclusively determined by anterior causes." It demonstrates that such symbols can refer "not just to some pre-existing reality . . . but to some . . . possible world" which they open up.[8]

Perhaps it is tempting to think that the eschatological referent of the eucharistic symbols has always been effective; the eucharist, Christians claim, is the anticipation of the heavenly banquet.[9] On the contrary, Ricoeur's analysis of symbolic power includes explicit attention to symbols' ethical force as well as their epistemological implications. Symbols are not innocent or neutral: they are "authentic or inauthentic according to the human 'interests' they express." Their "concealed intentions and interests" must be unraveled, and their "genuinely exploratory function" toward "a possible world of justice, equality and peace" must be critically sought. Symbols and the ideologies constructed of them are neither good nor bad except "by virtue of their ongoing reinterpretation by each historical generation of each social community."[10]

Viewing liturgy as ideology affirms the possibility of an authentic protest over the gap between the reformed liturgy and Christians' social consciousness. A group's symbolic expression of itself has ethical import: it can function in a conservative or a liberating fashion. One can ask, therefore, about the ideological status of the liturgy. Is it, or has it been, reactionary? Does it have the eschatological power implied in the paschal symbolism itself?

The communal set of images by which the pre-Vatican church represented itself to itself and others in the requiem masses were those of penance, satisfaction and sacrifice for the remission of sin and the punishment due to sin. The notion of salvation implicit in the ritual pertained only to the baptized; it did not suggest the world's salvation or Christians' role in the world. Isn't this a very restrictive expression of Christ's salvific power? Can it not be called an ideology of Christ's sacrifice? Did it not become even more reactionary under Vatican II's new ecclesiology?

But aren't the new images of resurrection, meal and the assembly of the baptized equally limiting? An ideology that is reactionary "conceals the gap between what is and what ought to be ... between our presently lived reality and the ideal world of traditional self-representations."[11] Isn't this the precise complaint being made, namely, that a gap exists between liturgy and the Christian action of worshipers? And is the notion of salvation implicit in the reformed liturgy any more faithful to the salvific power of Christ's death than that of the older liturgy? Is the reformed liturgy as much a restrictive ideology of meal as the pre-Vatican rite was an ideology of sacrifice?

Christian ethics as moral vision

A second reason for the failed link between liturgy and social action has not yet been examined, for one must ask what is meant by "Christian social action." Often mentioned is the failure of Catholics to give support to the American bishops' pastoral letters on peace and the economy. The application of moral principles is, however, an insufficient idea of Christian moral life, according to Stanley Hauerwas and other writers, who instead offer the notion of character, virtue and moral vision. Moral behavior is a matter "not primarily of choice but of vision.... We ... should be formed primarily ... by the stories and metaphors through which we ... intend the variety of our existence." The moral life is "a way of seeing the world ... [it] cannot be divorced from the substance of the world." Achieving good in this life is done "only by the hard and painful effort of the transformation of our vision.[12]

We are formed primarily "by the stories and metaphors through which we learned to intend the variety of our existence." Hauerwas states that he "purposely leaves vague the meaning of story and metaphor" to allow for a "variety of the different kinds and uses of stories."[13] For the purposes of this essay, "story and metaphor" are expanded beyond the notion of narrative in language to the narrative character of ritual enactment.[14] In the same way that Hauerwas argues that our formation comes about by "stories and metaphors," this essay asserts that we are also formed by the ritual enactment of these stories and metaphors; and, therefore, we are "formed" or "deformed" by ritual as ideology, whether it is reactionary or eschatological, dominating or liberating. That Christians are formed by eucharistic participation is not an unfamiliar assertion.

The argument that social effects result from the eucharist tightens: not only do ideologies have ethical import, but the source of moral vision and action is engagement with these ideologies. With respect to doctrinal claims made for the redemptive power of Christ, past and even present eucharistic liturgies can be considered ideologically reactionary. The repeated confessions of the sufficiency and universality of Christ's redemption and its sacramental representation, deprived first of the security of Christendom's legitimation and more recently of the illusory excitement of interconfessional polemics, sound less and less convincing in the face of the world's acute need for redemption.

The eucharist and moral vision

If the liturgy constitutes the symbolic and ritual enactment of the stories and metaphors by which a group understands itself and if the moral vision out of which people act is created by the same stories and metaphors as the accumulated result of their history, then change in the moral vision must come from the encounter between the ritual symbols and the symbols already at work within each of the worshipers. If liturgy is to become a source of moral action, the eschatological force of the paschal symbols — their power to speak and to enable the coming of the kingdom — must touch the worshipers' moral life, now named as their symbolic life.

All elements of a good liturgy contribute to liturgy's power: the presider's sensitivity and transparency, the power of the well-proclaimed word, the depth and appropriateness of the homily, a generous measure of bread and wine for food and drink and the aesthetics of measured gesture, symbol, sound and silence. Less often articulated is the need for symbolic expression of the community's life and the life of the world in which it lives.[15] Still less well integrated into liturgical practice is belief in the Holy Spirit as the true source of sacramental effects, chief of which is hearts converted to the eschatological moral vision that arises in the disclosive encounter between the symbols of Christ's liberating death and resurrection and those of the world struggling for liberation.[16]

Behind the failure to bring the community's life to symbolic expression often lies the pastoral failure to discern and cultivate the Christian life that is already in the community. That the social concerns of Christians elsewhere can usurp those of the community present is surely another kind of ideological distortion. Churches who have named their crises are less apt to err here. In Brazil, the scenario of a worker tied to a chair in the sanctuary while other workers name the bonds that hold him — low wages, unemployment, lack of housing — forcefully brings worship's liberating power into the life of the masses. In an urban parish, the sight of the brother who is the backbone of the parish's housing, soup kitchen and thrift shop ministries presiding at a Lenten prayer for reconciliation was experienced as "heart-rending" by long-time parishioners. At the root of the occasionally deeply moving funeral or wedding is often some human aspect of the situation very well symbolized; that good symbols can happen more frequently and in ordinary situations must become conviction.

The Spirit, present and active in worship, is alone the author of the community's eschatological vision; the Spirit more easily moves hearts toward that vision when the symbolic expression of the community's life can be juxtaposed with the paschal symbols themselves. Sacraments "work" through symbolic causality: new meaning is disclosed through the encounter of the foundational symbols with the available life symbols. The meaning will be eschatological insofar as the Spirit of God living in the baptized is allowed full play.[17]

Liturgies scorned as ritualistic, didactic or propagandistic may often be exactly so: instead of experiencing their vision of the world as being confronted symbolically by the power of Christ's death and resurrection, worshipers may be subjected to unvarying routine, harangue from pressure groups or manipulation by unskilled liturgy planners. These situations may result from the inability to bring parish life to symbolic expression, or tragically, the cause may be the community's very lifelessness. Evangelization and conversion are the remedy more than liturgical expertise.

If the link between church and larger world parallels that between liturgy and life, William Dych's prescription for the church may be helpful for liturgy. He proposes that we see the world as the helpless masses of Matthew 25, in whom is the declared presence of the suffering Christ. Their continuing suffering, Dych says, requires that we replace the "soteriology of expiation" with a "soteriology of compassion.[18]

With the mention of "expiation" arises once more the concept of sacrifice. Reference has already been made to sacrifice as Jesus' heavenly offering. Ordinarily "the intercession of the exalted Jesus has been interpreted as the sequel of his completed sacrifice ... a priestly work but different from the sacrifice."[19] But H. E. Symonds says that "a right interpretation of the Epistle to the Hebrews demands the view that Our Lord in Heaven is offering Himself, that is to say, His sacrificed Body to the Father. ... If the action of Christ in heaven is parallel to that of the Jewish High Priest on the Day of Atonement (Heb 9:24) it would seem he is offering sacrifice in heaven."[20]

Critical study of the concept of *expiation* reveals, however, a contrast with popular understanding just as striking as the shift in the locus of Christ's sacrifice from the cross to the resurrection. Several decades ago Stanislas Lyonnet showed that while the Greek term *to expiate* meant to placate an angry God by sacrifices, for the Israelites to placate God was always a function of prayer.[21] Understanding expiation as prayer combines with the "heavenly sacrifice" of Hebrews to slant the meaning of sacrifice in a decidedly cultic direction, over against a penitential or an ethical one.

Is such a cultic understanding helpful in regard to the desire that the eucharistic liturgy affect Christian social-justice behavior? Can a "soteriology of compassion" comprehend all that has been contained in the classic "soteriology of expiation"? Put another way, is the notion of "sacrifice" as the continual intercession offered by Christ at the right hand of the Father able to ground a "soteriology of compassion"[22] and thus provide a firmer base for Christians to be confirmed in a moral vision that is an eschatological vision of the world?

At first sight, of course, mention of Jesus' heavenly sacrifice suggests another round of the "hermeneutics of suspicion"; Jon Sobrino rightly criticizes preaching the resurrection as a "symbol of universal hope" that can unleash emotions in a liturgical celebration but has little effectiveness for historical life." But his hermeneutic proposal also speaks directly to the argument for symbolizing in the liturgy the history of the community. When the church speaks of the resurrection, Sobrino asserts, it must be united to the "numberless other crosses *in...history*" [emphasis added] with all their "insanity and scandal" because there is "not enough history to lend lucidity" to the language of the resurrection itself. He too invokes the language of Matthew 25 to claim that "in the crucified of history...Jesus has returned — showing his wounds more than his glory...but really there."[23] He proposes an understanding of the resurrection as God's response to the criminal actions of human beings; it is not a matter of one's personal survival but of the triumph of God's justice over injustice.[24] But the issue is the symbolization of this community's history; even commitment to such worthwhile causes as the Sanctuary movement will be "ideological" if the living reality of the worshiping community is itself symbolically invisible.[25]

This essay has proposed a retrieval of the eucharist as sacrifice, a commitment to a symbolization of history in the liturgy and a recognition and dependence on the Spirit of God as the elements necessary to create a link between liturgy and Christian social action. The shift being called for in the paschal symbolism is from an accent on Jesus' sacrificial death to an accent on his sacrificial risen life as the way God's redemptive power can become effective. From a grammar of sacrifice embodied in priest, altar and victim is emerging a transformative grammar in which the uniqueness of Christ's sacrifice is allowed full play among New Testament images of the kingdom: "present your bodies as a living sacrifice"; "as often as you have done it to the least of my brethren, you have done it to me"; "have you not read, 'I desire mercy and not sacrifice'"; "for we do not have a High Priest who is unable to sympathize with our weakness but one who was tempted in every way that we are, yet never sinned."

Attention to living symbols of the community life is required in each liturgy: a deepening personal witness must become evident in the power of lectors, the demeanor of eucharistic ministers and the presentation of candidates for baptism and confirmation. Life-enriching power must be available in well-prepared weddings and funerals. Personal and social ministries ranging far beyond the merely liturgical, centers of fellowship, care and concern within the parish — and all these brought to appropriate expression from time to time — will speak for themselves in the liturgical presence of persons transformed by their embrace of the eschatological vision.

Sacrifice, as the ongoing intercession of the risen Christ, effective through the Spirit's empowerment of the baptized community and creating in each an eschatological vision of ways to allay the sin and suffering in which we are mired, is sacrifice in which the ethical and the cultic are rightly joined, and under which the church's redemptive embrace of the world can flourish. Liturgy approached with anything less than such a vision will only continue to give comfort to our culture's increasingly privatized worshipers.

Notes

1. "Unfinished agenda" is the approach of John Egan, "Liturgy and Justice," *Origins* 13, no. 15 (1983): 47–53. The most recent address to the problem is that of Regis Duffy, O.F.M., who speaks of the "striking pastoral dichotomy... between the theoretical meanings of liturgy and participants' actions, shaped by their liturgies, in the public sphere where the mission of the church must also be exercised." "The U.S. Catholic Contribution to Liturgy," *New Theology Review* 1 (1988): 31. He shows also that the action-oriented character of the American liturgical movement made no mark on official teaching and documents. See also his *Real Presence: Worship, Sacraments and Commitment* (San Francisco: Harper & Row, 1982).

2. Myles Bourke, "The Epistle to the Hebrews," in the *Jerome Biblical Commentary* (New York: Prentice-Hall, 1968) II, esp. 393–96; H. E. Symonds, "The Heavenly Sacrifice in the Greek Fathers," *Texte und Untersuchungen* 93 (1966): 285.

3. Cf. the author's *Concept of Sacrifice in the Eucharistic Theologies of Donald Baillie, Thomas Torrance and Jean-Jacques von Allmen* (Ann Arbor, Mich.: University Microfilms, 1972), 268–74.

4. Alisdair Heron, *Table and Tradition: Toward an Ecumenical Understanding of the Eucharist* (Philadelphia: Westminster Press, 1983), 174.

5. Richard Kearney, "Religion and Ideology: Paul Ricoeur's Hermeneutic Conflict," *Irish Theological Quarterly* 52 (1986): 111.

6. Ibid., 111–12.

7. For example, Tissa Balasuriya, *The Eucharist and Human Liberation* (Maryknoll, N.Y.: Orbis Books, 1979).

8. Kearney, "Religion and Ideology," 116–17.

9. The Decree of the 13th session of the Council of Trent on the Most Holy Eucharist speaks of the eucharist as a "pledge of future glory." DS 1638.

10. Kearney, "Religion and Ideology," 118–19.

11. Ibid., 112–13.

12. *Vision and Virtue: Essays in Christian Theological Reflection* (Notre Dame: Fides Publishers, 1974), 34, 71, 36, 44. Hauerwas works substantially out of a critical analysis of the philosophical ethics of Iris Murdoch. See her "Vision and Choice in Morality," in *Christian Ethics and Contemporary Philosophy*, ed. Ian Ramsey (New York: Macmillan, 1966), 195–218. W. H. Willimon makes good use of Hauerwas in *The Service Of Good: How Worship and Ethics Are Related* (Nashville: Abingdon Press, 1983), 21–37.

13. Ibid., 71, n. 5.

14. David N. Power has addressed this issue in *Unsearchable Riches: The Symbolic Nature of Liturgy* (New York: Pueblo, 1984), 136–37: "the ritual or bodily element in liturgy is metaphorical [and] is taken to represent the holiness and power of God among the people and in the world... things and actions... directly representative of the ordinary and the daily are proclaimed to be symbols of God's presence and action."

15. *Unsearchable Riches*, 71: "Self-knowledge is mediated by a projection into image, language and action — most of which are provided by... culture and society... [as] a mirror which reflects the person back to the self."

16. Geoffrey Wainwright develops the pneumatological scope of the eucharistic celebration with the intention of correcting our christomonist one and shows how word and spirit are active in the eucharist. See his "As with the Word, so with the Spirit," in *Eucharist and Eschatology* (New York: Oxford University Press, 1981), 94–102.

17. The work of the Holy Spirit is, I think, the "living hermeneutic" referred to by Don Saliers: "... the tacit range of meaning available is always selected out by the living hermeneutic of the worshiping assembly and given emotional focus in the societal perceptions and orientations we have been invited to bring" (*Worship and Spirituality* [Philadelphia: Westminster Press, 1984], 55).

18. William Dych, S.J., "The Dualism in the Faith of the Church," in *The Faith That Does Justice,* ed. John C. Haughey (New York: Paulist Press, 1977), 63–64. The anthropology proposed by René Girard, with its chief note the human willingness to wreak violence on "others" made into victims and scapegoats, can also be seen as enjoining "compassion" as the redemptive force. Cf. his *Violence and the Sacred* (Baltimore: Johns Hopkins University Press, 1978) and *SEMEIA* 33 (1985).

19. Bourke, 394.

20. Symonds, "The Heavenly Sacrifice," 285, 280.

21. Stanislas Lyonnet, "Scriptural Meaning of 'Expiation'" *Theology Digest* 10 (1962): 227–28; see his complete study of the New Testament's redemptive vocabulary, *De Peccato et Redemptione,* II (Rome, 1960).

22. Hebrews 4:14–5:1 is titled "Jesus, the Compassionate High Priest" in the JBC II, 389, and in the New American Bible, although the term "compassion" is not in the text.

23. Jon Sobrino, *Jesus in Latin America* (Maryknoll, N.Y.: Orbis Books, 1987), 157.

24. Ibid., 149–50.

25. The pastor of a San Francisco church, noted for its continuity with the past and engagement with the present, attributes the effectiveness of worship "not to the preaching but to the Eucharist, which 'draws people in and somehow informs them of the source of life that is present at the heart of worship'" (Robert Bellah et al., *Habits of the Heart: Individualism and Commitment in American Life* [New York: Harper & Row, 1985], 238).

8

The Soul of Black Worship

WYATT TEE WALKER

American Christians are fully aware of the different dynamics of worship that exist in white, mainline Protestant churches as compared with those of churches peopled by worshipers of African descent. Succinctly stated, black folks' worship is vastly different from white folks' worship. That is not to say that one or the other is necessarily superior or inferior to the other; it is only to establish that they are different.

The root of this difference is in the peculiar social history of black and white relations in the United States. For nearly *250* years, Blacks were subjected to the most brutal and obscene form of human bondage in the history of humankind. Following the Civil War, the reconstruction period brought only a brief respite from chattel slavery. Before long we were plunged into the quagmire of legal segregation, which was sanctioned by the highest court of the land (Plessy vs. Ferguson, 1896). The system of segregation shaped the social mores of this land in regard to black and white relations. Its legal sanction was not ended until the Supreme Court decision of 1954 (Brown vs. Board of Education). No real effect of that decision was felt until Martin Luther King, Jr., and his nonviolent devotees swept through our southland.

Once again a brief period of euphoria ensued, and rapid cosmetic changes took place in the republic's social arrangement; but the good times did not last any longer than reconstruction had. Richard Nixon came to power, and the fortunes of Blacks and those similarly situated have been in general decline ever since. The statistical census kept by the National Urban League over the last ten years tells the story. There has been marked improvement in the lives of some individual Blacks, but for most of the black community conditions are worse.

From *Liturgy: In Daily Life* 7, no. 3.

Sources of spiritual strength

How is it that this black community has been able, over and over again, to weather the continuous assault inflicted by the systemic racism of American society? The answer, undoubtedly, lies in the character of our religious faith, 95 percent of which finds expression in one or another form of Protestant Christianity.

Eugene Genovese, a Marxist historian, spent nearly eleven years pursuing a socioeconomic study of American slavery.[1] Viewing slavery from the internal evidence — the slaves' own perception — he concluded that the slaves were able to survive the rigors of their bondage only by means of their religious practice. Though as a Marxist historian he was ideologically unsympathetic to the notions of God and religion, Genovese was nevertheless so impressed by the quality and substance of black folks' religion during the era of slavery that he named his monumental work after a spiritual, "Roll, Jordan, Roll."

It is no different today than it was in slavery times. The vitality of black church life and the worship that accompanies it are a tribute to the God who is worshiped and to those who worship. In the best of times, which have been few, and the worst of times, which have been many, the black church and its worship dynamic have sheltered their adherents from the thousand demons unleashed by racism in America.

Our peculiar social history has finely honed our worship skills. The "stuff" of worship must be relevant to the everyday circumstance of those who worship; this is almost always true of black people at worship, despite the critics and detractors of our traditional worship style. Who knows better than we that "God moves in a mysterious way, his wonders to perform"? Who knows better than we that "the Lord is my light and my salvation — whom shall I fear?" Who knows better than we how to "sing the Lord's song in a strange land"? Many black worship services explode with emotion when someone starts to sing:

> If it had not been for the Lord on my side,
> (Tell me) Where would I be? Where would I be?

Thus the peculiar social history of Afro-Americans and the dynamics of black religious faith have produced an amalgam of religious experience that warrants attention, scrutiny and analysis. Such study can also be most instructive to the larger Christian community.

Black worship involves three primary support systems: preaching, praying and singing.[2] These are not the only ingredients, but they are the essential components of our liturgy. Authentic black worship does not proceed unless they are present and operative.

Until I commenced doctoral study in 1972, I had assumed that the progression of our religious development began with preaching, which was then followed by singing and praying in some uncertain order. How great my error. On the North American continent singing preceded preaching as the first by-product of the oral tradition that survived the barbaric Atlantic slave trade.[3]

Thus preaching and praying are colored by the idiom of that folk-base in song. In this essay I explore all three of these essential components of our unique black religious experience, emphasizing their interrelatedness and the priority of the oral tradition.

Preaching, the heart of black worship

Preaching in the black religious experience, that is, in the folk church, has been and is primarily oral in function and practice. The tradition out of which it developed as an art form is an oral tradition. It is, of course, very difficult to analyze oral material on the same basis as literary or written texts, the accepted bench marks of the west.

The preaching tradition of the black religious experience is heavily influenced by the persona of the black preacher-figure. There is a striking parallel between the African priest-doctor and the Afro-American pastor. Each presides over and is involved in the life crises of the community he or she serves: birth, death, sickness, puberty, trouble, domestic discord, marriage.

The renaissance of interest in the black preacher as a central figure in black people's affairs has created a parallel interest in the pastor's craft — preaching. Whatever else he or she may do, the folk-base has been primarily the preaching of the sermon. The combination of the centrality of preaching and the dominance of the preaching person has left an indelible imprint on the style and content of the black church enterprise, the institution of primary influence among Afro-Americans.

Despite imperfections, the preaching and theology of black preachers gave cohesion and unity to an oppressed people. From the vantage point of history it seems that sheer genius coupled with the providence of God enabled black Christians to survive slavery at all. What is more, black folks emerged from their collective traumatic ordeal with a clearer conception of the Jesus-faith than the masters from whom they learned his name.

The substantive role of the black preacher has changed little since slavery. The task remains essentially the same: to provide a sense of hope in a hopeless situation. The pain predicament of black people remains constant; only the time and places have changed. The black preacher stands between two juxtaposed realities: Ronald Reagan is in the White House and God is still on the throne. The otherworldliness of black folk religion is necessary because this world (slavery, segregation, Reagan and racism) is unbearable. The black preacher-person, if he or she is anything, is existentialist in matters of faith, and the centerpiece of that faith proclamation is the theological conclusion of our slave ancestors: "I know de udder world is not like 'dis!"[4]

The form of black preaching is rooted in the oral tradition of West Africa. To suggest that slavery had the positive result of introducing heathen slaves to Christianity is to distort history. Monotheism was not new to the transplanted Africans. Naive Europeans erred in interpreting the ceremony and dynamics of traditional African religion. They confused ancestor reverence with ancestor worship; they mistook the intermediaries of the High God for the lesser gods and assumed we were polytheists. Slavery was no stroke of providence by which we found our way to the true and living God.

Africans knew the one God as early as the fifth century B.C.E., when Europeans were still dressed in animal skins and living in caves.[5] The Jesus-faith, new to the Africans transplanted to America, had fertile ground in which to grow and develop because we possessed a religious heritage founded on the "one God" principle. Christianity might not have taken hold as it did had Africans not had a theological orientation to the High God and to a concomitant view of humanity and nature.

The root and soil of black preaching is the oral tradition of mother Africa. The authenticity and legitimacy of the black preaching phenomenon, verified by its track record in mobilizing humanity for Christ, claims our attention as the centerpiece of the liturgy of black worship.

The content of black preaching

In a religious context, preaching is our literature. Study and analysis of the content of black preaching will reveal much about us as a people. It details our hopes and aspirations, our fundamental responses to the changes in our lives, the facility with which we cope with crises and much more.[6] The substantive characteristics of our preaching have more to do with what is preached than with how it is preached.[7]

Black preaching has always been deeply biblical. Authentic preaching in the folk tradition comes out of the Bible. The central focus of preaching is Jesus Christ, crucified, dead, buried and risen on the third-day morning. Black clergy, of course, make use of all the scriptures, but our preaching is always heavily christocentric.

Black preaching is cross-centered, and black preachers are sometimes criticized for "always taking us to Calvary." Paul himself acknowledged that the cross was a stumbling block to the Jews and foolishness to the Greeks, but "unto them that believe, it is the power of God unto salvation." The glory of Christ is in the cross! Not by force of arms or by fascination of ritual or by glamour of learning or philosophy has the gospel entered into human life and transformed it but by the inherent power of the cross of shame. Warring only against sin, the gospel has lifted human life to higher levels, working moral miracles and glorifying everyday existence. The black preacher knows that the man who died on a cross outside the city wall has the power to change lives.

The overarching genius of the black preacher is the innate ability to take the "old, old story of Jesus" and make it live for today. The contemporary interpretation of scripture is one of the broad avenues down which the black preacher parades his or her considerable skill. Black preaching has always been faith-filled. In this high-tech era, black preaching continues to proclaim the message that is at the heart of preaching: God can do anything but fail. That embraces all the possibilities of human circumstance over which Jesus presided in his earthly ministry. The preaching in black worship services is heavily laced with the assurance that every once in a while God steps into human circumstances in extraordinary ways to let us know we are cared for. Black preaching proclaims that signs and wonders and miracles are by no means locked into the first century C.E.

Two other characteristics, each related to the other, bear mention. The black preaching tradition is marked by its otherworldly character, which leaves it open to the persistent criticism that it is irrelevant to the real world in which the devotees exist. The nature of religion itself, at bottom, involves an abiding concern with the metaphysical aspects of life after death.

The related characteristic is black preaching's concern with eschatology. The Greek root of this word means "ultimate" or "last things," in the biblical sense. The eschatological character is intertwined with the otherworldly in the spiritual, "God's gonna destroy this wicked race and raise up a nation that will obey!" In the judgment, all will reap what they sow.

Praying, the strength of black worship

The second support system of black worship is prayer: the act of lifting one's consciousness to God in some physical or verbal manner whose end is to blend the worshiper's will with that of the omnipotent God. Praying is the means by which we "talk" with God, as well as the medium by which God directly or indirectly answers the petitions of heart and spirit.

Each of the three support systems under scrutiny possesses elements of the others, and all share a direct link to the oral tradition of West Africa. After intensive study, I am almost sure that singing precedes preaching and praying. Preaching and praying most likely developed in parallel fashion close on the heels of the creation of the original musical art form, the spiritual. In our music as in our preaching, there is always a prayer content.

Like the other two disciplines, praying has been colored by our peculiar history. The subject and content of black people's praying were and are set by the social conditions around us. The prayers of our ante-bellum ancestors evidence an insatiable appetite for freedom — that is, political liberation. The sociological circumstance directly influenced the construction of the prayer utterances, then and now.

Prayer's chief function in the black religious experience has been to cope with the uncertainties of our continuing North American experience. It has never been easy for black people in this land. Relatively speaking, only time and place have changed. Slavery, segregation, second-class citizenship, economic dislocation — these are only the specifics of the systemic racism that touches every waking moment of our existence and every fiber of our being, one way or another. How we wish it would go away, but it persists. Thus, with no relief in sight, we turn it over to God.

The resiliency of spirit necessary to endure what we have to endure is due largely to our tradition of prayer, which is the strength of the black religious experience. If preaching is indeed the heart of black worship, then praying has been its strength.

Biblical and theological themes

It is safe to assume that when black folks first started to pray within the context of the Jesus-faith, they formed their early prayers on the biblical tradition of prayer. This is not as simple and straightforward as it sounds. The introduction of Christianity to slaves had a single purpose: to make better slaves. Yet the result was just the opposite; the slaves became more restive, and insurrections and runaways abounded.

The planters quickly regrouped. No religious services of any kind were permitted without tight monitoring by the planters and their overseers. The celebrated Cotton Mather prescribed that only "selective" passages of scripture should be shared with slaves, lest the system of slavery be disrupted.[8] The great biblical revelations on liberation, justice and equality in Jesus Christ were methodically extirpated from the catechism. The strict prohibition against slaves learning to read or write further controlled the doctrine forced upon new world Africans. Yet somehow, in spite of these obstacles, our ancestors discovered what the Bible really said. In some mysterious way, still unknown, we fastened our praying on the models of the biblical tradition.

Praying in the black religious experience is largely thematic. In talking to God, certain touchstones are always observed. Frequently the opening prayer of a formal service will touch all these bases; sometimes it will be the prayer at the communion table or the prayer at the close of the weekly prayer service or the prayer to open or close the monthly meeting of a church club or auxiliary. The tradition of black prayer is that whenever we talk to God in collective worship, we feel "duty bound" to bring certain items to God's attention on our behalf — even though God, of course, already knows all about them.

The most prominent themes in the prayer discipline of the black religious experience are "praise" and "thanksgiving."[9] We know that God is a great God and worthy to be praised. The thanksgiving begins as soon as the worthiness of God has been established. The next theme that is struck early on is sorrow for sin — "repentance." The praying of black folks is almost always at some point "intercessory" and "petitionary." Petition in black prayer ranges over a wide field but with great specificity.

Critics of the black religious experience say there is too much dependence on God. In my view the critics are misreading the ultimate submission of the worshiper to the will of God. This element of submission is present in much of the liturgy of black prayer, for example:

O Lord, we would not leave this praying ground without recognizing that you have the whole world in your hands. Accept the desires of our hearts, and we trust your wisdom to do that which we ask. We know that you're going to answer our prayers, one way or another, and we bow in submission to your holy and righteous will....[10]

No self-respecting black pray-er would think of closing a prayer in a service of worship without clear mention of "last things." As preaching is eschatological, so is praying — perhaps more so.

One last comment summarizes the themes of black prayer. The centrality of Jesus is evident in every instance. In every portion of the prayer, the invocation is made interchangeably to God and Jesus. When black folks say "Lord," they mean Jesus. The fabric of black prayer is always generously laced with direct reference to the Lord Jesus Christ.

Praying within the context of the black worship experience has been the strength of Afro-Americans. Our tradition began when we could do little more than pray, but pray we did. We learned that God answers prayer.

Singing, the joy of black worship

The third essential support system of black worship is singing. Music is an integral part of the liturgical mode of worship in the black religious experience. In 1975, I completed a doctoral study on the music of the black church.[11] It hinged on one simple yet profound idea: a people's faith-music is a mirror of their sociology. Simply put, I argued that if you listen to what black people are singing in religious contexts, it is a clue to what is happening sociologically.[12]

The musical tradition of Afro-Americans is rooted in Africa and shaped in the ante-bellum slave experience. The new-world Africans who survived the machinery of the Atlantic slave trade were distributed about the south with careful attention to language differences in order to reduce the chance of rebellion or insurrection. Snatched from their homeland, raped of their culture and language, these transplanted Africans could not be robbed of the music in their souls. The penchant to sing was constant in spite of enslavement. That deep-seated cultural tradition of song was kept in place via the oral tradition.

The oral tradition can be defined as "transmission by word of mouth, song, drum and folk wisdom of the mores, customs and religious rites of African peoples that persisted through the Atlantic slave trade and influenced the worship forms and patterns of Afro-Americans."[13] Thus, as I wrote in my dissertation:

> To understand the depth and deep-rootedness of the oral tradition, one must appreciate several facts about African life and culture that not only antedate the Atlantic slave trade but are also apparent today.... African history has been preserved in its music. Troubadours, storytellers, and griots (official village historians) have been the history keepers. Within the context of holistic theological systems

of Africa, all life is manifestly religious. The events of life — birth, death, puberty, fertility, harvest, famine, marriage, tragedy — have religious rites that give expression to that event. In the absence of any prescribed formula as to what is done and when, the music and the companion ceremony have been the key to the orchestration of events and the primary preservative ingredient of tradition.[14]

This passage underscores the importance and dominance of music in the life of indigenous Africans, past and present. In spite of the process of Americanization, persons of African descent in North America stand in the direct line of inheritance of that tradition.

The music tree

Historically, all music born in America has felt the influence of the base-line musical art form commonly known as the spiritual. Visualizing a tree will aid our understanding of the development and relationship of the music that has its origins in black life-experience.

The roots of the "music tree" are the slaves' chants, moans and cries for freedom. Once the slaves had developed the facility of "pidgin English" — our best attempt to speak the language of the planters — we created the trunk of the tree with a variety of musical forms under the umbrella designation "spiritual." The spiritual forms included "praise songs," the "field spiritual," the "shouts" and "hollers," among others.

At emancipation, the sociology of the new-world Africans underwent drastic changes as chattel slavery came to an end. The vagaries of reconstruction and postreconstruction induced such grave ironies of freedom that a large quarter of black life became disillusioned, and many lost hope. Those who kept the faith utilized the spiritual mode to leave an imprint on meter music, which was European in origin.

With a marked increase in literacy at the turn of the century, Blacks stamped the Euro-American hymns with the imprimatur of improvisation. The confidence born of that syncretism led Blacks to produce gospel, and the influence of secular musicality, in turn, helped to produce modern gospel. That, in a nutshell, is the route of development of the music of the black religious experience.

This seeming digression is necessary to understand the inherent nature of the music of black worship as well as its contemporaneity. For Americans of African descent, the holistic character of our worship generally — and of our music particularly — necessitates the weaving of daily life events into our music and liturgy. This tradition remains very pronounced because of the dominant influence of music in the character of worship in the nation's free black churches.

It is this writer's firm conviction that given our historic social predicament, it is essential that the music Afro-Americans use in worship be relevant to our circumstances. That same conviction is shared by other black pastors and worshipers. The unique circumstances of our daily experience account for the contrast between black-style worship and the worship styles of white America.

Notes

1. Eugene Genovese, *Roll, Jordan, Roll: The World the Slaves Made* (New York: Pantheon Books, 1974), 280.

2. Wyatt Tee Walker, *Somebody's Calling My Name* (Valley Forge, Pa.: Judson Press, 1979), 22.

3. Ibid., 29.

4. Traditional spiritual.

5. John S. Mbiti, *African Religions and Philosophy* (Garden City, N.Y.: Doubleday, 1970), 167.

6. Wyatt Tee Walker, *The Soul of Black Worship* (New York: Martin Luther King Fellows Press, 1984), 13.

7. In *The Soul of Black Worship* I suggest that there are additional superficial characteristics of black preaching, but they are not germane to the discussion in this article.

8. C. Eric Lincoln, "The Development of Black Religion in America," *Review and Expositor* 70, no. 3 (Summer 1973): 304.

9. Walker, *The Soul of Black Worship*, 33.

10. Traditional-style folk-prayer.

11. Walker, *Somebody's Calling My Name.*

12. Ibid., 17.

13. Ibid., 27.

14. Ibid., 28–29.

9

Sense of the Seasons: *Proclaiming the Paschal Mystery*

SAMUEL TORVEND

Every celebration of the Christmas cycle proclaims the paschal mystery of the Lord's passion, death, resurrection and sending of the Spirit.

For many Christians and countless North Americans, the Christmas season has been reduced to the celebration of the birth date of Jesus or the more generic practice of good will, public charities and consumerist frenzy. Another intention appears, however, when we consider the historical origins of a feast marking the incarnation, the readings appointed in the lectionaries, the liturgical texts proclaimed at worship and the sustained reflection of liturgical scholars.

Together these various sources suggest that the Christmas cycle draws its ultimate meaning and purpose from the three great days of the springtime paschal season. In other words, the Christmas cycle of feasts — and indeed all Christian celebrations — are rooted both historically and theologically in the meaning of the last days of the Lord Jesus: the supper and the foot washing in the upper room; the arrest, trial, condemnation and crucifixion; the resurrection appearances, the breathing of the Spirit and missionary mandates. Thus the Christmas season looks to the paschal season as the still point of the turning liturgical year.

We might see here a parallel between the Gospel accounts and the origins of the church's liturgical calendar. Mark's Gospel, for instance, simply begins with Jesus' preaching, focuses on his passion and death, and ends with the disciples seemingly stupefied by the messenger's words: he has gone before you to Galilee. The Gospels of Luke and Matthew, from whom we derive so much Christmas imagery, offer a different perspective, one that is quite interested in Jesus' conception, birth and early infancy. Certainly these Gospels proclaim with Mark that the redeemer of the world is revealed precisely in his self-giving death on the cross, but from the viewpoint of the exaltation of Jesus as the risen Christ,

From *Liturgy: The Christmas Cycle* 9, no. 3.

they look back into the early life of Jesus and see God's loving purposes being signaled at an early stage. Where Mark remains silent concerning the birth of Jesus, Luke and Matthew see the events of the last days of Jesus' life already appearing in the events that surround his conception, birth and early life.

In parallel fashion, we now see that the earliest "Christian" feast was not all that interested in Jesus' birth but in the living memorial of his death made into life by the saving power of God and the presence of the Spirit awakening faith in the first followers of the risen Christ. Gathering weekly "on the Lord's Day," the early Christians celebrated the presence of the crucified yet risen Lord among them in the proclamation of his words, and in the breaking of bread and sharing of cup. From this weekly celebration of the Lord's death and resurrection, there developed the annual celebration of the paschal mystery in the Mediterranean springtime. Thus *whenever* Christians gather to celebrate, they gather to mark in word and meal the saving power of God revealed in the life, death and resurrection of the Lord Jesus.

How Christmas came about

But what of Christmas and the feasts that cluster around it? Only at a later date do we find evidence for a feast celebrating the Lord's nativity; it was inspired by the Gospels of Luke and Matthew as well as the Christian missionary concern to celebrate the Gospel within the pagan feasts of the winter solstice. Those feasts were marked by an abundance of food and drink during winter's meager provisions, by welcoming the sun's return from winter's darkness and by giving gifts to family and friends.

More recent scholarship suggests, in fact, that the emergence of a feast celebrating the nativity of the Lord was inspired by the biblical calculation of his birth date drawn from the belief that he was conceived on what would be the day of his death. Thus, nine months from the spring vernal equinox would lead to the winter solstice: conceived in the spring and born in winter's darkness.

Whether the origin of the nativity feast was missionary concern for pagan winter feasting or the evangelical calculation of the savior's birth, the fact remains that only at a later date do we find Christians celebrating the nativity. And when we read of their celebrations, we see they recognized that the One who made their worship possible was the crucified and risen Lord in their midst, proclaiming his saving word and feeding them on his life-giving death in bread and cup — yes, at the celebration of the nativity.

If we assume, then, that Christians gather today to celebrate the birth of the Lord, we must be careful to assert that in this Christmas celebration we already celebrate his death and resurrection. As William Dix wrote over a century ago in the beloved Christmas carol, "What Child Is This?"

> Why lies he in such mean estate,
> Where ox and ass are feeding?
> Good Christian, fear: for sinners here

the silent Word is pleading.
Nails, spear, shall pierce him through,
the cross be borne,
for me, for you.
Hail, hail, the Word made flesh,
the babe, the son of Mary.

Indeed without the rigor and realism of the last days, the Christmas cycle is simply turned into a pagan feast of light in winter's darkness or at best a sentimental celebration of the Lord's infancy. When, however, the worshiping assembly gathers to offer thanks to God for the great acts of salvation, in particular the saving death of the Lord, and to share that death in bread and cup, it is rescued from liturgical and biblical amnesia: the assembly holds in hand and tastes on lips the truth that the One feasted in at winter's solstice is the One who died and rose at spring's equinox; that the Word made flesh, Mary's son, is at last pierced in death's dreary darkness, making this the time and place of God's new dwelling with us.

The tree of Christmas

Perhaps we can suggest that the Christmas tree — so beloved of Christians from northern climes — shares in the same liturgical parallel, the same liturgical logic. Certainly the cross, as an instrument of cruel torture and public death, became at an early stage the preeminent symbol of the Christian faith and the paschal mystery. But in the thinking of Christians, the "wood of the tree" on which hung the savior of the world was typologically linked with the tree of life in the Edenic garden: the tree of death, washed in the savior's blood, had become the tree of life, filled with delicious fruits hanging on evergreen boughs, a tree whose leaves — as the Seer of Patmos wrote — are filled with healing for the strife-torn nations of the earth.

And so in customs of various nations, the link between the tree of life in the garden, the tree of death on Calvary and the tree of Christmas has been sustained through the centuries, so that the tree we decorate with burning lights in the midst of a northern winter's darkness is also the tree of Christ's suffering for us. Thus the tree we take down, cleared of lights, its needles dropping one by one, soon appears as that solitary tree from which the One celebrated at Christmas reigns as the suffering savior in his death. In other words, through the eyes of faith the tree that stands in home and church throughout the Christmas season already silently marks the truth of the paschal mystery. Already the sentimentality that surrounds and infuses so much winter feasting and Christian worship is corrected, sharpened and focused by the knowledge that the Christmas season and its symbolic tree are linked inextricably to the last days, the paschal season and its tree of life.

Already the scripture readings for the Christmas cycle reveal the bond between the two seasons: a vengeful and unjust ruler hears of a "new king's" birth and is afraid; he sends his troops with orders to slaughter the innocent; blood is shed and all seems lost, but One is brought back from Egypt, the old "house of bondage, house of death." Already the Gospel writers herald that which is to come: the incarnation already celebrates the passion, death and resurrection. Already the meal of bread and cup, celebrated and shared in the Christmas cycle, proclaims the death of the Lord until he comes to gather to himself the dead and the living.

What are we really celebrating?

The Christmas cycle celebrates the ongoing incarnation of the Word in human life and history.

With the toleration of Christianity by the imperial government in 313 and the establishment of the church as the state religion in 381, Christian leaders and their imperial benefactors were able to build churches over those sites recorded in the Gospels where Jesus lived, worked and spent his last days on earth. This development, in turn, made it possible for Christian pilgrims to tour these "holy sites," to go back in time and view the places where significant biblical events had taken place, to trace the savior's steps.

The "Holy Land tour" mentality, however, had disastrous effects that remain with the churches today; in effect, it suggested that the most significant actions, the salvific actions, took place in the past and remain in the past. That mentality further suggested that for those who live in the present, there simply remains the possibility of remembering those actions and being inspired by dramatic reenactments that are produced in the present moment.

Thus for many contemporary Christians, the celebration of the Christmas cycle appears as the opportunity to return to old Bethlehem of the past, to hear again the favored stories that surround the season, to be inspired by the music and colors of the holidays.

Since we cannot return through time to the past, we perform simple or elaborate Christmas pageants reenacting the Christmas past, place plastic dolls in mangers near altars and speak of the celebration as a "birthday party for Jesus" as if he were being reborn again and again. Almost unthinkingly, we return to a time that cannot possibly exist again and are satisfied with our return to the degree that the music, decorations, costuming and affectation of the actors inspire a range of emotional responses. In other words, we celebrate events of the past (e.g., the birth of Jesus) and leave them in the past since they are completed and cannot take place again. Thus our imaginations are often restricted to biblical pageants and churches decorated as stables.

For familial, ethnic or cultural reasons, we may lavish the feast with an extraordinary expenditure of money and energy. Is it possible, though, that some Christian communities have forgotten one salient point in their attempts to capture some of the "charm" of the "first Christmas"; namely, that *the incarnation of the divine Word*, celebrated in the Christmas season, *is not yet complete in human life and history?* Could some of us have forgotten that all Christians, all Christian communities, are called to serve as heralds and midwives of that ongoing birth of the Word in the present moment? Is this not the intention of the author of "O holy Child of Bethlehem, / Descend to us, we pray; Cast out our sin, and enter in, / *Be born in us today*"?

Rather than viewing the Christmas-cycle celebration as a nostalgic trip to old Bethlehem (or the old England, Germany or Italy of our immigrant past), where for a few hours or days we return to a most significant time, the rigor of the liturgy proclaims another purpose for our feasting: "Today a savior is born." One hears the words and thinks, "Yes, born hundreds of years ago," but the liturgical proclamation should be taken at face value: born today.

Thus the liturgy of the season asks the question of those worshiping: *Where is the savior being born today?* Where is the Word taking on visible life in forms that might seem as unexpected, as surprising, to us as to those who 2,000 years ago found it incredible that a mere infant could be the human form of the invisible Creator of the universe?

If the question is asked, "Do we prepare for and celebrate Jesus' birthday throughout the Christmas season?" we would have to answer "No," if by those words is meant a journey into the past for a few simple hours or days, a much needed respite from the pace of life pursued by so many in North America. If the question is rephrased: "Do we celebrate the incarnation of the Word, indeed the ongoing incarnation of the Word in human life and history today?" we must emphatically answer, "Yes!" We celebrate this incarnation and pray that its power may find a more profound dwelling within us, our communities, our larger world, in the midst of our often hurried and distracted lives. For if the incarnation, the ongoing birth of the Word, does not continue through the agency of the Spirit in our life and times, what possible meaning can this feasting have other than wistful, wishful thinking, a nostalgic impulse for what could have been?

Is our worship a return to the Bible lands of the past? Is it a matter of putting on plays about a past to which we cannot possibly return? In either case the worshiping assembly is simply transformed into a group of spectators who might be inspired by eloquent preaching or beautiful music. But if Christian worship views past events as paradigms, models, hints, of what is taking place in the present moment, then preaching, music, the arts and religious education are inspired and challenged to ask the question that ought to resound in the hearts of all worshipers: How are we assisting in the present advent, incarnation and epiphany of the Word?

Three movements, one theme

Recognizing, then, that the Christmas cycle is not intended to be a return to the past but the celebration of the ongoing incarnation of the Word in the present, we need to assert with equal emphasis that the church's calendar marks *a season of celebration* rather than a few days of unrelated feasting.

Historians of the church year point out that the earliest celebrations of the incarnation developed along slightly different paths in the Eastern and Western regions of the early church. In the East, greater emphasis was accorded the manifestation, the epiphany, of the Lord as light for all nations. As the feast developed in the West, greater emphasis was given to the Lord's birth, his nativity as light shining in the darkness of sin. Consequently, the Western church developed — in parallel fashion to Lent — a period of preparation prior to the feast of the nativity: what we know today as Advent. The entire incarnational cycle, then, was marked in time by three movements: advent-nativity-epiphany (and the feast of the Lord's baptism).

From a pastoral liturgical perspective, we must ask ourselves if this overall view of the season has, in fact, become the basis on which preaching, music, intercessions, environment and art, catechesis and household prayer are planned and implemented for the worshiping assembly. Do we not often find instead churches simply worshiping in accord with the socioeconomic "calendar" of North American culture, one that tends to reduce a season of liturgical celebration to two days: Christmas and the New Year?

If, for instance, one is preparing to preach throughout the season, does it not make good liturgical and homiletic sense to have an overview of the scripture readings for the entire cycle in order to grasp the movement from the Baptist's preaching to the inauguration of Jesus' preaching after his baptism in the Jordan? One might ask: How is the congregation being called to proclaim, preach and herald the advent, incarnation and manifestation of the light in the particular age and culture in which it exists?

Likewise, if one is preparing the worship space, how might one envision an environment that signals the movement of the entire season from Advent through the Nativity to the Epiphany? Or if one is preparing music for the assembly, how might the integrity, the unity, of the entire cycle be assured (a refrain sung throughout the season, perhaps), while the distinctiveness of each movement is highlighted (the hymns and canticles cross-referenced to the lessons for each Sunday and feast day)?

When one considers the movements of the entire cycle, the history of its development and the readings appointed for proclamation in worship, a single theme emerges that articulates the unity of the season; namely, *welcoming the light*. When one contemplates the readings for the first Sunday of Advent (the sudden appearance of the Lord clothed in light), the Nativity (the light born in the middle of night) and the Epiphany (the light of the star guiding the visitors), the appearance of the Lord's saving activity is metaphorically cast as the emergence of light in the midst of human darkness: "Arise, shine; for your light has come," sings Isaiah, "and the glory of the Lord has risen upon you."

Thus it is not so much for dramatic effect that Luke speaks of Jesus' birth in the middle of the night as the desire to make a theological-soteriological statement: that in the midst of human suffering, in the darkest hour, *God is with God's children*, sharing their pain and struggling with them.

So it is that the church celebrates the Nativity in the hours of darkness on Christmas Eve, welcoming the light in song, word, gesture, image and meal. In this celebration of light at the northern winter's solstice, we see once again the parallel to the church's celebration of the Lord's resurrection in the springtime: light burning in the midst of Easter Vigil darkness. Thus the unity (welcoming the light) and the distinctiveness of the Christmas cycle (Advent-Christmas-Epiphany) serve as the framework for the preparation of winter worship.

The season's center: the eucharist

Centered around the table of the Lord, the congregation celebrates in word and meal the living presence of the crucified and risen Christ, named in the Christmas cycle, God-with-us, Emmanuel. In every celebration of the Supper, the congregation is rooted in the past (the birth, life, death and resurrection), in the continual presence of the risen Lord (gathering the community through the agency of the Spirit), and in the future (the "second advent" when all shall be seated at the messianic banquet).

To proclaim "Jesus our Emmanuel" in the worship of the Christmas cycle is to participate in that most intimate act of sharing his death given for human life: the breaking of the bread, the sharing of his cup. No amount of singing, candle holding or pageantry can be a substitute for this act by which the Lord Jesus gives himself to his sisters and brothers.

We will be taken by surprise

The incarnation of the Word celebrated in Advent-Nativity-Epiphany takes place where it is least expected. A young Jewish girl from the hill country, a wild preacher on the fringes of Israelite society, a group of smelly and sleepy shepherds, a confused and frightened carpenter, an infant born in a stable, a band of curious visitors from the East, a retired couple in the temple precincts: this odd array of characters underscores the *paradoxical* nature of the season; that is, the divine Word is *not* revealed where one might expect such a revelation-among persons of social standing, economic influence or political power. Rather, the Word makes his dwelling among those who consider themselves unworthy or incapable of receiving a visitation of grace, peace and hope, a visitation from the Most High God, the Ruler of the universe.

For those who have eyes to see, however, the Word continues to visit us when and where we least expect it: the elderly sick in a nursing home, the poor single mother struggling to care for her children, the often stumbling words of the preacher, the people of the earth who are confused and frightened, a taste of bread and sip of wine — the meal that is hardly a meal. Indeed, the Word, the Light, casts his lot among those who are suffering, fearful and lonely. In our worship we sing of "Peace on earth, good will toward all," but we know there can be no peace without forgiveness and self-sacrifice, no lasting good will until the little ones of this earth experience some measure of their God-given dignity.

Does our worship simply reinforce the *status quo* of the worshipers? Is it a sedative dulling the senses to the world's pain and the Word's incarnation in that pain? Or does it enlighten the paradox of the season: that the little child of Bethlehem is the abandoned and crucified rabbi who is the risen Lord still giving himself in those places and times to those persons and groups whom our society says should not expect such a gracious visitation?

An apostolic feast

The beginning of the season is marked by the appearance of the risen Lord at the end of time, that day — one prays — of merciful judgment for the peoples of the earth. The season ends with his manifestation, his epiphany, to the gentiles — those who do not know him yet — and the celebration of his baptism into a ministry of proclaiming the presence of the gracious reign of God. John emerges from the wilderness of solitude to announce the advent of the Lord; the angelic messengers appear to Mary, Joseph and the shepherds with good news; the shepherds rejoice that they have witnessed the astounding birth; in Jerusalem, the Eastern visitors relate the birth of a "new king"; Simeon and Anna sing praise to God in the public precincts of the Temple.

In scripture reading and festive song, the congregation hears and sings of numerous persons who could not remain silent in the presence of the silent Word. The impulse of the season, from Advent to Epiphany, shares to no lesser degree in the apostolic fervor of Easter and Pentecost. Only a "literalist" reading of the church year could lead one to conclude that the Christmas cycle merely introduces one to the public ministry of Jesus and his followers.

Instead, *we know the end of the story:* he was born, he preached and healed, he died and is now risen among us through the power of the Spirit. We cannot return to ancient Bethlehem just as we cannot return to Jerusalem's Golgotha. But we can celebrate the cycle of feasts as the model, the paradigm, of Christian life and witness today. The congregation can indeed be invited to take its "missionary cues" from those who witnessed the first advent, nativity and epiphany of the Lord. The Christmas cycle itself invites the churches to contemplate their participation in the ongoing work of redemption wherever they find themselves.

Christian initiation

The Christmas cycle is the framework and content of catechesis for those preparing for Christian initiation at Easter. As the witness of the ancient church makes clear, the worshiping assembly is the primary teacher of those preparing to enter the Christian community. Those charged with the formation of such persons should resist the temptation to turn the season into a seminary curriculum that treats of systematic questions and doctrinal concerns.

Rather, those being introduced to the faith are rooted in the readings appointed for the season. The theology of the season is carefully drawn from the readings and liturgical-musical texts that are used. The movement of the season is noted as the question is asked: How does such movement shape the experience of deepening conversion to the grace of Christ? How is this community being called to serve as heralds of the reign of God today? How are we serving the poor, unwed mothers, the sick and elderly, the widows and orphans? How can the light of Christian faith best be communicated in this city, town or region of the country?

The One who gathers the assembly for worship is, in the end, the Spirit. The One who is the ultimate teacher of the faith is the Spirit working in the hearts of believers. The Spirit's tools are the community, its common worship, its acts of service. Let the liturgy, the worship of the church, do its work. And then may we confirm that work in acts of worshipful service to the larger world.

10

The Origins and Shape of Lent

Thomas J. Talley

Renewed considerations of the rites of Christian initiation in this century have vastly heightened our consciousness of the profoundly public and communitarian nature of these rites. Gone for the foreseeable future if not forever is the presumption that baptism will be administered outside the times of general liturgical assembly in an intimate gathering appropriate to what once seemed the familial and relatively private nature of that act.

This renewed appreciation of initiation as an inherently public act of the gathered body of Christ leads us as well to a renewed appreciation of initiation as a process rather than a discrete act. The rite for the initiation of adults in the Roman Catholic church and similar rites in other churches reveal once again the fully processual character of initiation. Initiation is a process of growth that leads to ultimate participation in Christ's death and resurrection as the type and sign of our understanding of human life. This process was a significant dimension in the life of the early church. It shaped every aspect of that life, including its ordering of the time that we know as the liturgical year.

A paschal theology

Of the time for the administration of baptism, the New Testament tells us nothing, though some have supposed that certain New Testament documents reflect a practice that was later taken as normative, the administration of baptism in connection with the annual celebration of the paschal mystery. Paul's theology of baptism in Romans 6 suggests that the association of initiation with this festival was aboriginal, and some writers believe that this association can be seen in such books as 1 Peter. These findings probably claim too much, yet recent research into the history of the Christian Pascha indicates that this feast was a modulated continuation of the observance of the Jewish Passover, rather than a yearly festival created *de novo* in the second century: As such, the Christian Passover was

From *Liturgy: Putting on Christ* 4, no. 1.

observed originally on the traditional day, in the night from the fourteenth to the fifteenth of Nisan, on whatever the day of the week that might fall. In the second century the paschal fast was extended to the following Sunday throughout most of the church, though Christians in Asia Minor continued to cling tenaciously to the traditional date, the fourteenth of Nisan. For this reason, they were called Quartodecimans.

The earliest clear testimony to the association of baptism with Pascha comes at the opening of the third century, in the treatise on baptism by Tertullian. Although the nineteenth chapter of this work is careful to observe that baptism may be performed at any time, it insists that the most solemn times are Passover and the Pentecost that follows. Some writers have suggested that this practice reflects a custom that was already observed by the Quartodecimans of Asia Minor, and that it might through them reach back to the apostolic period. None of the documents remaining to us from the Quartodecimans, however, make any certain reference to paschal baptism. Thus, any attempts to limit baptism to the paschal season are impossible to demonstrate until well after Tertullian.

Shortly after Tertullian, Hippolytus made a similar suggestion of Pascha as an appropriate time for baptism in his *Commentary on Daniel* (I.16.1–3). Most commentators suppose, moreover, that the baptismal liturgy described in the *Apostolic Tradition* a work usually ascribed to Hippolytus, unfolded in the course of the paschal vigil, though that is not explicitly stated. Even if the initiatory process described in the *Apostolic Tradition* was carried out at other times in addition to Pascha, still Pascha was one such focus of baptism. Therefore, we may take it that the separation of the candidates for baptism from the other catechumens and the subsequent daily exorcisms of those candidates described in the *Apostolic Tradition* occurred in the days or weeks prior to Pascha. Those daily exorcisms over an unspecified period may well be the seed for the season of Lent at Rome because, as research in the twentieth century makes clear, Lent began as a season of preparation for baptism, a season given to and shaped by the formation of candidates for Christian initiation.

Fasts and special disciplines

Two centuries later Socrates, the historian from Constantinople, reflected on the varieties in the shape of the fast before Easter. He called it "the fast of forty days" but also observed that those at Rome fast only three continuous weeks (H. E., V. 22). This surely was not the case in the fifth century when Socrates wrote, but it is interesting that later Roman documents such as the *Gelasian Sacramentary* and *Ordo Romanus XI* focused baptismal scrutinies in the third, fourth and fifth weeks of Lent, and that focus is much older surely than those documents. These three weeks perhaps underlie the assertion of Socrates; certainly they are a vestige of the special disciplines applied to candidates for baptism first mentioned in the *Apostolic Tradition*.

By the late fourth century, the total length of the fast at Rome was six weeks, the last of those weeks being the generally older Holy Week. A decretal of Siricius, bishop of Rome, to the bishop of Tarragona, Himerus, reflects the establishment at Rome of a period of forty days for the preparation of candidates for baptism, though Siricius evidently knows as well of places where an even longer period was customary. His letter to Himerus also makes it clear that Rome actually considered Easter and Pentecost to be the only appropriate times for baptism, since Lent, the forty-day preparation time occurs only in the weeks before Easter.

About this same time, in the last quarter of the fourth century, a Syrian testimony attempts to distinguish between the fast of forty days and the older paschal fast of Holy Week, which Syria had observed since the first half of the third century. According to the *Apostolic Constitutions* (V. 13), the fast of forty days began on a Monday and ended on a Friday. The fast was then broken off for two days, Saturday and Sunday, and the paschal fast of six days began on the next Monday. As it was generally true (outside Rome) that Saturdays and Sundays were always exempt from fasting, the statement that the Saturday and Sunday before Holy Week were exempt from the fast must have had a stronger meaning, namely, that this Saturday and Sunday were festal days, separate from either the Lenten or the paschal fast.

The Byzantine tradition

This pattern of two fasts can still be discerned in the Byzantine liturgy. Lent begins on a Monday and continues through an unbroken period of forty days until it ends at vespers on a Friday evening six weeks later. A troparion reflects the transition from the fast to the festal day that follows: "having completed the forty days that bring profit to our soul, let us cry: Rejoice, city of Bethany, home of Lazarus. Rejoice, Martha and Mary, his sisters. Tomorrow Christ will come, by his word to bring your dead brother to life." This text reveals the nature of the celebration on the following day: it is the Saturday of Lazarus, the celebration of the raising of Lazarus from the tomb at Bethany.

Throughout Lent the Gospel readings of the eucharistic liturgy in the Byzantine rite are taken from the Gospel of Mark, from its beginning through Mark 10:32–45. On this Saturday, however, there is an abrupt shift to the Gospel of John, the only Gospel to contain the story of Jesus' raising of Lazarus. The following day, Sunday, is Palm Sunday, and its Gospel is also taken from John. The theme of that Sunday, the celebration of Christ's triumphal entry into Jerusalem, has given its name to all the days of the preceding week; each day is a day "of the branches," and Saturday is called the "Saturday of the branch-bearer, memorial of the holy and just Lazarus."

That day is just one week before the great Easter Vigil, the principal time for baptism in the Byzantine tradition of the patristic period. Yet, in the liturgical books of the ninth and tenth centuries, which clearly continue earlier tradition, this Saturday of Lazarus is celebrated with a full baptismal liturgy during which the patriarch administers baptism in the little baptistry while the word liturgy continues in the church. The patriarch introduces the neophytes into the church after their baptism and chrismation. As on other baptismal days, the choir sings, "as many as have been baptized into Christ have put on Christ," instead of the Trisagion, the regular entrance chant. This baptismal troparion still replaces the Trisagion on this day.

This solemn baptismal liturgy just one week before Easter is surprising, but note that it marks the baptismal climax of the fast of forty days. It seems likely that these two days, Saturday and Sunday, which the *Apostolic Constitutions* reported as falling outside the two contiguous fasts, were observed as commemorations of the raising of Lazarus and the entrance into Jerusalem even prior to 383, the year in which the pilgrim Egeria described at Jerusalem a visit to Bethany on Saturday afternoon and a procession with palms down the Mount of Olives on Sunday afternoon. These practices are clearly secondary reflections at Jerusalem of the liturgical themes of those days already established elsewhere, and probably at Constantinople. It is perhaps the same situation that just a bit later is reflected in Chrysostom's *Homily on Psalm 1,15* (PG 55.519ff.).

From the available data, then, we can distinguish two forms for the observance of Lent in the fourth century. One, in Syria and Constantinople, treats the fast of forty days as a continuous period over six weeks, observed apart from Holy Week. According to the later data on Constantinople the last of the six weeks was seen as leading to Palm Sunday, every day of that week being designated "of the branches" or "of the palms." That six-week period concluded in a baptismal celebration on the "Saturday of the Palmbearer, Memorial of the Holy and Just Lazarus." This memorial led into a second festal day, Palm Sunday, and this day concluded that week of the palms.

The second Lenten pattern treats Pascha itself as its term and major baptismal day. This pattern also consists of a total of six weeks, the last being the one we know as Holy Week. Such a Lent was observed at Rome and elsewhere in the west, and is evident also at Alexandria, according to the *Festal Letters of Athanasius*. These letters, however, make no reference to preparation for baptism, and a Coptic codex of a later time (but probably based on historical information) offers evidence that baptism was not celebrated at Easter in Alexandria until the first year of the patriarchate of Theophilus, 385.

The Festal Letters of Athanasius are concerned to establish the "Fast of Forty Days" at Alexandria, but they also reflect the people's resistance to a fast that appeared to them to be a novel practice. Since these letters also afford our earliest reference to the forty-day duration of the fast (the first letter dates from 330), we might wonder whether our Lent is not a conflation of the two traditions, a period of baptismal preparation on the one hand and a general fast of forty days on the other. Gregory Dix, in *The Shape of the Liturgy* (354), insisted that the association of Lent with the forty-day fast of Jesus following his baptism in the Jordan derived from what Dix took to be only a fourth century interest in traditional commemoration of the historical details of Christ's life, and had, therefore, nothing at all to do with the beginning of Lent. He further observed that such a historical commemoration would have had to follow immediately after Epiphany as the celebration of Christ's baptism.

Increasing attention has been paid in the last two decades to the consistent and firmly held Coptic tradition that insists on just such a pattern. This tradition says that in early Alexandrian practice the fast of forty days began immediately after the Epiphany celebrated at Alexandria as the baptism of Jesus. That fast, medieval documents say, came to a climax in the administration of baptism during the sixth and final week of fasting. The fast itself was finally broken on the following Sunday by the "Feast of Palms," while Pascha was still observed weeks later at a time independently established.

Baptism was performed on this special day, it is said, because that was the day on which Jesus baptized his disciples. This assertion is problematic since the only Gospel that can be construed to refer even obliquely to the performance of baptism by Jesus is John's Gospel, and it contains no references to Jesus' fast in the wilderness. This fast is reported only in the synoptic Gospels, which in turn say nothing about baptism by Jesus. The puzzle concerning the source of this assertion indicates a need for caution with regard to this entire Coptic tradition.

In 1958, however, Morton Smith of Columbia University discovered at the Monastery of Mar Saba near Jerusalem a manuscript copy of a hitherto unknown letter of Clement of Alexandria which is now widely accepted as genuine. Written late in the second century, the letter refers to and quotes a peculiar version of the Gospel of Mark used in the church of Alexandria but read, as Clement says, "only to those who are being initiated into the great mysteries" and otherwise preserved in secrecy (see Smith's *Clement of Alexandria and a Secret Gospel of Mark* [Cambridge: Harvard University Press, 1973]).

The passage quoted follows Mark 10:34, and inserts at that point a story of Jesus' raising from the dead a young man at Bethany, clearly a parallel to the story of the raising of Lazarus. Unlike the Johannine version of that story, however, in this account Jesus subsequently (after six days) performs an ambiguous initiation of the youth into "the mystery of the kingdom of God." This account of an initiatory ritual performed by Jesus must be the source of the strange tradition associating the early Alexandrian baptismal day with the performance of baptism by Jesus. Its insertion into the Gospel of Mark, already revered as the protopatriarch of Alexandria, accounts for its influence.

We could easily imagine, then, an ordering of the first part of the liturgical year in early Alexandria around a course reading of Mark's Gospel: the beginning of the Gospel with its account of the baptism of Jesus on the Epiphany, its continued reading during the six weeks of the fast so as to arrive at the tenth chapter by the final week, the added story of Jesus' raising of the youth of Bethany on the baptismal day of that final week, and the consummation of the entire pattern with the celebration of the entrance into Jerusalem (Mark 11) on the following Sunday. It is also fascinating to observe that between Jesus' entrance into Jerusalem and the beginning of Mark's Passion narrative (events that are not connected chronologically) falls a body of Jesus' teachings without any chronological line. Such a collection of teachings might have been read as needed during the weeks between Palm Sunday and the beginning of the paschal fast.

A complex development

After Nicea, all the evidence agrees that the fast of forty days either precedes Holy Week directly or otherwise includes that week so as to precede Pascha itself. Coquin has even suggested that the prepaschal placement of the fast may have been a dimension of the paschal agreement forged at Nicea. In any case, we can see that the prepaschal fast for baptismal preparation and the commemorative fast of forty days in imitation of the fast of Jesus are in no way opposed to one another. Both came to their climax in the celebration of baptism, at Easter in Rome, on a day commemorating the raising of Lazarus in Alexandria — and on both of those in Constantinople where the pattern of the Alexandrian Lent was detached from Epiphany and situated prior to a broadly understood Pascha, i.e., prior to the six-day paschal fast. So it was that the concluding festival of the ancient Alexandrian Lent, the Feast of Palms, came to fall on the day before the paschal fast and, eventually, to become the opening day of Holy Week, sharing that day with what Rome had earlier known as "Passion Sunday." From this progression arises the complex double theme of this day so beautifully interwoven by our liturgical poets: "Ride on, ride on in majesty, in lowly pomp ride on to die."

From such a complex history we can see that the themes presented in our Lenten readings reflect no artificial catechetical schema but bear us back to the earliest roots of our tradition where the patterns and contents of the liturgical year flow from the patterns and contents of the Gospels themselves as, for example, the Gospels for the first Sunday of Lent and the fifth Sunday in Year A, and especially Palm Sunday itself. Thus, the liturgical year is itself a development closely bound to the formation of the gospel tradition. For a much longer time than we might have thought, the season of Lent has set the pace and prepared us for our participation in Christ's death and resurrection, a participation that is in the first instance baptismal but is also for that very reason our entrance into Christ's ministry.

Note: For more extensive documentation see Thomas J. Talley, "The Origin of Lent at Alexandria," *Studia Patristica* 18, ed. by Elizabeth A. Livingstone (London: Oxford University Press, 1982), 594–612.

I I

The Assembly: A Priestly People

Barbara O'Dea

"The assembly, gathered for worship, is nothing less than the really present, fully visible Body of Christ." This bold proclamation issued by Roy Rihm to participants of the Southwest Liturgical Conference in 1985 is not without historical and theological foundation, but it can hardly be called a prevalent understanding in popular religious consciousness. A major challenge of current liturgical renewal is to recapture a sense of the identity of the liturgical assembly.

Identity lost

The history of the liturgical assembly is long and circuitous and bound up with a sense of Christian and ecclesial identity. Ralph Kiefer suggests that the rise and fall of the assembly can be paralleled with the history of the eucharistic prayer.[1] The *Didache*, which contains the earliest extant eucharistic prayer, describes how eucharistic worship is to be conducted:

> In regard to the Eucharist, you shall offer the Eucharist thus: First, in connection with the cup, "We give Thee thanks, Our Father, for the holy vine of David Thy Son which thou hast made known to us through Jesus thy Son; to Thee be glory forever." And in connection with the breaking of bread, "We give Thee thanks, Our Father, for the life and knowledge which Thou has revealed to us through Jesus Thy Son; to Thee be glory forever. As this broken bread was scattered upon the mountain tops and after being harvested was made one, so let Thy Church be gathered together from the ends of the earth into Thy kingdom, for Thine is the glory and the power through Jesus Christ forever."[2]

A lengthy prayer of thanksgiving follows, and a prayer that the Lord deliver the church from all evil and make it perfect in love. The fact that no commemoration of the last supper is included is noteworthy, though the memory of Christ is invoked in the Johannine image of the vine (John 15:1). Thus by allusion the

From *Liturgy: The Lord's Day* 8, no. 1.

Didache links the church's thanksgiving meal to the Lord's supper with his disciples on the night before he died. It is the community of the baptized who celebrate the sacred meal in memory of Jesus dead and risen.

Early in the third century the Apostolic Tradition reflects this tradition and also includes the seeds of an institution narrative. The epiclesis invokes the Holy Spirit on the assembly's offering. The holy assembly offers gifts, at the same time offering itself as gift, thereby praising God through Christ. In these prayers, as Rihm points out, the gifts are sacred because the action is sacred, not the reverse, and the prayer centers on the consecration of the assembly.[3]

Ambrose in the late fourth century signals a major turning point. In his treatise *De Sacramentis*, Book IV, Ambrose includes an institution narrative.[4] Commenting on the text, he notes:

> Look at these events one by one. It says: "On the day before He suffered, He took bread in His holy hands." Before it is consecrated, it is bread; but when Christ's words have been added, it is the body of Christ. Finally, hear him as He says: "Take and eat of this, all of you; for this is my body." And before the words of Christ, the chalice is full of wine and water; when the words of Christ have been added, then blood is effected, which redeemed the people. So behold in what great respects the expression of Christ is able to change all things. Then the Lord Jesus Himself testified to us that we receive His body and blood. Should we doubt at all about His faith and testification?[5]

Clearly in this text the bread and wine, and not the liturgical assembly, are transformed into the body and blood of Jesus Christ. It is no longer clear, or even apparent, that it is the assembly, the church in a particular time and place, which offers eucharist to God.

Once this theology became popular, it was inevitable that the institution narrative would become the focal point of the eucharistic prayer: the all-important moment in eucharist. The dominant theological question became how bread and wine are changed into Christ's body and blood. Moreover, since only the ordained presbyter could confect eucharist, the unique role of that minister increased, while the assembly's role decreased in importance. Gradually, the worshiping assembly became a passive audience whose members were engrossed in their own private prayers. No longer was the liturgy "the work of the people" but a sanctuary activity of ordained clerics, ordinarily but not essentially, with a congregation in attendance.

Tradition rediscovered

Vatican II attempted to reverse this development. Harking back to an earlier tradition, the bishops in council stated that "in the liturgy full public worship is performed by the Mystical Body of Jesus Christ, that is by the Head and members. From this it follows that every liturgical celebration . . . is a sacred action surpassing all others" (Constitution on the Sacred Liturgy [CSL], para. 7).

Thus the liturgical assembly and the body of Christ are not two separate realities but one. Indeed the liturgical assembly is the body of Christ present in a particular time and place.

Numerous postconciliar statements have underscored this central and essential role of the assembly at worship. Referring to the baptized as the royal priesthood of believers, the General Instruction of the Roman Missal reiterates that the eucharistic celebration is the action of the whole church. Regarding the liturgical assembly the document states:

> The worshiping community is the people of God, won by Christ with his blood, called together by the Lord, and nourished by his word. It is a people called to offer God the prayers of the entire human family, *a people which gives thanks in Christ for the mystery of salvation by offering his sacrifice.* It is a people brought together and strengthened in unity by sharing in the body and blood of Christ. This people is holy in origin, but by conscious, active and fruitful participation in the mystery of the eucharist it constantly grows in holiness (GIRM, para. 5, emphasis added).

The liturgical assembly is sign and symbol of God's people. *Environment and Art in Catholic Worship* tells us that no symbol in the liturgy is more important than the assembly of believers. Indeed the document states that "the most powerful experience of the sacred is found in the celebration and the persons celebrating, that is, it is found in the action of the assembly."[6]

Finally, a relatively obscure statement published over a decade ago by the Roman Catholic Bishops' Committee on the Liturgy (BCL) begins with the daring statement: "The greatest liturgical symbol is the assembly of the Christian community transformed into the Body of Christ."[7] Not only does the assembly offer Christ, the sacrificial victim, to the Father in the Holy Spirit; the faithful, as the body of Christ, offer themselves as a living sacrifice.

The rediscovery of the assembly's centrality has moved the church to a fundamental reorientation confronting basic issues. The contemporary church has begun to grasp the meaning of its baptism and corporate ecclesial identity, of liturgy and commitment. Many decades will pass, however, before the full meaning of these insights will be shared by all the faithful.

Ecclesial identity

To understand the liturgical assembly and its calling, one must understand how it comes to be. For it is a common baptismal vocation that Christians express in worship and mission. In the restored praxis of the Roman Catholic communion, the paradigm for the formation of new Christians is initiation. A twofold purpose marks initiation: the personal commitment of the neophyte to Christ and to a way of living based on the vision and values of God's reign proclaimed in the gospel, and his or her incorporation into the community of believers who share this faith and mission.

The baptismal rite, particularly when expressed in the robust symbolism of immersion, gives ritual expression to both purposes. Each candidate's dying and rising with Christ becomes palpable as she or he is immersed in the waters and raised up again. Anointed with the Spirit, each comes forth from the font and puts on a baptismal garment. Next, they are led back to their places to stand as full members of the liturgical assembly. Then for the first time the neophytes celebrate eucharist with the rest of the faithful. At the Lord's table their baptismal covenant is expressed, nourished and sustained. Henceforth, they will assemble each week to be formed by the word of God, to nourish and deepen their baptismal commitment in eucharist and to be sent forth into the world as salt, leaven and light.

Gathering and scattering are the rhythm of Christian life: we come together to act out our faith in ritual celebration; we go forth to live it in the midst of family and marketplace. Every Sunday the baptized, Spirit-filled, priestly people of God, renew the covenant. United with Christ, the gathered community offers itself to God on behalf of the world. One in Christ, the assembly is the primary agent at worship.

What contemporary churches have rediscovered their earlier counterparts knew from experience. Liturgy, as its etymological roots indicate, is the "work of the people," a public work, done on the people's behalf. Thus understood, private mass is a contradiction in terms. It is not simply desirable that believers assemble to offer eucharist, it is essential. Liturgy is an action that requires the full, conscious, and active participation of the assembled community (CSL, para. 14).

Current liturgical praxis is more than a renewal or even a reform. It represents a revolution, a 180–degree turn in understanding and attitude. Generations of believers striving to express this concept in community worship will be needed to understand its meaning fully.

Liturgy, the work of the people

Twenty-five years of postconciliar liturgical experience has moved the church toward an assembly-centered worship. As church, we have learned that Christ is indeed present in believers gathered in his name. What then has experience and reflection taught us about the tasks that this holy and priestly people are called to do?

We remember not only that the assembly is a privileged locus of Christ's presence in eucharist but also that Christ is present in his word, since it is he who speaks when holy scripture is read in the church and who nourishes us in the eucharistic species (CSL, para. 7).

But what does that mean? Behaviorally, the action of the assembly parallels the ritual framework of the eucharist. All present, regardless of their particular liturgical ministries, are primarily members of the worshiping community gathered to exercise their priestly identity and role. That is most important to an appreciation of the nature of worship, the centrality of the assembly and the variety of liturgical ministries. All other liturgical ministries exist to enable the assembly to fulfill its role, which it does by celebrating and responding to the threefold manifestation of the Lord's presence in eucharist.[8]

The ministry of the assembly

- To gather as a community: Members recognize the importance of welcoming one another as they know the Lord's presence in the "here and now church" gathered for worship. Aided and prompted by ushers who are more ministers of hospitality and less custodians of the collection basket, worshipers greet one another as they enter the church. Encouraged by competent music ministers, the assembly prepares to unite heart and voice as the gathering rite begins. A well-executed gathering rite enables the baptized, Spirit-filled assembly to recognize Christ's presence in its midst and to prepare itself to encounter the Lord in word and sacrament.

- To listen, reflect, respond: The Christian assembly, catechumens and faithful, are formed by the word of God. Sunday after Sunday, the word proclaimed with faith and preached with conviction enters the consciousness of assembled believers. The hearers' faith that God has spoken, not only in the past but to believers now, gives the word its power to transform and shape their consciousness. Sandra Schneiders, professor at Berkeley's Graduate Theological Union, says that the word of God becomes revelation when it touches a human heart and elicits a response. The Sunday assembly is called to listen and ponder the word the Lord speaks to each one, to respond to it and to acclaim it in faith, so that it may by the Spirit's power become revelation in all hearts.

- To remember and give thanks: The assembly recognizes the Lord's presence in gifts transformed by its consecratory prayer into Christ's body and blood: gifts not only of bread and wine but of the assembly themselves now offered to God as a covenanted people. Each week the covenant is deepened and renewed as the assembly sings "Amen" to the wonderful mystery of faith celebrated in its midst and lived out in the week that follows.

- To be in and to receive communion: Called by the word of God, united with the whole Christ in eucharist, the assembly has only to come together to the table to partake of the covenant meal.

- To scatter for mission: It is finished. The gathering of believers assembled to worship God and to renew its common commitment has achieved its end. The presider sends them forth to continue Christ's presence and mission in the larger world. There the Christian vocation is lived out and Christian spirituality expressed. These believers and others like them are the only presence of Christ that many will ever know. Their lives as expressions of the vision and values of God's kingdom is a contemporary witness and proclamation of the gospel.

Significant in itself, rediscovery of the centrality of the assembly is part of a still larger picture. As Robert Hovda so aptly expresses it:

We are beginning to recapture the meaning of initiation, baptism, corporate ecclesial commitment, as a bending of our lives to serve the world by seeking the freedom and the oneness of all people.... [We are beginning to understand that] the one begins with the assembly as a whole, if one would understand Church, liturgy or ministry.... And we are beginning again to understand... mission as a ministry that belongs to the entire covenant community, not just the clergy, and that it is not exhausted in liturgical celebration but essentially expressed, inspired and renewed therein.[9]

Notes

1. Roy Rihm, "Let the Sunday Assembly Speak," (Address given at the Southwest Liturgical Conference, San Angelo, Texas, January 1985).

2. "Didache or Teaching of the Apostles," in *The Apostolic Fathers,* trans. Francis X. Glimm, Joseph Marique, S.J., Gerald Walsh, S.J. (New York: Christian Heritage, 1947), 178–79.

3. Rihm, "Let the Assembly."

4. Do you wish to know how (the eucharist) is consecrated with heavenly words? Accept what the words are. The priest speaks. He says: "Perform for us this oblation written, reasonable, acceptable, which is a figure of the body and blood of our Lord Jesus Christ. On the day before He suffered He took bread... and giving thanks, blessed, broke, and having broken it gave it to the Apostles and His disciples, saying: 'Take and eat of this, all of you; for this is my body, which shall be broken for many.'" Take note. "Similarly also, on the day before He suffered, after they had dined, He took the chalice,... saying: 'Take and drink of this, all of you; for this is my blood.'" Behold! All these words up to "Take" are the Evangelist's, whether body or blood. From then on the words are Christ's: "Take and drink of this, all of you; for this is my blood" (in *Saint Ambrose, Theological and Dogmatic Works,* trans. Roy J. Deferrari [Washington, D.C.: Catholic University of America Press, 1963], 304–5).

5. Ibid., para. 23, 305.

6. Bishops' Committee on the Liturgy, *Environment and Art in Catholic Worship,* (Washington, D.C.: United States Catholic Conference, 1978), 18.

7. Bishops' Committee on the Liturgy, "The Assembly in Christian Worship," in *BCL Newsletter* (September 1977) reprinted in *Assembly, a People Gathered in Your Name* (Washington, D.C.: Federation of Diocesan Liturgical Commissions, 1981). For a popular presentation of the liturgical ministry of the assembly see Eugene Walsh, *The Ministry of the Celebrating Community* (1977) and *Giving Life: the Ministry of the Parish Sunday Assembly* (1982) (Glendale, Ariz.: Pastoral Arts Associates of North America).

8. Robert W. Hovda, "The Primacy of the Ministry of the Assembly" (Excerpts from a talk delivered at Union Theological Seminary, New York, July 1980), in *The Assembly, a People Gathered in Your Name* (Washington, D.C.: Federation of Diocesan Liturgical Commissions, 1981), 16.

12

Leadership in the Filter of Culture

Catherine Gunsalus González

Theology, as Christians profess it, contains profound statements about God's attitudes and actions toward humanity. Scripture reveals these gracious, surprising acts of God as examples for us. We are to forgive one another as God forgives us and love one another as God has loved us. This is familiar biblical material, yet in the church's actual life such examples and injunctions are sometimes short-circuited because the influences on us encompass more than our theology.

We are also significantly affected by the presuppositions of our culture. As Christians we find it hard to recognize the implications of the gospel that run counter to the social assumptions of our lives. Moreover, the effectiveness of the liturgy can be seriously impeded by unwitting contrasts between what we say about God and what we do as church. Since such contrasts are more easily perceived if they are shown to be embedded in another culture and time, I have chosen to look at a specific example: the thought and action of Leo the Great. His sermons clearly enunciate an inclusive theology, but his administrative decisions in the appointment of appropriate leaders of the church's worship prevented his theology from coming through with power and clarity in the midst of the worshiping assembly.

Contrasts in Leo's culture

Born late in the fourth century, perhaps in Tuscany, Leo was educated in Rome and was soon recognized as a Roman church official of tremendous ability and promise. In 440, while he was away from the city on business, he was overwhelmingly acclaimed as the new pope, though at that point he was an archdeacon and not a priest.

His papacy coincided with a crucial time in European history. The barbarian tribes were rapidly entering and conquering the western section of the Roman Empire. Leo possessed exceptional administrative skills, which he used in the

---

From *Liturgy: Ethics and Justice* 7, no. 4.

church and in the wider society. His Roman education with its emphasis on organization, polity and ethics, and his deep Christian commitment were used to great advantage. The Christian populace as well as the barbarian invaders recognized his stature and skill.

In addition the church, particularly in the eastern portion of the Empire, was racked with theological debate and division over the relationship of the human and the divine in Jesus of Nazareth. Leo wrote his opinion in the famous *Tome*, which was incorporated in the final decision of the Council of Chalcedon in 451. The incarnation was of central importance to Leo, a fact reflected in his sermons, particularly those written for the feast of the Nativity. Two passages from these sermons indicate the power of the incarnation to affect the fate of humankind:

> Any believer in whatever part of the world that is reborn in Christ, quits the old past of his original nature and passes into a new man by being reborn — and no longer is he reckoned by his earthly father's stock but among the seed of the Savior, who became the Son of man in order that we might have the power to be the sons of God (Sermon XXVI.II).
>
> He took the form of a slave without stain of sin, increasing the human and not diminishing the divine; because that "emptying of himself" whereby the Invisible made Himself visible and Creator and Lord of all things as He was, wished to be mortal, was the condescension of Pity not the failing of Power (Sermon XXII.I).

Leo exhorts his hearers to gratitude and faithfulness to the one who has condescended to enter their poor condition and redeem them. But an exhortation to emulate God in this respect is not present, nor does he emphasize the significance in the church's life of the notion that our common descent is from the Son of God rather than from human families. The radical ethics of the gospel in regard to human community is not developed.

In fact in his administrative work he comes to very different conclusions. Leo writes to the bishops in the provinces concerning several irregularities in the church that he seeks to eliminate:

> Men are admitted commonly to the Sacred Order who are not qualified by any dignity of birth or character: even some who have failed to obtain their liberty from their masters are raised to the rank of the priesthood, as if sorry slaves were fit for that honor; and it is believed that a man can be approved of God who has not yet been able to approve himself to his master. And so the cause for complaint is twofold in this matter because both the sacred ministry is polluted by such poor partners in it and the rights of masters are infringed so far as unlawful possession is rashly taken of them. From these men, therefore, beloved brethren, let all the priests of your province keep aloof and not only from them, but we wish you to keep away from others also who are under the bond of origin or other condition of service: unless perchance the request or consent be intimated by those who claim some authority over them. For he who is to be enrolled in the divine service ought to be exempt from others, that he be not drawn away from the Lord's camp in which his name is entered, by any other bonds of duty (Letter IV.II).

Two distinct issues are raised in this letter. The first is whether or not a slave should be ordained. The answer is no; somehow low birth is an impediment to high office. The second issue is more practical: Can someone who owes service to a human master be free enough to carry out the duties of the priestly office?

Leo was not alone in raising this second question. The Apostolic Constitutions of the late fourth century prohibit a slave's ordination without the consent of the master, consent that includes the slave's freedom (VIII.XLVII.82). Particularly in regard to the first question, however, Leo seems strongly influenced by his own culture. Offices in the church should be held by those whose social status makes it appropriate for them to hold those offices.

Yet if we go back to the theology espoused in the Christmas sermons, several other issues of "appropriateness" could be raised. If God condescends to take on the low estate of a slave, why is it not highly appropriate that persons in that estate be also ministers of the gospel? Why would the gospel's power be diminished by such lowliness if God's power has not been diminished? If all the baptized are now part of a new family, equal in dignity to other family members in spite of the great differences in original families, why cannot this equality carry over into the office of ordination? If by baptism we are no longer reckoned of our earthly father's stock but among the seed of the savior (Sermon XXVI.11), why then should "dignity of birth" be viewed as a requirement for office? More than inconsistency is involved here. What is lost is an opportunity to make crystal clear the surprising newness of the gospel itself, a loss caused by the imposition of cultural assumptions about what is appropriate. Roman views of social hierarchy have been allowed to intrude between theology and the life the faith community.

The implications

Leo is not very different from most theologians in this matter. His writings clearly indicate the inconsistency, however, because he writes both sermons and administrative decisions. But let us look at what Leo might have been able to carry out administratively had he used the example of God's action as a model for theology and for the behavior of the community.

If those of low birth had been allowed to preside in worship, perhaps with others whose family origin had been socially high-ranking, then the significance of a sermon about the common dignity conferred on us by Christian initiation would have been clearer to the congregation. What does it mean to hear a theological statement about the dignity of the baptized within the sermon if no evidence of it is apparent in the life of the church? If the assumptions of Roman culture are not disregarded within the church, then why should the gospel proclamation — the heralding of a new life in which such barriers are destroyed — be taken seriously anywhere? Wouldn't the introduction of clergy who themselves are witnesses to this new order force the congregation to take such words seriously? What effect would that have on those of the faithful who are of high birth? Would it not demonstrate that such factors are no longer the criterion for life in the church? And when there is no such witness, what does the liturgy's actual performance say about the content of the sermon, the prayers or other parts of the celebration? The church's mission and credibility can be greatly enhanced only if God's graciousness is used as a model for the leadership of worship.

The second matter, the clergy's need to be free from all other duties, has some practical basis. But here too, assumptions other than those of the gospel may be at work. Even in a society that has rid itself of slavery, is anyone free of bonds and obligation? Don't we all have to learn how to balance parental obligations, civic duties and other responsibilities to family and the larger society with our specific duties as worshiping Christians?

Why is the situation different for clergy? Couldn't our prayer leadership be exercised by one who lives under various obligations during the week — even to an employer — and wouldn't such leadership make better sense of sermons that address our call to community, mutual assistance and love? Is the ordained minister who appears to have no personal obligations to others really the best interpreter of God's work among us? Would not a variety of responsibilities among the clergy help to clarify what the gospel is about?

The theology embraced in a sermon or other part of a liturgy can be no more compelling than the actions and behavior exemplified by those who implement the liturgy. Even though our cultural assumptions differ from Leo's, our situation is not unlike his. We have a clear idea of the criteria for appropriate worship leadership, including the kind of appearance, voice and speech that we can approve, and variations seem unfitting. We are as unprepared to have our assumptions challenged as Leo probably was. Yet they arise from the surrounding culture and continue to impede gospel proclamation.

The God who does strange and unexpected deeds for the world's salvation creates a church in which those actions continue to lead people to salvation. The leadership of worship is not an irrelevant item in the gospel's proclamation and comprehension. If the church only approves for ordination the persons whom the wider society also approves for leadership positions, then Christians will see little in the gospel that is revolutionary. On the other hand, if church leaders are called on the same basis as we are called by God, namely, unafraid of losing status by being lowly and calling all sorts and conditions of humanity into a new order, then it would be very difficult for even the most insensitive to overlook the fact that the gospel is a life-transforming reality.

13

Not on Bread Alone
Shall We Live

ROBERT W. HOVDA

Because we believe in the God of Jews and Christians, the God of the biblical covenant, who in the Christian view is incarnate in Jesus the Messiah; and because the covenant community is not a specialization but a way of living, we dare not get sidetracked in one particular area of expertise. "Not on Bread Alone Shall We Live": "Not on any specialization alone shall we live." People who are "into liturgy" or "into its environment and arts" in this kind of exclusive way should be considered as much of a problem as people who are into computers in a special way. This way is no way to live. Aptitudes, skills, talents, training become excuses to absent oneself from the human task, alibis for noncommunication, narcissistic indulgences.

A human need and hunger

To recognize this danger is not to take the concerns of the environment more lightly, but rather to take them more seriously. As believers we must try to understand why the churches generally are still so insensitive to the human hunger for an experience of surpassing goodness, truth and beauty in the environment in general and the worship environment in particular. Why do we so rarely find imaginative design and striking beauty in the formation of worship spaces and in every object, utensil, book, vestment, furnishing, image used in that space? Goodness, truth, beauty, unpretentious and unprevaricating quality in things — our love for one another is expressed in our care for the created things we commonly use. Why are such expressions so rare?

One would think that the worship environment would have an unquestioned priority in a community like the church, which is created in liturgy, regularly

From *Liturgy: Dressing the Church* 5, no. 4.

contacts its primary sources in liturgy, and both nourishes and expresses a critical aspect of its life in liturgy. Because there is goodness and truth and beauty in the worship environment, we humans glimpse transcendence and are moved to the silence, the reverence, the wonder without which public worship loses the quality of common prayer.

It isn't that human beings have ceased to recognize their need for beauty, harmony, simplicity and grandeur in order to feel their best and to be at their best. We flock in great numbers to the sea, the mountains, the forests, and frequently for precisely the kind of experience liturgical life should afford. We turn to the elements of earth and air and fire and water to renew ourselves.

But we do not think of liturgy and church in this way because we are too specialized. Until we give the Sunday assembly the same total human meaning and bring to it the same expectations we bring to the grandest manifestations of nature, until we see this word-sacrament event as one that pulls every aspect of our lives together, makes us whole and glad to be human — until then, we are condemned to the cramped exercises of a compartmentalized obligation religion. And it's a vicious circle, because those realizations depend to a great extent on the kind of experience that much of our past and present Sunday gatherings do not encourage.

Here and there, an island

The church in our country, even in its most dismal periods, has been sometimes graced and sometimes cursed by little islands of concern for the worship environment and the arts. A parish here and there which, by virtue of some priest or some particularly motivated and bold member, has acquired a reputation for "liturgy." Perhaps it pays attention to the visual arts or has good music, or perhaps it has trained its members for good proclamation, or has active congregational participation and a variety of ministries.

The grace of such islands is obvious, for that is the way things happen in the church. We learn from each other, and leadership in reform rarely, if ever, comes from those in authority. It emerges prophetically here or there, is tested and refined in a crucible of resistance and criticism, and if it is true and of the spirit, finally wins approval and becomes "what we have always taught." For the church is never finished, but always growing, developing, like the world of which it is a part.

Such islands, however, can also be a curse, if the particular area in which they excel is pursued as our self-conscious specialization, isolating us from our total human and ecclesial life. Nor should we be surprised at this. Jesus said the weeds and the wheat have somehow to grow together until the harvest. Contradiction and paradox are part of our pilgrim's path to the reign of God.

Finally, we are in times of broad and basic renewal. The enthusiastic worldliness of the incarnation and the passion for communication of epiphany are reasserting their claims on believers. We are recovering what David Steindl-Rast calls the basic religious experience, the experience of belonging, of being at home in God's world and able to say honestly and wholeheartedly, "I belong." When this is our experience, we will not need to exhaust our resources protecting ourselves against outsiders; rather, we will spend ourselves to communicate the vision of God's reign through, with and in that belonging.

A new springtime

In my old age there are few affirmations about which I have no doubts at all. But there are a few, and one of them is that the reform agenda initiated by the Second Vatican Council can lead all Christian bodies to the recovery of a pilgrim church, a constantly reforming and developing church, incomplete and in travail until the end of time. This recovery has placed you and me at the beginning of an era for which we should be profoundly grateful, a new springtime for the people of the biblical covenant.

One has to take the long view, of course. At the present moment, we have to admit that the atmosphere of the churches and their leadership is regressive and fearful of the risks and prospects of continuing growth. We are in a moment of reaction and retreat. Such moments are like the exception that proves the rule. Paralyzed limbs have already felt the stirring of life, and the body of the church will not yield again to torpor. You and I may not see in our short spans the fruitions we have hoped for, but that is not the point. The point is offering our lives and our energies to the process. That's what *living* is about!

So now every time the papers or television unload the latest batch of tired consternations from ecclesiastical housekeepers or the ruminations of a poet crushed by the commonness and fluidity of texts once imagined to be fixed eternally, I can laugh. And every time they unload the outrage of novelists or playwrights whose comfortable foil (dependable for centuries) will maintain a rigid pose no longer, or the anger of military, political and economic powers whose private preserves do not suffer the invasion of newly aroused consciences gladly — every time the media or the defenders of that old fortress church unload this kind of stuff on me, I can laugh. The laughter may be a bit rueful; it's embarrassing that the church's prophetic element doesn't grab the media like popes and other bishops sometimes do. The media, with their vast resources, are so captured by stardom, commerce and the status quo that they hardly ever dare serve the progress of humanity as they might. But the laughter is real, nonetheless.

Once I couldn't laugh at all about such things because I was so dependent on secondary sources for my faith attitudes and orientation. But reform and renewal, even in these early stages, have plunged me down to the basics, down to the very foundations of the structure: the symbols of faith, the word proclaimed and the deed done in the Sunday assembly. Now I am not a spectator. I am right there, and these primary sources are mine, along with a still cautious but increasingly brave effort to discern the signs of the times.

The solidarity of hope

As we help one another to move from dependence on secondary sources to the primary ones, we will be helping our legitimate specializations and hopes. The orientation and the attitudes fed by those primary sources are the medicine we need to rid ourselves of the otherworldliness and the privatization that have reduced liturgy to a mere service station for individuals, and the church, the covenant community, to a mere bureaucratic organization. Part of this fundamental renewal is an appreciation of incarnation and epiphany that relieves our alienation from humanity and its arts and our loss of a sense of church as humanity's corporate servant.

Likewise, that fundamental reform has to make it apparent to all, eventually, that our concern for worship, environment and the arts belongs in solidarity with the other reform elements pressing for life and growth in the church.

Prophetic elements in the church should be the very last ones to ignore their solidarity. We can't afford internecine quarrels. None of us can do everything, and therefore specialization is both inevitable and appropriate. But a specialized mentality is neither inevitable nor appropriate for Christians. If we, for example, with our commitment to the environment and the arts cannot appreciate the relevance of the women's movement for real equality, or the revolutionary political and economic implications of a church whose business it is to proclaim the reign of God, or efforts to supplant authoritarian models of office with collegial ones, or black and Hispanic challenges to Anglo-cultural dominance, or the demands of people who are struggling daily to find both happiness and responsible faithfulness in their God-given human sexuality whatever orientation it takes, or the anguish of the powerless in general who know that the church, as society's jester and liminal critic, should of all institutions be least affected by the status quo — if we cannot appreciate our solidarity with other reform and prophetic elements, then it seems to me we are still suffering from a basic sickness, an alienation from humanity. And no matter how expert we are in our little area, that alienation will vitiate whatever we try to do.

Now we can sympathize with the feelings of those ecclesiastics who regard the church's aim not as the reign of God but as the Good Housekeeping Seal of Approval. Renewal is messy, and a church that is committed to "semper reformanda" is always going to be messy. To gain a sense of belonging is to accept the tensions and the travail.

One who seeks escape, or the island, or the fortress, who regards humanity as a trial and the world only as a testing-place for a future existence, simply cannot (and therefore does not) take as a real commitment the world's institutions, its systems, its colors and textures and shapes. We have to make our home *here*, quite deliberately, before environment and art and anything else that belongs here become matters of real concern.

A biblical faith

What the bishops of the Second Vatican Council called "a new humanism, one in which the human person is defined first of all by a real responsibility toward all the sisters and brothers and toward history"; and what a visionary like Pierre Teilhard referred to as the emergence of a new humanity — these are tremendous steps that enable us to understand the biblical message far better than our ancestors did. The bishops and Teilhard reject that unbiblical cast of faith that regards all human industry and art with bored amusement or contempt, that places itself above the grubby economic and political life of ordinary mortals, that may claim a respect for goodness and truth but categorizes beauty and all the sense experience of sacraments as "externals." With that kind of "not here," "not now" approach to life, the reign of God is only after death, and the organic relation of means and ends is ignored. All that constitutes our present existence is discounted.

A biblical faith says to this: "Oh, no! The focus of faithful life is here and now. This is the moment we have, and this is our responsibility. The church is in service to the world, as salt and light and leaven." We do not try to make a life "in the church." The church is not our life, our scene, but rather our life's search for inspiration and meaning. Our life, our scene, is the world.

The practical significance of this biblical focus for liturgical celebration is obvious. If the church is thus related to the rest of the world, then its job is not to exhaust or protect our time and energies but to nourish us, inspire us, for a life to be lived elsewhere. That means the church has to get busy. It can't rely on a castle moat any more, or on protective walls. It has to utilize to the full the limited time, energy and attention that the baptized community can give to its corporate formation and celebration. Our business as church is the inspiration for a life to be lived outside the ecclesiastical sphere and without the prop of culture. The Sunday assembly, the gathering, will become again a unique contact and reinforcement mutually gained around the common and primary sources of our faith orientation and attitudes.

Then everything about our proclamation of the living word, our attempt to interpret the signs of the times, our celebration of the symbolic actions we call sacraments — everything about these things becomes critical, an object of concern and care. Because a church that rejects self-sufficiency and self-service, that accepts the covenant, that initiates new members and revives the old ones not into a culture, or a shelter, or a total life-system, but into a worship and support group whose life and mission is in the rest of the world — such a church needs a Sunday assembly that is not commonplace but remarkable, not ordinary but festive, not a daily portion but an occasional excess, not a maintenance procedure but an inspiration. Unfortunately, we clergy are not yet being prepared for this. Clerics whose world is the ecclesiastical island, and who are therefore drained by its inconsequential demands, consumed by its spiritual narcissism, breathless from its ritual busy-work, will never be able to preside in, or even understand, the Sunday assembly that a living faith community must have for its survival.

Art and wholeness

We are not dealing with mere "souls" any more, but with persons — persons who are not larvae awaiting their metamorphoses at death, not simply brains with ears attached, but whole human beings — each with body, senses, sex, memory, imagination, all of which function as one person, whose faith orientation must be whole. Such a faith experience must leave no human faculty untouched, no agency of reason or will unmoved. Worship, environment and the arts not only have the keys to all the human parts that our capitalist, pragmatic and scientific culture has neglected; they also communicate with a power least easily eroded by differences of place and time.

In his 1970 Nobel acceptance speech, A. Solzhenitsyn articulated a truth about art and beauty that many of us perceive but cannot express:

> ...a work of art bears within itself its own verification: conceptions which are devised or stretched do not stand being portrayed in images; they all come crashing down, appear sickly and pale, convince no one. But those works of art which have scooped up the truth and presented it to us as a living force — they take hold of us, compel us, and nobody ever, not even in ages to come, will appear to refute them. So perhaps that ancient trinity of truth, goodness and beauty is not simply an empty, faded formula as we thought in the days of our self-confident, materialistic youth?

In that case, Dostoyevsky's remark, "Beauty will save the world," was not a careless phrase but a prophecy.... Falsehood can hold out against much in this world, but not against art (see *Washington Post,* August 27, 1972, B1).

Not only the symbolic act, then, in which the communication is so clearly not primarily verbal or rational (e.g., the solidarity of the eucharistic meal, the fresh, new beginnings of the baptismal bath), but also the word proclaimed and the signs of the time with their mute appeal for our discernment — all these avenues of revelation, these sources of faith, deal with us as whole human beings. None of them is satisfied with a merely cerebral approach.

At the center

All communication among human beings, including revelation, puts environment (its shapes, colors, textures, smells, flavors, tones) and all the imagining and skills that we call the "arts" right at the center of the enterprise. They *are* in great part the communications enterprise. So when we talk about environment and the arts we are not "adding something on," like a bit of embroidery on the pillowcase. We know the way these concerns are frequently dismissed: "If there's something left over, then we just might...." What the deluded creatures who dismiss environment and art considerations in that way are really doing is dismissing incarnation, epiphany and communication, dismissing the *whole* way in which God reveals the divine design to us, the *whole* way in which God loves, to say nothing of the mission God has given us.

There is nothing "precious," nothing at all luxurious, about what we seek: to proclaim the symbolic word and do the symbolic deed wholly, with all the beauty that God's creatures can summon, with reverence — never in a careless or mechanical way. It is not merely the aesthetic sense of the refined at stake; it is the Christian revelation and the whole biblical message of salvation, in which the inching of the world toward the reign of God depends on human presence and on a church not withdrawn from but devoted to the rest of the world.

I wish I knew how to hasten this process. All I am sure of is that, like a title of one of Eric Gill's books, "It all goes together." What we are here seeking is at the heart of the Christian enterprise. Every facet of our conciliar reform and recovery is related: reform in our self-understanding as church; reform in the way we initiate our members; reform in our economy, property and budgeting; reform in moral maturity and doctrinal expression; reform in qualifications, training and lifestyle of ministers; reform in administration and organization; reform in a grownup sense of mission and of economic and political responsibility, and reform in liturgical practice. If we are fully human, none of these tasks is distasteful to us. And if we are not supportive of them, then it really doesn't matter what we do with our specialization on our island — it will be irrelevant in any case.

To sum up, I have tried to do two things: to encourage us, to encourage the interests, the talents, the vision that brought us here; and to make an appeal. The encouragement is based on my conviction that both our human nature and our faith demand the time, the effort, the expense, the care, the quest for beauty, that you and I clearly feel is vital in the worship of the church. The massive indifference and sometimes hostility we meet are not aesthetic problems only but deeply rooted faith problems. In pushing these issues, we are pushing the gospel in central and essential ways.

And the appeal — not to get disoriented by isolating our own specialization — is analogous to the general cultural situation in our society. It is natural that each oppressed group should concentrate on demanding justice for itself. Those chronically imprisoned in substandard conditions of education, work, housing, food, clothing; women; black and Hispanic and other minority groups; gay and lesbian persons; old people; AIDS sufferers and others who are chronically ill or disabled — all are victims of our society's injustices and prejudices. But the common suffering of these groups and others should make for solidarity, for the recognition that what oppresses you oppresses me, and for a common front.

In the same way, our commitment to worship, environment and the arts and the uphill nature of any reform and renewal effort in the history of the church should make us supporters of all gospel-oriented efforts toward reform. We must not allow ourselves to be isolated or set against each other by the forces that resist change. For those forces are always present and are at this moment considerable. We cannot afford the jealousy, the pride, the sectarianism and narrowness that divide. Those who seek their own lives will lose them, and those who lose their lives for the Lord's sake and the gospel's — they are the ones who will find out what life is all about.

Part II

The Languages of the Liturgy

"The language of liturgy and devotion is not the denotive language of explanation. It is, rather, poetic or pictorial; it calls from imagination to imagination. It orients us to reality as we are grasped and redirected by a new story that we recognize to be in some sense our story or by a new picture in the mind that freshly orders our inner and outer worlds."

—Daniel B. Stevick in *Liturgy: Central Symbols*

14

Tension and Transformation in Public Prayer

Catherine Vincie

New concerns about participation, language, distribution of roles and decision making confront the Christian community with hard questions. Especially during liturgical celebration, change or its absence can send our anxiety levels skyrocketing.

But should the church's public prayer be the occasion for such disturbance and uncertainty? Or to ask the question another way: Ought we to struggle during liturgical celebrations with new understandings of self, community and ministry or with new patterns of intra- and extra-ecclesial relationships? Is the assembly the right place to experiment and redraw with trembling hands our images of God?

We are not talking here about the tensions created by a poorly celebrated liturgy. If gestures are awkward, readings mumbled, preaching poor or ritual lacking flow or rhythm, many participants will feel angry, bored or anxious. The questions raised by this article, however, presume good celebration. For us the key issue is how liturgy fits into the Christian community's life as a pilgrim people. Such a church is a community of disciples or learners; it is not a complete or perfect community but one that always stands ready to grow into its fuller self through the dynamics and interrelationships of liturgical and social change.

Peace versus growth

Recent experience suggests that there are two quite different approaches to this issue. The first suggests that we should grope, struggle and learn outside liturgical space, then turn to corporate worship for healing, consolation and a respite

From *Liturgy: The Healing Word* 7, no. 2.

from troubling community concerns. Proponents of this view are threatened by any changes in the liturgy, including the initial postconciliar reforms and more recent adaptations. For them change is an inappropriate modification of what is already correct and sufficient, and the incorporation of problematic issues into the liturgy only introduces divisiveness into a community that worship should unite.

The second approach conceives of liturgy as one among many vital moments in the community's social process. This interpretation permits a freer reaction to the dynamics of liturgy. Adherents of this view can allow for liturgical development to take place in fits and starts, and with mixed success; they can relax enough to allow a certain turmoil to have its place; and they can live more easily with tensions, apprehension and anger. They believe that healing, growth and transformation may come through our uncertainty, turmoil and struggle as a Spirit-filled community.

The premise of this paper is that community concerns about meaning, identity, mission and belief have their proper place in the liturgy and that their presence, even in an unresolved state, is the norm. Though difficulties arise as we try to live with unresolved dilemmas, impertinent challenges and increasing pluralism, our task is to grow in our acceptance of the relationship of liturgy to a community in the midst of change and to learn to live with greater ease and grace as we struggle together to find new answers. Before the liturgy can be a healing and transforming word, the pain it often causes should be acknowledged.

Ritual and social process

Cultural anthropologist Victor Turner has contributed much to our understanding of the place of ritual in the social process. His work was done mostly with the Ndembu tribe of Zambia, in a cultural situation vastly different from the North American situation, so his findings may not be directly applicable to our own. Some of his insights, nonetheless, are helpful.

Turner stresses that his study of the Ndembu would be incomplete and deeply flawed if he did not attend to this people's ritual. The social data he collected "became fully intelligible only in the light of the values embodied and expressed in symbols at ritual performances."[1] He further argues that ritual holds an important place in the whole social process. It functions to express, support and enforce the society's major values, but it also serves as the setting where these values are tested, challenged, reshaped and reconfigured to adapt to new societal needs. Not only is ritual expressive, then; it also shapes the nature and character of the society.[2]

For the Ndembu the society's values are those expressed in the ritual, and the society's conflicts are those brought to light in ritual. Participation in ritual is not mandatory with us in the same way, nor is there as much uniformity about social values. In our mobile society, an individual may be part of many communities, making it difficult to argue for a tight connection between rituals and social process.

While in complex, postindustrial societies like our own the connection between ritual and social process is not clear, the situation within the church is somewhat different and perhaps closer to Turner's research community. From apostolic times the church has always named itself a worshiping community. Acts 2:42–47 tells how the early church gathered for prayer, praise and the breaking of the bread. More recently, Vatican II's Constitution on the Sacred Liturgy asserted the intimate connection between the liturgy and the church's identity and mission.[3] Though the liturgy never exhausts the activity of the church, whether Catholic, Protestant or Reformed, the church is inconceivable without its corporate worship. We can expect to find, therefore, an intimate bond between the church's ritual process and its social process.

Shaping the imagination

The liturgy is a privileged place, though not the only place, for establishing a community's meaning.[4] As the occasion when most of the community interacts with the tradition and with one another in word and symbol, liturgy is a particularly powerful tool; it carries a people's tradition from past to present to future and invokes the name, power and presence of God in the process.

The following are examples of how liturgy and community meaning intertwine:

The church names itself in its worship and shapes its members in terms of that naming. Before Vatican II, for example, the Catholic church often spoke of its members as "sinners" and laid heavy emphasis on the ritual of confession. Vatican II named the church "people of God" and stressed the relationships forged by baptism and eucharist.

In liturgy the church publicly establishes relationships among its members by ritual interactions and transactions.[5] Consider the different relationships established between a priest and a layperson as lay penitent kneels at the feet of the priest, or the two sit or kneel together in prayer for God's forgiveness. Consider also the changed relationships that result as laity and ordained touch and distribute the eucharistic bread and wine.

The church professes its belief in God and forms images of God in its members through prayer, song and the worship environment. Compare the use of more abstract names for God, such as "almighty" or "everlasting," with the repeated address "Father" in all eighty-four of the Roman Catholic proper prefaces. Consider also the absence of feminine images for God in any of our approved prayer texts or in our liturgical art.

In each of these examples liturgy is a principal shaper of the ecclesial imagination, providing a vocabulary in symbolic language that enables the community to understand itself, its relationships and God. It forms the community not through rational discourse or argumentation but through images, gestures, spatial relationships and various types of prayer formulas, all of which powerfully affect the whole person.

Variety and quality in liturgical celebration are important factors in deepening the community's imagination. The richness and the multiple layers of meaning disclosed through liturgy's symbolic language yield multiple interpretations and diversity in appropriation. These factors permit changes in the community to happen gradually, often imperceptibly and with great unevenness.

The larger context of liturgy

The imagination that has been renewed and transformed within a liturgical context bears fruit far beyond the confines of liturgical space. Meanwhile, the religious imagination is also being shaped by life outside the liturgy. Again the liturgy is one moment among many in which community meaning, identity and mission are established. Lay participation in all aspects of ecclesial life has increased tremendously in the last two decades. Experiences of building up the community through participation in the pastoral care of the sick, joint decision making on the local level, adult education and the rites of Christian initiation have also significantly helped to shape the ecclesial imagination.

The community brings its imagination to the liturgy — its sense of meaning, identity and mission — which has been shaped by prior liturgical experience and other ecclesial and nonecclesial experiences. Therefore, the church's ongoing struggles will inevitably be found in the midst of the assembly gathered in corporate worship.

Questions about ordination and the priesthood of the laity find liturgical expression in our choice of a worship leader; questions of power show up in decision making regarding liturgical norms and approved rites and in the immediate preparation of a liturgy and its celebration. Political issues such as sanctuary become liturgical concerns as refugees come to dwell in the house of worship, and questions about women in the church surface in the roles they assume in the worshiping assembly and in decisions about liturgical texts, lections and translations.

Readers can undoubtedly provide many more examples. Whatever the conflicts, we are becoming increasingly aware that liturgy is not a place of refuge from the church's most pressing concerns; if anything, it is the arena where those concerns become publicly articulated, often loudly and painfully.

Because the liturgy carries ecclesial meaning, because it names the self, the community and God, the community's investment in the liturgy's shape, style and content will be high. That is not to say that participation, enthusiasm and unanimity will necessarily be the order of the day but that worship will confront the community with existential questions. The community will either affirm its established identity, its images of God and its ministry inside and outside the church, or it will find itself struggling with the incongruities between its identity and beliefs and the image it projects in the liturgy.

The power of symbolic language

The language of liturgy is symbolic language. Liturgy employs speech, gestures, sound and ritual action to disclose divine and human realities without ever letting us forget that these realities contain a superabundance of meaning that can never be completely disclosed. The reality of God always escapes our naming, whether we say "Father," "Mother," "merciful," "almighty" or a combination of these words.

Our identity as individuals and as community also escapes our naming. Yet the continual effort to name God and ourselves is important, and we are not excused from the task because of its difficulty. In liturgy we are called to speak what we already know, but we are also called to explore the mysteries of God and self that remain unknown, a task that calls us to become what we are not yet.

The philosopher Paul Ricoeur helps us to understand how liturgy's symbolic language nurtures our self-becoming. Symbolic language, metaphor in particular, opens up worlds of possibility for human being and action.[6] Language is not a second moment after the perception of reality, a kind of reproduction of perception; rather, it has a creative function, enabling us to see a new and different world.[7] What we say makes a difference; our speech enables us to perceive ourselves, our relationships and all other reality in a new way.

Poetic language in the liturgy, for example, does not function to describe the reign of God as it now is but to speak of it as it might yet be. To include women deliberately in our liturgical language makes them visible and acknowledges their significance, and so enables us to imagine a church that truly values women in word and fact. Symbolic language invites and challenges us to grow into a new future, a new way of being church.

This type of language sparks the imagination and makes it important. Change is too difficult to accomplish unless we can imagine how things might be different from the way they are. But reordering our ecclesial imagination is as hard as it is frightening. We have become accustomed to our way of seeing God and the church, and to alter our vision is jarring. When Jesus asked the man at the pool of Beth-zatha (John 5:1–16) if he wanted to be well, the man could only reply with memories of his past experiences of infirmity. Our tendency, too, is to remain with what we know rather than to risk the unknown.

Challenges for the church

To take up Ricoeur's invitation to live in the world of symbols is a challenge for the believing community. We have to learn how to take our rituals and symbols seriously yet not literally. This means taking the time to attend, to participate in and even to create our own rituals.

Popular "pious practices," alternate liturgies, prayer services and charismatic prayer groups are valuable because they place the ritualizing process in the hands of the whole community. Pressing concerns find easy entry into these nonofficial liturgies and once admitted stretch the community's imagination. Such practices foster ease in symbolic expression and understanding, thus facilitating a natural flow between the social process and the ritual process. Liturgical reforms in the past have often failed to take into account these nonofficial liturgical actions.

A second challenge is to allow symbols — symbolic objects, actions and speech — to be themselves. We must respect their primary meaning even as we explore their second and third levels of meaning. Bread should look like bread; washing should be done with more than a thimbleful of water; mythic, poetic speech should be evocative rather than didactic. Whatever senses they appeal to, symbols should be generous enough to fill those senses. And, as noted above, there is a nonidentity between the symbol and the reality symbolized. Consciousness of this nonidentity prevents our falling into the trap of idolatry. This is particularly important in our language for God. Resistance to new metaphors for God may indicate that we have forgotten that God is always more than our naming.

The liturgy calls us to attend to symbols in our lives, to allow ourselves to be touched by water, bread and cup, word and people. We must open ourselves enough to symbols that they can shock us into new ways of seeing and thinking. To be committed to a community that claims ritual as an essential part of its life is to be committed to the learning, change and struggle that occurs in ritual's symbolic language. For as Ray Hart suggests, the imagination can only be shocked by language spoken in its own tongue;[8] that is, by the kind of evocative language in which liturgy specializes. The shock, as we all know, can be disturbing, unsettling and sometimes deeply threatening.

It is not possible, moreover, to change only part of our religious imagination, for the imagination's role is to integrate all new experience into a meaningful whole. A single symbolic statement can be the catalyst for a whole new world view. Those who think it does not matter that laypersons now distribute the eucharist fail to recognize the power of a single symbol to reorder the entire religious imagination.

Deeper awareness of the power of symbols also challenges us to be willing to hear another symbolic word besides our own. We have not all been formed through the same experiences of church or society. The identity, meaning and beliefs that various members of a community bring to ritual will be diverse and mutually challenging. The potential for personal and communal transformation depends on the willingness to listen to another's word. Since the last word of Christian faith and practice has not been spoken, we dare not indulge in the luxury of refusing new words, images and symbols. However painful, disturbing or incomprehensible the word may initially be, the challenge is to allow our ritual to play its part in the community's larger social process.

The role of homogeneity

If openness to diversity is so important, is there still a place for rituals developed out of homogeneous communities? We know very well that people often choose a worship community for its like-mindedness. Some will choose to participate in a Latin mass, others to attend a university chapel. Some will organize an experimental liturgical gathering; others will join another parish. But if liturgy is an appropriate place to struggle with questions of community, identity, meaning and mission, then several answers suggest themselves to the question of the possible positive role of homogeneous communities.

The answer is a definitive "yes" if homogeneity allows a particular community to enlarge its ritual vocabulary and thus find its voice in a way that has not been possible before. Johannes Cardinal Willebrands stressed that the ecumenical dialogue must embrace the question: "What was it that we did not address that caused you to break away?"[9] That question is pertinent in each church community.

Yet we must qualify our "yes" by adding that there is room for such experimentation only if there is a commitment to bring those new insights and expressions to the wider church community. Since resistance to change is extremely strong, the onus for openness to the dialogue is often on the status quo.

The answer to our question of homogeneous community will be "no" if that implies that the dialogue, if there is to be one, can only take place outside liturgical space. To declare the liturgy exempt from community conflict and struggle is to remove it from the social process, and with it, the possibility that the struggle with real issues and conflicts can be the occasion for the transformation of individuals and communities on levels that only symbolic language can touch.

Pastoral suggestions

If the liturgy is not to become an ideological battleground, opportunities must be provided apart from it for reflection, explanation, evaluation and critique. Time must be provided in which to review changes in light of the community's tradition, history and existing structures of ecclesial authority and human experience. There is room in this dialogue for ecclesial authority (in terms of legislation or standing commissions), liturgical scholars and worship participants. It is a time to assess the varying claims of authority, scholarship and immediate experience. In present church experience we are only beginning to learn how to engage in this kind of exchange.

A few additional pastoral guidelines may help us work our way through the social and ritual process:

Patience is the preeminent virtue — patience with one another and with the process. No one has absolute answers, but we have deep convictions that need to be heard. The process of change and transformation is messy and slow. Demands for "grammatical" correctness, for example, need to be matched with an equal ardor for adequacy to experience and tradition.

The shock dealt to the religious imagination by liturgical change can affect persons at deep levels. Because of the connection between ritual and the social process, strong reactions to change or strong demands for more change should be understood as appropriate responses to important issues. We must give ourselves and one another permission to have those reactions, and we must take time to understand them.

Commitment to the dialogue is our principal challenge. The decision to continue struggling with the thorny questions of liturgical change is a decision to keep liturgy at the heart of Christian life and praxis. Because of the difficulty and the seeming hopelessness of the dialogue, the tendency can be to move toward separatism and homogeneous worship experiences. Though this tendency may be necessary for a time, it cannot remain the only answer. The power of liturgical transformation lies in reordering the religious imagination and opening up new ways of seeing all reality. We can tap into the creative function of symbolic language only if we enter and live in its world. To open ourselves to that world is to allow ourselves to be called to openness and courage, risk and transformation.

Notes

1. Victor Turner, *The Ritual Process: Structure and Anti-Structure* (Chicago: Aldine, 1969), 7–8.

2. Victor Turner, *The Forest of Symbols: Aspects of Ndembu Ritual* (Ithaca, N.Y.: Cornell University, 1967), 20.

3. *Sacrosanctum Concilium,* nos. 2 and 10.

4. For an in-depth analysis of the relationship between liturgy and ecclesial meaning, see Margaret M. Kelleher, "Liturgy: An Ecclesial Act of Meaning," *Worship* 59 (1985): 482–97.

5. See Mary Collins, "Critical Questions for Liturgical Theology," *Worship* 53 (1979): 302–17, for an extended discussion of the significance of changing transactions with eucharistic bread.

6. Paul Ricoeur, *Freud and Philosophy: An Essay on Interpretation,* trans. Denis Savage (New Haven: Yale University Press, 1970), 15–16.

7. Paul Ricoeur, *The Symbolism of Evil,* trans. Emerson Buchanan (Boston: Beacon Press, 1967), 278. See also a discussion on the development of Ricoeur's thought on language and the imagination in Mary Aquin O'Neill, "The Anthropology of Ambiguity and the Image of God," in *The Pedagogy of God's Image: Essays on Symbol and the Religious Imagination,* ed. Robert Masson (Chico, Calif.: Scholars Press, 1982), 31–53.

8. Ray L. Hart, *Unfinished Man and the Imagination* (New York: Herder and Herder, 1968), 216.

9. Johannes Cardinal Willebrands, "The State of Roman Catholic Ecumenism," Washington Institute of Ecumenics, Catholic University of America, Washington, D.C., May 8, 1987.

15

The Uses of Liturgical Language

MARK SEARLE

In his autobiography *Surprised by Joy,* C. S. Lewis describes how the attempt to "think about what one was saying" while saying one's prayers so drove him to distraction and despair that it was a major cause leading to his adolescent loss of faith. Looking back on this agonizing experience from a later and more mature viewpoint, Lewis recognized that he had simply been badly instructed in the art of prayer. Still, the exhortation to "mean what you say" is one that no serious believer dare ignore. Whereas previous generations were concerned primarily about the Orthodoxy of their prayer, we, as a generation, are more likely to be concerned first and last about its authenticity. Do our words come from the heart? Do we really mean what we say?

If this distraction creates a problem for private prayer, the problem is compounded for liturgical prayer. At least in private prayer, one can say what one wants when one wants to say it; in the liturgy, neither of those options is available. Liturgical prayers have become fixed in texts, and the texts have been assigned for use with no regard for the particularities of the people who use them or the circumstances under which they will be used. Small wonder, then, that in this era of vernacular liturgy, celebrants often take it on themselves to adapt the preformulated words of prayers and invitations or dispense with them altogether, replacing them with some spur-of-the-moment improvisation more congruent with the time and place of the celebration. The community as a whole, of course, does not enjoy such liberties: either we all say the same prescribed words, or we say nothing. Perhaps this explains why so many people, even after years of the "new liturgy," either pray privately or complain that they cannot pray at all during the liturgy.

The problem, as it is posed here, concerns the difficulty of turning preformulated texts into authentic prayer, but it touches on the broader and more fundamental problem of what it means to participate in liturgy at all. The same problems of authenticity, the same dangers of empty formalism, attend all the

From *Liturgy: Language and Metaphor* 4, no. 4.

other dimensions of liturgy: the chants, the gestures, the postures, even the fact of being present in a congregation. How can those be authentic acts of prayer if they are required and preordained?

Saying and doing

One way to approach the problem of fixed formulae in the liturgy is to begin from a consideration of how language is used in ordinary discourse and work back from there to a fresh view of the way language works in prayer.

It was an English philosopher, John Austin, who first developed the theory of "performative language" in a little book entitled *How to Do Things with Words* (1975). He began by observing that it is a fallacy to suppose that the sole, or even primary, function of language is to communicate information or to convey thoughts. On the contrary, when we speak, it is not merely to say something but to do something: we order, pledge, bet, promise, dedicate, apologize, congratulate, urge, judge, flirt, rebuke and perform a thousand other actions by our words. Thus words are not only used to describe and communicate existing states of affairs; they can also bring about new states of affairs. To say, in such instances, is to do.

To suggest that words "work," that they cause effects, sounds rather like "word magic." There are, however, some things we need to consider about these "speech acts."

In the first place, it will be noted that the effectiveness of such "performatives," when they are effective, is in the realm of interpersonal relations. As a result of what I say (in making a promise or issuing an order or praising a friend), the network of relationships that constitute my world are subtly, even profoundly, altered. The one who makes a promise and the one to whom the promise is made stand in a different relationship to each other after the promise is made than they did before. Speech-acts, therefore, hold human society together and keep it in continual movement, as relationships are continually enacted, affirmed, modified or broken. More than mere transmission of information, language permits all sorts of activities to go on; indeed, it is the medium through which those activities take place. It is therefore entirely misleading to separate words and actions too precisely. There are very few instances in which to speak is not at the same time to act or, better, to transact, for the human community is founded on and sustained by such interactions.

Another way of putting this is to say that such actions are conventional insofar as a word means what a given society agrees it shall. In the case of speech-acts, however, the effect is part of the meaning, and the effects are also subject to convention. Thus, I can say "I congratulate you" but not "I insult you." Under the Mosaic Law a man could rid himself of his wife by saying "I divorce you" and putting it in writing, whereas in our own society the formalities, or conventions, of divorce are rather more complicated. Some countries do not have a convention for divorce at all, just as most countries no longer have a convention whereby one person can challenge another to a duel.

Such examples may appear to be moving us from casual conversation to complicated legal processes, but we have not really shifted our topic, for the development of law is merely an extension, in matters important to society as a whole, of the conventions that attend all speech-acts. A promise is a promise, and promises are more or less binding, depending on the solemnity with which they are made and the importance of the matter promised. Therefore, in the case of promises that need to be taken very seriously if society is not to fall apart, such as marriage or multimillion-dollar contracts, the conventions are formalized and made explicit in minutest detail in enactments of law.

All this should not distract us, however, from the point; namely, that speech-acts are social in character and have to do, not with the putting of thoughts into words but with forms of social interaction. They are performatives, ways in which human beings interact. What they achieve, consequently, depends on convention in the society in question, that is, on what the society as a whole (not the individual speaker) intends them to achieve. For example, only a judge can pass sentence. The witness may declare the accused guilty, but that doesn't count, no matter how sincere the witness may be. And only someone who is unmarried can marry, no matter how often the bigamist may say "I do." It is not the honesty, sincerity or zeal of the speaker that counts but whether the conditions for a valid or lawful "speech-act" have been fulfilled. Speech is governed not only by the rules of grammar but by the rules of social interaction as well.

It is also worth noticing that many of these speech-acts are more or less ritualized. Making a bet or a promise will often be accompanied by a handshake. Witnesses may be called. The naming of a ship, the opening of a new building, the dedication of a public park, acknowledgment that a student has successfully completed a course of studies, are examples of speech-acts most often accompanied by ritual actions. Even congratulations or commiserations can call for some ritual accompaniment. Words and action go together, and both are usually stereotyped or ritualized.

Liturgical speech

I suggest that liturgical speech, like ordinary discourse, is best understood as performative; that is, it is on a continuum with the examples cited above and subject to the same sorts of conditions. There are many parallels between liturgical speech and performative language in everyday life.

In the first instance, many of our liturgical practices, especially the celebration of the sacraments, become more intelligible when we think of them as speech-acts governed by the conventions of the society that employs them, namely, the church. "I absolve you from your sins," for example, is a conventional formula whose conventional effect in the life of the church is forgiveness and reconciliation with the community. "Joseph, I baptize you..." or "Mary, be sealed with the gift of the Holy Spirit" are formulae of admission into the community. There are conventions (canon law) governing who may say these words and under what conditions. The effects are also conventional. Said by a priest or bishop in a liturgical context, they are deemed effective. Pronounced by an actor in a play or a seminarian in a liturgy class, the words are the same, but the convention is not invoked. On the same grounds, it is clear that no drunken priest can consecrate a bakery full of bread by pronouncing the words of consecration: as the convention cannot be invoked under such circumstances, the conventional effect does not follow.

This may sound like reductionism, comparing baptism to a legal contract, until we remember that the society that uses these particular conventions is the church, the body of Christ. Precisely as acts of the church these conventional acts have more than merely societal implications. Because the life of the church is rooted in the life of God in Christ, the acts done in the name of the church have repercussions at the deeper level of life with God. The speech-act and its social effect on life in the church is the *sacramentum* of the newly configured relationship with God that, theologically, is said to be the effect of the sacrament.

Although derived from modern language theory, this approach to the sacraments links up with scholastic teaching on the *res* and the *sacramentum* to emphasize the importance of the empirical, ecclesial dimension of sacramental acts. The effectiveness of the sacraments cannot be separated from the question of their context in the social life of the church. Sacraments are not private communications with God but social actions of a human community. Their supernatural dimension is dependent on the supernatural dimension of the church: its credibility as a sacrament of life with God in Christ.

Liturgical prayer

If we seem to have wandered far from C. S. Lewis and his scruples and from the person who complains that he or she cannot pray during the liturgy, the time has come to return to them.

Human speaking, or speech, is hardly if ever the pure communication of information or the mere externalization of private thoughts and feelings. Yet that is the model usually implied in "meaning what you say." The effect, in liturgical practice, is to feel uncomfortable with preformulated prayer and this, in turn, has two results. First the celebrant will alter the prayers to make them more expressive of what the celebrant thinks or feels, or thinks the community ought to think or feel. Second, liturgical planners and presidents will feel it incumbent on them to work the congregation up so that they do feel the appropriate feelings.

Such labors to think this or feel that, if liturgical language is full of speech-acts, is largely beside the point. For example: "I confess" is an act of confessing, not the externalization of some presumed guilt-feelings; "I believe in one God" is not a statement of opinion but an act of giving oneself over to God; "Heaven and earth are full of your glory" is not a statement about the cosmos but an act of praise. These acts may or may not be accompanied by appropriate feelings: what matters is that they are done. Shaking hands with someone I dislike does not make me a hypocrite: it can be a heroic act of affirmation of the other person. Similarly, if you confess, you confess; if you praise God, God is praised; if you say "Amen" you have committed yourself.

What is involved here is more a matter of *attitude* than of appropriate feelings. Such is the nature of speech-acts, or performative language. To mean what you say is to be willing to go along with what the words commit you to. This may not sound like much, or it may sound like a lot, but it is crucially important to liturgical prayer for this reason: it de-centers those who pray. This does not remove all responsibility from our shoulders, for our presence and participation is, in the first place, our more or less free response to the God who calls us in convoking the assembly. But once we are there, the prayer is not our own. We are invited to lend ourselves to the prayer rather than to pray out of our own meager resources. We are invited, not to express our feelings or thoughts but to submit to the convention of this common prayer, to try it on, to adapt ourselves to its demands: "It has a personality five times that of ours."

All liturgical prayer is for this reason spoken in the first-person singular or plural. The prayers in the book can be taken up and tried on by anyone and all of us but only if we are prepared to put ourselves into that anonymous first-person role: "we praise you, we bless you, we glorify you, we give you thanks"; "we are not worthy to be called your children"; "Lord, have mercy upon us." The prayers and texts of the liturgy invite us to assume the attitudes required by these conventional prayers; not to express feelings or thoughts we may not have but to find ourselves in the words. "Happy are we who are called to his supper" is not the same as saying "We are happy to be here today": a common example of the dangers of improvisation.

But there is more. We say above that speech acts are social acts, governed by the conventions of the society that uses them and having the meaning and effects that society attributes to them. So it is with liturgy, the performative language of the church. The church understands its assembled people to be the visible sign or sacrament of the presence and action of Christ. Indeed, our tradition goes so far as to say that the prayers and actions of the liturgy are the prayers and actions of Christ directed to God and to us. From this perspective, the performative character of liturgical language is extremely important. It is the fact that the prayers are not our own but are given to us to try on which makes us aware that it is not we who pray in the liturgy but Christ who prays. The attitudes of praise, confession, trust, pleading, confident hope and so forth to which we commit ourselves in the speech-acts of the liturgy are the attitudes of Christ himself. We are to lose ourselves in Christ's prayer by allowing our immediate feelings and concerns to be swallowed up in his cosmic priesthood before the throne of the Holy One. We can only do this if we are willing to de-center our ego, and allow the prayer to be prayed, the hymns to be sung, the acclamations to be made through us, rather than by us.

Conclusion

This may have seemed a long and tortuous route to take, only to arrive at such a simple conclusion. But, as the purpose of this article has been to highlight how liturgical language operates, we had to consider some of these mundane qualities of ordinary human speech. Doctrinal and theological statements can appear admirable but remote from the world in which we live. Liturgical language, I have tried to suggest, is very like ordinary language, though not in the way we normally think. It is concerned less to express our thoughts and feelings than to impress them, that is, to shape and form them by shaping and forming our attitudes, to conform them to those of Christ, the only liturgist.

This conclusion, if accepted, must influence the way we see our pastoral-liturgical agenda. We need to catechize less on the contents of liturgical prayers than on the way to pray them. Our congregations need to know that they come, not to vent their faith and feelings but to submit to the discipline of the rite, to learn, from the images it proposes and the postures it puts us through, who we are, who God is and what it means to have the mind of Christ Jesus. Conversely, those charged with liturgical planning and celebration need to be of that mind themselves, deeply conversant in the ways and words of the tradition. This will not only govern our decisions about whether or not to improvise prayer texts, it will also influence the kind of music we use and the ritual innovations we make (is "pinning our sins" to the cross on Good Friday the same as, or better than, kneeling to kiss it?). The question we must ask is whether and how the community might be able to join not merely in this collective activity but also in this moment in the priestly activity of Christ and the liturgy of heaven and earth.

It is the fact that the texts and rites of the liturgy do not always express who we think we are that constitutes their potential to transform us. Were we to allow ourselves to grow into them, to let ourselves and our minds be transformed by them, then the liturgy's impact on life might be rather greater than anything we can hope for by jazzing up the music or anointing the prayers with doses of our own personal unction — all of which merely leaves us celebrating who we are in our own eyes.

Rather, our aim should be to let the prayer pray in us, the ritual be enacted through us, the song of heaven resound in us. We need to lend ourselves to the convention of the liturgy, that convention — that coming-together — of the church as a historical and social community but also that convention or congruence of the liturgy we celebrate now with the ever-living liturgy that Christ celebrates perpetually before the throne of God. Ultimately, every congregation that gathers to celebrate and pray needs to make these words from the Eucharistic Prayer of Serapion its own: "Give us Holy Spirit, that we might be able to speak and expound your unspeakable mysteries. May the Lord Jesus Christ speak in us, and Holy Spirit, and hymn you through us."

16

The Water of Life

Daniel B. Stevick

"If there is magic on this planet, it is contained in water." The comment is from the late scientist and man of letters, Loren Eiseley.[1] It comes to mind as I sit beside a New England pond on a day in late summer. The attraction of this place is partly practical. Since the day is hot, the water and the air around it provide a pleasant relief. But there is also the magic that Eiseley speaks of. On days like this, tens of thousands of us are drawn to streams, lakes and ocean beaches, partly by the fascination of water itself. One who is under a magic spell cannot analyze the experience very well, but I can try.

I begin by looking into the lake from where I sit. The water at the edge is clear, and on a sunny day like this, one can see every pebble and blade of grass. Shapes are defined; colors are bright. But starting a few feet from the shore, the water grows murky, shapes become indistinct, and the dark vegetation is appropriate only to its strange underwater world. From there the water shades off into depths the light does not reach today — and seems never to have reached.

The water is not quiet. Reflections on the surface are broken and full of movement. The sunlight toward the far shore creates rippling silver bands. An occasional breeze makes cat's-paws here and there. Tiny wavelets maintain their gentle and ineffective assault on the shore. Yet despite the motion of light, air and water, the lake is a place of stillness and peace. The craggy irregularities of earth, rocks, shrubs and trees end where they meet the level surface of the water. I do not come here for the restless busyness but because beneath the variety, change, surprise and movement, there is about this lake a quiet serenity.

I observe that as I think about the lake I think about what it imparts to me. Of course this lake is what it is; it exists on its own terms. I shall not see it, know it or love it truly unless I respect its complexity, its mystery, its otherness. Yet it contains magic — magic that I find potent. I come here to be spoken to,

From *Liturgy: Central Symbols* , no. 1. This article first appeared in *Christian Initiation Resources,* vol. 2 (New York: William H. Sadlier, 1981). Used with permission.

ministered to. And the lake does not fail me. There is a profound bond between the mystery out there in the water and the mystery within myself.

Water in human experience

I use these observations from my lakeside seat to introduce some procatechetical reflections on baptism, for the central ritual action of becoming a Christian confronts us with water. Baptismal customs differ as to whether much water or little is used — though liturgists prefer much water, lest token quantity and overtidy actions trivialize the sacramental meanings. Liturgical traditions have placed important actions before and after the baptismal moment and have associated other signs, such as oil and light, with water. But the essential, indispensable element is water.

Of course the active reality in baptism is not water, but God in Christ by the Spirit. The corporate redemptive life encloses a new name. Baptism is effective not through magic but through faith. Christianity is not a religion in which we perform rites to secure the reliability of springs, wells and streams or to unite us with the movements and cycles of nature. Water in baptism is, rather, an instrument of the word. It is caught up in an action in which the gospel is proclaimed and enacted. In baptism the natural mystery of water is a means of engaging the mystery of a human person with the redemptive mystery of the living Christ.

But water is capable of being used in this expressive ritual because water is a meaning bearer. It can be a sign because it signifies. A convincing, authoritative rite does not impose alien meanings on its materials; rather, it uncovers, selects, uses or heightens meanings that are given in the materials themselves.

Water holds a rich capacity for carrying meaning. In its many forms it is all around us. The oceans cover more than two-thirds of the earth's surface. Then there is the water in the lakes, the rivers, the ground, the ice caps and the atmosphere. When the ancient Greeks began to speculate about the nature of the cosmos, one of the first proposals put forward was that the universe is basically composed of water. A related idea lies behind the biblical creation story. There the familiar world is pictured as floating on the flat bottom of a hemispherical opening created and maintained by God. This "firmament" separates the lower waters ("the waters that were under the dome") from the dome (sky) of upper waters (Gen 1:6–8).

Ancient peoples believed that one could verify this world picture by commonsense observation: The flat sea out to the horizon and the arching sky overhead are the same color; the waters above become apparent when on occasion some of them fall down, either gently or torrentially; the water below can be found by digging down far enough on any piece of land or by following a land route anywhere in a straight line until eventually one comes to the water in which the whole solid mass floats. This ancient cosmology is worth remarking, not because it was scientifically accurate — for of course it was not — but because it indicates an old and deep human awareness of the importance and prevalence of water in our world.

But now, as much as at any time in the past, water is everywhere close at hand. Is any other substance taken in by the senses so fully? A laboratory description might try to persuade us that a beaker of water is tasteless, odorless, transparent and soundless. But as we encounter water in actual experience, we feel it, taste it, smell, see and hear it. Water has cooled our skin or resisted our efforts to move in it; we know the refreshing feel of water when our mouth is dry, and we can identify the special taste of water from certain places; we recognize the smell of ocean spray or of a garden after a rain shower; we have seen water take on color from material it carries or from light diffused within it or reflected from its surface; and we have all said, "Please repeat what you said. I couldn't hear you. I had the water running."

This elemental, pervasive stuff is full of contradictions. At times water is gentle, manageable, our obedient servant; it turns aside for a pebble or a stick. At other times it is imperious, terrifying, refashioning the earth and destroying everything in its path. At times it is in motion; at others, completely at rest. Sometimes bright, sometimes dark. Sometimes noisy, sometimes silent.

Sacramental understanding is, in considerable measure, rooted in our imaginatively grasped experience of things. We speak of what may be beyond the here-and-now only through terms derived from our more or less rich, more or less discriminating here-and-now experience. We would be better sacramental theologians if we were better poets, or at least better observers.

I suggest here three functions of water that have substantial bearing on its baptismal meanings.

Water and life

One cluster of associations gathers around water and *life*. Even though water can appear to be so alive that some languages and cultures speak of water in motion as "living water," water itself is not a living thing. Yet nothing that lives does so without water. In arid land, a clump of trees indicates a spring; a line of green means a stream; a field of growing things is a field to which water has been led. The difference is dramatic. Where water is, life is possible. Where much water is, life can be abundant. Where water is removed, life ceases.

The dependence of life on water has a history. Life had its origin in the sea, and biological species lived in water for millions of years before they made their first uncertain ventures onto land. There is a chemical resemblance between sea water and the blood of vertebrates. We carry in our bodies evidence that unites us with the epochs in which rudimentary life forms, enclosed by thin membranes, were awash in warm, salt pools at the ocean shore.

Individually too, our origins speak of water. We live in water for the first nine months of life. At birth we come, with a shock, into the world of air, and we are not sure we prefer it!

This primal and never-ending dependence of all Life on water provides material for the human imagination. Waterless places, dry wells, fields without rain are obvious symbols of unproductivity, failed promise, the negation of vitality, creativity and hope. Mystics refer to unrewarding periods of the inner life as "dryness." A poet, despairing over his inability to write, cries to God, "Send my roots rain."

By contrast, water, fresh and abundant, suggests plenty and fulfillment. In a great vision the Hebrew prophet Ezekiel saw a splendid temple, with four sweeping rivers flowing from the gates of its four walls. As he explored the river to the east, he reported: "I saw... and on the banks, on both sides of the river, there will grow all kinds of trees for food. Their leaves will not wither nor their fruit fail, but they will bear fresh fruit with every month, because the water for them flows from the sanctuary. Their fruit will be for food, and their leaves for healing" (Ezek 47:12).

In biblical idiom, to live without a believing, thankful, obedient relation with God is to miss that for which we were made. It is a life so defective as not to deserve the name life at all. In the midst of life we are in nonlife. The gift of an open, loving relation with God makes persons alive who had been only dead before; it is like being newly born. Water is a powerful vehicle for such redemptive and baptismal meanings. The self-imparting divine life is like an unfailing spring, or the divine word is like the rain that falls from heaven (Isa 55:10–11). God offers water to the thirsty to drink (Isa 55:1; Rev 22:17). Celebrating God's steadfast love, a psalmist says, "You give them drink from the river of your delights. For with you is the well of life" (Ps 36:89).

The summit of such imagery is doubtless Jesus' invitation in the fourth gospel to anyone who thirsts to come to him and drink. In a somewhat paradoxical stretching of the figure, he promises that what began as a modest intake of water will turn into an abundant outflow, as the receiver becomes a source (John 7:37–38).

Symbolic thinking does not work by clear, tidy distinctions but by imaginatively grasped associations. In redemptive and baptismal imagery it is inevitable that water-out-there giving life to other things and water-taken-inwardly for one's own life become mingled. Both are the same substance, and both speak of life. The baptismal water is not drunk; its sacramental use is purely external. But in the early church some baptismal pools were decorated with mosaics of deer drinking, suggested by Psalm 42:1: "As the hart longs for flowing streams, so longs my soul for thee, O God." Baptismal psalmody also used Psalm 23, with its sheep beside still waters. Baptisteries picture the Samaritan woman (John 4:1–42) to whom Jesus spoke of the water that would put an end to thirst. Some early liturgical texts say that a cup of water as well as a cup of wine was used at the baptismal eucharist, surely expressing the sense of inward life and cleansing.

Water and death

Another equally accessible but quite contrasting group of associations suggests water as limit, boundedness, threat and *death*. Water is an alien element. While we cannot live without it, we cannot live in it. Water, in appropriate amounts and under control, supports life; too much water, out of control, can kill.

We are able to survive in water only by means of contrivances such as floats, rafts or boat hulls that separate us from the water, or by means of strenuous exertions that not everyone learns, few do well, and no one can keep doing indefinitely. This human awkwardness is a source of deep fear. It is also a source, over the centuries, of our fascination with the strange world under the sea and with the creatures that seem quite at home in that element that is so hostile to us.

Rivers and oceans are barriers. Boundaries on a map often follow river courses or shorelines. Our easy passage is stopped at wide bodies of water, except where bridges or ferries are available. Bridge builders, bridge defenders and courageous voyagers are among the heroes of our sagas. But even small streams can separate — estranging an "us" on this side from a "them" on the other.

Here too, imagination has psychologized and universalized this simple human experience. In the flood story in Genesis, water is a means of fearful divine judgment. In the story of the exodus, water covered Israel's oppressors (Ps 106:11; Exod 15:56). But judgment on Israel, through "the king of Assyria and all his glory," is also spoken of as a terrible flood. God will bring against the people "the waters of the river, mighty and many... and it will rise over all its channels and go over all its banks" (Isa 8:7–8).

Water can speak of that ultimate human boundary, death, and the ultimate fear associated with it. Greek mythology gives us the dark river Styx and its aged boatman. But water is a symbol also of those frightful moments of negation where in the midst of life we touch seeming annihilation. A psalmist speaks to God of his dejection in terms of drowning: "All thy waves and thy breakers have gone over me" (Ps 42:7).

This life-negating aspect of water touches a profound range of baptismal meaning. The various biblical idioms do not consider sin a trivial matter that can be dealt with by a slap on the wrist. It is a wrongly set course of life (individual and collective) that incurs judgment and death. But a passage is opened from death to life by Jesus Christ: the representative one who died and rose for the many. It is possible now for sinful persons to die creatively in the death of another. As a participant in Christ's death and resurrection, one dies to a sin-dominated existence and lives in a new, fulfilling lordship.

When baptism is seen as a ritualization of the gospel, and the gospel is depicted in this essentially Pauline idiom, baptism is a death — an acceptance of the verdict of God against a false, destructive mode of life. But since it is a dying with Christ it is not a futile death; it is death as a way to life. The dramatic force of this idiom requires that there be no short cut to life. We pass to life by a cross and a dying, and not otherwise. In this perspective, death is an indispensable part of the gospel and of the gospel sacrament of baptism. Thus baptism draws on the associations between water and death.

Perhaps these associations are so powerful and so negative (and hence only penultimate) that they need to be underlined in baptismal ritual with some reserve. But it should be possible to use and yet control this forceful imagery. One thinks, for example, of the widespread early Christian custom of making baptismal pools in the shape of tombs, or sometimes of crosses. The candidate for baptism entered such a pool by descending some stone steps — usually three steps, representing Jesus' three days in the tomb — and left by going up on the other side. Even the least subtle baptized person must have caught the rich evangelical meanings.

Water and cleansing

Water attracts yet other associations around its power of *cleansing.* When my hands are soiled, I cannot eat or shake hands with my friends or touch anything beautiful. I am acceptable neither to others nor to myself. But by the application of water my hands are restored to usefulness and I am restored to my full world, my full community and my full self-esteem.

Here again a simple feature of water offers a symbol of profound moral and spiritual realities. A condition of sin or alienation is spoken of in terms of defilement. One thinks of the bloodstained hands of Lady Macbeth. The condition is remedied by an act described as a washing. A psalmist, oppressed by a sense of unworthiness, calls out for divine cleansing: "Wash me through and through from my wickedness" (Ps 51:2, 7).

This third image can seem weaker than the first two. Cleansing, for one thing, seems too external an act to serve as a symbol for moral reality. The human problem is too serious to be compared to a little dirt, and the necessary remedy is hardly measured by the analogy of a good scrubbing. The symbolism of washing seems to lack the ultimacy and finality of life-and-death terms. Life is imparted once, and we die once, but we bathe often.

Perhaps such objections to the imagery of cleansing are most persuasive in a modern, middle-class world where soap and running water are taken for granted and dirt is easily dealt with. In the world in which the Bible and the sacramental tradition originated, water was scarce. All of it, for all household purposes, was obtained with effort and had to be used frugally. Indeed, in much of the world this is still the case. Water is always a finite resource, and getting it to where it is needed calls for work and ingenuity. Modern ecological awareness (along with regional summer shortages) may remind us that having enough water — enough *clean* water — is a collective responsibility, if it is not to be a collective crisis.

Moreover, contrary to the appearance that it only deals with surfaces, there is an unexpected profundity in the ancient image of sin as defilement or contamination. This image diagnoses the human fault as a condition of the self rather than as a series of offending acts. When I speak of myself as bearing a stain too deep for me to remove by my own effort, I am saying that more fundamental than this or that specific sinful action is the kind of person I am. And when I speak of the availability of cleansing for so deep a stain, I draw on the good news that something can be done about the self beyond what my futile efforts at self-reformation can accomplish.

Beyond our ego-centered moralism, the image of a soiled thing being washed speaks of gift and grace. It points to a fountain opened for sin and uncleanness (Zech 13:1). The language of washing describes the transformation of an old condition into a new. It announces that however deep and seemingly ineradicable the stain may be, a cleansing is available. It declares, "Though your sins be as scarlet, they shall be as white as snow" (Isa 1:18). When we take a shower after particularly strenuous work or play, we often say, "I feel like a new person!" We are not at the time speaking theologically, but we are using language of continuity and radical newness, of transformation that is yet restoration. It is the same I and yet a new I; it is the new I and yet the same I, newly enabled to fulfill its intended purposes. Such language is an analogue of the gospel of forgiveness and fresh beginning that we enact in baptism.

As to the seeming inadequacy of a casual, repeated action to speak of final issues, we may ask whether allowing a common, frequent act such as washing to symbolize baptism actually weakens the sacramental meaning, or whether instead the connection of baptism with Christ and the gospel redefines what is meant by this one special washing. Baptism touches the transcendent; the fundamental actor in the sacrament is God. In redemption God is doing a new and decisive thing. The sign in water uses the act of washing to point to that one, determinative act of triumphant love.

Again a vision from Ezekiel comes to mind. The prophet sees a new age in which God's name will be vindicated. Israel will be restored, the people will be given a new heart, and God's spirit will be put within them. God inaugurates that radically new relationship by a ritual act of divine washing: "I will sprinkle clean water upon you, and you shall be clean from all your uncleanness, and from all your idols I will cleanse you" (Ezek 36:25). This unique and definitive cleansing is an unrepeatable moment in the unfolding purpose of God.

These prophetic themes inform the initiatory rite of the Christian community. The work of Christ brought in a new age, an age of the Spirit. The church, the people of the new age, came into being in a momentous, unique baptism of the Holy Spirit at Pentecost; and each individual life within it is begun in an unrepeated baptism of water and the Holy Spirit. The principal background of the washing imagery of Christian baptism should not be the washing of my soiled hands, which I do many times a day. Rather, its background is the once-for-all event of redemption in Christ.

So considered, the washing imagery is fully as strong as the images of life and death. Baptism speaks of final things — of the cleansing in Christ for the race. Its meaning comes from everyday washing only as that practice is caught up and transformed, as it must be if it is to be a demonstration of the gospel. This sacramental act is a washing in some sense like all other washings; but at the same time and most importantly, it is a washing unlike any other. We must bathe repeatedly; we are baptized once. There is no final act of physical washing; but there is no repeated baptism. The uniqueness of this sacramental washing speaks of the finality and completeness of what God has done in Christ.

Taking in the symbol

This essay has now distinguished three somewhat obvious functions of water: water supports life, it can destroy life, and it can make soiled things clean again. These functions are the basis for three clusters of meaning for redemptive and sacramental faith. Each of these images has a force and consistency of its own. Each can carry aspects of meaning that the others miss. What God does in, to and for human lives cannot be expressed except by image talk. But it cannot be captured or defined by any single image. The images discussed here do not divide a unit of meaning into thirds, so that we can just add them together. These multiple images suggest and convey a single, unitary reality.

We explore the infinite depths of our relation to God in Christ through the complementarities and tensions among these baptismal images. We draw on our common experiences of water, on the symbolizing capacity of the imagination, and on the specific development that images receive in the texture of the Bible. We combine these images with others that are not related to water — images such as anointing and light. We pass from one image to another with a sense of play and paradox. Cyril of Jerusalem in the mid-fourth century explained to some recently baptized persons: "At the selfsame moment, you died and were born; and that water of salvation was at once your grave and your mother."[2]

The language of liturgy and devotion is not the denotative language of explanation. It is, rather, poetic or pictorial; it calls from imagination to imagination. It grips and orients us to reality as we are authoritatively grasped and redirected by a new story that we recognize to be in some sense our story, or by a new picture in the mind that freshly orders our inner and outer worlds.

The meaning of baptism, of course, derives from Christ. Water is silent and full of ambiguities. By itself it cannot give us a ready-made baptismal theology. Our experience of water serves our understanding of baptism only after it has been ordered and clarified through the Christian story and faith. But God is not arbitrary in marking the human link with the divine by an outward sign that uses water. There is an inherent appropriateness in the chosen sign material. That being so, we shall be open to more of the meaning of Christ as conveyed in baptism if we are open to that magical sign material on its own.

We must let the luminosity and wonder of things impress themselves on us. Water, in its wordlessness, makes its own self-revelation. Its very ambiguities and multiple significances mean that our interpreting, inquiring minds will never come to the end of their work. For a renewal course in sacramental theology, I recommend sitting beside a New England pond on a hot summer day.

Notes

1. Loren Eiseley, *The Immense Journey* (New York: Random House, 1957), 15.
2. Cyril of Jerusalem, *Mystagogical Catecheses* 2.4.

17

Liturgy as Art

DON E. SALIERS

From the outset we know that liturgy is indeed art. It is not simply that we employ various art forms within the liturgical assembly, though such forms are essential; rather, the very nature of gathering about the book, the font and the table is intrinsically a matter of order, form and dramatic coherence. As Gerardus van der Leeuw observes, "Look at the liturgy: among the forms of Christian art, it is the transcendent and dominant one; the Spirit of God itself formed it, in order to have pleasure in it."[1]

Yet the liturgy is not primarily a "work of art." The point of worship is not the production of aesthetic experience but the encounter and dialogue with a living God. "The beauty of the liturgy belongs among the glorious gifts of God which are granted us when we seek the kingdom of God. In any other instance, the liturgy becomes a spectacle and a sin."[2] By this, van der Leeuw reminds us of the history of tension between the beautiful and the holy as heard in the prophets.

So "art" in the sense used of liturgy is not to be confused with "work of art," any more than prayer is to be exhausted by specific prayer texts. Any talk about the role of art and symbol in the liturgy requires a recognition of the primary intention of liturgical celebration: participation in the mystery of God's self-giving in word and deed. This lies behind Aidan Kavanagh's claim that "the liturgy thus is said to 'use' symbols and art only to the extent that it is itself artful symbol in the first instance."[3] We begin with the art of liturgy as ritual enactment, proclamation and prayer. Yet there can be no ritual enactment without gesture, movement and shared significant form; there is no proclamation without human utterance and common rhetorical forms; there is no prayer without the intrinsic music of sound and silence, speaking and listening, seeing and beholding. The poetics of liturgy emerges in the actual celebration of specific assemblies.

From *Liturgy: The Art of Celebration* 8, no. 3.

Liturgy as artful symbol

The church gathered is the gathering of the gifted, as St. Paul reminds us in 1 Corinthians 12, Romans 12 and elsewhere. At the heart of worship is the mystery of our having been called into common life and having been given gifts for the praise of God. In the very act of gathering, the community assembles to sing, to hear, to pray and to celebrate the meal and the water bath. For these things to take place the community needs singers, preachers, celebrants, servers, environmentalists, ministers of hospitality and a host of other ministers. These are themselves gifts that differ now brought together in the new event of this particular day, time, place and people. Many members, one body; many gifts, one Spirit. And the primary minister is the assembly itself. So we must speak of the art of celebration that both engenders and requires the gifts of God's people brought together.

At the center of liturgical worship are the corporately shared forms and patterns into which the faithful are invited and through which they are formed in and give expression to adoration, praise, thanksgiving and supplication. This is because liturgy is more than texts and rubrics governing the correct performance of the rites. The means of participation are not abstract rules but embodied forms that open up levels of reality for the assembly. The very means of singing, praying and the ritual actions confer a harmony on the whole. The early church knew this well. St. Basil, in preaching on the psalms, speaks of them as "a bond of unity harmoniously drawing people to the symphony of one choir."[4] St. John Chrysostom observes that

> ...the psalms which occurred just now in the office blended all voices together and caused one single full harmonious chant to arise; young and old, rich and poor, women and men, slaves and free, all sang one single melody....Together we make up a single choir in perfect equality of rights and of expression whereby earth imitates heaven.[5]

These luminous passages remind us that the various graced capacities given to those who lead the assembly are for the coming alive of the whole body. Words, musical forms and sign-actions with light, water, wine, bread, oil and human hands shape and express the community of faith in the presence of God. All the arts employed are born of human response to the created order, so liturgy seeks to constitute these into an ever-fresh unity. When the doxa of God is sought, the primary languages of our humanity are released, not as individual virtuosity but as a unity of praise, thanksgiving and petition. Whether festal or ferial, the liturgy is our common morphology, that is, the shape of our common humanity when attracted to the glory and holiness of God.

Such a gathering is formed to acknowledge the transcendent mystery of the holy one; to confess, to hear, to remember and take to heart that what God says and does in Jesus goes well beyond our intellect. Liturgy is far more than doctrine well dressed. There is truth to be sure, but it is truth in the form of music heard so deeply that we are the music; stories told so well that we become actors in the story; prayers prayed with such integrity that we become prayerful; a meal celebrated so graciously that we are nourished and become bread for others.

Our participation begins with the concretely experiential dimensions of the rites, but it points to that which can only be received through, with and in the forms: the mystery of God's self-communication. Participation is certainly to be "full, conscious and active" as the Constitution on the Sacred Liturgy commends, but such participatory activity on the part of the people is itself to become symbol: the assembly as church. This in turn cannot remain merely an ecclesiastical or sociological realization. For participation in the forms as church must be suffused with the reality of the paschal mystery itself in all its range. These, then, are three interrelated levels of participation: in the aesthetic phenomena of the rites, in and through the rites as church, and finally in the grace and mercy of God.

Of course such interrelated levels of participation take time and catechesis and discipline. The task as well as the gift of the liturgical assembly is to become always and everywhere an artful symbol of the church in communion with the divine life. In so becoming, all the various arts find their origin and their true end in the uncreated energies and glory of God.

Humanity at full stretch

Christian liturgy in its whole economy — from the rites of initiation, eucharist, the daily offices, the cycles of time (both temporal and sanctoral) through the rites of passage and pastoral offices — possesses great formative and expressive power over human imagination, emotion, thought and will. Such power may be for good or for ill. Liturgy thoughtlessly performed, without deep affection and imaginative range, will be far less likely to awaken us to the realities of biblical faith and to the things signified, divine and human.

At worst the liturgy has, in certain times, formed communities in deep enmity (as against the Jews) or has perpetuated social indifference and the privatization of faith. But those who are alive to the reforms and renewal of liturgical and sacramental life in the twentieth century work for the rediscovery of liturgy's primal formative and expressive power. This requires, among other things, the liberation of the multiple ranges of meaning given by the primary symbols. And this has to do with respect for the aesthetic and imaginative range of the texts, sign-acts and symbols in their interaction.

Classical definitions of liturgy speak of the glorification of God and the sanctification of our common humanity. This is best understood as an ongoing journey that simultaneously takes us into the mystery of God's being and act, and into the depths of our humanity. Authentic worship lures us into our own best being in relation to God and neighbor, that is, into our humanity at full stretch. If Jesus Christ is, by the animating life of God's Holy Spirit, at the center of all our assemblies, then the image of the humanity of God at full stretch is always before us — whether in healing, reconciling or feeding; in prophetic fierceness or in weeping; or in Christ's arms outstretched in blessing and shalom. At the storm center of God's mercy, justice and love is the offer to us of our true humanity. This is certainly behind what St. Irenaeus meant in claiming that the glory of God is the living human being.

We catch a glimpse of such a range of image and passion in the psalms. For they are the artless songs of faith stretching toward the God who is "enthroned upon the praises of Israel." They cry out our longings and laments, our desire for God, our terror and anger, our mortality and anxiety, our joys and our hope.

The biblical psalms and canticles are metaphors for the whole formative and expressive power of Christian liturgy. So far as our repertoire of song is reduced to the pleasant, the comfortable, the domesticated and the immediately accessible, so far is the emotional power of common prayer diminished. Similarly, so far as the words we speak are dull, banal, self-serving or unctuous, so far as the style of presiding and the modes of participation are utilitarian and perfunctory, so far is liturgy's power to awaken us to awe, wonder and joy diminished. But if the texts we sing and pray, and the style of our common participation in the ritual acts and primary symbols are resonant with the mystery proclaimed and signified, liturgy's power to reach our depths will become clear.

Here is the art of it all: Christian liturgy is itself symbolic, parabolic, metaphoric; it is an epiphany of the divine self-communication in and through the created order. So the arts that serve and the art of common prayer and ritual action must lead to participation in that which theology cannot finally explain but only apprehend in wonder, gratitude and adoration. As St. Augustine reminds us, when we receive the eucharist, it is our own mystery we receive.

> The liturgy, well celebrated over time, forms us in the way of living signified by the words: to repent, to love, to be thankful, to seek justice and mercy, to hope, to love and serve the neighbor, and to look for what is yet to come from the promises of God to this world and cosmos. So the patterns of emotion and intention formed by liturgical life are those aligned with real human life. Creation, birth and death, sin and grief and heartbreak, truthfulness in the inmost being, hope and faith and compassion, are the realities signified and into which we are formed over time in word and in sacrament, in prayer and in discipline.[6]

The aesthetics thus have to do with the well formed and the beautiful, and with the sensate activities of participation. All these artful features of liturgical celebration are what led Romano Guardini to define Christian liturgy as holy play — a wondrous set of improvisations on the cantus firmus of the song of the incarnation and the resurrection: "Glory to God in the highest."

A permanent tension

The symbolic value and the beauty of the liturgy's various elements derive from the material and form of each, while the holiness derives from the mystery of the events celebrated in, with and through Jesus Christ.[7] These points are based on the theological claim that God has created all things and called them good, and has become incarnate in Jesus Christ, gathering a historical community that is always culturally specific for worship and service in the world of space and time. In this sense liturgical aesthetics and the art of liturgy are rooted and grounded in the doctrines of creation, incarnation and redemption. All things are rendered holy by virtue of God's creative and redemptive action. All things are to be regarded as holy and brought to expression in sight, sound, gesture, movement and environment. Liturgical worship respects the difference between creature and creator, employing the things of earth to refer to and invoke the glory and mercy of God. This, of course, calls for a fundamental religious sensibility oriented to splendor and to appropriate sobriety and awe in the use of language, music, symbol and the other languages of the rites.

Yet there is also a permanent tension involved in the use of material objects, the domain of the human senses and the use of the imaginative power of human art. This is because human beings are not in full harmony with the created order, nor is any human community or culture congruent with a fully transformed world. All our liturgical celebrations remain "east of Eden" and captive to the limits of human cultural codes and perception as well.

In short, Christian communities remain sinful and culturally bound. This means that whatever significant form is realized in liturgical celebration, we still "see through a glass darkly." Furthermore the expressive forms must always negotiate between the symbol-breaking iconoclasm of the cross and the symbol-enriching glory of creation and resurrection. Liturgical art must always point to an eschatological self-critique of its own forms.

This permanent tension in liturgy as art is but a reflection of human existence and the fragility of faith. We do in fact live in a good but fallen creation, between the initiation of redemptive history and its consummation. Any given liturgical aesthetic belonging to a particular time and culture requires a counterpoint in the mystery of faith which transcends cultural forms to that "which eye has not seen, nor ear heard," which God has prepared for the children of earth. This eschatological dimension of all common prayer implies a question of style.

The question of style is not a matter of human technique. If it were, we could produce awe-inspiring rites by the simple manipulation of lighting, sound and surface effects. But the artful dynamism of authentic liturgical celebration is just the opposite of manipulation and magic; it is the opening up of the interrelations between the divine and the human. This opening is a matter of attentiveness to the form and the matter, and to the whole environment of the assembly's worship. Each unit of the liturgical rite and each "subrite" invites a specific quality or disposition which is appropriate to the nature of that rite and its contexts. These qualities are part of the artful symbolism, together with honesty and integrity of materials and the aesthetic range and power of the forms.

The assembly as a whole shares mutual responsibility and accountability for the art of liturgy well prayed. The presider and other specific ministers become focal points and representations of what is called forth from the people. The acts of gathering, singing, attending to the word, bowing, touching, eating and drinking, and blessing all require a heightened sense of receptivity. The cultural variables are many, since different cultures exhibit differences in behavior and manner in the course of such actions.

The poetics of celebration requires examination of the assembly's cultural context. In our postconciliar period, new emphasis is being placed on the modes of expression indigenous to the social and cultural history of the people gathered. If the liturgy is to signify interaction between the divine and the human, the modes of appropriating the basic symbols must be mediated in and through the language, music and bodily style of the people. The aesthetics of liturgy thus demands that we know the differences between, for example, Hispanic and African-American sensibility and a North American cultural tradition formed principally in Northern Europe.

At the same time, the symbolic action points to realities that are in tension with all inherited cultural assumptions and patterns of perception and communication. The permanent tension in the art of liturgy is between the necessity of local cultural modes of expression and interpretation, and the common culture of Christian faith and life. Only by maintaining those tensions can we also assert the specificity of Christian faith and life over against the assumptions of much postmodern and technological culture.

Though each subculture has its own integrity, there is still a manner of celebration that is Christian, stemming from the particular claims of the paschal mystery. There is a way of enacting the rites that is ultimately the human reception of what God has done in creation and in Jesus Christ. This has been referred to by Joseph Gelineau and others as the "paschal human in Christ": a manner or style always enacted in particular cultural languages that evidences "both reserve and openness, respect and simplicity, confident joy...and true spontaneity."[8]

Liturgy belongs to the created world and thus is an art, for the created order is God's handiwork. The aesthetics of authentic liturgy concerns the intrinsic means, not simply the external decoration or ceremonial elaboration, of the rites. Without such aesthetic considerations as quality of materials, appropriateness, proportionality and integrity of performance style within the liturgy and the art forms employed, the whole liturgy may be lessened in symbolic power. Yet, lest we take delight only in the beautiful forms we have produced and not discern the enabling grace of God in and through the forms, the final word must be eschatological. All artistic effort in service of the liturgy is itself proleptic as well as participatory in God's creativity. The mystery celebrated is never exhausted or fully contained in any act of worship. Liturgical rites authentically celebrated point to the vision and the heavenly liturgy of Christ of which all earthly celebrations are but hints and guesses.

It is, of course, given to us from time to time to experience this vision in part. Some feasts are themselves dedicated to this, but all — whether at Easter or in ordinary time — partake of it. The vision of a created order transformed and reconciled to the life of God should animate all our art. In that place all that is creaturely will be permeated with light, dance and song, with the *splendor veri.* Insofar as we experience the prefigurement of that reality in particular times and places, the art of liturgical celebration becomes congruent with the holiness and beauty of the triune life of God, at once incarnate in the world yet transcendent in glory beyond all created things.

Notes

1. Gerardus van der Leeuw, *Sacred and Profane Beauty: The Holy in Art*, trans. David E. Green (New York: Holt, Rinehart & Winston, 1963), 110.

2. Ibid.

3. Aidan Kavanagh, "The Politics of Symbol and Art," in *Symbol and Art in Worship*, ed. Luis Maldonado and David Power, Concilium: Religion in the Eighties, no. 132 (Edinburgh: T. & T.; New York: Seabury Press, 1980), 38.

4. St. Basil, *Homilia in psalmum* 1.2 in *Patrologia Graeca* 29:212.

5. St. John Chrysostom, *Homilia* 5.2 in *Patrologia Graeca* 63:486–87. Cited in Joseph Gelineau, *Voices and Instruments in Christian Worship: Principles, Laws, Applications*, trans. Clifford Howell (Collegeville, Minn.: Liturgical Press, 1964), 82.

6. Don E. Saliers, "When in Our Music God is Glorified: The Music of Liturgy and Life," in *Weavings* 4, no. 4 (July/August 1989): 13.

7. Material from this section is taken in large measure from passages in a forthcoming article, "Liturgical Aesthetics" in *The New Dictionary of Sacramental Worship*, ed. Peter Fink, S.J. (Wilmington, Del.: Michael Glazier, 1990).

8. Joseph Gelineau, *The Liturgy Today and Tomorrow* (New York: Paulist Press, 1978), 113.

18

The Concept of Sacred Space

Walter C. Huffman

Everything as it moves, now and then, here and there, makes stops. The bird as it flies stops in one place to make its nest and in another to rest in its flight. A man when he goes forth stops when he wills. So the god has stopped. The sun, which is so bright and beautiful, is one place where he has stopped. The moon, the stars, the winds he has been with. The trees, the animals, are all where he has stopped, and the Indian thinks of these places and sends his prayers there to reach the place where the god has stopped and win help and blessing.[1]

An old Dakota wise man formulated this aboriginal theology of prayer and place for a report to the Bureau of Ethnology in 1898. The spatial image he proposes is an arresting one: "...the Indian thinks of these places and sends his prayers there to reach the place where the god has stopped."

The study of sacred space in human experience is grounded in the assertion that certain objects, essences, spaces, hold traces of divine presence. Special places exist that engender hope, evoke memory and yet fill us with a sense of the present. They prompt our prayer. Transparent, they inevitably point beyond themselves.

In his work among the Ndembu people of northwestern Zambia, Victor Turner discovered that every ritual use of space and time contained an element that pointed beyond itself. The Ndembu were aware of this phenomenon and called it *Chijikijilu*, a word borrowed from the vocabulary of hunters that literally means "to blaze a trail" — to slash a mark on a tree to point the way home. These symbols, the "molecules of ritual," link known territory to unknown. Used as a metaphor for ritual, *Chijikijilu* "...connects the known world of sensorily perceptible phenomena with the unknown and invisible realm of the shades. It makes intelligible what is mysterious, and also dangerous."[2]

In primitive tribal societies, space is a heterogeneous experience, a clear demarcation between the sacred and the profane. Profane space according to Mircea Eliade is characterized by disorientation and deterioration. In contrast,

---

From *Liturgy: Dressing the Church* 5, no. 4.

sacred space is the locus of regeneration, creativity, and transformation.[3] Sacred space becomes a point of reference around which one builds and organizes existence. From this center, which is "an anchor in the ultimate" one can face the hazards of the larger environment.

A common perception of sacred space by *homo religiosus* is that its shape has been provided by divine plan to serve as an earthly microcosm of the cosmic realm in which the gods abide. Amid the vicissitudes of human experience, sacred space is a place fit for the gods to visit, a meeting place between heaven and earth in which prayers are heard and blessings bestowed.

> In this way the place becomes an inexhaustible source of power and sacredness and enables man, simply by entering it to have a share in the power, to hold communion with the sacredness.... But however diverse and variously elaborated these sacred spaces may be, they all present one trait in common: there is always a clearly marked space which makes it possible...to communicate with the sacred.[4]

In Eliade's view, this experience of the sacred is all but impossible in contemporary culture. Modernization has meant the loss of any capacity to experience time and space in any way other than homogeneous and profane. The once bracing and suggestive connection between prayer and place no longer exists. As a people we have become spatially and spiritually disoriented.

The house of the church

"Among the symbols with which liturgy deals, none is more important than this assembly of believers."[5] "The true identity of the Church is constituted and revealed by this assembly in Jesus Christ...."[6] The liturgical movement in our day is marked by its stress on the Christian assembly. In our formal theology and prayers of dedication "the people are the place." Hippolytus is invoked to remind us that the church is not only a place; it is also the "holy assembly of those who live in righteousness." The history of church architecture fluctuates between views of the church as the *domus dei* versus the *domus ecclesiae*, but our modern choice for the *domus ecclesiae* is part of an important midcourse correction touching the heart of Christian worship.

It is certainly naive to think that a Christian worship space can be ecclesiologically indifferent — only a protective skin over the assembly. Even buildings designed as *domus ecclesiae* are meaning specific; they continue to speak after the liturgy has concluded and the assembly disperses. The building creates a symbolic landscape that is not only instrumental in the action of the assembly but also an ongoing sign of a living tradition. The simplest meeting house remains charged with the life of the people who worship there.

Because the Society of Friends has often set itself against the concept of holy places, the affirmation of this idea in an article from *The Friend* is significant:

> Places and things do not hallow people, but the enduring faith of the people may hallow places. Where you are sitting in that calm cool place, there has been un-

broken prayer and worship generation after generation. In the outward and inner silences there...you may realize that...“we are surrounded by a great cloud of witnesses.”[7]

We can affirm the Quaker’s “sacrament of meeting” as a primary place where “the god has stopped,” but sometimes we forget that the gathering has a physical and historical embodiment. The building has an integral relationship to the living temple as community, and even though we place the locus of holiness in the people we cannot exclude the participation of the building from this same holiness: “We must say that even the *domus ecclesiae* exhibits a holiness derived not from mere external association with the holy community but from intimate and organic participation in its life.”[8]

For a dozen years, a young pastor poured his love and energy into a Christian congregation. He described his final Sunday in that place where, after morning eucharist and farewell luncheon, he stopped into the community’s worship space for one last solitary visit. It was a “boundless moment,” for the empty room was full of faces and noises from those years of worship and communal activity. A thousand memories crowded his consciousness. What had always been until now a rather inadequate cinder-block structure became for him a sacred place, and deep cathartic prayer welled up in him.

The possibilities of “liminal space”

Anthropology’s insights into the human experience of space and especially Victor Turner’s germinal suggestions about “transformative liminal space” need to be more fully appreciated and explored. Challenging the conclusion of Eliade, Turner proposed that all human cultures — contemporary as well as pre-industrial — can experience sacred space. He believed that such “liminal space” is inherent to all personal and social processes. Existing in “space/time pods” or sanctuaries, these are places in which deep ritualization has occurred. Often a key to their effectiveness are the “ritual elders” who manage their thresholds and boundaries and who lead the ritual activities that modulate and transform the space in the experience of a specific community.[9]

These protective zones act as counterpoints to other spaces in our lives that so often structure and reflect the driven, production-oriented nature of our society. Indeed our “kingdom play” begins in such liberated spaces. Their sabbatical nature prompts a sense of the spaciousness of the spirit that supports and encourages an environment of prayer.

It may well be that the alternating quality of such spaces will emphasize that which is elemental for us today. Perhaps they should permit us to synchronize our lives with the changing rhythms of day and season. Here we use and reverence objects — water, wine, bread, light — in their natural state. If such spaces are ritually inscribed with the great ancient memories and great visions of the community, then we can know them as “houses of prayer.”

The church which has devoted great energy to the categories of time and sacred history needs to remember also that history has a geography. We need to listen to the work of those who study the human experience of space. We need a renewed theology of space, not just for the sake of sound scholarship but for the health and spirituality of our people whose lives cry out for places of refuge, of sanctuary — for places where the "god has stopped."

Notes

1. James Owen Dorsey, "A Study of Siouan Cults," 11th Annual Report of the Bureau of Ethnology, 1889–90, Washington, D.C., 1894, 435. (Cited in Claude Lévi-Strauss, *Totemism* [New York: Beacon Press, 1963], 98).

2. Victor W. Turner, *The Ritual Process* (Chicago: Aldine Publishing Company, 1969), 15.

3. Mircea Eliade, *The Sacred and the Profane: The Nature of Religion* (New York: Harper & Row, 1961).

4. Mircea Eliade, *Patterns in Comparative Religions* (New York: Sheed and Ward, 1958), 367–69.

5. *Environment and Art in Catholic Worship*, Bishops' Committee on the Liturgy (Washington, D.C.: United States Catholic Conference, 1978), 17.

6. Eugene L. Brand, *Worship Among Lutherans* (Geneva: Department of Studies, The Lutheran World Federation, 1983), 5.

7. F. J. Nicholson, "A Hallowed Place," *The Friend*, 132, no. 12 (1975): 288.

8. Harold W. Turner, *From Temple to Meeting House* (The Hague: Moulton, 1979), 327–28.

9. For a discussion of the nature and dynamics of sacred space in the thought of Eliade and Turner, see Chapter VI, "Space and Transformation in Human Experience," in Robert Moore and Frank E. Reynolds, eds., *Anthropology and the Study of Religion* (Chicago: Center for the Scientific Study of Religion, 1984).

19

The Place of the Dead: Christian Burial and the Liturgical Environment

WILLIAM SETH ADAMS

The relationship between the liturgical rites of the church and the liturgical environment is rich and subtle. The more care we take in our liturgical theology and our exploration of the sacraments, the more the findings of that exploration should be expressed in the place where those rites and sacraments are celebrated. This attention is required because the liturgical space plays such a powerful and enduring role in the formation of the liturgical community that uses it.

It is increasingly common for the liturgical, theological and pragmatic necessities of eucharist, proclamation and baptism to exert their happy influences on building committees and designers of liturgical spaces. The spaces they create are testimony not only to the insights of designers but also to the centrality of table, ambo and font, and to the needs of the assembly and the one who presides.

We have to stretch the normal limits of design considerations if we are to look at the relationship of the liturgical environment and the burial of the dead. In doing so, we will look briefly at three aspects of the matter: first, the relationship of the liturgical space to the rites of burial; second, the actual place of burial; and third, the relationship between the remembrance of the dead and the continuing formation of the liturgical community.

Buried from the church

It may seem a curious thing to say to some communities, but *The Book of Common Prayer* makes a point of suggesting that "Christians are properly buried from the church."[1] Curious because one would think it so obvious — surely the

From *Liturgy: And at the Last* 10, no. 3.

community of the faithful gathers to remember and celebrate the life of one who has died, and surely, remembrance and celebration happen logically where the church's other celebrations occur. Yet in some traditions and for many people, the experience of this final rite of passage is increasingly associated with chapels in funeral homes and not with the church building. So perhaps we must first urge as forcefully as possible the return of the rite of the burial of the dead to the church building, the community's liturgical space. This is the place where the ecclesial memory of the community is set in motion, where the primordial stories are told and retold, where the central signs and symbols of the faith are in evidence.

Though the specific space requirements for Christian funerals are modest, the space must clearly accommodate the particular needs of the rite and the community. From the tradition of which I am part, this would mean an entry and/or gathering space that would allow for the reception of the body (coffin), the act that typically begins the liturgy of burial.[2] This reception is accompanied by prayer and the action of draping the coffin with a pall.[3] Under the best circumstances, those who receive the body would include not only the presider and those who assist with the draping but pall bearers and family members, as well as members of the congregation. These persons would then participate in the entry procession.

Following the reception of the body, the procession from the entry to some central location (often a place near the altar/table) requires a sufficiently broad aisle, so that this solemn movement can be accomplished with ease and visual clarity. Typically accompanied by the recitation or singing of words of great power ("I am Resurrection and I am Life, says the Lord . . ."), this procession is a sign of the "passage" and "pilgrimage" that lie at the heart of the rite. The procession, therefore, should be seen.

The coffin should be placed in such a way that those present can see it, yet it cannot be an obstacle to movement in the rite. If, for example, the eucharist is celebrated and if the liturgical room is arranged so that the logical position for the coffin is at the foot of the chancel stairs as it might be in a Gothiclike building, then the coffin can become an impediment to those who move toward the altar/table for communion.

At the same time, consideration needs to be given to the *inclusion* of the coffin in the embrace of the liturgical community as well as in the liturgical action. Our faith persuades us that those who die in the Lord remain in communion not only with God but also with the living, so the physical exclusion of their mortal remains contradicts our theological intent. Solving the "obstacle" problem, then, must not result in the exclusion of the coffin.

Since "[t]he liturgy of the dead is an Easter liturgy" (*BCP,* 507), wherever the coffin is placed it should be accompanied by the lighted paschal candle. The candle could be carried in the entry procession and placed in its stand, next to the coffin, as the coffin itself arrives at its proper place. If carried in, the candle might also be carried out, as the coffin is removed to the burial place.[4] And since the symbols used in this first part of the service (the pall, candle and water) are also reminders of the baptismal liturgy, some churches find it fitting to place the coffin near the baptismal font (or pool) if that space is visible and meets the other criteria for inclusion of the deceased.

All of these environmental details need to be considered at the design level. For our purposes, these details lead us, in turn, to consider the actual burial place and the connection between the remembrance of the dead and the formation of the liturgical community.

The place of burial

The history of Christian burial practices lays out before us the church's increasing interest in the place of burial. In the earliest life of the church, burial places were outside the city walls, since this was the civil custom of the times. As time passed and Christian theology matured, however, we began to do two things that changed our sense of the rightful placement of the dead. First, we began to meet at burial grounds for commemorative prayer, celebrating saintly lives at the burial site. Second, we began to build churches in association with burial grounds, in order to house and shelter our prayers and commemorations. Over time, these churches and burial places came to be included *inside* the geographical limits of the city or town, as these communities grew around them. The town came to surround the burial place, and the liturgical place associated with burial became an integral part of urban life. And so the living were accompanied in their daily life by reminders of the dead. Burial places were no longer relegated to locations outside the walls — remote, removed. In a world in which the lines between visible and invisible, between the spirits of the living and the dead, were blurred, the sense of the companionship of our holy dead must have been very powerful, the sense of the presence of the communion of saints almost palpable.

In our time, many of us suffer the deprivation of powerful and palpable reminders of such communion. To be sure, plenty of cemeteries dot our urban and suburban landscapes, but very few of them exist in any physical or geographical association to the liturgical community. For most of us, the churchyard is not a burial ground, even though well into the eighteenth century such an association would have been our common inheritance.

In recent years, an increasing interest has arisen in returning, in some way, to this earlier practice. This interest usually expresses itself in the design and construction of columbaria, burial places inside the church building or its environs intended to receive the cremated remains of the dead. One such example is the floor of the chapel of Christ Church (Episcopal) Cathedral in St. Louis. The pavers that comprise the floor cover the tops of burial niches and bear the names and life dates of the persons whose cremated remains are kept below them. The Episcopal Church of the Holy Spirit, Lake Forest, Illinois, a creatively reordered Neo-Gothic building built at the turn of the century, has recently added a sizable memorial chapel that adjoins the principle liturgical space and houses a large number of niches with places available on their covers for names and dates. In both of these examples, the room that houses the columbarium is a room intended to be used, visited, enjoyed by the living.

In other instances, outdoor gardens serve as the locus for the burial of the faithful, either in columbaria or by direct interment into the ground itself. Such places serve not only as burial places but also places for contemplation or social interaction. If such a garden possesses a pool or fountain, the garden could well be used for baptism in those churches that permit this rite outside the church building. A similar possibility exists in an interior space. Given what has been said above about the link between the symbols used in funerals and their counterparts in the baptismal liturgy, churches might think about a building design that links in some creative way the space for baptism and a parish columbarium. A columbarium could be built in an extant baptistery, or a baptismal space could be incorporated into an area designated for a columbarium. In any such instance, where better to enact and accomplish baptismal death and resurrection than in a burial ground surrounded by the living and the dead?

Space to form community

More important, however, than any of these benefits ancillary to the actual burial of the dead is the role that such places themselves would play in the formation of the liturgical community. At the very heart of our liturgical life and our liturgical formation is the work of remembrance. The liturgy is our "remembrancer," our storyteller, our memory bearer. The liturgy gathers up the past and re-presents it to us now — its effects, its influences, its impact, its benefits. And in this remembrance, we hear the narration of our identity. What the liturgy remembers with power shapes us, forms us, identifies and describes us. The remembrance of the liturgy protects us from a kind of amnesia, and the calendar of commemorations is clearly a central agent of these acts of recollection.

Throughout the year, customarily the church remembers before God our holy dead people whose lives give definition to our hopes, shape to our intentions and substance to our identity. We the church hold these in sacred memory. It would be a wonderful aid to this work of remembrance if our liturgical action were done in a setting that was common to the living and the dead. This, it seems to me, is the strongest argument for the return of burial places to the church grounds and buildings. The presence of these reminders of the lives of "the saints" would, as it were, have their way with us. With subtle and enduring power, they would remind us of God's promise about death, a promise made to the living by One who has risen.

Further, if the liturgical community were to celebrate God's saving activity in physical proximity to the burial place and if we were to proclaim in such a place our convictions that death has been overcome, how better could we declare to a *death-denying* world our intent to be faithfully *death defying*? Surely it would prove a remarkable testimony!

The burial office in *The Book of Common Prayer* (p. 499) contains the following language, part of an anthem borrowed from the Orthodox tradition: "All of us go down to the dust; yet even at the grave we make our song: Alleluia, alleluia, alleluia." If burial places were restored to the church and its environs and if the liturgical community were "taught" to understand itself as part of the community of lives memorialized in those burial places, then surely we would more readily see that *every* shout in praise of God, *every* alleluia, is *always* made at the grave. And that is how it ought to be.

Notes

1. "Concerning the Service — The Burial of the Dead: Rite One" in *The Book of Common Prayer*, 468. A similar point is made in the Ministers Edition of the *Lutheran Book of Worship* (Minneapolis: Augsburg Publishing House, 1978), 37. *The Roman Catholic Order of Christian Funerals* (*OCF*) makes this point about the funeral liturgy, i.e., normally the funeral Mass (#131), but not about the vigil and related rites, which may be "celebrated in the home of the deceased, in the funeral home, parlor or chapel of rest, or in some other suitable place" (#55).

2. "The anthems at the beginning of the service are sung or said as the body is borne into the church. . . ." *The Book of Common Prayer.* Similar gestures of welcome are suggested in the Lutheran and Roman Catholic rituals as well as in other revised books.

3. Other actions at this time might include sprinkling the coffin with holy water as a reminder of baptism and the placing on the coffin of appropriate Christian symbols, such as a Bible, cross or the open Book of the Gospels (see *OCF* #161 and 163), though as the Minsters Edition of the *LBW* reminds, "the ceremonies or tributes of social or fraternal societies have no place within the service of the Church."

4. In the Roman Rite, the candle is not to be carried in procession but "placed beforehand near the position the coffin will occur at the conclusion of the procession" (OCF #162).

2O

A Place for
Burial, Birth and Bath

S. Anita Stauffer

About water and baptism can be said the same things: they mean life and death and bathing. Without water people and animals and plants wither and die. Water extinguishes fires; it cleanses and refreshes. God created water for life and death and bathing. It is God's instrument for salvation and destruction. As the waters of the flood brought death, so the waters of the exodus — "swept by a strong east wind" — brought life.[1]

Christian baptism is also water for life and death and bathing. Wherever abundant water flows, there is a setting for baptism: Jesus was baptized in the Jordan River (Mark 3:9–11), and Paul baptized Lydia in a river near Philippi (Acts 16:13–15). Rivers, lakes and the sea continued to be the usual sites for baptism for two or three centuries.[2] In the second century, however, because Christians were still under persecution, baptism may sometimes have occurred in the bathing rooms and courtyard fountains of private homes and in small public baths.[3]

Early baptisteries

In the third and fourth centuries, particularly after the Emperor Constantine ended the persecutions in 313, special places for baptism were constructed or adapted. Baptisteries were buildings, or sometimes separate areas within buildings, that contained baptismal pools known as fonts. At that period in church history, adult baptism was the norm, and baptism generally occurred during the Easter Vigil. To accommodate all the candidates for baptism and to provide privacy,[4] the baptisteries in the West were usually detached or only loosely attached to churches.

From *Liturgy: Dressing the Church* 5, no. 4.

136

Examples of such early baptisteries still exist in Italy in such places as Ravenna, Grado, Lomello and Rome (San Giovanni in Laterano) and in Frejus, France. In addition, excavations have revealed other important paleo-Christian baptisteries in Italy: San Tecla in Milan (the Ambrosian baptistery), Castel Seprio, Torcello, Concordia Sagittaria, Aquileia and San Marcello in Rome. The form of these early baptisteries and their fonts varied by geographic area and related to the architectural origin, the sacramental mode and the theological meaning of baptism.[5]

The baptisteries seem to have at least two architectural antecedents. First, they have been influenced architecturally by martyria and mausolea, which were often quadrilateral, circular or octagonal. The fourth-century baptistery of San Giovanni alle Fonti at San Tecla in Milan, for example, was modeled after Maximian's mausoleum at San Vittore. Moreover, its plan bears a striking resemblance to the extant chapel of San Aquilino, attached to San Lorenzo in Milan, which was originally built as a mausoleum and was also modeled after the San Vittore mausoleum.[6] Also remarkable is the eleventh-century trefoil baptistery at Concordia Sagittaria, Italy, which exactly reproduces the nearby fourth-century trefoil martyrium; the martyrium itself, in fact, may have been transformed into a baptistery for a period of time.[7]

A second architectural antecedent of baptisteries seems to have been the *frigidarium,* the cold section of Roman baths that was usually octagonal, circular or quadrilateral. The baptistery of San Giovanni in Laterano in Rome is one example of a baptistery built over a preexistent bath. In the Constantinian era, its plan was very similar to two *frigidaria* in Pompeii.[8]

Interpreting the font

Fonts, more than the baptisteries in which they were located, deserve our particular attention, since it now appears that separate or detached baptisteries would contradict an emerging ecumenical consensus regarding baptismal theology and practice. According to this consensus, baptism is part of corporate worship, to be celebrated in the congregation's presence and with their involvement.

The oldest font known to us dates from the early third century. Found in a house church in Dura-Europos (in what is now Syria), this font had the rectangular shape of a coffin. In Italy from the fourth century on, hexagonal and octagonal fonts became common. Round fonts were also found in many areas in the early church, including the earliest font at the Lateran baptistery in Rome. Cruciform fonts (in the shape of the Greek cross) existed in Greece, Asia Minor, Syria and Egypt.[9]

The shapes of fonts have been interpreted according to differing theological emphases, especially burial, birth and bathing.[10] Paul stressed the paschal nature of baptism in his letter to the Romans:

> Do you not know that all of us who have been baptized into Christ Jesus were baptized into his death? We were buried therefore with him by baptism into death,

so that as Christ was raised from the dead by the glory of the Father, we too might walk in newness of life (Rom 6:3–4).

This paschal motif was central in the baptismal theology of Ambrose, Cyril of Jerusalem, John Chrysostom and Theodore of Mopsuestia,[11] and it is a common theme in patristic writings about baptismal fonts. In the late third century, Origen referred to the font as a sepulchre.[12] A century later Chrysostom wrote that "it is as in a tomb that we immerse our heads in the water."[13] Ambrose of Milan, also in the late fourth century, described the font as being like a grave and a tomb.[14]

It is not surprising that baptism was usually celebrated at the Easter Vigil or that many early fonts were interpreted as symbolizing this understanding of baptism as death and resurrection with Christ. Octagonal fonts, which probably originated in the Ambrosian baptistery in Milan and can still be seen in excavations there, symbolized the Eighth Day, the day of resurrection, the eschatological dawning of the new age. The fifth-century Lateran font, which can no longer be seen, was also octagonal.

Hexagonal fonts suggested the sixth day as the day of Christ's death. Such paschal symbolism was particularly powerful when a hexagonal font was in an octagonal baptistery — an arrangement that can still be seen in Italy in Aquileia, Grado and Lomello — because when the candidate for baptism "entered the hexagonal font, he knew he was to die with Christ, but as he left the font and stood once more in the eight-sided room he also knew that he was to walk in newness of life."[15] Another shape, the cruciform font, symbolized the victory of Christ's resurrection.[16]

A second major theological emphasis connects baptism with birth as in this text from the fourth gospel:

> "Very truly, I tell you, no one can see the kingdom of God without being born from above." Nicodemus said to him, "How can anyone be born after having grown old? Can one enter a second time into the mother's womb and be born?" Jesus answered, "Very truly, I tell you, no one can enter the kingdom of God without being born of water and the Spirit" (John 3:3–5).

Theologically, the font was seen as a womb or a mother. Clement of Alexandria wrote in the early third century that God "begot us from the womb the water."[17] Almost two centuries later, Augustine described the font as "the womb of the church."[18] The fifth-century Latin inscription that can still be seen on the architraves in the Lateran baptistery includes many phrases interpreting baptism as birth. Leo the Great, who may have composed the Lateran inscription, also preached about the parallelism between baptismal water and the womb. Round fonts have also been interpreted as suggesting this birth imagery.

A third theological understanding is of baptism as a bath for cleansing us from sin. Paul wrote to the Corinthians: "You were washed, you were sanctified, you were justified in the name of the Lord Jesus Christ and in the Spirit of our God" (1 Cor 6:11). In the second century, Justin Martyr described baptism as a washing.[19] In the next century, Cyprian of Carthage wrote frequently of baptism as washing and cleansing. It is interesting that some early baptisteries were located near or constructed over Roman baths; whether this was done for symbolic reasons or simply to provide a source of water is a matter of debate.

Despite their varying shapes, early fonts — literally pools — were always large and held abundant water. The Lateran baptismal pool was twenty-eight feet in diameter — easily accommodating the two most common modes of baptism. Immersion involved dipping the candidate's head in the water; affusion involved pouring the water over the candidate's head. In both cases, however, the candidates were standing in the water when they were baptized. Affusion as well as immersion suggested burial: water was poured over the candidate just as earth was cast on a corpse.[20] Submersion (completely plunging the candidate under water) does not seem to have been practiced in most places in the early church because the fonts were relatively shallow.

From the sixth to the eighth centuries, adult baptisms declined in number[21] — probably due to the high infant-mortality rate and parental fears resulting from Augustine's doctrine of original sin. When fonts no longer needed to be large enough for the immersion of adults or to be located in detached baptisteries to insure privacy, they were placed inside churches, usually near the main entrance. They were still relatively large — to accommodate the immersion of infants — and traditional in shape, either octagonal (suggesting resurrection), hexagonal (death with Christ), rectangular (tomb) or round (birth).

The loss of primary symbols

From the Middle Ages until the present time, baptismal space has deteriorated both functionally and symbolically. As affusion (pouring) and aspersion (sprinkling) became widespread, the fonts became smaller and smaller. What was originally a river and then a pool eventually became a shallow "birdbath" and finally a small bowl. In addition, in the thirteenth century, when people began stealing the consecrated water in the font to use for witchcraft, locked covers were placed over the fonts.[22] The covers soon became elaborate and decorative, and eventually the covers — not the water itself — became the primary visual symbol, until it was no longer possible to interpret the font with its water as either womb or tomb or even as bathtub.

As a result, today's popular understanding of baptism is often trivial. Baptism is seen as a nice little ceremony, rather than as a consequential event of death and life. Few of us perceive baptism as the profound event that Cyril of Jerusalem described in a sermon to newly baptized Christians in the fourth century: "You died and were born at the same time. The water of salvation became for you both a tomb and a mother."[23] Indeed, so little water is commonly used for baptism today that even the washing or cleansing motif is impossible to perceive.

Baptismal space today

The trivialization of fonts through the centuries resulted largely from deterio-
rating baptismal practices. Now, these practices are changing for the better. New
and revised baptismal rites across the ecumenical spectrum have attempted to
let the rite itself — its texts and actions and setting — demonstrate its profound
meanings. Because we learn the meaning of the sacraments from what we do
and what we see, the poor baptismal practices of centuries have taught us a poor
baptismal theology.

One of the most important changes in baptismal practice today is the growing ecumenical awareness of the sign value of water, and thus the use of more
abundant water in the rite. The Roman Catholic Bishops' Committee on the
Liturgy has written: "To speak of symbols and of sacramental signification
is to indicate that immersion is the fuller and more appropriate symbolic action in baptism."[24] The remarkable ecumenical document *Baptism, Eucharist and
Ministry* agrees:

> In the celebration of baptism the symbolic dimension of water should be taken
> seriously and not minimalized. The act of immersion can vividly express the reality
> that in baptism the Christian participates in the death, burial and resurrection of
> Christ."[25]

Four centuries ago, in 1519, Martin Luther also affirmed the practice of
immersion. He wrote that it is

> demanded by the significance of baptism itself. For baptism...signifies that the
> old man and the sinful birth of flesh and blood are to be wholly drowned by the
> grace of God. We should therefore do justice to its meaning and make baptism a
> true and complete sign of the thing it signifies.[26]

Immersion and even affusion — if the pouring is done with an abundant
amount of water — more fully convey the meaning of baptism than mere sprinkling. The point is not how much water is necessary for baptism to be efficacious
but rather how much water it takes for us to realize the radical nature of baptism.
A few drops cannot communicate the rich biblical meanings of baptism.

Renewing our baptismal spaces

Baptismal space in a church building will encourage or inhibit a congregation's
development of mature baptismal practices and understandings. An insignificant
font kept in a corner and moved out for occasional use does not signify the
permanent baptismal foundation of the Christian life. A font in any location,
if it holds only a minimal amount of water, does not teach us to understand
baptism as burial or birth or bath. A small bowl of water placed on the altar for
baptism does not reflect the centrality of baptism in the life of the church.

Form follows function and meaning. If baptismal practices are to be renewed
to make clear the meaning of baptism, then our baptismal spaces must also be

renewed to enable those practices and that meaning. Water is the central symbol of baptism:

> All the things suggested by water — washing, life sustenance, refreshment, drowning, birth, creation, flood, Exodus, Jordan — support and enrich the proclamation of incorporation. The first five of these meanings connect with people's experience of water outside of liturgy, and they communicate in a supraconceptual way. For example, one cannot really explain the refreshment a shower brings after a strenuous game. The latter four meanings are conditioned or learned, and they depend on one's knowledge of biblical history. It is water signaling on all these levels that gives depth and breadth to what is proclaimed about incorporation into Christ. Baptism is not solely a verbal event; it is a total experience.[27]

The most important factor about the font is the amount of water it can hold. *The Lutheran Book of Worship* (1978) suggested in its rubrics that "a font of ample proportions for the Sacrament of Holy Baptism should be part of the furnishings of the church."[28] In the same year, *Environment and Art in Catholic Worship* advocated the same principle. A font should be large enough to accommodate at least the immersion of an infant, or ideally, the immersion of an adult. (A good example of the former is the font at St. John the Evangelist Roman Catholic church in Hopkins, Minnesota; and of the latter, at St. Peter's Lutheran Church in Manhattan.) Even if immersion is not now practiced in a parish, the profusion of water will help people recognize the biblical water images used in the baptismal liturgy.

To communicate central baptismal imagery a font should contain enough water that one could bathe or even drown in it. If possible, the water should be running and heated. Also, in our era when good stewardship of the earth certainly involves water conservation, the water in a font should probably be recirculated.

What, then, should be the shape of a font? The ancient octagonal and hexagonal shapes still have much to commend them. With good pastoral teaching, the shape of the font can help convey the meaning of baptism as burial and resurrection with Christ. Such emphasis seems especially important in our culture in which the denial of death is pervasive and the scandal of the cross less appealing than cheap grace.

Round, cruciform, quadrilateral and other shapes of fonts are also possible; a remarkable new cruciform font for the immersion of adults has been constructed at St. Charles Church in London. Care should be taken, however, to avoid "cute" shapes such as shells.

Before determining the shape for a new font, a careful study of symbolism should be undertaken by the planning committee — to be followed by a program of thorough and ongoing catechesis with the entire congregation and prospective members when the new font is completed. The shape of the font is less important than its size, however, and this, too, is a matter for good catechesis.

It is not necessary for the font to be adorned with symbols. The water it holds is the central symbol, and the font itself — its size, shape and location —

is also a symbol. Other symbols on the font may detract. This is not to disparage art but only to suggest that symbols on symbols are not necessary. Likewise, it is no longer meaningful to put covers on fonts. In our culture baptismal water is not considered supernatural (though it is used for a holy purpose) or magical, and there is no need to prevent people from stealing it as they did in medieval times. It is far better to let the water be visible and tangible.

The location of the font is a matter of symbolism and of good liturgy. First, the word of God, the eucharist and baptism are three separate ecclesial acts. As there are three worship acts, so there should be three worship spaces, the pulpit, the altar and the font. Placing the font in the chancel obscures this distinction. In addition, as it minimizes the amount of movement in the liturgy, it reduces everyone's participation to passive roles.

Second, what is symbolized and enabled by the location of the font? The most appropriate location seems to be inside the main entrance to the worship space, with adequate space around it. Such a location symbolizes baptism as entrance into the family of God, the church. It is good for the font to be located so that the people must walk around it as they enter the nave, and thus be reminded each Sunday of their baptism. When baptism is celebrated, the baptismal party (and perhaps others in the congregation, especially children) gather around the font; the rest of the congregation turns to face it (even as it turns to face a bride when she enters for a wedding).

The area around the font is known as the baptistery. The paschal candle may be placed near the font (except during the weeks of Easter, when it is located near the altar) as a reminder of the primary connection between baptism and Easter.

A small shelf or table is also useful in the baptistery to hold items needed for baptism, such as oil for anointing, a towel, the baptismal garment and the small baptismal candle.

Proclaiming the profound

Baptism is a profound and radical act — profound because it draws us deeply into Christ and the paschal mystery, and radical because it grafts us onto the very roots of the Christian faith and into the body of Christ. Baptism is a cosmic and individual act because it makes each of us part of salvation history. It is also a profoundly personal act with radical corporate consequences because it makes each of us a child of God and simultaneously incorporates us into the communion of saints.

Baptism is an act of termination and new beginning, a time of *transitus* — the most important passage of our lives. The words of Ash Wednesday remind us abruptly of the reality of life on earth: "Remember that you are dust, and to dust you shall return." All too soon we, too, will be but skeletons disintegrating into dust, like the remains that stare out at us from the burial niches of the catacombs. Born from the wombs of our mothers, we move inexorably toward tombs in the earth.

But there is another reality of life in Christ: reborn in the font, the direction we move in is reversed, for the font is both a watery womb and a life-giving tomb. In baptism we move from death to new birth, from burial to resurrection, from darkness to light, from the stain of sin to the cleansing power of grace, from ourselves into the family of God. We are never the same again because the chaos and self-centeredness of our lives are washed away, and we are joined to Jesus Christ. The waters that drown us are also the waters that give us life.

Baptism is a profound and radical act of burial, of birth and bath. The sacrament is not a trivial event, but it is trivialized by insignificant fonts and small amounts of water. Baptism is no time for minimalism; it is, rather, a time for signs and actions consistent with its radical and profound meaning. Large fonts holding abundant water can proclaim and enable baptism's wonderful consequences: death and life and salvific cleansing.

Notes

1. For more about the significance and symbolism of water, see Martin E. Marty, *Baptism* (Philadelphia: Fortress Press, 1977), 9–19; and Alexander Schmemann, *Of Water and the Spirit* (St. Vladimir's Seminary Press, 1974), 38–40.

2. I. G. Davies, *The Architectural Setting of Baptism* (London: Barrier and Rocklift, 1962), 2.

3. Richard Krautheimer, *Early Christian and Byzantine Architecture*, 3rd ed. (New York: Penguin Books, 1979), 24. See also Clement F. Rogers, *Baptism and Christian Archaeology* (London: Oxford University Press, 1903), 314–15.

4. Public bathing was done in the nude in ancient culture. Patristic literature interpreted baptismal nakedness, e.g. Cyril of Jerusalem: "Having stripped yourselves, you were naked; in this also imitating Christ, who was naked on the cross" (*Mystagogical Catecheses* 2:2).

5. What follows is a very simplified summary of a complex matter that is subject to scholarly research. One interesting approach is provided in A. Khatchatrian, *Origine et typologie des baptistères paléochrétiens* (Mulhouse, France: Centre de culture chrétienne, 1982).

6. See Richard Krautheimer, *Three Christian Capitals* (Berkeley: University of California Press, 1983); Mario Mirabella-Roberti and Angelo Paredi, *Il Battistero Ambrosiano de San Giovanni alle Font* (Milan: Veneranda Fabbrica del Duomo, n.d.); and Mirabella-Roberti, *Milano Romana* (Milan: Rusconi Immagini, 1984).

7. A. Khatchatrian, *Les baptistères paléochrétiens* (Paris, 1962), 77. For excellent photos of Concordia, see Bruna Forlati Tamaro, Luisa Bertacchi, et al., *Da Aquileia a Venezia* (Milan: Libri Schweiller, 1980).

8. See Joseph N. Fête, "The Cultural Background of the Roman Ritual of Baptism" (unpublished S.T.M. thesis, Yale Divinity School, 1981).

9. Davies, 22.

10. Aidan Kavanagh has suggested that the birth and cleansing motifs were predomi-

nant prior to the late fourth century, when the burial motif became emphasized. See his *Shape of Baptism* (New York: Pueblo, 1978), 46.

11. See Hugh M. Riley, *Christian Initiation: A Comparative Study of the Interpretation of the Baptismal Liturgy in the Mystagogical Writings of Cyril of Jerusalem, John Chrysostom, Theodore of Mopsuestia, and Ambrose of Milan* (Washington: Catholic University of America Press, 1974).

12. *In Romanos* 5:8.

13. *In Joannem* 25:2.

14. *De sacramentis* 2:20 and 3:1.

15. Davies, 21.

16. Walter M. Bedard, *The Symbolism of the Baptismal Font in Early Christian Thought* (Washington: Catholic University of America Press, 1951), 38–41.

17. *Stromata* 4:25.

18. *Sermones* 56. *De oratione dominica ad competentes.*

19. *First Apology* 61.

20. Davies, 26; and Rogers, 356.

21. Kavanagh, 67. See also J. D. C. Fisher, *Christian Initiation: Baptism in the Medieval West* (London: SPCK, 1965).

22. Davies, 69–70. See also Francis Bond, *Fonts and Font Covers* (London: Oxford University Press, 1908), chapter XVII.

23. *Mystagogical Catecheses* 2:4.

24. *Environment and Art in Catholic Worship* (Washington D.C.: United States Catholic Conference, 1978), 39.

25. Faith and Order Paper No. 111 (Geneva: World Council of Churches), Baptism V.18.

26. Martin Luther, "The Holy and Blessed Sacrament of Baptism," in *Luther's Works,* ed. E. Theodore Bachman (Philadelphia: Fortress Press, 1960), 35:29.

27. Eugene L. Brand and S. Anita Stauffer, *By Water and the Spirit,* Pastor's Guide (Philadelphia: Parish Life Press, 1979), 25.

28. *Lutheran Book of Worship Ministers Edition,* 30.

29. See Kenneth Nugent, "Church Art and Architecture: New Life for an Old Church, *Clergy Review,* 69, no. 10 (October 1984), 361–64.

2 1

Comparing the Rites
of Christian Initiation

Laurence H. Stookey

A remarkable progress in the practice and understanding of Christian initiation
has occurred in the last two decades. This is most evident when one compares
the recently revised liturgical texts of Roman Catholics, Lutherans, Episcopalians and United Methodists, among others. Not that the emerging consensus
in the new rites tells the full story. Such agreement as we have now reached only
encourages us to continue our dialogue and to work for change in areas about
which there is no unanimity at present.

Four areas especially need to be explored in this broader ecumenical context:
mutual recognition of baptism; the nature of the catechumenate and its relationship to the age of candidates; the status of confirmation and its relation to
the episcopacy; and the use of rites in addition to water baptism, particularly
the eucharist.

The mutual recognition of baptism

Since the reformation, baptism has been a divisive rather than a uniting issue
in many quarters. One can draw an imaginary line between those Protestants
who, along with the Orthodox and Roman Catholics, have considered baptism
a sacrament, and those who have not. On the right, or conservative side, were
the Lutherans and the Calvinists (Presbyterians, Reformed Churches), the Anglicans (who adapted their doctrine from both Luther and Calvin), and later
the Methodists. To the left, or radical side, were the Anabaptists, together with
the later groups that emerged to form what we now call the "Baptist" family.
Zwingli also was to the left of the line, though at times he seemed to straddle
it. The Zwinglian influence, however, on groups on both sides of the divide, is
too complex a matter to discuss here.

From *Liturgy: Putting on Christ* 4, no. 1.

The crucial point is this: in general, those churches to the right of the line have recognized all baptism because of its sacramental nature. Those to the left of the line have not recognized the baptism of those to the right — and sometimes not even of other bodies on the left. For if baptism is nonsacramental, its validity is bound up with age, mode, belief of the candidate, and sometimes, even a membership agreement within one particular congregation.

We can be encouraged that the point of division is increasingly a dotted rather than a solid line. A growing number of Baptist congregations will accept into their membership persons who have been baptized at any age or by any mode, though these same congregations will impose both age and mode restrictions on unbaptized candidates who come to them for initiation. Accepting the already baptized is a policy decision that individual congregations have to make, and it is very rare. By contrast, the congregations of The Christian Church (Disciples of Christ) evidence a more general acceptance of this kind of policy. The Disciples are participants in the Consultation on Church Union, and their general assembly has commended COCU's "mutual recognition of membership" policy. Because of their congregational polity, individual congregations of Disciples are not bound by this action. Most of them, however, seem to have accepted this stance of open membership.

Compliance is difficult to achieve in denominations that have a congregational polity. But even in churches that can legislate uniformity, there are mavericks. For example, the Roman Catholic priest who "rebaptized" President Lyndon Johnson's daughter acted long after Vatican II's Decree on Ecumenism had made clear Rome's recognition of all Christian baptism. This highly publicized incident served the church well if it ended noncompliance by Roman clerics, but many Protestant clergy have yet to learn the lesson. Then, too, there are undoubtedly hosts of laity in all our churches who assume they have been baptized into a denomination rather than into the church catholic.

This is unfinished ecumenical business, therefore, and it is twofold. First, we must continue to dialogue with those groups who do not yet recognize the baptism administered by other Christians. Second, we need to create understanding and acceptance within those bodies that do recognize such baptism, if only formally.

The catechumenate

The post–Vatican II restoration of the adult catechumenate in the Roman church is a significant reform. It affects not only liturgical celebration but also the attitudes of Christians to the process of initiation, including the initiation of infants and children as well as adults. Nothing like it can be found on the Protestant landscape; among the possible reasons for this are the following:

1. The centralized nature of the Roman liturgy provides its revisers with a global perspective from which to view the needs of Christians in areas where the church is assimilating large numbers of adult converts from non-Christian

backgrounds. By contrast, Protestant liturgical revisions are rather narrowly nationalistic; revision committees of Protestant denominations based in the United States have little awareness of the needs of congregations elsewhere. In all likelihood such a committee will not include representatives from Africa, for example, even though the denomination may have a significant number of congregations in Africa. While this may allow the African congregations to develop thoroughly independent, indigenous rites, it also causes a great loss of insight to churches in the United States. International consultation for future revisions has become a pressing matter for many Protestants.

2. In the past, the lines between Roman Catholic and Protestant affiliation have been rather rigidly fixed and different in character. Either one was a Roman Catholic by birth or deliberate choice, or one was a Protestant of some sort — perhaps by accident or cultural absorption. Anyone not in the former camp was presumed to be in the latter category — never vice versa. The language for changing was significant: a person "converted" to Catholicism if s/he were Protestant but merely "transferred" from a Lutheran to a Methodist congregation. Even when certain Protestant groups did require those seeking admission to go through new rites of baptism or confirmation or both, the persons who made such a change were not usually thought of as "converts." This led Catholics, even before the development of the RCIA, to view the reception of non-Roman adults far more seriously than Protestants viewed the reception of other Protestants (or even former Catholics).

3. A corollary is this: because Protestants have assumed the existence of some pan-Protestant background (no matter how vague) on the part of adults joining the church, Protestants have not come to terms with the secular orientation of new Christians the way Catholics have. It has not yet dawned on American Protestants that adults living in our current culture may need to undergo a conversion to Christianity at least as drastic as that of an animist in Africa; and the situation is likely to get worse rather than better. Meanwhile, many continue to suppose that a pastor's class for "inquirers" is all that we need, notwithstanding that those classes usually extend for only four to six sessions, two of which are devoted to such matters as denominational polity, local church organization, and the promotion of the parish program and budget.

4. How much change can denominations assimilate without undue loss of membership? When Roman Catholics dislike all of the innovation set before them, either they stay at home or they seek out a parish where the reforms have not yet been implemented. They usually do not become Lutherans — unless for other reasons. But United Methodists who feel put upon by change quite readily become Presbyterians, or Baptists or something else. Liturgical revisers, sinners like the rest of humanity, know about the numbers game and act accordingly. Even when the motive against innovation is less base — a genuine pastoral concern rather than statistics — the practical result is the same. Extensive reforms such as the RCIA exemplifies may have to come about much more slowly within Protestantism.

For these and other reasons, the careful consideration of the restored catechumenate is a major piece of unfinished business before us. Among the problems it poses is the status of infants and children as candidates for baptism. Some Catholic Christians see the benefits of the RCIA so clearly that they are ready to jettison the baptism of infants — or at least to consider baptism as an extended process that culminates in the administration of the water only after the catechumen, enrolled in infancy, has reached a degree of maturity, however maturity is defined. Some Protestant Christians also propose to do away with the baptism of infants, though for slightly different reasons. Still others are ready to defend to the death the immediate and indiscriminate baptism of all for whom it is requested, infants or adults.

So many opinions indicate that many hard questions have yet to be considered. Is baptism a means of grace to such a degree that it can never be denied or deferred, or is it so bound up with adult understanding and commitment that it cannot be completed except by adults? If the latter, is adulthood to be defined chronologically, psychologically, socially or on the basis of some form of spiritual and ethical evaluation? What does it mean to accept the notion that the church is a covenant community and to believe the biblical affirmation that within the covenant the promises are given both to us and to our children? What kind of stamina will it take for both pastors and congregations to decline to baptize certain persons, and what can be done pastorally for those so refused? When persons who have been refused baptism in one congregation request the same rite of another congregation — one that practices a less sacramental discipline, perhaps — what kind of respect does the first congregation have the right to expect from the second? To what degree is this affected by whether the two are in the same or different denominations?

In all quarters, it is clear that the church's baptismal discipline is now being taken with new seriousness. How exactly that discipline will relate to a recovery of the catechumenate requires much more exploration.

Confirmation

Of all the formal aspects of the initiation process, confirmation is the most perplexing. Several denominations, in the process of liturgical revision, sought to abolish the word, if not the very concept. None could — for reasons far more related to popular expectation and vested interests in the field of administration than to theological assumptions. Nevertheless, the theological status of confirmation is by no means clear. Nobody any longer wishes to suggest that baptism is somehow deficient until it is "completed" by confirmation. But then, is this rite a separate sacrament, or not a sacrament at all, or something in between?

This problem is further complicated by the uncertainty surrounding the need for confirmation and its relationship to the bishop in episcopal churches. Among Methodists and among Lutherans who have bishops confirmation is now, as it always has been, a pastoral prerogative. Should a bishop be present, s/he will be

asked to preside, but this is for courtesy's sake, rather than a theological requirement. Roman Catholics in principle at least would have the bishop as presider
at all baptisms and confirmations, as would Episcopalians. Yet when adults are
baptized according to the RCIA, confirmation is effected even if the presider is
not a bishop. Except in carefully specified instances, however, the confirmation
of infants baptized before the age of catechesis is reserved to the bishop.

In any event, in addition to the confirmation formula, Roman Catholics require the placing of the administrator's hand (singular) on the forehead at the
time of chrismation; the laying on of hands (plural) which precedes this is not
the definitive sacramental action. For Episcopalians, in contrast, chrism may be
used by a bishop or priest at baptism, but this is optional. Confirmation requires a separate laying on of hands (plural), and only a bishop may perform
this action. Those who are baptized as adults by someone other than a bishop
are, according to the prayerbook, "expected to make a public affirmation...in
the presence of a bishop and to receive the laying on of hands." Chrismation is
not part of this separable rite of confirmation. But does "expected" mean "required"? Ambiguity in rubrics often results from the deliberate sidestepping of
a thorny issue.

This diversity of approaches to the confirmation rite is a clear indication
of the unfinished business that pertains to this aspect of initiation. It is not
surprising, therefore, to find that confirmation may not be accepted across denominational lines in the same way that baptism is. Christians agree that what
constitutes baptism is water, the trinitarian formula and intention, but they do
not agree on the matter or form of confirmation — nor even that confirmation,
in whatever form, is necessary.

Rites in addition to water baptism

Apart from the administration of the water, Protestants have far fewer liturgical
actions associated with initiation than do Catholics. Given the lack of attention they pay to the catechumenate, it is not surprising that Protestants do not
celebrate the making of catechumens. They do not practice the election or en-
rollment of candidates at the beginning of Lent, the scrutinies (let alone the
exorcisms) or the presentation of the creed and the Lord's Prayer. To inquire of
any Protestant, moreover, about the meaning of a postbaptismal mystagogy is to
elicit a response of total befuddlement; such a question cannot be understood,
much less answered. Yet there is a richness in these rites that Protestants must
not ignore, even if accepting them demands much adaptation.

Protestant circles are perhaps more ready to accept the signation with chrism,
the touching of the baptized, the giving of the white garment and the presentation of the lighted candle. Episcopal and Lutheran formularies mandate
signation with optional chrismation. The United Methodist rite suggests both
but requires neither. Except when confirmation is administered as part of the
rite, the Episcopal service provides for no use of the hand except at signa-

tion. Lutheran celebrants are instructed to lay hands on the newly baptized in conjunction with the prayer for the Spirit. United Methodists at this point recommend that other baptized persons gathered at the font may join in this laying on of hands with prayer. The directions of the Episcopal prayerbook suggest the giving of the candle but not of the new clothes. United Methodists and Lutherans suggest both.

It is not the diversity but the very possibility of such actions that is important here. While some congregations in each denomination will object to any such actions, and some eyebrows will be raised in every congregation, still these actions are now being referred to — and tolerated — in denominational documents. Such mention would have been unthinkable only a quarter of a century ago. Who knows? Perhaps even exorcisms and postbaptismal mystagogy will stage their comeback a couple of revisions from now!

A far more pressing concern is the relationship between baptism and the eucharist, both on the occasion of the sacrament of initiation and thereafter. It is now commonplace for liturgists to suggest that baptisms take place within the eucharistic service of the congregation. When those baptized are adults, there is no confusion; baptism admits them immediately to the Lord's table, at least within that denomination. But what about the communion of baptized infants and children? And what about intercommunion among those who respect each other's baptism?

Until recently, Lutherans, Episcopalians and Presbyterians took it for granted that confirmation constituted admission to the eucharistic banquet. Roman Catholics had a separate tradition of first communion before confirmation but well after the age of early childhood. Methodists allowed, even encouraged, reception of the eucharist by young children, though this was almost never taken to include infants on the occasion of their baptism. Now the entire question is up for grabs, and already a variety of tentative solutions have caused some distress.

Presbyterians at one point had a local-option provision, which meant, theoretically, that children granted communion in one congregation might be excommunicated if their parents moved to a congregation of a differing opinion. In one branch of Lutheranism, permission for children to communicate was given, then rescinded, producing excommunication by denominational rather than local action. The sad irony is that some liturgical reformers would abolish the baptism of infants while others would encourage the communion of infants. One expects that sooner or later someone will advocate the granting of communion to children who are not permitted to be baptized!

The question of intercommunion is an even more perplexing issue. How can communicant members of one denomination be denied (officially at least) the eucharist in denominations that recognize their baptism? That this question is far from new only intensifies the urgency of the work for a solution. There are two schools of thought. One is that legislation always lags behind practice. Therefore Christians should simply appear, incognito if necessary, at the tables of those churches that officially deny them access. The assumption is that when enough people have broken the laws long enough, the churches will be sufficiently embarrassed to reform the rules.

The other theory is that laws are best changed through the pain of having to obey them. Thus, Christians should attend services at which they are not permitted to receive communion and should refrain from communion. Their noncommunication presence will produce so much of what Reinhold Niebuhr somewhere called "sacramental agony" that all parties will be motivated to alleviate the pain by reforming the exclusionary rules. Probably either tactic can be effective; perhaps both approaches used together can complement each other. It is crucial that some way be found to resolve this dilemma: the denial of communion to those whose baptism is recognized.

Certainly the rites of initiation challenge us with many and complicated kinds of unfinished business, and there is important work to be done on every front. But given the central place to which the eucharist is being restored in all our churches, the extending of the sacramental body and blood to all who have been incorporated into Christ's ecclesial body through baptism is surely the most urgent piece of unfinished business confronting us.

2 2

Coming Together in Christ's Name

James F. White

Worship is the most important thing the church does, and coming together in Christ's name, the most important thing that happens in worship. It may also be the most overlooked.

One can trace in detail the evolution of the entrance rite of priests, but what about the entrance of people? Church interiors are designed with care; most people, however, arrive through a side door from the parking lot. Their gathering is treated as something to be hushed or smothered under loud organ music. Neither time nor space is allocated to signify the importance of coming together in Christ's name.

When we gather to meet our God we first meet our neighbors. Thus before anything is said or sung a very important event occurs; the church is formed by the gathering of those called out from the world to be the body of Christ. They gather to recognize the body of Christ in their midst (1 Cor 11:29); their gathering creates the body itself, the church. And they know that their risen head has promised to be with the body of Christ: "Where two or three have met together there I am in the midst of them" (Matt 18:20).

An important reality

Ministers everywhere panic at the thought of the electronic church. They fear that everything done on Sunday morning — prayer, preaching, music — will be done so much better by the highly skilled professionals on television that they and their congregations will be compared and found wanting. Most ministers forget that the incarnate church has gifts that can never be matched by the docetic church of the media. For the incarnate church assembles face to face. It is a meeting of real people who speak to and touch each other. In that speaking and touching in Christ's name the church happens. Our fears of the media show how little we have valued our assembly in Christ's name. The television set can

From *Liturgy: The Rites of Gathering and Sending Forth* 1, no. 4.

never duplicate the experience of Christ's presence in the midst of his people. Christianity is a religion of real people, not the chimera of dancing light images. I like to speak of Christian worship as speaking and touching in Christ's name, a definition that may not be very abstract but does catch an important reality. Only in the assembled church are both speaking and touching possible.

Christians in other times have sensed the importance of coming together. Indeed, we meet, assemble, convene, gather, collect, congregate or confer together, and the richness of our language serves to highlight the importance of our act. In Judaism the "synagogue" was both a place of assembly and the congregation itself. Christians could apply the term, too (Jas 2:2). For Quakers the term "meeting" serves as a synonym for worship itself, namely, "go to meeting." In Puritan New England the meeting house was the building in which the church met for worship and the town for town meeting. In some colonies, it was illegal to build a home more than a mile from a meeting house. New England developed little civic architecture until well into the nineteenth century because the meeting house served as the place where both church and state happened.

A royal priesthood, a people fully human

Why is the act of meeting so important? Robert Barclay, the seventeenth-century Quaker theologian, compared meeting to the way "many candles lighted, and put in one place, do greatly augment the light." If anything, Christianity is the flight of the together to the Together. John Wesley preached that "Christianity is essentially a social religion . . . to turn it into a solitary religion is indeed to destroy it." This is not to say that personal devotions are unimportant. But it is distinctive of Christian worship that we need to gather together to serve God through serving each other.

Baptism has made all of us part of a royal priesthood, a priesthood we exercise when we assemble. As Paul says: "When you meet for worship, each of you contributes a hymn, some instruction, a revelation, an ecstatic utterance, or the interpretation of such an utterance. All of these must aim at one thing: "for building up" the church (1 Cor 14:26). Our present gifts may be considerably less dramatic, but they all contribute to one aim: by praying together, by singing with each other, by listening to God's Word, we build each other up. Priestly people come together to minister to one another.

Another aspect may be less obvious. In my village, most of my neighbors spend the week on the seat of a tractor, in the cab of a truck or at home with the children. Most of them see few people other than family during the week. They come to church on Sunday to be human. Church is a humanizing experience for many people in our society, certainly not just for the elderly who look forward to "getting out to church." Gathering for worship is an important socializing occasion; its humanizing function ought not to be overlooked.

As we gather to recognize the Lord's body, we also learn what it is to be fully human. The body that takes shape on Sunday morning is a body already discerning the presence of the Lord in the flesh even as it gathers for worship. Therefore let us not be disturbed by the noise and shuffle of people arriving. Meeting is important; assembling is part of Christ's work among us. It deserves to be recognized with sufficient time and space.

Apportioning the time

A few examples of such recognition can be cited. In the United Methodist service book *We Gather Together*, even the name indicates an understanding that was carried throughout the basic services of worship that constitute the book. The first portion of each service — "A Sunday Service" (with or without the eucharist), weddings and funerals — begins with a section labeled "Entrance and Praise." Within this section the first act of worship is designated as "Gathering." In other words gathering is not just a necessary evil as it has so often been treated, but is specifically designated as part of worship itself. How much this understanding is shared by most ministers and church musicians is another question. Some still feel compelled to drown out all footsteps and conversation with loud organ music.

Word and Table, the manual of instruction for "A Sunday Service," suggests several possible ways of enhancing the act of gathering: conversation, informal singing, welcoming by the pastor, and rehearsal of new music or other unfamiliar service materials. It is hoped that pastors and musicians will begin to consider gathering an important part of every service: as worship rather than as a preliminary to worship. In certain types of services assembling has long been recognized as an important act of worship. The wedding procession is far more than a mere preliminary. Since it demands a significant number of participants, it receives considerable time. A procession with the coffin is also often part of the funeral service. Strangely, our arrival at the church in death may be granted more significant time than it was week after week in life.

The services in *We Gather Together* should help communicate the importance of coming together in Christ's name. The "basic pattern" indicates that "Entrance and Praise" is a portion of worship in which "the people come together in the Lord's name." Creative use of this portion of the services will depend largely on ministers, musicians and worship committee members. Once they grasp its significance, they will be limited only by the horizons of their imaginations. Their first step will be to consider gathering as a time of importance, as a meaningful time well spent. [See *The United Methodist Book of Worship* (Nashville: Abingdon Press, 1992), 16–17 — ed.]

A space for the gathering

But even the most imaginative worship planners are going to be frustrated if the building says that coming together in the Lord's name is insignificant activity. The quality of human interaction that occurs in the movement from the impersonal space of the car in the parking lot to the personal space of the pew in the church depends largely on the organization of space. If "good celebrations foster and nourish faith," surely careful planning of gathering space strengthens good celebrations.

We come together by various means. Most of us are brought to our baptism; all of us are brought to our funeral. We are ushered into other types of services: in the company of intimate friends at our wedding, in consort with our contemporaries at first communion or confirmation, and with all our fellow Christians at the Lord's Supper. Thus the designing of space for assembling is a complex matter.

The basic problem of course is that rarely have architect or building committee given it much thought. Absent from their minds is any recognition of how much the design of congregating space shapes the nature of human interaction as the church assembles for worship. Usually the worshiper is left to his or her own devices to make a beeline from parking lot to pew. That may save some energy but if so, that is its only advantage. European church builders have long recognized the importance of a transition space in which people can move from the world (street) to the kingdom (church). The magnificent atrium before St. Ambrose's in Milan is a prime example of space in which to gather, to cleanse one's hands, and to reflect as the church congregates. The columns of the arcade provide a magnificent alternating rhythm of light and shadow, beckoning one forward. Trees and shrubs can do the same thing in creating a processional path. It is important to sense in a processional path the rhythm of objects along the route: sculpture, benches, trees or columns. Too often these are treated as luxuries only, to be considered after the building is paid for.

Interior space for coming together is also usually considered of minor importance. What happens in the lobby or narthex is not often considered part of worship. Provision is made for cloakrooms and restrooms but not for forming the body of Christ. "Get inside the church as best you can" is the usual message. Fortunately nothing new is quite so bad as the eighteenth-century prison chapel that I saw in Lincoln, England. Absolutely demonic, it was so designed that no prisoner could see any other prisoner while entering or while worshiping. After that who can doubt that the devil takes architecture seriously?

I have found it a marvelous exercise for seminary students to observe a service, ignoring what is said or sung but noting all human interactions and movements, especially when people arrive and leave. Most students think worship is just saying the right words, but this exercise opens their eyes as well as their ears. Many learn that the quality of a community's life together is largely determined by the space they share in worship. Even the parking lot is important; we impatient ones can lose most of our Christianity before even reaching the street!

Three particularly well-thought-out buildings deserve our attention. One of the most successful new churches of the last decade is the Church of Saint John the Evangelist, Hopkins, Minnesota (George Rafferty of Rafferty, Rafferty, Mikutoski and Associates, architect; Frank Kacmarcik, consultant). Here an interior gathering space pulls people together from all parts of the church building and the world outside. They are led together from a rather dark space, past a mammoth granite baptismal font with the sound and sight of moving water, and directed into the well-lit church space.

An entirely different approach appears in a remodeling project at St. Peter's Catholic church, Saratoga Springs, New York (Frank Kacmarcik, designer). The front entrance of a conventional Gothic revival church was sealed off, the chancel walled up to create a small weekday chapel, and the interior reoriented to face one of the long walls. To enter, one comes from the main street of the town into a walled courtyard, beautifully landscaped with trees and flowers, then turns right to enter through what once was the easternmost bay of the nave. Thus, long before one enters a door something has happened: one has been brought into a people place and induced to mix with other worshipers. The various members of the body come together to be one in worship before the door is reached.

Edward Sövik has designed several churches with a "concourse." In First United Methodist Church, Charles City, Iowa, the concourse is a rectangular space with chairs and tables such as those found in old ice-cream parlors. This design invites people to come early and linger late after worship. It is obviously processional space; it leads into the worship space, but it has a low ceiling and an air of informality. Again it is a people place, bridging the transition from car to pew.

Other architectural possibilities can be envisioned. But they will only materialize as we realize that coming together in Christ's name is itself a vitally important part of worship. Once we realize that we gather to form the Lord's body we will find the resources to facilitate and enhance the act of coming together. A body needs space and time.

23

Liturgy for Healing

Elaine J. Ramshaw

Now he was teaching in one of the synagogues on the sabbath. And just then there appeared a woman with a spirit that had crippled her for eighteen years. She was bent over and was quite unable to stand up straight. When Jesus saw her, he called her over and said, "Woman, you are set free from your ailment" (Luke 13:10–12).[1]

Of all the Sabbath healing stories in the gospels, Luke's story of the crippled woman proffers the most interesting rationale for Jesus' action. There are two understandings of healing at odds here: the official religious line, that healing is work, and Jesus' counterinterpretation, that healing is liberation. The woman is bound by Satan; when Jesus lays hands on her, he says, "You are set free from your ailment." Healing is appropriate on the Sabbath not because it is a good, kind work but because it is liberation — and liberation is what the Sabbath is all about.

We usually think of the Sabbath as based on God's postcreation rest, which is the explanation given for it in the version of the commandments in Exodus 20. But in Deuteronomy 5, there is an alternative rationale for Sabbath keeping: "Remember that you were a slave in the land of Egypt, and the Lord your God brought you out from there with a mighty hand and an outstretched arm; therefore the Lord your God commanded you to keep the Sabbath day." Not only are you to rest, but you can't make your children or your animals or your slaves work either. It is to this motif of liberation that Jesus seems to be appealing. So you don't make your ox work, but you do untie it and lead it to water. You do set free a woman bound by Satan. All forms of liberation are connected here: personal and social, physical and spiritual. The Sabbath is about the end of slavery.

Healing in worship

What place does the concern for healing have in our worship? Would we say, too, that liberation from the powers of death and the freeing power of the resur-

From *Liturgy: Ritual and Reconciliation* 9, no. 4.

rection are source and goal of all our prayer? Can we, like Luke's Jesus, connect all the levels of liberation and see them as enactments of the reign of God? When slaves are freed, when workers are given the day off, when sins are forgiven, when crippling illnesses are healed, God holds sway. We need to pray for physical healing and for justice for the oppressed, not in a spirit of do-goodism (Help these unfortunate people; or, Send us out to help them) but in a paschal spirit, in the very same way we should pray for forgiveness. We are talking here about proleptic victories over the powers of death. In all these things, "we cry out for the resurrection of our lives."

The story of the healing of the crippled woman says another thing about the relationship between healing and worship: liberation leads to the ability to praise. If people in that time and place stood to pray to God, then it is no coincidence that the woman is enabled to stand up straight and praise God in the assembly. (People sometimes say you have to be brought to your knees to pray; I like this alternate image, that you have to be brought to your feet to pray!) When we are healed, we are set free to pray — not obligated to give thanks but freed to stand up straight and praise God (see Luke 13:13). So we need to ask ourselves two questions in response to this story: Can the community address the need for healing in its worship? But also, Does the community need healing in order to pray?

The eschatological task of the liturgy is to imagine the world whole, the community whole, each other whole. We are like Ben in Seymour Leichman's *Boy Who Could Sing Pictures,* whose songs miraculously made pictures in the sky above his head that others could see. Ben used this gift to sing away the great sadness he saw in the peasants for whom he sang:

> Once he sang an old farmer young again. And when the old farmer saw himself young, dancing above the heat waves, he remembered better days and smiled, really smiled.... For an old woman whose sons were away to war, he sang them back for a while. And she saw and she felt better.... He sang a man singing another man singing another man, and babies born in times to come. And oxen and warm fire and the sea gulls along the shore. And on and on he sang the Promised Land. The weary, he sang rested. The hungry, he sang full. The cold, he sang warm. And the great sadness, he sang all away. And then he sang no more.[2]

This is one aspect of what we do in worship — though we do it as a community, for each other and not as individual artists. We sing the Promised Land.

But do we? Do we imagine the world whole? Does our liturgy take on the reality of injustice and its sources, so as to imagine an alternative? Do we imagine the community whole? Is the power structure of the community as enacted in ritual a witness to wholeness? Do we imagine each other whole? Do our images of the self do more building up than breaking down? Do our rituals make room for the wholeness of our experience — not just gratitude, patience and hope but also protest, confusion and anger?

There is always a paradoxical, paschal character to this eschatological task of imagining the broken whole. We are both imagining a future wholeness and imagining the person whole now, in their suffering. By the cross we can see wholeness hidden in the brokenness. This paradox must not be used to legitimate suffering or to urge a patient acceptance of suffering as God's will. The wholeness can only be read backward from Easter. It is in the light of the final victory over the powers of death that we can both pray for a proleptic victory of physical healing and see in the unhealed person the wholeness of Christ.

Rites of healing

In the context of a community that imagines the world whole, many different rites may be enacted to bring healing to those who are sick. I want to begin with a discussion of traditional rites of healing and move on to a consideration of other rituals that may be appropriate components of the community's pastoral care for the sick. In connection with each of the ritual options, I want to raise some practical theological questions of meaning and effect.

Rites of healing may be celebrated by the whole congregation regularly (once a month, or a few times a year on appropriate feasts) or occasionally, as when a congregational rite of healing is held at the conclusion of a Bible-study series on healing. Rites of healing may also be celebrated in private or small-group settings; then it is most likely occasional, though ongoing small groups who feel a special need for healing, e.g., those fighting an addiction, may have a regular healing ritual.

The most basic ingredient of all such rites is intercessory prayer (on the part of the sick person, it would of course be a prayer of petition for the self). In praying for healing, we face all the questions that can be raised about the practice of intercessory prayer in general. For what is it appropriate to pray? How should we pray for it? What difference do we expect the prayer to make?

Petitionary prayer

Do we pray for something concrete? Or do we play it safe and pray only for "spiritual" benefits, such as courage or patience? On the whole, if people are willing to pray for any change in the external/objective world, they'll pray for healing and for world peace. But should we get more specific than "healing"? Is a specific request appropriate, based on Jesus' analogy of a child appealing to its father (Matt 7:9)? Or is a specific request a form of button-pushing, a sign of insufficient trust? One of the dangers of making a specific request is that we'll have to deal with the reaction, our own and others', if the hoped-for result does not transpire. I have students who will limit themselves to praying for spiritual goods including only the vaguest concrete goods ("healing"), on the grounds that people's faith may be threatened if you pray for something and the prayer is not granted. I suggest to them that in that case the question of petitionary prayer is a matter for ongoing education, preaching and discussion in their communities, and that in that process they should struggle with the story of Gethsemane, where Jesus prayed earnestly for something concrete which did not happen. (If they really want to stir things up, they can point out that John's Gospel explicitly contradicts the synoptic tradition on the question of whether Jesus asked to be delivered from death — a little intracanonical debate on how one should pray!)

The Gethsemane prayer brings up the will-of-God question, which raises the issue of whether petitionary prayer should be conditioned by the phrase "if it be your will." Some think this should be done all the time, some use it when praying for success but not when praying for peace or healing, and some never condition the prayer but leave it up to God to sort out the requests. Those who believe strongly that the witness of Jesus tells us that God is always for healing, always for abundant life, for liberation from bondage, would argue that to so condition a prayer for healing is particularly inappropriate, as if God might *not* will healing in this case. This approach entails believing that much of what happens in creation as we know it goes counter to the will of God, perhaps that sickness is part of sin's disorder rather than creation's original order. It's certainly true, though, that Jesus never refused to heal anyone on the grounds that sickness was God's will for them. "No, I'm sorry, I can't lay hands on you, it's God's will that you be sick."

Do you pray only for possible or likely outcomes, for outcomes that are reasonable to hope for? This can sound almost as wimpy as praying only for spiritual goods: don't risk praying for something that's not likely to happen. But the truth is we all do this to some minimal degree. None of us would be likely to pray for God to raise someone from the dead. But do you continue to pray for healing when the doctors have ruled it out? Will that support false hopes? Or is prayer not the means to educate other people's desires?

Prayer in symbolic action

The traditional rites for the sick are ways of praying for healing in word and symbolic action. There are three sorts of hands-on actions: the laying on of hands itself, anointing and tracing the sign of the cross on a person's skin. The first two, anointing and the laying on of hands, are sometimes conflated; the contemporary Roman Catholic rite clearly separates the two actions, with silent laying on of hands as well as an anointing, accompanied by the prayer for healing. Another action in the Roman Catholic rite is sprinkling with holy water, which is now interpreted within the rite more baptismally than penitentially. It's important to note here the centrality of touch, generally recognized to be extremely important to many who are sick, as a means of countering their isolation and fear. In addition, all forms of nonverbal communication take on particular importance where verbal communication is difficult or too distant.

We need to address the question of whether anointing with oil is recoverable as a living symbol. Anointing was done for scores of reasons in the cultures of the ancient world: in preparation for athletic events or wrestling matches (to slip through the opponent's grasp), as inauguration or investiture, as part of "secular" healing practices, as the final stage in all bathing, from the bridal ablutions to the preparation of a corpse for burial.

Anointing came into baptism as the natural culmination of bathing and into healing ritual as the paradigmatic healing act, which for us would probably be taking a pill. My own opinion is that if anointing with oil takes on significant meaning for us, it will only be the meaning we manage to bestow on it by using it in church ritual. It's not a living symbol grounded in the rest of our lives, as is bathing in water or sharing a meal. Liturgist Charles Gusmer says that probably the association that gives us best access to the symbol of anointing is the use of salves — but I find that less than adequate anthropological foundation. In fact, even skin diseases are often now treated by pills, with nothing at all applied to the skin. There are others who argue, though, that anointing has intrinsic qualities that recommend it: the oil is absorbed into the skin, which makes it meaningful as a symbol of grace permeating our selves; and besides, it smells nice, and the sense of smell is underutilized in our worship (another means of nonverbal communication).

For those who anoint at baptism, the anointing in the rite of healing can be explicitly related to baptism. If anointing or sprinkling is used or the sign of the cross is traced on a person's skin, it is important to make the baptismal connection clear. In baptism our life and death are brought into the paschal pattern of Christ's life and death and resurrection, and it is within this framework that we interpret our experience and by it that we shape all our praying. A Christian rite of healing must pray in the shadow of the cross, in the light of the resurrection.

Identifying difficult issues

A number of issues can be raised in connection with the practice of rites for the sick. One important issue is the question of who it is that acts and who is acted upon. Do we have here an active pastor and a passive patient, so that the ritual is yet one more procedure performed by a professional *on* the patient? And can the person seeking healing be empowered as a subject rather than an object of healing? "When he laid his hands on her, she stood up straight and began praising God." At the very least, the sick person should be involved as much as possible in planning the rite, choosing scripture readings and hymns, choosing among the various prayers and actions the ritual offers. Could the one who is sick bless the other participants in the liturgy? Could s/he give the homily?

Although I understand the logistics of getting hands on top of someone else's head, I'm disturbed by the power symbolism of congregational rites of healing where people are kneeling before clergy or for that matter, before laypeople with a gift of healing. It's interesting to note in this light that anointing with blessed oil for healing was not an act reserved for priests until after the Carolingian reform in the ninth century. Before that, the only clericalism involved was that the oil had to be blessed by a bishop. The blessed oil was then taken home from the eucharist by everyone to use, as Pope Innocent wrote in 416, "when their own needs or those of their family demand." Could one even anoint oneself? We may not like the "magic substance" quality to this practice, but at least it put the healing action in the hands of all Christians, including the sick themselves.

Another concern is whether we define a condition as sickness or a person as sick by performing a rite of healing. Most of the time that identification has already been made and is unproblematic, but that is not always the case. Some Roman Catholic rehabilitation centers for alcoholics have regular rites of anointing for the residents, which is considered acceptable only because alcoholism is understood to be a disease. Though that definition is widely accepted in the United States, it is still controversial. There is also the sensitive issue of drawing the line between disabilities and sickness. We don't want to perpetuate the notion that people with physical limitations, who have often compensated with abilities underdeveloped in the rest of us, are "sick." But the line is not always easy to draw. If someone is wheelchair-bound due to arthritis, yes; if due to an accident, no? But could one not pray for healing in the process of rehabilitation after an accident?

Another touchy area is emotional illness. Here the family-systems theorists have alerted us to the danger that treating the "identified patient" in a system will just reinforce that person's role as scapegoat or as distraction from conflict that can't be faced elsewhere. This raises a related issue: how our traditional rites of healing assume the Western individualistic view of illness and health. It's a fine thing to pray for the health of individuals, but we may need to balance this better with addressing the need to heal the whole community, family, congregation. Healing rites of traditional nonliterate societies often take better account of the communal dimension of healing than does our "sophisticated" approach.

There's another important issue relating to the definition of illness and health. Should we try to restrict healing rites to the situation of serious illness, as Roman Catholic canon law does? Is it trivialized if it is performed for minor problems? Charles Gusmer is bothered by the "indiscriminate anointing" that goes on even at Roman Catholic corporate rites of healing.[3] Why do so many who are not physically ill seek anointing or the laying on of hands in congregational services? Perhaps they want a personal blessing, and this is their only chance to get it. Equally important, though, is our interpretation of sickness and healing in broad ways, so that sickness is a metaphor for the human problem — replacing the traditional central Western Christian metaphor of sin — and healing is wholeness in all its dimensions. Is the use of the rites of healing with this broad application to be encouraged or not?

Perhaps it's about time we enlarged our repertoire of metaphors for the human problem. One could argue that healing is a more dominant metaphor or enactment of salvation (the same word in Greek, of course) in the Gospels than in the forgiveness of sins. I have difficulty, though, with the situation of some churches where a regular congregational rite of healing has clearly displaced the eucharist as the liturgy most highly invested with emotion and effort. Something is off kilter if a corporate rite of healing is the rite that constitutes the community or sets its self-understanding. With that critique in mind, though, we need to be alert to the reasons why the rite of healing may draw people more strongly than the eucharist.

Other rites celebrated in time of sickness

In addition to liturgies specifically designed to pray for healing, there are many other rites from the tradition, including the major sacraments, which may be used in a situation of sickness. First of all, there are the sacraments of initiation: baptism, confirmation (for some a separate initiatory sacrament, for others the laying on of hands and prayer for the Spirit in the baptismal rite itself) and first communion. An adult in the crisis of illness or at the prospect of death may request baptism; a baptized person who has not yet communed due to age or noninvolvement in the church may request communion.

In *Ritual and Pastoral Care* I told the story of a dying six-year-old girl who had heard her pastor talk about the eucharist in eschatological terms and said she wanted to be at God's party. He instructed her and celebrated communion with her and her family a couple of days before she lost consciousness. In that case the instruction and the celebration were a means of shaping the child's experience to the paschal pattern, a preparation for death and for life beyond death, and an enactment for the family of Christian community whose bonds survive death.[4] What I didn't say in the book was that there were people in the congregation who objected to the pastor's communing a child too young to receive. We may find such a complaint appalling under the circumstances, but it does go to show that Christian initiation is not a private matter, and the meaning of a community's ritual performed privately still has ramifications in the wider community.

Apart from prayer itself, the eucharist must be the rite most used by Christians in connection with the pastoral care of the sick. The main concern being raised now ecumenically about communion with the sick is the issue of its relation to the congregation's eucharistic celebration. Is it better to bring the bread and wine from the congregational eucharist, thus including the sick person in the very same meal? This practice allows laypeople to bring communion to the sick. However, some of the written rituals for this purpose convey the impression that they're saying, "Something really important happened while you weren't there," rather than inviting the communicant into a present reality of shared communion. Is it better, then, to celebrate the eucharist in the sickroom? When congregations have infrequent communion, there's usually no other option. The advice of recent ritual books in that case is to gather as much of a community in the sickroom as possible: visitors that come with the pastor, friends or family already there, or hospital or nursing home staff people.

Communion can be the best ritual care for those who aren't tracking well in the present, since it is more familiar to them than other rites. People may be neurologically impaired or mentally confused so as not to be able to follow the thread of a conversation for more than a few minutes, and yet ritual memory may carry them through an entire eucharist with the proper responses. It's helpful in such cases to find out what form of the liturgy is most familiar to the sick person. For an elderly person with neurological difficulties, the liturgy of their childhood may come back more clearly than the one they've celebrated for the past ten years.

When we speak of communing with those who are physically ill, we need to remember that the tradition speaks of communion as the "medicine of immortality" for soul and body, sometimes in ways so concrete as to surprise us who spiritualize the reality and gifts of the Lord's Supper. In the Large Catechism, Martin Luther wrote that this meal is "a pure, wholesome, soothing medicine which aids and quickens us in both soul and body. For where the soul is healed, the body has benefitted also." This incarnational, holistic understanding of communion's benefits is worth lifting up, along with the whole emphasis on communion as bringing healing and reconciliation as well as individually oriented forgiveness.

Another rite that the sick often request, and which is included at least as an option in most rites of healing, is the rite of confession and absolution. Certainly there are complex connections between sin and physical sickness. Not only do many believe with Augustine that sickness came into the world because of human sin, as a cosmic result of the Fall; but also the etiology of many illnesses involves matters of lifestyle, habits and choice. In addition, any stress, including the stress of dysfunctional, sin-warped relationships, can act to lower our immune response. Nonetheless we need to ask careful questions about the reasons behind a request for confession/absolution and the advisability of including it within a rite of healing. The danger is of reinforcing the primitive sense of punishment and guilt brought on in all of us at some level by bad luck. What did I do to deserve this? One can deduce one's own guilt in order to make the world make sense — or just feel guilty because something bad is happening. I'm being punished, therefore I must be bad. Now that isn't the only reason why people frequently make confessions to hospital chaplains. In times of crisis we reassess our lives, past and future, and may try to reorder our priorities and redirect our course. I may focus in my everyday life on work at the expense of relationships, for instance, and when I am unable to work, the experience of interacting with my visitors (or of lacking visitors) may bring me face to face with my relational failures. Even if one thinks that the guilt in a particular case is not neurotic and confession and absolution are called for, though, I would still argue that this act should be kept separate from a rite of prayer for healing. Sickness may be an occasion to examine oneself, but we should not ritually reinforce the popular theory, explicitly denied by Jesus on two occasions, that suffering is a personal punishment for sin.

Another rite that has been suggested for use with the sick is the affirmation of baptism. Lutherans, Episcopalians, Presbyterians, Methodists and members of the United Church of Christ now have rituals for affirmation of baptism, a repeatable rite in which people renew their baptismal vows and profess their baptismal faith, and are prayed over by the community (usually there is both general congregational prayer and a laying on of hands with prayer for the Spirit to continue its work in the person). In the Presbyterian trial-use volume on baptism, there are half-a-dozen forms of the rite of baptismal renewal tailored to various occasions, one of which is the "Renewal of Baptism for the Sick and Dying."[5] When there is a reassessment or deepening of faith in the situation of illness, this rite could be highly appropriate. For a person struggling with an incurable or chronic illness, an affirmation of baptism might seem more appropriate, more ego-syntonic, than a rite praying for healing. I can imagine using this rite, for instance, when a person has just received or assimilated a diagnosis of a serious chronic illness; in such a situation, an affirmation of baptism could be a way of claiming one's baptismal vocation in the new life task of living with illness.

A rite that is often overlooked and underappreciated is the ritual act of blessing. Blessing and praying for healing are two different things, though both can involve the laying on of hands, and they should not be viewed interchangeably. But there may be times when a rite of blessing can play a role in a healing process. I think, for instance, of a woman whose fetus died in the womb and had to be carried to term and delivered in the knowledge that it was dead. While different women will experience and symbolize such an event in various ways, I can imagine a blessing of the woman's body, of her womb, being appropriate in some cases. Her womb has been a place of death, and she, with others' help, might wish to bless it as a locus of life — possibly for another child but more fundamentally, for the woman herself. In a sense this is analogous to the practice of blessing a place where tragedy or evil took place — blessing a house that was broken into, or a hospital bed where someone died horribly, or the site of a suicide.

A friend of mine addressed the serious night fears of a little girl in his congregation by leading the family in a house blessing, which effectively exorcised the monsters. Who knows what "worked" in this case from a psychological point of view? Maybe it was the fact that the pastor took her concerns seriously, or the engagement of the whole family in addressing the issue constructively, or her own active role in the ritual. Whatever the mechanism, grace was at work here, healing a child's terror by an act of blessing.

Sometimes the ritual medium of healing may surprise us. Lutheran worship professor Walter Huffman tells of a woman who had recently received the diagnosis of terminal cancer, who was asked to participate in the imposition of ashes on Ash Wednesday. She was at first reluctant, thinking it would be too hard to bear, but after the liturgy she told how healing the experience had been for her. She realized that, isolated as she felt from all other, healthy people, she was not alone; we are all journeying toward death together. Only if our liturgy is honest about death and brokenness can it effectively proclaim the hope of healing. The honesty of Ash Wednesday is a necessary step in imagining the world whole.

Notes

1. This translation is from the New Revised Standard Version Bible, © 1989 by the Division of Christian Education of the National Council of Churches in the United States of America.

2. Seymour Leichman, *The Boy Who Could Sing Pictures* (New York: Holt, Rinehart & Winston, 1973), 31, 45–46.

3. Charles Gusmer, *And You Visited Me: Sacramental Ministry to the Sick and the Dying* (New York: Pueblo, 1984), 84–85.

4. Elaine Ramshaw, *Ritual and Pastoral Care* (Philadelphia: Fortress Press, 1987), 68–69.

5. *Holy Baptism and Services for the Renewal of Baptism* (Supplemental Liturgical Resource 2), prepared by the Office of Worship for the Presbyterian Church (U.S.A.) and the Cumberland Presbyterian Church (Philadelphia: Westminster, 1985), 92–93.

24

Weddings:
The Need for Ritual Practice

Ronald L. Grimes

After he had broken his engagement with Regine Olsen, the Danish philosopher-theologian Søren Kierkegaard was propelled into a lifelong career of reflecting on what he had done. He penned these words in his journal:

> In the marriage ceremony I must take an oath — therefore I do not dare conceal anything. On the other hand there are things I cannot tell her. The fact the divine enters into marriage is my ruin.... She can depend on me absolutely, but it is an unhappy existence. I am dancing upon a volcano and must let her dance along with me as long as it can last. This is why it is more humble of me to remain silent.[1]

Initially, Kierkegaard regarded his sacrifice as one of faith analogous to that of Abraham's binding of Isaac. Before he died at forty-two, he willed all his belongings to Regine, now long married to someone else. This time he concluded: "What I wish to give expression to is that to me an engagement was and is just as binding as a marriage, and that therefore my estate is her due, as if I had been married to her."[2]

Many modern clergy may consider this view of engagement pathetic rather than admirable, but couples will have even more difficulty sharing Kierkegaard's dread of the divine presence at the ceremony. Our view of ritual is so depleted that we often consider "the saying of vows" a synonym for a marriage rite, implicitly suggesting that the rite is reducible to verbal and promissory structures and ignoring its silences and actions, both of which are, wrongly in my opinion, construed as incidental or merely decorative. Certainly, fidelity based on promises is essential, but a marriage needs an ongoing ritual basis as surely as it needs a moral one. A ring, to take a simple example of a ritual object, lends concreteness to vowing, a moral act. Ritual tangibility is just as crucial to marriage making as moral seriousness is.

From *Liturgy: Celebrating Marriage* 4, no. 2.

Marriage making

If a wedding rite does not make a couple the way a tribal initiation rite makes a boy a man, it fails. Since ours is not a tribal society, we need to use the engagement period for building community and embodying symbols that wed us. The success or failure of a wedding is a major factor in marriage making, and engagement is, in turn, a crucial part of what I call "the work of wedding." We do not need more premarital counseling of the psychological or ethical sort but a more profoundly embodied way of ritualizing both the engagement and wedding. No matter how deeply couples "share" on retreats or learn, under priestly guidance, to "talk through" everything, they are not prepared to be wed until their insights are "somatized," made flesh, in ritual. It is a mistake for a priestly counselor to assume that couples automatically incarnate their own insights, just as it is courting disaster to relegate the work of embodying to the bedroom.

Since our culture presently lacks significant domestic rituals, having mistakenly imagined that ecclesiastical and legal ones alone were adequate, the tendency is for men and women to concentrate their ritualization on lovemaking itself. Both before and after the wedding they typically have few other ritual activities, or if they do, they lack power to engage the couple unconsciously and bodily, which is to say, spiritually. An engagement-wedding is best used as a time for discovering and constructing such rites in a manner that keeps sexuality from having to carry all the freight by itself and avoids making these rites mere acts of piety that duplicate or extend ecclesiastical ones.

I am not even remotely suggesting that domestic rites replace ecclesiastical ones such as the liturgy, nor am I advising couples to invent homemade vows, for, as Lance Morrow notes:

> The vows that couples devise are, with some exceptions, never as moving to the guests as they are to the couple. Too often the phrases, words overblown and intimate and yearning all at once, go floating plumply around the altar, pink dreams of the ineffable. Friends and family lean forward in their pews. The clergy-person beams inscrutably, abetting the thing, but keeping counsel. The guests are both fascinated and faintly appalled to be privy to such intense and theatrical whisperings.[3]

What I am urging is that religious leaders, particularly liturgists, help couples find and construct domestic practices of a symbolic nature that lead up to and away from a wedding. Marriage requires continual ritual practice; a few showers and a honeymoon are not enough. And interpersonal growth alone is insufficient.

Ceremonial realignment

The connection between a wedding and a marriage is often misunderstood. A wedding is a ritual that effects a transaction from the social state of being single to that of being a couple; much is packed into the term "effects." Strictly speaking, people are never single — never simply unto themselves. Rather, they are "the child of," "the sister of," and so on. Consequently, a wedding rite is a ceremonial realignment, not just an invention, of ties that bind a couple. The ceremonial aspects of any ritual are those that involve us in negotiating power and constructing alignments between people.[4]

In a wedding two people ceremonially make relatives of each other. Relative making, like lovemaking, is both dangerous and difficult. It is dangerous because made relatives (the in-law type) can be unmade by divorce and difficult because those things we make up, for example, our fictions and weddings, also make us up and may even outlive us. We cannot always unmake what we have made just by deciding to do so. When two people make love or make relatives, they generate or tap something (call it a "force," "thing" or "institution" — all are inadequate terms) outside themselves. It surrounds them or is between them, we might say. And this "something" does not go away just because warm feelings wane and couples fight.

When two people divorce, even priests are prone to attribute marital breakdown to social and moral factors. Seldom do they attribute it to ritual factors, even if they assess the breakdown spiritually. But — and this is my main point — wedding rites themselves can fail and not simply by the bride's tripping or the groom's forgetting his lines. There can be ritual failure as surely as there can be social or moral failure. I consider most Christian weddings in modern North America to be ritual failures; marriages succeed despite them, not because of them.

A ritual criticism

This failure, for which liturgists as well as couples are responsible, occurs for at least two reasons: lack of a ritual criticism and an overly expressivist view of weddings. By "ritual criticism" I mean training in diagnosing ritual needs, as well as a vocabulary and set of criteria for evaluating rites to decide whether they actually effect what they symbolize. By "expressivist" I mean any view of a ritual that considers its primary task to be the expressing of participants' feelings or the church's theology. Weddings fail *as* rituals when they only *express* ideals and aspirations, when they *describe* rather than actually *effect* new states of being. Weddings must wed, not merely anticipate that a couple will later somehow make a marriage.

I do not deny that weddings should express, but they should do more. They should transform. A rite is "performative" not just expressive. By "performance" I do not mean "pretense," so perhaps I should use Richard Schechner's term and call a wedding a "transformance."[5] A transformance is liturgical. By putting it that way, I do not mean "eucharistic" or even "Christian," though a wedding may, of course, be both. I mean something closer to the word's etymology: "the work of the people." A rite is liturgical in that sense when it "works" in addition to "expresses." Wedding rites do not automatically work. The goal is to wed, not just to ratify a legal transaction. Every couple approaching a wedding has a unique "work" (a *magnum opus)* to perform. The liturgist's role is first to divine that work and then, with the couple, effect it ceremonially and celebratively.

Great expectations

A wedding reaches both forward and backward in time. It reaches forward, thereby ritualizing the future, by formal vows and promises as well as informal devices such as wedding pictures, gifts, legal obligations and tacit understandings that outlast the ceremony itself. "Ritualizing the future" refers to those occasions after the wedding when the ceremony itself, rather than, say, feelings of togetherness or social expectation performs the work of wedding.

How a wedding ritual reaches backward into the past is less obvious. A priest may inquire about the couple's families and religious backgrounds. "Something old" may be worn, and so on. But the most important, and most overlooked, heritage from the past is a couple's "interaction ritual," the term Erving Goffman applies to their stylized, dramatic patterns of face-to-face interactions.[6] An interaction ritual encodes unconscious elements such as family scenarios and personal habituations, so it is utterly crucial that the "graft" between interaction ritual and wedding ceremony be, as the horticulturists say, on good "base stock." The ritual graft "takes" when the wedding rite itself permeates the marriage, when the ritual continues to wed. What is usually missing in premarital ritual preparation is any sense that ritual transactions between the individuals have been transpiring for some time before a couple ever approaches a priest.

Taken seriously, this idea implies far more than premarital counseling followed by an hour-long wedding and reception. It could imply — and here I can only suggest — a week-long wedding with individual, couple, friend and family phases preceded by certain ritual tasks (one might even say "trials") during the preceding engagement period (for instance, periods of solitude and sexual abstinence). These tasks would have to be designed to expose the dynamics of the couple's own interaction ritual. This tacit ritual would reveal both the strengths and weaknesses of their habitual patterns. Subsequently, a liturgist in consultation with the couple could design a ceremony to consolidate the strengths and compensate the weaknesses of the interaction rites. Within the ceremony a liturgy, in the strict sense of the word, could be celebrated in order to effect and ratify the ceremonial ties.

My calling attention to a couple's tacit ritualizing parallels the church's recognition, on a corporate rather than individual scale, of indigenous rites. Just as the church imbeds the eucharist in indigenous gestures and spatial idioms, so it ought to attend carefully to the layers of a wedding: the couple's interaction ritual, the priest's "divination" of that ritual, the ceremonial making of relatives and the liturgical effecting of the transition. If these occur as they should, celebration is possible; otherwise, it is not.

Such attention to ritual preparation is time-consuming and demands work both in the literal and spiritual sense of the word. Celebration in every culture is costly, and our effort to make it quick and expressive has led to its repeated failure. Our marriages are seldom better than the rites that make them. And neither a religious liturgy nor a civil ceremony suffices by itself. To enable a wedding to become a celebration of fidelity capable of permeating a marriage in these days of divorce, liturgists will have to learn to stitch together several pieces of ritual work into whole cloth.

Notes

1. Søren Kierkegaard, *Journals and Papers.* 5:IV A 107.

2. Søren Kierkegaard, *Kierkegaard: Letters and Documents,* Trans. Henrick Rosenmeier (Princeton: Princeton University Press, 1978), 33.

3. "The Hazards of Homemade Vows," *Time* (June 27, 1983), 58.

4. I have discussed the distinctions between ceremony, liturgy and celebration in "Modes of Ritual Necessity," *Worship* 53, no. 2 (1979): 126–41.

5. Richard Schechner, *Essays in Performance Theory, 1970–1976* (New York: Drama Books, 1977).

6. Erving Goffman, *Interaction Ritual* (Garden City, N.Y.: Doubleday, 1967).

25

Hope and Despair as Seasons of Faith

WALTER BRUEGGEMANN

The dynamic of "despair and hope" is scarcely a "rhythm" in the life of faith, for despair and hope do not predictably occur in sequence, nor are they to be nurtured and valued equally as conditions belonging to faith. Rather they are together a contradiction. Faith battles for hope against despair. Nonetheless, both despair and hope occur in the midst of faith, and we must address both in honest faith and honest worship.

Biblical faith begins when God asserts God's will and purpose against a present, disordered condition. Faith begins when God announces God's intention for an alternative to the brokenness of the present. This is how it was when at the outset, God addressed Abraham and Sarah with a promise, creating for them a new possibility in the *face of barrenness*. It is God's speech of promise that permitted Abraham and Sarah to act in hope: "Go from your country and your kindred and your father's house to the land that I will show you. I will make of you a great nation, and I will bless you, and make your name great, so that you will be a blessing" (Gen 12:1–2).

The same dynamic operates with Moses and the slaves in Egypt. Into a *situation of bondage*, God speaks a promise of liberation, which permits Israel to hope against the fated circumstance of the Egyptian empire:

> I have observed the misery of my people who are in Egypt, and have heard their cry on account of their taskmasters; I know their sufferings, and I have come down to deliver them from the Egyptians, and to bring them up out of that land to a good and broad land (Exod 3:7–8).

Or in a third sphere, the word of God intervened against the *power of chaos* and made creation possible: "God said, 'Let there be light'; and there was

From *Liturgy: Rhythms of Prayer* 8, no. 4.

light.... And God saw everything that God had made, and behold, it was very good" (Gen 1:3, 31).

The promise spoken to Mary is of exactly the same sort. The word is spoken *"in the days of Herod,"* that is, in the face of failure and despair. The word of Gabriel, messenger of God, moves powerfully against "the days of Herod:" "Do not be afraid, Mary, for you have found favor with God. And behold, you will conceive in your womb and bear a son, and you shall call his name Jesus" (Luke 1:30–31).

In all four cases, the word of promise from God is inexplicable. In each case the word speaks against fatedness: barrenness, bondage, chaos, Herod. And in each case, the response of the one addressed by promise reflects trust, permitting a new possibility to emerge beyond present circumstances. God's promise evokes faith and obedience in the one addressed.

In these four narratives (and many others), the Bible traces the dramatic way in which hope overrides despair. In this dramatic narrative way, the tradition also testifies to the character of this God who refuses to be contained in present circumstance, who holds and voices an alternative will, and who by the power of promise sets life in motion toward new possibilities. God is shown to be the shatterer of the old and the worker of the new. The stories also witness to the human practice of hope, for hope is embraced by Mary "who believed that there would be a fulfillment of what was spoken to her from the Lord" (Luke 1:45). The whole of biblical faith is a witness to the process of powerful promise and responsive trust that refuses to accept the world on its perceived terms and that refuses the present shape of life as the way it will be.

Same speeches, same God

Biblical faith is the deposit of these speeches of new possibility. Biblical faith is also the ongoing account of the way each new faith generation appropriates that deposit of promise for its own and acts on that promise in its own time and place. The process of deposit and appropriation is the way this community of faith, until our own time, continues to act in hope. The faith community affirms that the same speeches of possibility still count, and the same God who spoke then speaks and contends now for new possibilities beyond present circumstance.

Thus hope is rooted in the speech of God that men and women of faith receive as true and reliable. When that speech is trusted, it authorizes and permits daring action that may be judged impossible by present circumstance. That is the affirmation of the resounding "by faith" of Hebrews 11. That grand chapter names a sequence of those who have acted in daring ways beyond present circumstance because they believed that God's speech of promise counted for more than those circumstances. Note well that hope is not a general optimism or an inchoate sense that "things will work out"; rather, hope is intentional trust in a deliberate promise. It is a trust rooted in knowing the God who speaks, a trust expressed as concrete action that dares beyond present permit. This faith is indeed "the assurance of things hoped for, the conviction of things not seen."

A present tense

The story of faith, however, is not an uninterrupted account of hope. Women and men of faith, in the Bible and in the church's long history, know about despair, that is, about the nullification and abandonment of God's powerful speech of promise.

How can the power of despair drive out hope? I submit that despair has power whenever we absolutize the present, concluding that there is no new possibility spoken, no new gifts to be given, no alternatives available.

The present may be absolutized in two different, but equally powerful, ways. On the one hand, there may be coercive, oppressive power, that is, sheer force, which imposes its will on present circumstances so completely that it preempts all our thought and imagination about what is possible. The most obvious case of such an exaggerated sense of present circumstance is an authoritarian or totalitarian regime which so dictates life and precludes choices that one dare not imagine an alternative. From the massiveness of the ancient Egyptian empire to the comprehensiveness of recent South African apartheid, the present tense seems guaranteed to all thinkable futures. Indeed, to imagine a future that will not be an extension of the present is impossible in such circumstances.

The power of despair, however, arises not only in great public arenas of oppression. Despair may be a quite personal sense about the present's absoluteness. That experience may be the coercive sense of fatedness that comes from a worrisome financial situation, an unbearable work situation, a wrongly shaped primary relation, a devastating medical diagnosis or simply a sense of one's self that leaves one discomforted. At the core of our experience, any or all of these circumstances may lead to a conclusion of hopelessness because the present circumstance is so powerful and all-comprehending that it can never, ever be changed.

Conversely, a sense of fatedness may not come from coercion. It may be a gentler kind of seduction in which we are slowly but powerfully persuaded that the present arrangement is good for us, our right place, the condition in which we are destined to be, and therefore, we must grow comfortable and affirmative about it. Seductiveness is the main strategy of consumer ideology; it seeks to convince us that "it doesn't get any better than this." While the slogan may sound celebrative at first hearing, it is in fact a counsel of despair. Even in a beer commercial, the formula asserts that no new gifts are given, no new promises are at work, no new possibilities are offered.

In all these circumstances, public and personal, coercive and seductive, the powerful and pervasive claims of the present drive out the unsettling power of promise, silence the voice of an alternative and reduce life's option to the single one already in hand. The power of the present thus overrides God's speech about

newness. We are left alone with a relentless, unyielding, fated, present tense —
world without end!

Hopelessness countered by memory

The Bible is no stranger to this terrible combat between despair and hope, between God's speech of newness and the oppressive silence of the present. Two
examples of that conflict which appear in the Bible are cited.

In Psalm 77, the speaker voices despair. The poem on the one hand describes
the restless discomfort of trouble and loss of sleep:

> In the day of my trouble I seek the Lord;
> in the night my hand is stretched out without wearying;
> my soul refuses to be comforted.
> I think of God, and I moan;
> I meditate, and my spirit faints.
> You keep my eyelids from closing;
> I am so troubled that I cannot speak (vv. 2–4).

On the other hand, the poem voices the probing questions of doubt that begin
to forfeit confidence in God:

> Will the Lord spurn for ever,
> and never again be favorable?
> Has God's steadfast love ceased forever?
> Are God's promises at an end for all time?
> Has God forgotten to be gracious?
> Has God in anger shut up God's compassion? (vv. 7–9).

The despairing answer to these questions intended by the poem is yes. Yes,
God will spurn forever. Yes, God's steadfast love has ceased. Yes, God's promises
are at an end. Yes, God has forgotten to be gracious.

Preoccupation with present discomfort pushes God away. When God is
nullified, there can only be despair. Verses 1–9 are a full voicing of that despair.

This psalmic voice of hopelessness, however, is oddly countered by a vigorous
act of memory (vv. 11–20). God is brought back into the speaker's horizon in
these verses. The speaker for an instant turns attention away from the present's
debilitating power to recall former times when God was indeed faithful and
gracious.

> I will call to mind the deeds of the Lord;
> I will remember your wonders of old.
> I will meditate on all your work,
> and muse on your mighty deeds (vv. 11–12).

In verses 16–20, the poet recalls God's mighty work in the past with reference
to God's power and with concrete citation of the Exodus:

> Your way was through the sea,
> your path through the great waters;
> yet your footprints were unseen.
> You led your people like a flock
> by the hand of Moses and Aaron (vv. 19–20).

The recall of the Exodus is a model appropriated from a former situation in which the Egyptian empire seemed to be for perpetuity. Nothing was available to suggest that the situation of oppression would ever change. Then the winds blew and the waters parted. Inexplicably, there was transformation and liberation. This strange inversion is now recalled in the psalm and brought forcefully into the present. When this particular past is available, the present circumstance has to be experienced differently. Now the present may be no more closed than was the old Egyptian empire. Because YHWH is "remembered into the present," the present is reshaped. Graciousness and steadfast love may be operative even now and here. A reread present depends on a powerful and available past. Hope depends on memory.

In this psalm, the present is reread in light of a saving past, but that is all the psalmist is willing to share with us. We are not told anything about how the present was changed. Even more strikingly, we are told nothing about the speaker's new perspective on the future; the future is left unuttered. We may dare to imagine, however, that the intrusion of this past into the present is like hope intruding on despair. We may conclude that the fated sense of the present, which produced such a sorry preoccupation with self, was decisively broken. When the present is narrowly wrapped around self, there are no resources or energy for the future. But the powerful remembering of verses 11–20 introduces a new character into the present, a character who characteristically breaks the present and permits a future quite underived from the present.

Steadfast love, mercy, faithfulness

The book of Lamentations is literature in which hope engages in sustained battle with despair. That poetry is an act of grief over destroyed Jerusalem and the failure of Israel's public life. That situation contained ample grounds for despair, for believing that the loss of a sacred center meant the defeat of God and the closing of the present in an unending Babylonian hegemony. The voice of despair is unambiguous in the poem:

> My soul is bereft of peace,
> I have forgotten what happiness is;
> So I say, "Gone is my glory,
> and my expectation (*yhl*) from the Lord" (Lam 3:17–18).

The term rendered "expectation" is precisely Israel's word for "hope." The loss of Jerusalem leads the speaker to conclude that no new futures are possible.

Verses 19–20 are preoccupied with the defeat and loss. The situation has a compelling, destructive fascination; the speaker can think of nothing else:

> The thought of my affliction and my homelessness
> the wormwood and the gall!
> My soul continually thinks of it
> and is bowed down within me.

The poet goes over and over the data and can draw no other conclusion.

In verse 21, however, the poem takes an unexpected turn: "But this I call to mind, / and therefore I have hope (*yhl*)." The verse's wording is striking because the poet exploits the term just used negatively in verse 18. The remembering (*zkr*) in verses 18–20 is all negative, concerning the heavy burden of the present. In verse 21, there is another "remembering" but with a new reference. The same word "hope" was used in verse 18 to speak of the nullity; now in verse 21 it is used to speak positively, "therefore I have hope." The one with no hope now hopes. The two notions, "remember" and "hope," were both used negatively (vv. 18, 19), but now both are used positively (v. 21).

How could this drastic change have happened in this rhetoric? What is different that permits a dramatic rhetorical reversal? The answer is given in verses 22–23:

> The steadfast love of the Lord never ceases,
> God's mercies never come to an end;
> They are new every morning;
> great is your faithfulness.

What is remembered positively is expressed in three words that evoke the whole powerful memory of God's past fidelity and transforming capacity: *steadfast love* that never fails; *mercies* that never come to an end but are daily new; and *faithfulness* that is great. In these words, the poet gathers what is central, precious and characteristic in Israel's faith. The three words are more or less synonymous references to YHWH's enduring solidarity with YHWH's people. In these three words, the poet says what is most crucial about the very character of God, already enunciated in the old credo assurances of Exodus 34:6–7. Moreover, these three words recall the entire memory of concrete transformation in which YHWH's character is known. The three terms radically resignify the present that makes a way for a new possibility, even in this present circumstance.

The wonder of Israel's faith is that in the moment of a devastating present, the speaker has a vivid past, concretely available. The present is not set in a vacuum but linked to a contrasting past. Even in this present situation of despair, the old memories, phrases and words press in. When they are uttered, these words override the present and break its deathly power. Even in the present, when all things sacred had been nullified, the poet can now assert that "the Lord is good" (v. 25). In verse 32, the speaker again sounds the words "compassion" and "steadfastness" that completely characterize the present, permit energy and evoke possibility.

An alternative life

Our contemporary situation of theology and worship inevitably exists in the context of modernity. We are all inescapably children of modernity. The intellectual, social references of our common mindset are organized to magnify the present at the expense of the past and to live in the present with the assumption that in the present there is only us and those like us. As a Radio Shack television ad proclaimed, "You've got the whole world in your hands." Such an ideological claim, so powerful among us, so prevalent across the political spectrum, is a proposal for despair. Modernity affirms that there is only now, "world without end." There is only us. Despair then is not an accident or an occasional misfortune among us. Despair is the almost inevitable outcome of the value system and the ideology to which our society is largely committed.

Christian worship, rooted in the peculiarly Jewish act of hope, asserts an alternative conviction about reality. This alternative in principle means to subvert the ideology of despair championed by modernity. In Christian worship, then, the power of hope is voiced against the deathliness of despair. This voicing of subversive alternative includes:

1. The powerful recall of and reentry into the memory of transformations that witness to the power and fidelity of God.

2. The daring envisioning of futures contained in evangelical promises, visions rooted in memory but pushing beyond the present.

3. The odd characterization of God known in the memory and anticipated in the vision — God marked by steadfastness, mercy and faithfulness.

4. The radical insistence that the present exists between this memory and this vision, and is the arena where God's radical faithfulness is at work for us, beyond our poor capacity to choose life.

This fourfold affirmation leads to the subversive, startling affirmation that we are not alone but live as the beloved object of God's powerful care. This God does for us far more abundantly than all that we ask or think. This gospel intends to talk us out of our despairing modernity, summoning and authorizing us to withdraw our membership in it for the sake of an alternative life.

This practice of faith in worship is thus cast as a struggle of cosmic dimension between the established power of despair and the evangelical alternative of hope and its accompanying possibility of life. It is a struggle that has enormous scope, but it is staged, voiced and processed in daily acts of resounding adjectives of fidelity, of reiterated promises about the future, and genuine newness amazingly given. Such a daily practice seems almost commonplace, but it is a freighted activity. This daily act places us in deep crisis and invites us to the "nevertheless" of faith (see Hab 3:18).

Referring to hope and despair as a rhythm is hardly correct, for their recurrence is not so planned, predictable or desirable as that. Hope and despair constitute a rhythm only because we move back and forth between them. It would be better to term their relation a struggle in which the opposed forces wax and wane. First our life is tilted one way and then the other. On our good days, when we are held to the claims of the memory, the vision and the gospel, we can be as unambiguous as Paul:

> No, in all these things we are more than conquerors through him who loved us. For I am convinced that neither death, nor life, nor angels, nor rulers, nor things present, nor things to come, nor powers, nor height, nor depth, nor anything else in all creation, will be able to separate us from the love of God in Christ Jesus our Lord (Rom 8:37–39).

On other days, when our life seeps outside the range of the memories, when the visions are silenced and the adjectives are momentarily forgotten, we succumb to despair. Such an instance of defeat is reflected at the end of the book of Lamentations. Even after the great affirmation of Lamentations 3:21–24 that we have cited, matters end with a plea and an unanswered but anxious question:

> Restore us to yourself, O Lord,
> that we may be restored!
> Renew our days as of old!
> unless you have utterly rejected us?
> and are angry with us beyond measure (5:21–22).

In that moment of dread and pathos, the question lingers and waits for an answer clearer than those we have received. The poem is an honest voicing of how, in fact, it is with us. Our daily life, under deep threat, does indeed sometimes fall outside the evangelical claim of the memory. The last word, we say, has been spoken that answers our question, overrides our anxiety and vetoes our despair. The last word of the gospel is the best word we can speak, but it does not always and everywhere prevail. In the end we trust that last word to be true. It sounds like this:

> As surely as God is faithful, our word to you has not been "Yes and No." For the Son of God, Jesus Christ, whom we proclaimed among you, Silvanus and Timothy and I, was not "Yes and No"; but in him it is always "Yes." For in him everyone of God's promises is a "Yes." For this reason it is through him that we say "the Amen," to the glory of God (2 Cor 1:18–20).

Nothing important could be said after such a yes from such a source. The no of despair, however, is still heard, even in the land of this decisive, privileged yes. Sometimes the no of despair is believed among us. The yes of God is spoken into the despair. It can be trusted.

Part III

The Proclamations of the Liturgy

"Christians discover Christ's body in the softness of bread and Christ's blood in the sour, sweet tang of the wine. They hear Christ celebrated in song, feel Christ in the embrace of another. The sacramentality of liturgy allows the wholeness of God's being to penetrate the whole of creation."

—Anthony Ugolnik in *Liturgy: Central Symbols*

26

At Least Two Words: The Liturgy as Proclamation

GORDON LATHROP

"Here on earth," wrote the early twentieth-century theologian Adolph Köberle, "we can never rightly say the truth of God with just one word, but always only with two words."[1]

Whatever else the Sunday assembly of Christians is intended to do, there can be wide ecumenical agreement on this: the Sunday assembly means to say the truth about God. Indeed, we hold the gathering intending to proclaim the truth about God to whoever will listen — the assembly, visitors, the larger world, ourselves — and thereby to re-immerse those listeners in a view of the world as it stands before God.

That proclamation takes at least two words. Köberle is right. In this world speaking about God with just one "word" — one connected and logical discourse, for example — will almost inevitably mean speaking a distortion, even a lie. It will suggest that God is a consequent idea, not a burning fire and a mysterious presence. Or it will give up on God altogether, and talk rather about us. It will miss the powerful presence of the Holy Trinity. No, for us the mystery of God, for all that it may indeed be graciously present in human speech, must be proposed by triangulation. Words, even such contradictory words as "now" and "not yet" or "judgment" and "mercy" or "absence" and "presence" or "death" and "life" or "one" and "many," will necessarily be put side by side, like two candles near the altar or the two cherubim on the ark of the covenant, that we may meet the astonishing presence of God between them.

The great Christian tradition of the Sunday synaxis has known this. Nowhere in the traditional Sunday or festival pattern do we read only one reading. There are always at least two, side by side. These juxtaposed readings may speak different — even wildly contrasting — views. Then another reading, a psalm, a verse,

---

From *Liturgy: We Proclaim* 11, no. 1.

a hymn, are further juxtaposed, multiplying the diversity of voices and forms of verbal truth, and these "words" together, in mutual tension, are meant to speak "the truth of God." No, actually the tension is even greater. Next to readings and psalm and alleluia and hymns is set the sermon. Then the voice of the present speaker is meant to articulate the current meaning of all these ancient texts, sometimes even criticizing the texts to require them to serve the merciful truth of God in Jesus Christ. At the same time, the room still echoes with the surfeit of meaning present in the texts, and that meaning may be criticizing the preacher, requiring a larger, deeper truth than she or he may be articulating. The synaxis has been marked by at least two "words."

An ecumenical heritage

But the proclamation of the Sunday assembly, the speech of the assembly about God with its "at least two words," embraces even more of the whole liturgical event. Side by side with the "word" of the word service there is also the "visible word" of the table. This juxtaposition also is an ecumenical heritage. Thus the current *United Methodist Book of Worship* calls for the Sunday service to be a "Service of Word and Table."[2] And the Second Vatican Council proposed that no communal Sunday mass should be without preaching, the homily being regarded as an integral part of the liturgy.[3] Whatever the confessional or denominational reasons for these proposals, the shared pastoral reason for their urgency is the need for clear, reliable and profound speech about God. For such speech we need at least two words.

Without the scripture readings and the preaching, the "visible word" of the table service may be experienced as a sacred encounter with God in the present time but without any history or any future. Similarly, without the table, the "word" of the synaxis may easily become a lecture, a conjecture, a distant history with no "for you" that anchors it in present experience. We need at least two words.

Saying the truth of God

And we need them both for an even deeper reason. Finally, the speech of the synaxis is intended to juxtapose texts, song and preaching so as to speak Jesus Christ, his cross, resurrection and the faith that is through him, that people may live. That is what it means, in Christian terms, for the synaxis to "say the truth of God." But the present times are full of words, most of them mistrusted as slogans and lies. And there is a lot of talk about Jesus, by no means all of it life-giving. In the New Testament, the clearest speech Jesus makes of himself, his identity and mission, is when he says, "This is my body, given for you.... This is my blood of the covenant.... "

So in the Sunday liturgy, next to texts and speeches, there is this meal. It is the identity of the Jesus of whom the synaxis has been caused to speak. It is the continual touchstone, criticizing the word service, requiring the preacher to move toward saying in words what the bread and cup will say. In such a juxtaposition, the word service will also stand in tension with the table, calling us to make our circle larger, begging God to bring the time of the great universal feast, giving a name and a history and a future to our eating and drinking.

But word and table do these things only as they are held together, two "words" to speak the truth of God. If the danger of an earlier time was that we would forget preaching, focusing only on the holy action of the feast, the danger of the present time may be just the opposite. Sunday preaching without the table runs the considerable risk of being distortion, of wandering away in "my story," of acting as if one connected discourse captures the mystery of God, of missing the identity of Jesus Christ.

We need both words: visible word and audible bread and cup; a meal that speaks of God's mercy in Christ and a reading of texts and preaching that offers us words to eat as if they were the feast on the mountain when all tears are wiped away. And with these two principal words, we also need all the other "words" of the liturgy, juxtaposed: coming together and being sent away; singing and being silent; giving thanks and crying out the names of the needs of the world. In this assembly, texts next to preaching yield prayer before God for the world. Thanksgiving next to eating and drinking can yield sending food to the hungry and being sent ourselves. Word next to table can yield faith. The whole liturgy, this whole pattern of juxtaposed "words," says the faith of the church and the truth of God. The whole liturgy proclaims. It is precisely for the sake of this *proclamation* that we urgently need the continued renewal of the whole action.

Notes

1. A. Köberle, *Rechtfertigung und Heiligung* (Leipzig: 1929), 295.
2. *The United Methodist Book of Worship* (Nashville: United Methodist Publishing House, 1992), 33–50.
3. Constitution on the Sacred Liturgy, 52.

27

Reclaiming the Eucharist

Tad Guzie

The liturgical readings of the Easter season, especially the selections from the Acts of the Apostles, remind us of a simpler time when the Christian church had few of the structures we experience today. Sociologically, the early church was a loosely organized collection of household churches, a network of people whose Christian experience was characterized by intimacy and a sense of close fellowship. Not everything was warm fuzzies, of course. The letters circulated under Paul's name make it eminently clear that the early communities had some sticky problems with people and with basic Christian ideas.

The Christians of the first century did not have a systematic theology, any more than they had organized socioeconomic structures. And this absence of theology has important implications for understanding the development of the ritual of breaking bread and sharing a cup in Jesus' name. The early Christians practiced this ritual; and we practice it today. But if the people of Paul's day and Christians of the late twentieth century could have the opportunity to converse, it would be evident that they and we have difficulty understanding one another regarding the meaning of the eucharistic action. Many moderns would be surprised to learn that nonordained persons presided over the breaking of the bread in the early church. For their part, earlier Christians would be astonished at our elaboration of splendid ceremonies and settings of visual and musical beauty to adorn the eucharist and, at the same time, our contraction of the core ritual itself into a distribution of wafers barely recognizable as bread.

Changing ownership

Who really owns the eucharist? It is easy to say: the church, the Christian people. But that answer is much too abstract. Concretely, in the first Christian communities the eucharist belonged to household churches. It belonged to small groups of people who gathered to remember and recognize the Lord

From *Liturgy: Central Symbols* 7, no. 1.

in the breaking of the bread at meals of fellowship. Ownership of the eucharist has changed radically over two millenniums. Today, it is not the little
church, the small community, or even the church at large that owns the eucharist. Official church teaching talks about the eucharist as the action of the
whole church. But this seems to be a rationalization when it comes to the question of true ownership. The official church does not recognize the validity of
any eucharist celebrated without an ordained minister. Therefore, to speak concretely and practically, is it not the ordained who hold proprietorship over the
eucharist, at least in all the mainline Christian churches?

I have no intention of attacking the ordained ministry. Our Christian communities need competent and qualified leaders, and the institution of holy orders
is one way of providing this leadership. But the eucharist did not begin in or for
or because of the community of the ordained. Quite the opposite. Holy orders
came into being because Christian people were breaking bread and sharing a
cup in Jesus' name. It was only gradually, over a period of several centuries, that
the church at large began restricting control over the eucharist to those holding
positions of official leadership in the community.

Today, with our renewed sense of the church as the whole people, we are
increasingly concerned to reclaim the community's ownership of basic Christian
symbols like the eucharist. Many people are frustrated, especially those who have
some theological background. Why must one put up with bad liturgy? Why
should one wait for the "community" to become aware of itself, or for the liturgy
committee to get its act in order, when everyone knows that the pastor will do
his or her own thing anyway? When push comes to shove, the ordained person
is the real owner of the eucharistic liturgy, and there doesn't seem to be any way
around it.

Enacting eucharist

Although I can't offer any quick solution to this widespread pastoral problem, I
can point to some theological blockages that will need to be cleared away before
the Christian community as a whole can reclaim the symbol of the eucharist
as its own. I have been teaching sacramental theology for some twenty years,
mainly to Roman Catholics. Over the years, I have noticed two basic ideas that
have consistently been eye-openers for my learners, who have ranged in age from
young adulthood to old age.

The first idea is so simple that it may appear naive. In the context of dis-
cussing eucharistic theology, I ask: "What are the original eucharistic symbols?
Answer the question in silence." Then I ask, "How many of you answered bread
and wine?" The majority of any group says yes, that's how we answered. I then
go on to explain that, no, bread and wine are not the original eucharistic symbols. The original symbols involved *breaking* the bread and *sharing* the cup. The
original symbols are actions, not things.

We are still in the grip of a eucharistic theology that focuses on the elements

of bread and wine, rather than on the act of giving thanks (i.e., "eucharist-ing")
by breaking bread and sharing a cup.[1] Liturgically, we are still insecure about
enacting a table liturgy that speaks loud and clear: we are afraid of setting the
table, proclaiming the great prayer of thanksgiving, breaking bread and sharing
the bread and wine in a way that would vividly involve the entire community.
Isn't it the case that in most parishes, respect for the consecrated elements takes
precedence over the community's act of thanksgiving and sharing?

Returning to small groups

The second idea that pervades my memory of decades of teaching courses on
eucharistic theology has to do with a question that students have asked me,
rather than one I have asked them. After a bit of history and theological reflection, it becomes clear that Christians celebrated the eucharist long before
there was an institutional priesthood. In this context, it is natural to discuss how
families and small groups might rediscover the eucharist by breaking bread and
sharing a cup in Jesus' name, with simple prayers of blessing. Inevitably, in this
context someone asks, "What is a eucharist without a priest?" The only answer
I can give is that it is a eucharist without a priest.

In the give-and-take of this discussion, people make a connection between
theological ideas and their own experience. What I have observed over the years,
at an eminently teachable moment like this, is that my answer only affirms what
students already know in their heart of hearts: it is not the priest who makes the
eucharist. Rather, the body of Christ, the community of the faithful animated
by the Spirit of God, creates the sacrament of the eucharist and the presence
of Christ.

Again, the idea here is simple and theologically very basic. But it is difficult
for Christians, especially for those reared in a liturgical tradition, to understand
the saying of Jesus: "Where two or three are gathered in my name, there I am
in their midst" (Matt 18:20). This saying applies to families and small groups,
not just to large assemblies in a church. Certainly a particular dignity belongs
to a large gathering like the Sunday assembly. But this in no way diminishes
the dignity of a small group gathered in the name of Jesus. The presence of
Christ is no less "real" in a small group than in an assembly gathered around
an ordained minister.

The eucharist did not begin in large assemblies. It began in everyday Jewish
table fellowship. Such fellowship seems to have been a key part of Jesus' own
ministry. In Luke's Gospel, meals are the setting for much of Jesus' teaching.
When Levi the tax collector became a follower of Jesus, he hosted a dinner.
The legalists who knew him complained that Jesus was eating and drinking
with people who were unacceptable, who were excommunicates. By honoring
Levi's invitation, Jesus broke through the divisions that the professional religious
people of his time wanted to maintain. The meal became a healing and recon-

ciling event, and a sign of the meal that Jesus will eat and drink with us in the kingdom (Luke 5).

Later on, at a Sabbath meal, Jesus expanded on the same point. He insisted that Christian table fellowship should reach out to others, to the rejects of society, and not be confined to a comfortable in-group (Luke 14). A meal hosted by Jesus and his disciples was the setting for the great mercy parables, including the story of the prodigal son, whose homecoming and forgiveness were celebrated by a feast (Luke 15). And Zacchaeus, from his branch in the sycamore tree, received and accepted Jesus' offer of table fellowship; he returned to honesty and determined to share his wealth with the needy (Luke 19).

Local church, universal church

The Gospel of Luke offers us a "basic" eucharistic theology that is especially characteristic of small groups gathered in Jesus' name. What the breaking of bread conveys in this context is forgiveness, welcome and mutual acceptance, commitment to caring for others and sharing one's blessings. While these themes are not absent from large assemblies, they are bound to be experienced with greater intensity and clarity in small groups.

Assembly liturgy adds another dimension. Assembly liturgy focuses on the "great church," the *catholica,* the largeness of Christ, the universality of the message. The gospel and the great prayer of thanksgiving proclaim the largeness of God in history, the breadth of the story in which we are called to take part and the wonders of God that have yet to be achieved in this world, this community, this parish. The intimacy and close union that characterize small groups need to be complemented by the hope and vision of the "great church." Without this vision, microchurches tend to close in on themselves and focus only on their own concerns. The Sunday assembly is meant to provide a dimension of breadth and largeness to summon us beyond what already is. Here is the power and uniqueness of macrochurch liturgy. When it is done right, it provokes our growth; it prods our minds and hearts to think and feel more largely, beyond this place and time.

The symbolism of the eucharist is rich and multiform. The eucharist can be understood and enacted at different levels. The difficulty is that the eucharistic theology of our recent past begins and ends with the macrochurch, the Sunday assembly gathered around an ordained minister. This form of celebration is as valuable as it is powerful. Still, the household church, the microchurch, was Luke's context regarding the meaning of the breaking of bread. There has been little or no theological reflection on the microchurch. The result is that the church's theology is not yet complete. It does not take account of the eucharistic experience at any level other than that of the "great church."

The incompleteness of recent eucharistic theology helps to explain why it is difficult for ordinary Christians to claim ownership of the eucharist.[2] Most people's ideas about the eucharist are bound up exclusively with the macrochurch and its forms and structures. The theological "blockages" I mentioned above are spinoffs of that unilateral theological development that is no longer rooted in the really sacred experience of sharing a meal. Losing touch with the household churches resulted in a change of focus from sharing a meal to contemplating the food itself; it also led to a concept of the "real presence" focused on the elements of bread and wine rather than on the people who are the presence of Christ in this world; and, finally, it led to a transfer of proprietorship: the eucharist was removed from the community at large and given to the ordained.

To share a meal in peace and fellowship is a great grace and a precious gift of God. Many of us need to rediscover or recover this gift, and to experience at least some of our family meals in an atmosphere of thanksgiving would help. Begin with Sunday dinner, or with meals at special times: holidays, birthdays, anniversaries. Enact the eucharistic symbols: break bread and share a cup, with simple prayers of blessing.

Liturgical renewal at the level of the Sunday assembly can only go so far. Renewal of a ritual consciousness has to reach into the life of microchurches as well. The existence of an official liturgy does not negate the authentic eucharistic ministry that belongs to small groups and to every Christian household. Until we experience in our own households the holiness of a meal shared in Jesus' name, we will not really grasp the import and power of the eucharist as it is enacted in the great church.

Notes

1. I have developed some of the practical liturgical implications of these ideas in "The Art of Assembly-ing," *Pastoral Music* 11, no. 4 (April–May 1987): 20–25.

2. Further historical and theological background regarding different forms of eucharistic symbolism can be found in my study "The Church as a Eucharistic Community," *Chicago Studies*, 22 (November 1983): 283–96.

28

Biblical Images of Water

IRENE NOWELL

A waterfall, just south of Atchison, Kansas, is a special place for me. A friend first took me there about three years ago. It is a place to share with someone who understands one's spirit. It is also a place to be alone; but even when I am alone, a sense of presence fills this place, a sense of being loved, healed, whole.

The waterfall is never the same. Sometimes I can hear the rush of water some distance down the road. Sometimes it dries to just a trickle. In spring there are little fish trying to jump the cataract. In winter the water continues to run beneath a frozen mirror of itself. The rocks that form the ledge have been falling one by one, carved off by the constant flow. The pool at the foot of the falls and the channel that carries off the water are constantly changing shape and depth. But the waterfall remains. It is faithful; it is living water.

Life-giving water

Our need for water was present in the beginning. In one of the creation stories we read, "At the time the Lord God created the earth and heaven there was no vegetation because God had not sent rain on the earth, nor was there any human being to till the soil" (Gen 2:4–5). Both water and human labor are necessary for a fertile earth. The story continues to link the two. "Water flowed out of the ground and watered all the surface of the soil. The Lord God shaped the human being from the soil of the ground and blew the breath of life into his nostrils, and the human became a living being" (Gen 2:6–7). Then God plants the garden, and the biblical writer describes the great rivers that water the face of the earth. When water and human labor are present, then God brings the earth to fruition.

The image of water as necessary for life recurs throughout scripture. The Israelites are awed by a description of the promised land because it is a place of

From *Liturgy: Central Symbols* 7, no. 1.

rain, not like Egypt, that had to be irrigated "by foot, like a vegetable garden" (Deut 11:10–12). In the desert God gives thirsty Israel water from the rock to sustain them (Exod 17:1–7). In the same fashion the believer expresses trust in God who leads the sheep by streams of water (Ps 23:2).

On the symbolic level, water functions as an image of almost everything that is life-giving. Rebecca and Rachel, the patriarchs' wives and the mothers of future Israel, are found by wells (Gen 24:11–15; 29:1–10). The faithful person, nourished by meditation on the law, is like a tree beside living water (Ps 1:3). The law is like a river from which the teacher diverts a little brook for the sake of students (Sir 24:23–34). Salvation is like living water. "You will draw water joyfully from the springs of salvation" (Isa 12:3).

Even God is compared to water. "As the deer yearns for flowing streams, so I yearn for you, my God" (Ps 42:1–2). "My soul yearns for you like a dry weary land without water" (Ps 63:1). In Ezekiel's vision of the new Jerusalem, the water of God's life flows out of the temple, eventually rising to the height of a river that the prophet finds impossible to cross (Ezek 47:1–5). Here, the vision of the river of life from Genesis 2 is expanded; its waters have become a river teeming with life and its banks are lined with trees that bear healing and life forever (Ezek 47:6–12).

The waters of death

But if water is a force for life, it is also a dangerous and uncontrollable power that brings destruction and death. This is the image of water that appears in the other story of creation, Genesis 1, which describes the primeval chaos as an abyss of water over which a mighty wind blows; and again, in the great flood in Genesis 9, which destroys all creation. Only the just ones — Noah and his family — survive and the wildlife that they took with them into the ark.

This image of creation being drawn from the waters of chaos was a common one in ancient Near Eastern mythology; however, mythological language was used more blatantly in the psalms than in Genesis. "God . . . you split the sea in two and smashed the heads of the monsters on the waters. You crushed Leviathan's [the sea-monster's] heads" (Ps 74:13). "You control the pride of the ocean, when its waves ride high, you calm them. You split Rahab [the sea-monster] in two like a corpse" (Ps 89:9–10). God is always in charge of the chaotic waters. "The Lord's voice is over the waters, the God of glory thunders!" (Ps 29:3). God is always in charge of the sea-monsters. Psalm 104:25–26 says that God made Leviathan a thing to play with. The story of Jonah reveals a sea-monster more docile than a prophet of Israel.

Passing through the waters

One image above all others colored Israel's vision of reality: the exodus. Whatever Israel knows of God, whatever Israel knows of life, whatever Israel knows of itself, all is understood in the light of that one central experience. The center of the exodus experience is the crossing of the sea. The sea is the primeval image of chaos, the waters of death. But a strong east wind sent by God blows all night, and in the morning Israel is able to cross on dry land (Exod 14:15–30). Life has come from death. Not only has life come from death, but death has been destroyed in the waters. Israel's enemies are drowned in the returning waters.

The exodus, then, is Israel's creation story. Before it they were an enslaved group of sufferers; now they are a people, indeed, the people of God. When they were absolutely helpless, God delivered them, when death lay before and behind. God led them through the waters of death that lay before them and destroyed death in the waters that lay behind.

In time, the exodus became Israel's primary image for creation. The waters of chaos over which the mighty wind blows in Genesis 1:1–2 are the waters of the Reed Sea through which Israel came to life. The destructive waters of chaos in Genesis 9 are for the death of sin, which threatened the life of God's creation; the new creation, Noah and his family are delivered from death through the waters of death. When in the book of Joshua, Israel is separated from the promised land by the waters of the Jordan, it is again through water that the people come to life (Josh 3:1–17). The waters of exodus are death and life: death to chaos, slavery and sin; entrance to new life, new land, new creation.

Christ, the living water

The early church inherited Israel's water images and used them as Jesus had to express the new deed that God had done for them. In John 7, at the feast of Tabernacles, Jesus proclaimed himself the source of living water. "Let anyone who is thirsty come to me! Let anyone who believes in me come and drink! From that one's heart shall flow streams of living water!" (John 7:37–38). Earlier in the same gospel Jesus had told the Samaritan woman that, if she had only asked, he would have given her living water. "Whoever drinks the water that I shall give will never be thirsty again" (John 4:13–14). In the book of Revelation Christ is the shepherd who leads the sheep by streams of flowing water (Rev 7:16–17).

Thus, Jesus becomes the source of living water and the water of life. The water that is necessary for earth to flourish, for human beings to live, for Israel to reach the promised land, is found in Jesus.

Jesus also controls the waters of death. When the disciples are threatened by the storm at sea, Jesus speaks and the winds die down, the waters become calm. The disciples catch a glimmer of the action's significance and exclaim, "Who is this that even the winds and the sea obey him?" (Mark 4:35–41). Later, in complete possession of his power and wanting to be with the disciples, Jesus walks on the surface of a stormy sea. The disciples themselves, in the person of

Peter, are empowered to tame the waters of death. As long as his faith endures, Peter, too, can walk on water (Mark 14:22–33).

But the primary image for Christians, the image that colors all other reality, is the new exodus, the death and resurrection of Christ, which delivers them from the slavery of death and leads them to the promised land of God's kingdom. That event creates them as a people and gives them life.

Baptism is the people's entrance into that saving event, their passage through the waters of death into life. Paul says in the letter to the Romans "Do you not know that all of us, when we were baptized into Christ Jesus, were baptized into his death? By our baptism into his death we were buried with him, so that as Christ was raised from the dead by the Father's glorious power, we too should begin living a new life" (Rom 6:3–4).

As Christians, we stand with death before us and behind us. We look back to the death of sin; we look ahead at the waters of baptism beyond which lies the promised land. Only through the waters of chaos, the waters of flood, the waters of the sea, can we come to life. Only through the waters of baptism can we become a new people. Only through baptism into Christ's death can we hope for a share in the resurrection. Water is a symbol of death; water is a symbol of life. Water has become our way through death to life.

Water today

Our everyday experience of water is no less ambiguous. We stand helpless in the face of hurricanes and floods, which are certainly the waters of death. We look in horror at our own poisoning of the waters of life with pesticides, radioactive waste, organic pollution. Half a continent away from the great Atlantic and Pacific Oceans, we watch the waters of our life diminish as the Ogallala aquifer is drained, the Arkansas River is diverted, mountain waters are pumped away to quench the thirst of urban areas.

Yet our eyes are not closed to the wonder of peaceful waters. We are nurtured by rainstorms and fast flowing brooks in the country, and we are gathered into strong cities wherever rivers are bridged for commerce. Rain falls, and the reflection of traffic lights in street puddles seems almost to mimic the magic of people's lives.

More especially, we each go to our own waterfalls to be healed, restored. We stand in awe at the ever-flowing, ever-changing, clear, living water. We watch the living water changing the face of the earth, carving new channels, watering the growth of spring and summer, covering the repose of fall and winter. We go to water to find life.

Almost three thousand years ago a prophet cried out, "Come to the water!" (Isa 55:1). Jesus promised to give living water to all who asked for it. And the book of Revelation portrays the future as a time when the sea, the waters of death, will be no more, and the river of life that rises from the throne of God will flow crystal clear, nourishing trees of life on either bank (Rev 21:1; 22:1–2).

We come to the water of exodus, the water of baptism, the water of life. "The Spirit and the bride say 'Come!' Let everyone who listens answer 'Come!' Then let all who are thirsty come; all who want it may have the water of life, and have it free" (Rev 22:17). "Amen; come, Lord Jesus!"

29

Typology and Christian Preaching

GAIL RAMSHAW

The use of the Hebrew Bible in the Christian assembly has long been surrounded by one controversy or another. Already in the second century a man named Marcion proposed a list of books fit for public Sunday reading. Assured that Christianity worshiped a different God than the God of the Hebrews, he believed that the Hebrew Bible no longer had a place in the Christian assembly and even edited some of the Hebrew content out of Christian writings. The church came to reject this proposal absolutely, and as it condemned Marcion, began to draw up a list of books that were appropriate for public reading in the Sunday assembly. The church declared, *contra* Marcion, that the Hebrew Bible was to be read in the Christian assembly.

That Christians read weekly from the Hebrew Bible is no longer controversial, but why we do is once again a lively question. At a 1988 conference of liturgical scholars, when a meeting was called for anyone interested in the issues of the liturgical use of the Hebrew Bible, a standing-room-only crowd assembled. What readings select from the vast Hebrew books for Christian proclamation? How, if at all, are these texts related to the New Testament books? What shall we do about sexism, militarism, the notion that sickness is punishment? Some of our churches, as well as the Consultation on Common Texts, are reexamining the selections from the Hebrew Bible in their lectionaries, and dozens of issues are surfacing.

The most fundamental question is the hermeneutical one: With what intention do Christians read from the Hebrew Bible? Do we read it to learn ancient Near Eastern history? Do we see the Hebrew books pedagogically, a complicated but necessary way to learn, for example, the significance of the Passover? Do we read the narratives as proof-texts about morality? Do we hope to gain "wide truths of life," as my ninth-grade English teacher used to say, from these "Great Books"?

From *Liturgy: Preaching the Word* 8, no. 2.

Although all these hermeneutics are in evidence today, another quite different principle stands behind the classic lectionary and the ancient liturgies of the triduum: typology, the use of Hebrew Bible images for Christian meaning. Yet the historical-critical method of studying the Hebrew Bible has made several generations of preachers leery of typology. Many preachers are ill-equipped to use its imaginative method, and many scripture scholars condemn it as a naive and anti-Semitic misappropriation of Jewish material for Christian use. In what ways, in our critical age, can typology function as the key to Christian use of the Hebrew Bible?

Defining a critical typology

Of first importance is distinguishing a critical typology from much that has passed as typological interpretation in the church's past. By "a critical typology" I do not mean the simplistic prophecy-fulfillment formula with which we are too familiar. In this use of the Hebrew Bible, the principle of prophecy as ancient words spoken unknowingly about Christ's coming and divine promises fulfilled in Christ's mission controls Christian selection of Hebrew passages. Under this rubric, not only poems about future redemption but also speeches within Hebrew narratives are understood as actually referring to Jesus. Scholars rightly criticize this pattern of interpretation as naive and unstudied. Furthermore, this method too often disregards, with blatant Christian imperialism, God's continuing covenant with the Jewish people.

Nor would I defend the trivialization of the Hebrew Bible that accompanies the snippet approach to Bible reading. Here, in an effort to keep selections relatively short, verses are chosen here and there from longer stories in gargantuan editing stunts that effectively force the Hebrew texts to convey a meaning that was never intended. In the lectionary's use of 2 Samuel 12, Nathan's condemnation of King David's stealing of Bathsheba and murder of Uriah, several current lectionaries omit from the reading the prophet's primary curse on David: that his wives will be taken away and given to another. This story's original meaning has been significantly altered through judicious editing of the text. One hopes that another way could be found.

Perhaps it is such cavalier editing that has led to the concern that the Hebrew scriptures "be read in their own right." In these discussions one stumbles over the notion that there is some pure way the Hebrew Bible is meant to be understood. The rabbis tell us, however, that their scriptures were written for public reading and were read not as historical record but as vehicle of an intentional and expounded religious meaning. The question remains: If Christians read the Hebrew narrative as it was written, what does it mean for us?

Typology as extended metaphor

In this critical age we can no longer imagine typology as God's mysterious clues foretelling Jesus' destiny. I find extremely distasteful and unworthy of religion the idea that several thousand years of human struggle were an elaborate game God was playing. Typology is not the key to the divine mind but a requirement of human symbolic language. Typology is a form of extended metaphor. The faithful of every age try to tell of their experience of grace, but they rely on the words and images in their tradition to do so. Our fears and hopes are told in stories; those we humans tell to our children — whether of the big bad wolf or star travel — symbolize our search for meaning in the same categories we heard in our grandparents' stories.

Think, for example, of heaven: we cannot describe our longing for God adequately, but we repeat and build on a long tradition about the splendor of God's city, the beauty of gemstones, the power of angels, the necessity of light — all those conventions reaching their magnificent peak in the book of Revelation. We describe our hope for God in the extended metaphors of the final, glorious city. Perhaps we simply retell the old vision; perhaps we dress it up yet more. But the old metaphor is there to help us. The conventions of our language give us words to speak of grace.

So too with typology. The early church understood that the Hebrew Bible provided the church with many stories of God's grace. Before the Christian scriptures were written, these very stories of God's intervening mercy were the gospel for Christians. When Paul writes that Jesus was raised "according to the scriptures," he means the Hebrew Bible; and when the Christians depicted the resurrection in the catacombs, they drew the story of Jonah. Christians continued to keep the Passover, not because they were conserving Jews but because the narrative of the Israelites' exodus across the Red Sea was the early church's primary metaphor for the resurrection of Christ.

Thanks to the superb editing of British scholar Avril Henry, we now can study one of the medieval church's monuments to typology at its best, the Biblia Pauperum. From the thirteenth through the fifteenth centuries, hundreds of these books circulated in Europe, first as manuscripts and later as blockbooks; their existence helps discredit the charge that medieval Christians did not know their Bible. Indeed, I would be delighted if the preachers in our churches knew the Bible well enough to make use of a Biblia Pauperum.

Each one of the forty pages in the Biblia Pauperum focuses on a single event in Jesus' life or in the end of time. Circling around a picture of that event are four prophetic texts, two pictures of stories from the Hebrew Bible, two blocks of explanatory notes and three interesting, sometimes cryptic, phrases that hint at the complex levels of relationship between the images in the stories. Henry's commentary adequately refutes the assumption that such a book was an aid to illiterate preachers, suggesting instead that any such book might have been a meditation guide for highly learned and pictorially sophisticated people who were well acquainted with Christian use of Hebrew images. To see typology at its best, let us open the Biblia Pauperum to its double-page spread on the crucifixion. In the pictures of the four Hebrew narratives, we see most clearly typology as extended metaphor.

But before we look to the Biblia Pauperum, we must stop to ask ourselves: What is the meaning of the crucifixion? The death of Jesus was a secular execution. To become the central event of a religion, the historical event of an execution had to acquire religious meaning. That is, it assumed layers of pious interpretation, images of holiness, religious labels and sanctified language that the unbeliever would reject but that were essential for understanding the event as religiously significant.

We say that Christ's crucifixion is the sacrifice that saves us; the cross gives us life; from this death the church is born; and from this body flow the sacraments. These are astonishing claims to make of an execution. The New Testament writers and subsequent hymn writers, preachers and theologians used the images and metaphors in central stories of the Hebrew Bible as their categories of religious meaning. These stories give us the words, then, with which to describe God's grace in Christ. In the Biblia Pauperum four such significant stories tell us the meaning of the crucifixion.

Telling the ancient stories

The first of the four stories from the Hebrew Bible pictured alongside the crucifixion is the so-called sacrifice of Isaac from Genesis 22. Abraham is about to lower his medieval-looking sword; Isaac is piously praying; beside the altar is a cruciform pile of wood; the ram is waiting in the foreground; and the angel descends from heaven to halt the sacrifice. The pairing of this enigmatic story with the death of Christ demonstrates the complexity of typology at its best; even the Biblia Pauperum's own explanatory sentences offer inadequate exposition of the imagery. Here is no simple parallel: one child saved, one ram provided, one adult executed; one sacrifice halted, one sacrifice completed, one execution perpetrated. Probing the connections between these two stories would take another article; to say the parallels simply is to say them poorly. The sacrifice of Isaac is not a simple simile of the crucifixion but an extended metaphor, in which complex possibilities beckon.

The second of the stories pictured occurs in the gospel of John as a metaphor of Jesus: the serpent in the wilderness. The Israelites stand behind Moses, and some of the company writhe on the ground entangled in a den of snakes; on a pole before them hangs a great serpent. The narrative in Numbers 21 tells that the complaining Israelites were punished by fiery snakebites, and that Moses called the people to gaze at the brazen serpent in order to be healed. Here again is no simple simile.

For surely this story of the people's devout worship of a brazen serpent is an unexpurgated memory of their participation in Canaan's goddess cult. The

Canaanite mother-goddess Asherah was depicted as a pole, a cross or a tree, and
the serpent in the ancient Near East was a feminine symbol of divine regeneration. Excavations have unearthed Canaanite figurines of Asherah holding snakes
in each hand. The Bible tells of several times the Asherah pole found its way
back into the temple, but those narratives absolutely condemn any use of the
mother-goddess image; and one of the reforming kings destroys the brazen serpent. Yet here the pagan symbol of holiness becomes a vehicle of God's grace.
The old story of mother-goddess worship is used as a metaphor for religious
devotion to the God of the covenant and later as a metaphor for Christians'
faithful gaze at the cross.

The third story pictured is of the creation of Eve from the side of Adam. The
stories of the first human beings have provided grist for everyone's interpretation
mills: Christian tradition has been plagued with rigorous teaching of this story
as proof of the subordination of woman; modern scholars see the story as a
version of other myths of the original hermaphrodite split into two sexes. But
the Biblia Pauperum uses the story metaphorically as an image of the meaning
of the crucifixion. The illustration of Christ on the cross depicts the legend of
the soldier healed of blindness by the blood flowing from Christ's spear wound.
Adam too has a wounded side, from which comes health and life for all. The
image introduces Paul's old Adam/new Adam metaphor as one explanation of
the fruits of redemption.

The fourth story pictured is from Exodus 17, the water from the rock. In the
illustration, Moses stands before the Israelites and with his rod brings forth a
stream of water from the rock. Paul also uses this story as a metaphor for our
life in Christ. Recalling the rabbinic legend that the rock followed the people
of Israel throughout their forty-year journey, Paul says that the rock was Christ.
Here Paul is not teaching a literal christology, as when John's prologue says that
the word was at the creation of the world. Rather, a metaphor is being employed,
using the water story to illustrate our life in Christ. The medieval artist followed
Paul's lead, juxtaposing the image of water flowing from the rock with that of
blood flowing from Christ.

Here then are four stories: a boy is saved from sacrifice, the people are healed,
life comes forth from the wound, water flows from the rock. These stories are
the tinted glasses worn by those Jews who knew the details of Jesus' death; these
stories and other tales of the Hebrew Bible provide the interpretative framework
for the meaning of the crucifixion.

As we said above: Christ's death is the sacrifice that saves us; the cross gives
us life; from this death the church is born; and from this body flow the sacraments. To substantiate these claims, we tell the ancient stories, borrowing their
imagery for our experience of human need and divine grace. Such a use of Hebrew narrative as extended metaphors for the benefits of redemption is what was
primitively understood as typology. Even the name Jesus, which is Joshua, and
the title Christ, which means the anointed one, are examples of such typology,
Hebrew images reused to describe God's grace in Jesus.

Awakening a consciousness of grace

Such an understanding of typology suggests that a good deal of revision is necessary in our selection and preaching of texts from the Hebrew Bible. Seminaries must think hard about how to teach the Hebrew Bible. It does little good for preachers to know the presumed dating of a biblical passage if they cannot tell its meaning for Christian proclamation. On the famous typological altarpiece at the monastery in Klosterneuburg, the Latin inscription declares that the Hebrew Bible depictions are "to make the results of redemption plain and to awaken in the people consciousness of grace." We hear readings from the Hebrew narratives that we may better know ourselves as saved from sacrifice, healed from the snake's poison, newly born as Eve, nourished from the rock. How startlingly different are these images of the crucifixion than, for example, Martin Scorsese's depiction of Jesus as a neo-Platonic male tortured by an identity crisis — a portrayal that offers salvific images to no one.

Perhaps some preachers would try to expound the Hebrew Bible images as extended metaphors of human need and divine grace. But we do not need a news report on the preacher's spiritual journey or the latest Semitic studies; we need the metaphors within which to cast the life of Christ and the images of need and grace that tell the meaning of the Christian story. Such preaching uses the Hebrew Bible "to make the results of redemption plain and to awaken in the people consciousness of grace." The central stories of the Hebrew people offer preachers more than enough material, and as the years pass by we can see the images of grace slowly unfolded, the metaphors of mercy tried one way and another.

30

The Sacramentality of Preaching

Harold Dean Trulear

Divine worship is eschatological, revelatory and dramatic. It declares the ultimacy of God and God's reign and points to the day of "the fullness of the times; that is, the summing up of all things in Christ, things in the heavens and things upon the earth" (Eph 1:10).

Divine worship reveals the perspective of almighty God from which the devoted are bid to interpret or to reinterpret all the activities of everyday life: eating, sleeping, personal relationships, working, playing. Worship defines being in the world in a different mode from that offered by the world itself.

Divine worship provides the context for the rehearsal of life in the reign of God; it is a call for believers to take their places in the unfolding of eschatological history and to act out life in Christ to the fullest.

These three qualities of worship are ever present and interrelated; each sheds light on the task of preaching. They are also powerfully present in the experience of black preaching and worship, and serve as lenses within that particular experience through which we can view the universality of the Christian witness. My task in this essay is not to examine the totality of black Christian experience and spirituality.[1] Rather, given our focus on the central symbols of worship, we will use the insights of the black Christian tradition and its emphasis on the crucifixion and resurrection to reflect on the task of preaching.[2]

Rite and symbol in the Afro-American church

My own fascination with the relationship between preaching and worship in the black church tradition and in the whole of Christian witness was spawned during a conversation with a graduate student early in my teaching career. Aware of my decision to enter the Baptist ministry after twenty-plus years as an Episcopal layman, she remarked "I don't see how you could have handled being an Episcopalian." Curious about her remark and still in love with the communion of my

From *Liturgy: Central Symbols* 7, no. 1.

youth, I bid her qualify that statement. "Well," she continued, "week after week you use the same prayers, the same mass, the same service. Where is the room for spontaneity? Where is the room for the Holy Ghost?"

My response to her did not consist of a defense of Anglican liturgy. Instead, I found myself thinking about the major role that liturgical order plays in the black free church traditions.[3] Examples of order, symbol and sacrament come quickly to mind. There is liturgical order in the procession of black church choirs, their members often dressed in brightly colored robes, reflecting the joyous nature of life in Christ.[4] There is deep meaning in the symbolic gesture of handshaking, i.e., greeting one another during worship as the radical recognition of mutual personhood under the auspices of God. This eschatological identity stands in stark contrast to the depersonalization inherent in the institutional and personal racism in the world. There is sacramental reality in the preaching event as the preacher declares the gospel with an accompanying ecstasy that assures the congregation of the "real presence" of grace. In short, I found myself excited about the spiritual intuitiveness of a people from whom many of the rites and symbols of the Christian tradition had been withheld but who nevertheless captured the meaning of the gospel and created their own rites and symbols, which are faithful to the witness of tradition.

Subsequent study of and participation in black church worship revealed to me that the black preaching event is a microcosm of the whole of good Christian worship. There is the declaration of eschatological reality, the proffer of the divine perspective and the invitation to take one's place in the dramatic movement of God in this life. All three of those hinge on understanding the connection between the Easter event, its liturgical expression and contemporary life. In the black church tradition, it is imperative that one see the reality of everyday life mediated through the crucifixion and resurrection of Jesus Christ. Preaching in the black church and in any church gains its authenticity from its ability to relate the sufferings of Christ, as well as the victory of the resurrection, to what's happening now.

Eschatology and marginality

The preaching event announces a new order; a new reality has come. Eschatological preaching derives its power, in part, from declaring a distinction between the old order and the new, *nomos* and grace, the suffering of this world and the victory of the next. It is a hollow victory that is announced without a recounting of the reality of the battle, i.e., the suffering that is part and parcel of life in this world. The resurrection has meaning precisely because of the crucifixion.

Black preachers have always taken suffering seriously, since it presents itself as an ever-present reality for our community. Slavery, segregation and discrimination on one hand, depersonalization, miseducation and inequality of opportunity on the other, have created the conditions of marginality that are painful in a world that celebrates the value of belonging. Conformity to the majority opin-

ion is an itch engendered by the powerful to enhance the sale of all sorts of
scratching devices designed to make one depend on anything but God to be fully
human. Being marginal hurts; it leads to psychological damage, the withholding
of goods and services and literal physical danger.

But marginality also begets a sensitivity to suffering that enables the marginal
community to understand something of the Passion. Jesus' suffering becomes
recognizable, as pain wears a neighbor's face and the crucifixion's hammer has a
familiar ring. The joy that comes as a result of preaching the gospel — the good
news of the kingdom and the eschatological reality ushered in with the resurrection of Christ — is manifest because that reality stands in stark contrast to
the reality of current suffering and marginality. The resurrection means "trouble
don't last always"; it announces that there is an alternative to the predicament of
complicity in this world as a determinant of personhood.

Could it be that it is in failing to realize the marginality of the Christian
message that we fail to impress its power on the congregation? Could it be that
in failing to enable people to see the pain of this life, we also fail to help them
see the glory of the next? Could it be that people can't see the power of the
resurrection because they have been anesthetized to their own passion and hence
are numb to the Passion of Christ? Could it be that the Easter they see is more
a baptism of Western prosperity than the announcement of a new humanity
available in Christ?

The point is not that Blacks own any spiritual superiority but that conversion
to a new world rests on dissatisfaction with the old. When the preacher declares,
"We're all God's children," the words are radical for those who have constantly
been told otherwise. Perhaps this means that the Easter preacher must break
open the experiences of his or her community in which the new eschatological
identity is being eschewed in favor of idolatry, narcissism and alienation.

Preaching as revelation

This does not mean that Easter preaching degenerates into a lengthy harangue,
listing the sins that so easily beset us. Preaching is more than a moral diatribe.
Preaching does not read us the riot act; it does something far more radical. It
dares to say that God is watching the world, and then it declares what God
sees. God sees and knows the world in which people must live. God knows
their suffering, even as God knew the awful Passion of Christ. Preaching not
only declares that God's eyes are on the world, but in the best of the black
tradition, it claims to represent those eyes and to say what they see. In this sense
perhaps more than any other, preaching is sacramental, and the preacher herself
or himself becomes the symbol of grace in the midst of the congregation.

Drawing on the rich images of the Hebrew Bible prophets, New Testament
evangelists and African storytellers and priests, the black preacher mounts the
pulpit as God's mouthpiece, God's spokesperson. The preacher is expected to
declare what "thus saith the Lord." With the preaching event elevated to central

status in the ritual, all eyes and ears are focused on the man or woman of God; the preacher has become a symbol of God. The use of impressive vestments, a central pulpit and eloquent language all point beyond the preacher to images of God: the robes declare God's holiness, the pulpit declares God's authority and the language evokes images of beauty and intelligence. To be sure, there are other sensibilities at work and other liturgical tools available, but they are subservient to the preacher's ability to be a sacramental presence.

If the preacher in the black church can rehearse the struggles of the people, he or she does more than stir up wounds and heartaches. He or she fashions that trouble into a litany in which every sentence of sorrow is punctuated with an exclamation point of God's care. Using the words of familiar songs, the preacher declares, "Jesus knows all about our struggles," or "He knows just how much we can bear." Or heightening the empathy between the Passion of Jesus and the trials of the congregation, the preacher recalls the words of the old spiritual:

> Nobody knows de trouble I see
> Nobody knows but Jesus
> Nobody knows de trouble I see
> Glory, Hallelujah!

There it is: the sentence of sorrow punctuated with joy. And joy comes because Jesus knows; i.e., God sees the difficulty of this life. Sorrow and joy, crucifixion and resurrection — the hearers recognize their own story in the preacher's words.

Watchers for God

The preacher as sacramental presence must not only see; he or she must also offer an interpretation of life. C. L. Franklin, regarded by many as the prince of black preachers until his death in 1984, talks about this interpretive role in the recorded sermon, "Watchman, What of the Night?"

> That cry was an inquiring cry, "Watchman, What of the Night?" What are the times? What time of history is this? What time of trouble is this? For after all history is God's Big Clock . . . and inasmuch as we cannot see within the next five minutes in our system of time, in God's system of time, in God's clock of history we can't see. We must call out to our prophets as Edom or the Edomites did in those long days of bygone days. Men who can pierce the future. Men who can interpret the future. Men who can see beyond now . . . and inquire of them, "Watchmen, What of the Night?"

The preacher as sacramental presence is a listening presence. Therefore, Franklin hears the cry of the people and is in touch with their passion. He even plays their part: "We are blinded by the mystery of history" and the "destiny of time." We are unable to "read the writing" on God's scroll of history:

> Only God can reveal it to us, or reveal it to His men of mystery. And so, as the Edomites did thousands of years ago, with anxiety of the future, with questions of

the future, we inquire to the men of vision who walk upon the lofty walls of God's inspiration, "Watchman, What of the Night?"

Franklin then performs the role of the watchman, as he reports on the tense state of international affairs. He covers events from the emergence of Sudan as an independent nation to the Hungarians' resistance to communism. The report highlights the struggle of oppressed peoples around the world. These struggles are indicative of the human predicament. The signs of international struggle indicate a seemingly unpredictable future:

> We're living in times that are like the nighttime
> We don't know what the morning will bring.
> We see oppressed people
> Not only abroad
> But also in our own lands
> Becoming impatient for full citizenship.
> Not only in Africa,
> Not only in Egypt,
> Not only the Arab world,
> Not only Germany,
> Not only China
> Not only India,
> But we see —
> We see Montgomery, Alabama,
> We see Florida,
> We see other parts of our own land
> Impatient for world brotherhood and full citizenship.

He has captured their struggle in his words and therefore has announced that God sees. In relating the community's suffering to global suffering, he shows just how big God's vision is. More succinctly put, the sacramental presence is that of an omniscient God. But God not only sees, God acts!

God will win, declares Franklin. We have to wait, but waiting is not passive. Franklin calls for an active waiting:

> Just a few more days. A little while to wait, a little while to pray. A little while to sing. A little while to labor, a little while to watch."[5]

Resurrection is sure to come. The presence of a seeing, saving God guarantees it.

Drama in black preaching

The reality of trouble in this life has been identified, and it has been proclaimed that God is watching the people's passion. The eschatological age has been announced in the declaration of the resurrection. But one task remains. The congregation must now participate in the ritual of worship as the celebration of new life. They must take their places in the drama that moves from crucifixion to resurrection.

Here, the dialogical nature of black preaching becomes a way of inviting participation in the drama. As the sermon rehearses the reality of suffering and passion, the images and examples used evoke participatory responses from the congregation. The difficulty of hard labor is captured in the image of "our foreparents toiling from 'can to can't'" (i.e., "can see," meaning dawn, to "can't see," meaning dusk or night). The pressures of urban life are recited, from "drugs on every street corner" to "nobody knows your name downtown." The reality of employment problems that cut across class lines is called to mind: "We're the last hired and the first fired." Voices from the congregation affirm each proposition. "That's right," "Tell it," "Amen," "Well." People are hearing *their* stories from the pulpit!

How important it is, then, that the Easter preacher knows the congregation's Good Friday stories. The responses may not be verbal or overly demonstrative, though one may argue that they ought to be, if there is liberty in Christ. But when people hear their Good Friday story, their own passion narrative, they are bound to respond. A nodding head, a wincing face, a heaving sigh, a knowing glance, may be the roots of response coming to bloom.

The black preacher has other homiletic tools that invite participation in the drama. Such admonitions as "Are you prayin' with me?" "Can I get a witness?" and "I believe somebody here knows what I'm talking about" are standard invitations to dialogue. More stern phrases such as "You don't hear me," "If you can't say 'Amen,' say 'Ouch'" and "Wish I was in the right church" push a recalcitrant worshiper to witness to the truth, even if it is painful.

As the sermon progresses and the stories of the congregation have been effectively identified with the Passion of Christ, the preacher must now proclaim the victory of Christ through the resurrection. That the new order has come has already been announced. But having led the people through their passion and the Passion of Christ, the even greater announcement is that now the new order has come *to you!* In black preaching, this announcement comes in power as the closing section of a sermon. Sermon closings have long been of great importance to black preachers. The ofttold story of Martin Luther King is that he frequently began developing his closing first and then worked on the rest of the sermon.

As the preacher approaches the closing, the emotional intensity mounts. It is clear that she or he is preparing to describe the word of Easter victory, if only by noting the intensity of the conflict inherent in the Passion story. Soon, the preacher indicates that the Holy Spirit's power is manifesting itself, either through the declaration "I feel my help coming on" or through the development of a chanted and more rhythmic style,[6] or even through increasing the volume and animation of voice and body.

While some may view this as theatrical antics, the reality is that all good worship is theatrical or better put, dramatic. When done properly and in awe of the one whose gospel we preach, this move into an intense spiritual state is the same as the priest invoking the presence of Christ in the eucharist. It is the transubstantial moment in which the word is most intensely sacramental. "I feel my help coming on" is a moment in which the word is consecrated in a manner not unlike the elements in the eucharist. The ensuing ecstasy of both preacher and congregation are, then, celebrations of the real presence.

Three formats of sermon closing are traditional in black preaching. All derive their power from the crucifixion-resurrection motif; all involve passion and victory.[7] The first is the preacher's own testimony. Sometimes she or he recalls the events of her or his own conversion, often embellished in great figurative language:

> I was on my way to hell.
> Not fit to live and too mean to die.
> When Jesus stepped in
> And spoke peace to my dying soul.
> He picked me up, turned me 'round
> Planted my feet on solid ground.

At other times the testimony is about victory over some trouble in the preacher's life. Financial difficulty, problems securing education or employment, confrontations with racism or a battle with some other "messenger of Satan" will be recalled and the victory affirmed in the words of another popular song:

> Trouble in my way
> I have to cry sometime
> Lay awake at night
> That's alright
> Jesus will fix it, after awhile!

In the second format, the preacher paints a picture of heaven. Whether in the general language of "No more cryin' there, no more dyin' there," or whether made peculiarly relevant in words such as "no more racism, no more 'Yessuh boss,'" it is clear that the predicament of this life *will* end and that a new order *will* emerge. The implication is, of course, that this new order engenders hope to live in this world.

The third format is a rehearsal of the actual crucifixion and resurrection. Black preachers have gone to untold lengths to portray vividly the events of Passion week. Good Friday's heartache is given clear view:

> They put him through the mockery of a trial.
> They put a crown of thorns on his head.
> They whipped him all night long.
> The crowd yelled, "Crucify him!"
> Soldiers laughed at him
> Bystanders mocked him
> Disciples deserted him
> Clouds began to gather
> Sky grew dark
> Lightning played its zig-zag games of tag
> And with a loud voice,
> Jesus cried and gave up the ghost.

"But," cautions a seasoned preacher, "don't leave him in the grave."

> But early Sunday morning
> While the dew was still on the roses
> An angel rolled away the stone
> And Jesus...
> My master
> Jesus...
> My redeemer
> Jesus...
> My savior
> Jesus...
> Lily of the valley
> Bright and morning Star
> Jesus...
> Rose of Sharon
> Jesus...
> Mary's baby
> Jesus...
> The only Son of God
> Got up from the grave
> Declaring
> "All power is given unto Me in heaven and in earth."

Worship has come full cycle. The same God whose eschatological order has been proclaimed to be the ultimate reality raises Jesus from the dead. As Jesus is raised from the dead, so too are the hearers, for their stories have been identified with the Passion of Christ. Joy comes as the people are raised to new life in Christ in vicarious resurrection through the preacher's rehearsal of the crucifixion-resurrection motif. The celebration is not a shadow or a sham. It is the rehearsal of reality. Christ has been present in the word, identifying with the passion of the hearers and ushering in a new life by the resurrection.

Notes

1. See Luther E. Smith, Jr., "Spirituality and Social Freedom," *Liturgy: In Spirit and Truth* (Washington, D.C.: Liturgical Conference) 5, no. 3 (1986): 47–51.

2. Perhaps the volume that deals best with black preaching and its implications for the universal homiletic task is Henry Mitchell's vastly underrated *The Recovery of Preaching* (New York: Harper & Row, 1977). See also H. Beecher Hicks, *Preaching Through a Storm* (Grand Rapids: Zondervan Publishing House, 1987), and Gardner C. Taylor, *How Shall They Preach?* (Elgin, Ill.: The Progressive Baptist Publishing House, 1977).

3. This idea is expanded in the author's "The Lord Will Make A Way, Somehow: Worship and the Afro-American Story," *Journal of the Interdenominational Theological Center* 13, no. 1 (1985): 87–104.

4. The late Wendell Whalum, one of the finest church musicians and musicologists to dedicate his talents to black church worship and liturgy, details this and parallel

phenomena in "Black Hymnody," in Emmanuel McCall, ed., *Black Church Life-Styles* (Nashville: Abingdon Press, 1986), 83–103.

5. Gerald L. Davis, *I Got the Word in Me and I Can Sing It You Know: The Performed African American Sermon* (Philadelphia: Westminster Press, 1985), 59–60.

6. Mervyn Warren calls this "effects style"; see his *Black Preaching: Truth and Soul* (Washington, D.C.: University Press of America, 1977). See also Pearl Williams-Jones, "The Musical Quality of Black Religious Folk Ritual," *Spirit* 1, no. 1 (1977): 21–30, and Willis Laurence James, "The Romance of the Negro Folk Cry," *Phylon* 16, no. 19 (1955): 15–30.

7. The following sermon-closing examples represent a composite of recorded messages from "Black Worship and Religious Identity," a research project undertaken in 1984 with sponsoring grants from the Association of Theological Schools of the United States and Canada and the New Jersey State Historical Commission. These sermon excerpts, preached by Fred LaGarde, William A. Jones, Ernest Lyght and Ruth Satchell, could have come from any number of preachers who could consider these phrases to be in the public domain. So often do they occur in black preaching that William B. McClain, professor of homiletics and worship at Wesley Theological Seminary in Washington, D.C., considers them part of "The Black Litany."

3 1

The Text Is Not Enough

Anthony Ugolnik

A familiar torment plagues the monster Grendel in the Old English epic *Beowulf.* Grendel endures longing, then rage when he hears from afar the songs and laughter of feasting in the great hall of the king. The joyful company of the feast intensifies Grendel's pain because the monster, in isolation, cannot enjoy it. The laughter of the warrior Danes deepens Grendel's sadness because he is condemned, in his bone-chilling alienation, to take everything so seriously — jokes, after all, require company. Grendel's world has no center; and in the bloody violence of his revenge it implodes and collapses. Grendel shows us the wisdom of an Old English insight. There is no solace in the self. Alone, outside the feast, there is no meaning.

Liturgy is the feast in our postmodern experience. In the former Soviet Union, for example, the Russian Orthodox liturgy sent its echoes across the cynicism and isolation of contemporary urban life, and the song and laughter of that great feast drew in a host of young and vibrant Christian thinkers. In American Christian life, however, we have yet to recognize the power, the pure force of meaning, that resides in the communal, liturgical act. Still isolated in the privacy of the individual intellect, still following the postenlightenment models of individual rationalist inquiry, Americans search for the joy of the gospel where Grendel failed to find it — crouching alone and isolated in the fastness of the moors.

The loss of the body

The liturgical act, the joy of the feast and the celebration of our God-given materiality as rational creatures has sustained the church through the centuries. The West, however, has lost trust in it. This failure to trust in liturgy afflicts almost all traditions. Liberal scripture scholars, assembled in seminar quests for the "historical Jesus," toss out chunks and gobbets of scripture with abandon. If there

---

From *Liturgy: Central Symbols* 7, no. 1.

211

is any "historical Jesus" left after the process, he is surely too pale and anemic a hero to inspire songs and stories at the feast. Conservative fundamentalists, in a heresy to rival any of those that afflicted the early church, recast scripture as a textbook in postmodern rationalism. Ignoring the mystery of language, which can only reflect and celebrate truth, they make of the text a literal absolute. Scripture for them is a text without context; and the great, heroic song of the king in their revised system has all the mystery and power of a statistical index.

Christians, even in liturgical traditions, have sacrificed the body to the mind. Liturgy has become a "grand incidental" — nice, perhaps even necessary but hardly vital. Flower arrangements can be left to a committee, and disputes over vestments or the order of services can be relegated to specialists. But these are not matters that strike at the heart of Christianity. In an age when, through athletics and diet and the intensity of exercise, we have rediscovered our physical bodies, we have neglected the "body" of our Christianity. Liturgy is the sensuality of the Christian experience, the muscle of our mysticism. And we have treated it with all the regard we would pay to a huge, pastel marshmallow.

The text in context

One result is all around us. Fundamentalism flourishes. And evangelicalism, which is perfectly compatible with a rich liturgical life, also falls under the influence of the unadorned, absolute and utterly isolating text. A part of this problem has been a crisis of faith among those who love liturgy: enjoying themselves fully at the feast, they have forgotten how to invite others to join them. Or perhaps even those at the feast have forgotten that gift of self-abandon that makes others want to join in. It is crucial for liturgical Christians, who have the full authority of tradition and our holy forebears in the faith, to become assertive. It is time to explain how liturgy is a social act, even a necessary act. For liturgy is a hermeneutic, a "way of making meaning." Just as a social context is necessary to reading and understanding every text, so also a social, liturgical environment is necessary to make meaning of the scriptures. Liturgy creates the context within which the text can take on its meaning.

This, I realize, is a bold assertion. We are accustomed to seeing the book, the text, the Bible, as the source of meaning for us. Yet for a thing to "mean" something, it is necessary to look at two things — the thing itself and also the mind that assigns it meaning. Even the fundamentalist, then, cannot look exclusively at the text. At some point the fundamentalist has also to look at the person who reads the text, the interpreter. When we look in this way at the phenomenon of meaning, we can see the intellectual power inherent in liturgy. For liturgy does two important things: it brings an audience together to discern meaning, and it also places the objects of inquiry, the things that have meaning, within a context. Liturgy is a material as well as an intellectual act; it is replete with sense experience. Thus liturgy liberates. It liberates us, the interpreting subjects, from isolation. And it liberates the objects, the things that have meaning for us, from autonomy and abstraction. Liturgy makes things real.

Those barbarian warriors whom the monster Grendel so envied, those Danes with golden wires twisted about their arms, had an interesting name for baptism: *fulwihtes baeth*, which means "the bath of full being." Only later, when theologians worried about textual accuracy, did they assign the latinate name "baptism" to the act. But "baptism" can only be understood when we divine the full meaning of that Old English word *baeth*.

In Anglo-Saxon poetry, the sea is the "bath" of the gannet, the white bird that hovers over the waves, then folds back its black-tipped wings and hurtles headlong into the churning surf. The Finns experience this "bath" when they bake themselves to a sweat in a wood-scented sauna and then leap into a cold, crystalline lake, drinking deep of the water as they emerge into the ripple-shattered sunlight. This is the "bath" that the liturgy of baptism recaptures and sets in the midst of those people who will receive the baptized into the new fellowship, the new being of the reborn. Baptism touches us all and celebrates our God-given materiality. Baptism lives in us, not in the text that inspires it.

Back to the flesh

There is a sense in which we must constantly translate the words of scripture back from the cold abstractions that things become in normal, rational discourse and place them once more in the immediacy and sensuality of daily language and experience. We must discover the "bath" hidden in the "baptism." Triteness is a thief. It robs the most vital, the most profound, realizations of all meaning. And any of us who has nodded off during a Sunday sermon realizes that triteness can steal immediacy from scripture itself.

Liturgy confronts us with the materiality of our being. In engaging all the senses, it prods us awake and once more centers meaning in the concrete materiality of the world around us. In blessings and hallowed water, in water sprinkled and water washing and water wetting the hands and dotting the face with the cold little shocks that make children giggle, there we rediscover water. There we rescue a mystery from triteness and rediscover what those wise barbarians meant when they called that central sacramental act "the bath of full being." We feel a bit of what Jesus felt that cool morning when he plunged into the Jordan.

This realization is not a trick of poetic discourse, nice but somehow "softer" than the real, intellectual realization of what baptism is. Liturgy, in its sensuality, puts flesh on the bones of rationalism. The modern mind has localized meaning, especially religious meaning, in the act of reading. And this is not the loud, lips-moving act that the ancients used to perform, or that the Orthodox Jews do today, for then the spoken word rings out even through the private apprehension of meaning. Reading is for us a manifestly private act.

The communal quest for meaning

The discovery of meaning has also been envisioned for us as a private quest. Most of our "icons of genius" celebrate a bold seer, an inspired poet or perhaps a dedicated researcher, thrusting out alone against all odds and rescuing meaning despite the hindrance, even mockery of the crowd. A Shakespeare, a Mother Teresa or a Madame Curie become not the expressions of communal forces, those who are able to express or concentrate the insights of an entire people but individuals carved like giants in a Mount Rushmore of the imagination. The reader, the seeker, even the Christian, becomes an individual and somewhat isolated agent.

The tradition of the church has been the grand corrective in this process. Again and again over the ages, in the Arian and Donatist heresies and in a hundred others, a segment of the church's body has veered from the historical community and found a moment's solace in apparent certainty. Tradition, so often viewed as a conservative principle, is in actuality a charismatic concept. Those who liberate themselves from its guidance find that they are condemned to repeat mistakes made so often before. Thus tradition, as the theologian Georges Florovsky asserts, actually constitutes a freedom from the past. Liturgy, the celebration of the word that binds us together as a people, frees us from the prison of private apprehension. Meaning is not the product of individual determination, for none of us is born in a cultural vacuum, removed from grounding in materiality. Meaning is a communal quest.

Thirteen hundred years ago, the church was engaged in a massive struggle over precisely this phenomenon of meaning. The Byzantine emperors rose up to crush the icons and images that they thought threatened the spiritual nature of the Godhead. Icons were too "visible," too "material." How could the very God who was in essence incomprehensible and immaterial, mused Constantine V, the iconoclast, be represented in material form? "Is not the ink in the most Holy Gospel Book material?" responded John of Damascus. And at the Seventh Ecumenical Council in 787, the church gave a resounding endorsement of materiality. Materiality was the vehicle, after all, for the incarnation. Therefore, the council decreed that icons and the concept of the image were indeed in the tradition of the church. The text of the gospel cannot exist in isolation, separated in some rational incubation from the material world in which we have our being. Images, then, are of equal benefit with the gospel insofar as they reflect it. "For those things which point mutually to each other undoubtedly mutually signify each other."

For thirteen hundred years, then, the church has been confident that the incarnation initiated a process of knowing and of coming to understand. In the concreteness of liturgy we continually discover the materiality of our world, and we acknowledge our own grounding as material beings. The materiality of this world, in all its sense-dazzling immediacy, can signify the gospel in mutuality. The incarnation means, not only that Jesus became flesh for us, with all its vulnerability even unto death on the cross; Jesus became *story* for us as well, a story that we celebrate liturgically.

This story, like all great stories, organizes us socially. Like those warrior Danes who gathered to sing their tales in the great hall of the king, we gather in our temples to sing Christ's praise and sacramentally enact the deliverance our hero has given us. The liturgical feast grounds us in the concreteness of the world and assures that we will discover God's meaning together, as a people, not as isolated and individual seekers. The self, as Grendel discovered, is but a lonely prison.

A dialogic anthropology

In our culture, to break free of that prison of self is not easy. The key to liberation lies in an understanding of language. This ancient, vital church has a polyglot wisdom. We have subsisted in a bewildering variety of tongues, and we have celebrated the feast in a multiplicity of rhythms. It is difficult for us to place trust in absoluteness as expressed in any tongue. It takes a profound naiveté to declare that "literal truth" resides in any text. For in which form will that literal truth reside? If in fact it resides in the original language of the ancient text, then it will take an ancient speaker of that tongue to express or comprehend its literal truth. And then even the ancient speaker (and not any poor scholar's imitation) would be able to treat us moderns to but a vague translation. Any linguist who has worked with the intertwining fabric of languages knows how a language can fuse to consciousness. No, language and hence scripture can convey only the icon of truth, truth's image. And that for us is enough.

Language is a communal enterprise. Each of us can seize our mother tongue and forge it into a multiplicity of ideas, but whatever we do with that language is the product of an intimate contract. The meanings of its words were conveyed to us by others. The understanding of those words belongs not only to us but to those who receive them. As Christian theology has taught through the ages, we are reciprocal beings. Or as some modern Christian thinkers, like the Soviet critic Mikhail Bakhtin, have developed the idea, we are dialogic beings. Our very identities and all our notions are born in the constant interplay of our dialogue with those beings around us.

Like Mikhail Bakhtin, Christians steeped in liturgy can innately recognize their interdependence. Liturgy is a grand, continuing dialogue between a presider and a people. In life's process, liturgy is even a dialogue between us (as we once were) and ourselves (as we now are), continually over a lifetime being shaped by and steeped in the word of God. Liturgy is the expression of our communal, dialogic being.

This, then, explains that wondrous thing that happens to the Christian "agent," the Christian who comes to understand. Liturgy firmly seats that Christian in the materiality of this world. Liturgy also insures that Christians will in truth be "communal beings," dialogically intermeshed and free of any illusions of autonomy. The liturgical Christian cannot commit those serious, ancient errors to which the fundamentalist can fall victim. Fundamentalists, like the ancient followers of Mani, see themselves as the repository of all good and everyone else as the alien "other," the embodiment of evil; such neomanichaeism reads prophetic texts in such a way that one's own identity is exalted and one's political enemies are scripturally committed to hellfire. Such notions, of course, have no grounding in tradition. The liturgical Christian has a "reciprocal self," of necessity implied and embedded within the whole people of God gathered in every nation, the whole mystical body of Christ, which celebrates and proclaims the word together.

Restoring creation's center

But liturgy, as has been claimed, does more than seat the Christian interpreter firmly within tradition. Liturgy also promotes an understanding of the "object" of Christian thought. Liturgy not only restores the wholeness of the "interpreter," it also profoundly affects the act of interpretation. It is not only individuals who suffer alienation and isolation when they find themselves sundered and segmented from each other. God has bound us intimately to the creation in which we are placed. When we see ourselves as alienated and autonomous beings, the things within creation suffer from an alienation and autonomy as well. Creation loses its center and fragments into a chaotic meaninglessness.

Alexei Khomyakov, a Russian Orthodox teacher, warned us about this chaos in the nineteenth century. Exposed to Western empirical, rationalist thought, he rejected its implications. He did not judge it by its results — technologically, of course, it produced many benefits that assured its continuance. But Khomyakov judged it by its very process. He saw individualist, rationalist thought as distinguished by its segmentation. Its method is to separate, classify and resolve a thing into its component parts. Khomyakov feared the results of such a methodology. Would it not, he wondered, be impossible to see things any more in terms of "wholes," in terms of integration and resolution, of the oneness and unity of God?

Dostoyevsky played with the results of this rationalist framework in his *Notes from the Underground*. Deprived of any integrating principle, the underground man sees experience as chaotic and consciousness itself as nothing more than a disease. Postmodern art and literature are beset with such disintegrations and fragmentations. Contemporary literary theory presumes the experience of "deconstruction," and modern experience confirms the dissolution.

As a compiler of an archive collecting the narratives of Vietnam veterans and as one who himself shares their experience, I have dug into thousands of broken, isolated but vivid impressions resulting from the chaos of war. The memories are like the carnage of war itself — seared faces, scattered and bloody pieces of a once-whole body, a boot heavy with the severed foot yet inside. When the center gives, the structure collapses. Meaning implodes when things lose their connections, when objects no longer have any relation to other objects nearby.

Fundamentalism, working independently of any real Christian tradition, has valiantly struggled to restore the center in the immutability of the "literal" text. No matter what errors I think these neomodernists have fallen victim to, I cannot fault them for sheer courage of the will. The problem lies not only in their neglect of the historical "community of interpreters" but also in their denial of the world in which they live. If there is to be meaning in the world, then things must have meaning — *things*, concrete, material, sense-bound things. We cannot read scripture "outside culture" — we must make meaning of it as we make meaning of anything else. We must, to overcome the fragmentation of modernity, reconnect the text to the concrete materiality of sense experience. Liturgy dissolves the isolation and autonomy of objects and integrates them once more into the wholeness of an integral Christian experience.

John Meyendorff, a scholar and theologian of the Orthodox Church, has written that the liturgical "blessing" of an object releases it from the autonomy of the secular vision and restores it once more to the integration of a Christian world view. In liturgy, the object is inescapable. Christians discover Christ's body in the softness of bread and Christ's blood in the sour, sweet tang of the wine. They hear Christ celebrated in song, feel Christ in the embrace of another. The sacramentality of liturgy allows the wholeness of God's being to penetrate the whole of creation. Liturgy thus "mends" creation and with great deliberation places the pieces back together again. Liturgy, as we see in Russia or in the vitality of the liturgical revival in the Orthodox Church in Finland, can heal the sores of modernity. A liturgical vision sends members of the Orthodox Lay Academy in Finland plunging into the woods to collect medicinal herbs or tramping in knee boots through a course in organic gardening. Liturgy helps us to knit back together the raveled threads of creation.

Liberation from tyrannies

Finally, liturgy not only gives us a glimpse of the freshness and wholeness of things but also enables us to overthrow tyrannies, to eliminate those dimensions of our lives that limit and distort. "We are fools for Christ's sake" (1 Cor 4:20). The Russian Orthodox Church in particular has celebrated such "fools for the sake of Christ." The crazed, beautiful domes of St. Basil's on Red Square, in their riot of color and form, celebrate just such a saint. The holy fool refuses to accept the structures by which the world makes judgments. The holy fool reminds God's people that the structures by which the princes of this world prevail are less than "transitory" — they but show, in their narrowness and cramped cherishing of worldly power, what God will never be. The fool mocks the standard by which the cross is seen as "tragic," for the gospel is the very antithesis of tragedy.

Intellectual tyrants and worldly powers take themselves very seriously indeed.

The fundamentalists and literalists tend to echo that seriousness and to envision the dominion of God as expressed within those very structures of worldly power. The gospel mocks that seriousness. Liturgical celebration of the gospel brings Christians together in community, where, in structures of "dialogue," they re-create the terms by which they interpret this world. In liturgy there is a majestic celebration of a great alternative, the "otherness" of God. In liturgy the Christian overthrows the kingdom of this world and celebrates the kingdom of the Trinity. This is the social and religious structure within which the poor are enriched, the meek vindicated, the oppressed made into monarchs. Liturgy is a subversion of the structures of tyranny. It demands that we see this flawed and blasted world as renewed in Christ, that we sinners stand as redeemed. Liturgy does not announce, in monologue, the good news. Liturgy dialogically "celebrates"; it enacts the plan of God.

Liturgy, then, if it possesses capacities so great, should not lull those Christians who love it into so profound a quietism. The fundamentalist vision, like atraditional visions in the past, suffers a disturbing success. Yet in its profound individualism, and in its flesh-denying and unincarnational literalism, it is a part of the very problem that afflicts Christians in modernity. Liturgical Christians must demonstrate the courage of their tradition, like their forebears in the faith, and speak in condemnation of this — one must not hesitate to use the word when it is aptly placed — heresy. This literalist ideology, and the unfleshed, televised abstraction within which it flourishes, is a sometimes courageous, sometimes reprehensible, assertion of essentially false principles.

Yet coupled with the condemnation must also be a confidence in our own vision. Liturgy grounds us in each other, and there must be a revival of those principles of communal trust whereby we can be reasonably assured that the liturgy of one week will not fall victim to the fashion of the next. Liturgy is grounded in the senses, and liturgical Christians can confidently use liturgy as an expression of Christian materiality: "high" liturgy can reach very deep down, in fact, to engage the whole body in worship. And finally, liturgy possesses a controlled anarchy. It cannot freeze itself into cold constructs of signification: like the holy fool, it must in a grand irony challenge the structures of this world in order to renew it.

Charged with divinity

"Symbol" is not a nice word sometimes. It can imply that a liturgical, sacramental act is only a suggestion of something else. A "symbol" can, in fact, provide an indictment of materiality if it is interpreted to mean that materiality is not enough. Liturgy plunges us into the senses; it connects us with the immediacy of the object. Bread and wine do not "symbolize" the body of Christ; water does not "stand for" our rebirth; the richness of perfumed oil is not an "emblem" of our life in the Holy Spirit. Through these accessible avenues of sense experience, God effects the divine mysteries.

The events that transpire are so great, so incomprehensible in their significance, yet they are expressed through the material channels available to us. As the incarnation poured God forth into materiality, so the sacraments bathe us in divinity. The text, quite simply, is not enough.

The mind of modern rationalism, even while it denies transcendence and asserts the primacy of materialism, shrinks from the body. Lenin in his tomb is more certainly a "symbol," an emblem of something that waxened flesh is not, than any Christian sacrament. And even sex in our consumerized society becomes curiously defleshed, insufficient in itself and but a means to attain some yet higher state of being. It is as if the skull-encased mind, in touching the flesh, feels the cold firmness of death that will soon reside there. Liturgy, seated in the body that celebrates its own five senses, embraces the flesh even as it proclaims its resurrection. The world, in the liturgical vision, is charged with a significance that can reflect and point to the gospel. And the senses, which the modern mind indulges and yet so profoundly mistrusts, can be truly and certainly enjoyed. For in liturgy we take part in the feast. In liturgy we find the senses redeemed.

32

Entering into the Message

PAUL W. F. HARMS

There is, perhaps, no greater hardship at present inflicted on people in civilized and free countries than the necessity of listening to sermons. No one but a preacher has, in these realms, the power of compelling an audience to sit silent, and be tormented. No one but a preacher can revel in platitudes, truisms, and untruisms, and yet receive, as an undisputed privilege, the same respectful demeanor as though words of impassioned eloquence, or persuasive logic fell from the lips....

[The preacher] makes God's service distasteful. We are not forced into church! No: but we desire more than that. *We desire not to be forced to stay away.* We desire, nay, we are resolute, to enjoy the comfort of public worship; but we desire also that we may do so without an amount of tedium which ordinary human nature cannot endure with patience; that we may be able to leave the house of God, without that anxious longing for escape, which is the common consequence of common sermons.[1]

So writes Anthony Trollope more than a century ago in *Barchester Towers*. He states the case for the opposition with the eloquence that the opposition finds wanting in sermons. Whoever would speak otherwise dare not forget Trollope's statement and the thousand others like it, or the opposition of the opposition will harden even more.

A contemporary author is no less harsh and no less accurate than Trollope: "The gravest handicap of much pulpit preaching is that it doesn't matter. It does not concern primary damage, it is no life-and-death enterprise."[2]

Dorothy L. Sayers, a Christian author and theologian, put it unflinchingly:

Not Herod, not Caiaphas, not Pilate, not Judas ever contrived to fasten upon Jesus Christ the reproach of insipidity; that final indignity was left for pious hands to inflict. To make of His story something that could neither startle, nor shock, nor terrify, nor excite, nor inspire a living soul is to crucify the Son of God afresh and put Him to an open shame.... Let me tell you, you Christian people, an honest writer would be ashamed to treat a nursery tale as you have treated the greatest drama of history.[3]

From *Liturgy: The Art of Celebration* 8, no. 3.

The second and third critics, if not the first, were people committed to the Christian enterprise who spent much of their energy relating the Christian story. Their criticisms will not admit of hasty dismissal.

The wellsprings

What then are the wellsprings of preaching? Well, what are the wellsprings of the liturgy? Adoration — the first and always the first response of the creature to the creator. "Worship is the acknowledgment of transcendence: that is to say, of a reality independent of the worshiper, which is always more or less colored by mystery, and which is there first.[4] Worship is the response of the creature also to the re-creator of the re-creation as it was forged in the atomic-energy intensity of the cosmic crucifixion. Worship and liturgy — and preaching, as an integral part of worship and liturgy — have their wellsprings here. So also their midpoint. So also their end point.

Whatever else preaching is, it is an act of awe and adoration before the mystery that is the cross and resurrection of Jesus Christ. The response to the cross is the preaching of the cross. Paul speaks of the foolishness of preaching Jesus Christ, "the one who was crucified." "This Jesus whom you crucified, God raised from the dead," says Peter. And Luke writes:

> Then [Jesus] told them, "This is what I meant when I said, while I was still with you, that everything written about me in the law of Moses, in the prophets and in the psalms had to be fulfilled." He then opened their minds to understand the scriptures, and he said to them, "So you see how it is written that the Christ would suffer and on the third day rise from the dead, and that, in his name, repentance for the forgiveness of sins would be preached to all the nations, beginning at Jerusalem. You are witnesses to this" (Luke 24:44–48).

This story constitutes the power of God for the restoration of all things, and it is the gospel of which Paul is not ashamed. Alongside this story Paul was determined to know nothing else.

Joseph Sittler chose this language:

> By that story, I simply mean what our ancestors called "The drama of divine re-demption." The great story begins with the affirmation of faith that the whole cosmos in all its structures and processes, including man, is of divine origin. It is not just nature; it is creation.... This story comes to its tragic apex in the destruction, the crucifixion, of God's action. And that which is a tragic moment is also the most joyful proclamation in the Gospel because if God does not enter into our abyss, if God does not become our isolation and our desolation, that God is not God enough for human life, because human life is characterized by abysmal despairs, isolations and desolations, loneliness, failures and lack of honor.... It's a story that proclaims both its profundity and its truth by its sheer congruity with the contours of actual human life.[5]

Does the well spring?

"But, of course!" you may say. I am not now speaking, however, of believing with Sittler the story of divine redemption; I am speaking of preaching that story when the faithful gather to worship. At a eucharist marking the twentieth annual and final gathering of a pastors' conference, the bishop did not preach the gospel. At the funeral of a prominent Christian, his pastor of some twenty-five years did not preach the gospel. Nor did I hear the gospel preached on World Communion Sunday or on Christmas Eve or on New Year's Day or on Transfiguration Sunday or at a midweek Lenten service. And if not on these special days, what becomes of the gospel on the Twenty-Third Sunday after Pentecost?

If Sittler's statement of the gospel is accurate, who would not want to preach it on every occasion, especially Sunday after Sunday when the faithful gather for worship? Why should a preacher want to avoid preaching this message that addresses "all sorts and conditions of people" by its "sheer congruity with the contours of actual human life"? What else is there with which to serve the people?

"The greatest disservice that the church does for itself and for the world," wrote Emil Brunner, "is to withhold the gospel." I would question whether pulpit activity that does not preach the gospel can even be called preaching by any careful definition of that word.

Preaching is rooted in the preacher's response to the gospel of the crucified and risen Christ, the creator and re-creator of all things (Colossians 1). As preaching goes about its work, it proclaims the one who called it into being. It is an eternal dance.

The awe and wonder inspired by the crucifixion and resurrection is the stimulus that moves the preacher to preach.

The nature of this good news is to be forever bursting the boundaries of the self. The one who adores invites others to adore. In fact, adoration is not complete until it shares the object of its adoration, until all creation adores. That is why the liturgy says, "Therefore with angels and archangels and all the company of heaven we laud and magnify thy glorious name." Nothing and no one is to be left out of the "Holy! Holy! Holy!" that reverberates throughout the world. This worship, praise and adoration of the one "through whom all things were made" shapes preaching and makes it inviting and seductive.

When this sense of wonder is lost or diminished, the preacher and the congregation drift "into the shoals of nonchalance." Ennui and malaise transform preaching into the delivery of sermons. No longer is it a sharing of the organic life of God. Preaching ceases to be a life-and-death matter and so is conveyed in less than a life-and-death manner. Preaching then becomes ritualistic, not life-giving. Information usurps transformation. Words take the place of oxygen. A cardiac lecture replaces heart-transplant surgery. Pulpit activity may continue to have sermonic characteristics, except for one essential quality: significant life. And the sermon exists to transmit the very life of God.

The dominical wellspring

As the Word made flesh transmitted the very life of God by being responsive and responsible to the One who sent him, so preachers are called to be responsive to that living, lively "Word made flesh." To embody, to incarnate, to body forth "an epiphany, an almost miraculous manifestation of the inner core of life at a specific moment,"[6] is the calling and the task. The whole body, the whole person, must be responsive to the gospel being preached. The hearer must be able to sense, see, touch, taste, feel the preacher's responsiveness to the sermon. It is not enough for the preacher to state (as may well be the case) that s/he believes in the heart what the mouth says. While sincerity is a sine qua non, it no more gives authority to preach than it does to perform heart-bypass surgery. Too often inadequate preaching is excused on the basis of "good content" or the preacher's sincerity.

There is dominical precedent. "Who though being in the form of God did not insist on exploiting the prerogatives of being God's equal, but emptied himself, and took upon himself the form of a servant." "Except a grain of wheat fall into the ground and die, it will remain alone." "Who though he was rich, yet for our sakes he became poor so that we through his poverty might be made rich." "The one who loses life shall save it, and the one who seeks to save life will lose it." Through his death Christ created life. What is reliable in our faith is also reliable in our preaching of that faith. As the preacher loses the self in embodying the preaching, the gospel achieves its genuine goal.

When the focus is taken off the preacher — "It is not ourselves that we proclaim" — then the Christ whom the preacher came to proclaim is in fact proclaimed. When the focus is on the one who said, "Let light shine in the darkness" and when that one now shines in our hearts with the light of God's glory, then the preacher is using the gospel to serve others.

When the Word came, he did not come as a disembodied voice. The Word came enfleshed. The flesh and the Word were fully congruent and coalescent. The flesh told us who the Word was, how the Word felt, how the Word reacted, what the Word meant to do, how disappointed the Word was, how exhilarated the Word was. So congruent and coalescent were the Word and the flesh "that we beheld the very glory of God full of grace and truth." Grace and truth came to their full flower in the crucifixion and resurrection. Separate the words spoken from the flesh through which they were spoken and see how the meanings change! Ripped flesh, crowned with thorns, now suspended between heaven and earth by nails in hands and feet, flesh nailed and dying, is the posture.

Out of that tortured flesh comes the Word. We listen, if we can bring ourselves to listen at all. Then, when we hear, "Forgive them for they know not what they do," we hear, see and feel through the flesh of that man on the cross,

suffocating his way to death. Whenever we speak forgiveness without the crucifixion connection, grace becomes a principle, not an event made possible only
by the full trinitarian energies. "For without the shedding of blood, there is no
forgiveness of sins."

As a communicating agent, as a preacher and teacher, Christ was charged
with many offenses but never with a discrepancy between words and actions or
between word and flesh. For him word and flesh were all of a piece. And it
must be the same with us. With due regard for our fallibility, the words and
the flesh of the preacher must be coalescent and congruent so that the hearers
may now, as the hearers did then, "behold the glory of God in the face of this
Jesus Christ."

The dry well

This total involvement of the preacher in the gospel, though evident to the
hearer, is hard to come by. In many mainline churches, at least, there is a culture
or tradition that not only fails to practice full responsiveness to the sermon but
even cites biblical and other sources to oppose such responsiveness. "It is the task
of the preacher to get out of the way of the message," the argument runs.

And that is true, but the usual manner of doing so is false. A preacher gets
out of the way of the message by fully entering into it, by losing the self in the
message, by stretching out with full might to grasp the fullness of that which
cannot ever be fully grasped.

What hinders this coalescence of words (Word) and flesh in the contemporary preacher? Hans-Reudi Weber says that we are suffering from the flip
side of the Gutenberg Galaxy. The printed, frozen word has impinged its arctic
rigidity on the liveliness that is the spoken word. One printed page, even in the
Bible, is much like any other. Ruth, 2 Chronicles, Revelation, Esther and Jude
all look alike on the printed page. When read aloud, they sound much alike.
The three-year lectionary is read much like the one-year lectionary. The sounds,
postures and gestures of the readers are the same, though the readings are as
varied as "Ten Little Indians" and Johann Sebastian Bach's *Mass in B Minor.*
Print homogenizes what voice and body would particularize.

Print is not the only villain. In oral communication 93 percent of the communication is nonlinguistic.[7] That is not to say that the 7 percent that is verbal
is unimportant or to be neglected. The truth is that most preachers give that 93
percent very little attention. Many a homiletics text gives the nonlinguistic little
more than the back of its hand. Often a textbook on preaching will simply say
that the sermon should be lively and energetic, and then offer a few suggestions
on how to be faithful to this 93 percent of the sermon. As a result, many a
well-intentioned preacher does not know that the 93 percent of each sermon is
unintentionally neglected, the 93 percent that gives the 7 percent meaning for
the hearer.

A fresh well

The art of theater concentrates fiercely on having a text mean for the hearer and viewer what its author and director want it to mean. The church, above other organizations, claims to make meaning for time and eternity. Yet the church, whose goal through the centuries has been to communicate with disciplined care, neglects the resources of a discipline of more than a thousand-years' standing.

What is the communicating artist's concentrated focus? The nonlinguistic — sights, sounds and gestures. What determines the particular orchestration of the sights, sounds and gestures? (Here is where the words come in.) The text. How does this sermonic text feel when it speaks? What is the felt-sensing of this text? What is the truth behind the words? What kind of speaking does this text invite? And then, once the felt-sensing is determined, how may the preacher embody the sights, sounds, gestures that are the sermon, so that it will achieve its intended meaning for the hearer at each particular moment?

No less than a musical score, the sermonic score calls for a broad range of nonlinguistic responses. Fortunately, each preacher has a range of responses utilizing voice, vision and gesture that is orchestral in its breadth. To be sure, preachers all too seldom utilize their rich resources. "One estimate is that the human ear normally discriminates some ten thousand qualities of the human voice.[8] Pitch, volume, timbre, pace, pause, timing and intensity in their infinite, intricate, varied interplay make it possible for the sermonic text to have its intended meaning for the hearer. Most sermons would show a marked improvement if only their preachers responded with silence when their texts asked for silence, rather than with hurry and scurry until words have been exhausted.

"Students of gesture have estimated that there are at least seven hundred thousand different symbolic physical manifestations (gestures) that are capable of conveying fairly precise meanings."[9] Ray L. Birdwhistell tells us in fascinating detail of the sounds, gestures, postures and expressions by which the human body seeks to encompass the communicative acts that constitute life. He tells us, for example, that there are some 250,000 different expressions of which the human face alone is capable.[10] If that is true, then what hinders a preacher from so responding to the life-and-death matter that is preaching the gospel? If the sight that the hearer sees, as preaching progresses, is immobility rather than action, random activity rather than concentrated focus, what will be heard is what is seen — dullness rather than life. Homogenization of sounds, immobility of action, translate into death rather than invigorating, abundant life, the fullness of joy that Christ promised to give.

At Westminster Abbey and St. Paul's Cathedral, I repeatedly saw musicians and choirs faithfully embodying their texts, the adults as well as the children. They had come to praise. Not only their words but their voices and their bodies spoke awe for all to see and experience. In contrast the preachers were markedly unresponsive to their sermonic texts. The sermons could not mean what they were meant to mean because they were not appropriately embodied.

If the musicians and the choirs had so responded, they would soon have been dismissed.

It may sound almost idiotic to say so, but preaching includes speaking. Preaching is speaking. Preaching is oral, not written. When preaching is not oral, the sense of immediacy is lost. When preaching is not oral, it impairs visual contact with the hearer. When preaching is not oral, it impairs a sense of engagement with the hearer. When preaching is not oral, the event of divine intervention becomes, at best, a report. The vitality we exhibit in an everyday, spirited conversation we abandon in preaching. That which makes speaking what it is — the full engagement of the total resources of the person: mental, emotional, physical, psychological, intellectual — is largely and freely and tragically abandoned in speaking the word of life.

"To interest is the first duty of art," writes C. S. Lewis, "no other excellencies can even begin to compensate for failure in this, and very serious faults will be covered as if by charity."[11] People will forgive everything except dullness. The preacher's vivid realization of an idea at the moment of utterance lets the hearer know that the preacher, at least, is interested. Even if the preacher's persuasion persuades no one, all will be persuaded of the preacher's persuasion. The gospel demands that preaching have a quality of first-timeness, a quality the listener is looking for. The caring preacher seeks to give the sermon that quality, for the preacher, too, is listening to the preaching. In preaching the preacher also asks, "If this were my last sermon, as it may well prove to be, what would I preach?" Preaching, then, also has the quality of last-timeness, the quality of earnestness for the sake of the gospel and the sake of the listener.

Preaching is adoration of the creator, who created the preacher and the whole cosmos. Preaching is adoration of the re-creator, who gave the preacher new birth, molded by the spirit. Preaching invites all others to adore that same creator and re-creator. In preaching, the preacher seeks to embody faithfully the text of the liturgy, the scripture, the prayers, the day, the eucharist, his or her own reflections on the gospel, the listener, the world, the Word made flesh (who is Lord over church and world) and the text of the sermon created by these texts.

Notes

1. Anthony Trollope, *Barchester Towers* (Cleveland: Fine Editions Press, 1952), 252, 426.

2. Richard R. Caemmerer, *Preaching for the Church* (St. Louis: Concordia Publishing House, 1959), 270.

3. Paul Scherer, *For We Have This Treasure* (New York: Harper & Brothers, 1943), 134.

4. Evelyn Underhill, *Worship* (New York: Harper & Brothers, 1957), 3.

5. Joseph Sittler, "Conversation with Sittler," *Partners* 1, no. 3 (June 1979): 8.

6. Wallace A. Bacon, *The Art of Interpretation*, 3rd ed. (New York: Holt, Rinehart & Winston, 1979), 51.

7. Haig A. Bosmajian, *The Rhetoric of Non-Verbal Communication* (Glenview, Ill.: Scott Foresman, 1971), 4.

8. Giles Wilkenson Gray and Claude Metton Wise, *The Basis of Speech,* 3rd ed. (New York: Harper & Row, 1959), 12.

9. Robert T. Oliver, Harold P. Zelko and Paul D. Holtzman, *Communicative Speaking and Listening,* 4th ed. (New York: Holt, Rinehart & Winston, 1968), 180.

10. Ray L. Birdwhistell, *Kinesics & Context: Essays on Body Motion Communication* (Philadelphia: University of Pennsylvania Press, 1970).

11. C. S. Lewis, *They Asked for Paper* (London: Geoffrey Bless, 1962), 69.

33

What Is Liturgical Preaching?

Gerard S. Sloyan

Liturgical preaching is preaching that is done in the worship of the church, called by some communions but not by others the liturgy. But all divine service has a worshipful character. Therefore all preaching, from the fact that it is preaching, is liturgical. Or can be.

Preaching is liturgical if it has an intimate part in the worshipful character of the act. Liturgy is, by definition, a "people's act," a deed of the assembly. If those gathered are truly active in this prayer of praise, the word of God expounded within it will be their activity. If every word and movement of the ministers of worship invites them to a passive response, they will be an audience of consumers when the word is spoken.

Whatever is imposed on the hearing and the sight of people cannot be worship in spirit and in truth. Liturgy, which must be so defined, is not a presentation submitted for audience critique. It engages people, inviting them to criticize themselves.

Preaching is part of the total engagement. Preaching that does not engage the hearer is a word that comes down from heaven like the snow and rain of Isaiah 55 and returns fruitless to its source.

The word that is reflected on and explained is the word of God, not a human word. Yet not every word that God speaks in the church and in the larger world is a word of the Bible. It would be presumptuous to confine divine communication to this one source, inspired though it be. All that is found in these books of scripture, however, is looked on in faith as a word of God. All else that God says to a believing people is somehow an extension or exposition of what is uttered there.

The entire service of churches that use liturgical formularies is biblical. Occasionally, as in the baroque period, humanist scholars incorporated touches of classical learning into prayer forms like the hymns of the day hours. Two hundred years after the Reformation some of its heirs departed from biblical

From *Liturgy: Preaching the Word* 8, no. 2.

patterns and began to speak the language of popular wisdom in prayers and sermons.

Today, when liturgical teams or engaged couples "write their own liturgies," they often produce prayers that have the merit of earnestness, and even beauty, but are not liturgies. Many do not know the Bible well enough to produce even the briefest liturgical text. God only knows how many prayers have gone straight to the heavenly throne from people who possessed minimal familiarity with the Bible; but that is another question, being God's business and the business of people who pray. When the church prays publicly it always — repeat, always — prays in the spirit of the Bible, most often in the adapted words of the Bible.

Biblical preaching

Is liturgical preaching, then, "Biblespeak"? There are deep questions here, and the various churches of Christendom have resolved them differently. There are, in brief, various ways to preach biblically. Christian communions need to tread gently in declaring their way the sole acceptable way or even the best way. The Armenian Church, for example, both the apostolic and the catholic, has its traditional way of preaching the Bible. So do the black churches of North America. Developed over centuries, these two general ways are quite different from each other, but both preserve the word of the Lord as a biblical word.

To take the first example (and the churches of the east coming after Chalcedon are in this matter like Armenia), Orthodoxy and the Catholic East preach the Bible as the church preached it. This mode is continuous with the liturgy that is its setting. Patristic homilies comment on the text of the Bible and the texts of the many feasts and prayers as if they make up a seamless garment. Modernity does not enter in, though the conduct of Christians in any age is an ever-present subject of preaching. This pulpit discourse is carried on as if heaven were totally present to earth and earth to heaven.

In churches of the Christian east on this continent, the preaching that is faithful to the tradition, as most is, resembles patristic preaching, when it is not that preaching itself. This is liturgical preaching because it is thoroughly biblical, both as to quoted text and constant allusion, and is always an intimate part of the worship at hand.

The gifted preacher in a predominantly black church knows the text of the Bible well but in another pattern of usage. Modes of oral discourse apart (though manner and matter are all but inseparable), these preachers and their hearers have hundreds if not thousands of biblical verses committed to memory. Exact recall is not of great consequence here, nor was it in the early church. Knowing the spirit of a text is what counts. The result is a juxtaposition of texts, sometimes in dizzying speed and sequence. Leviticus may be followed by Philippians, then Mark, Isaiah and Daniel. Is it a hodgepodge? For the gifted preacher it is far from that: it is a mosaic. Often the relation between successive texts will be a word or a phrase in one that triggers the same or a similar one in the next.

The modern, biblically trained mind is likely to ask, What of the context? Context is where the preacher places the texts. Good preachers are masters of that art. They are in complete control. If any of them should contrive a dissonance among texts, their hearers, even the nonliterate, will pick it up immediately. The congregation knows when the word is being preached with or without power. The mosaic technique at its best employs shadings. Light blue fuses with deeper blue into dark blue. There is never a patchwork in which square is set side by side with squares of another hue. This style of preaching has the backing of antiquity. It is the way the Bible was employed in the patristic era, though the latter adjective is often unfamiliar to the preachers and people who do it best.

There is another type of biblical preaching found in predominantly white churches of evangelical conviction. It is a tissue of biblical texts, often memorized, all quoted exactly as the Authorized or American Standard Version gives them. They are frequently marshaled to prove the truth of the gospel of faith in the cross, "that every mouth may be stopped, and all the world may become guilty before God" (Rom 3:19*b*). This is biblical preaching; it may or may not be liturgical preaching.

There are two reasons why the latter can be the case. One is that this preaching has a certain amnesic quality, a forgetfulness of all that the church has been and done since the faith was first delivered to the saints, as it is thought, in inspired writings. While the church has always proclaimed its scriptures publicly once it received them, it has never confined its activity in the assembly to proclaiming its scriptures. That proclamation resulted in a living body that has always acted out its biblical faith in symbol. Liturgical preaching, therefore, happens in those churches where whole persons respond corporately to the word proclaimed and do something worshipful more than assent in mind in a spirit of faith.

The act of preaching

Liturgy is deed, liturgy is act. It is acceptance of a message heard, to be sure, but it is more than that. What constitutes the "more" is an important question. Inspirited song? Yes, of course. Bodily movement? That too. Rite, stylized behavior, bespeaking an encounter with the living God? That is of the essence. It can be the celebration of what are called sacraments in some churches and ordinances in others. It may be the observance of marriage in Christ or the commitment of a dead Christian to the earth, the soul commended to God until it rejoins the body on the last day. Processions and chanted litanies, dancing and music making, going vested in bright costumes — all are liturgical behavior.

In brief, liturgy is a living presentation of the received word of God as worship, its translation into deed. Liturgical preaching is the biblical preaching that fits into that matrix. It may *be* that matrix. Any other preaching is a lecture on a sacred theme set in a prayer meeting with choral accompaniment. Not at all a bad thing but not liturgical preaching.

In the Roman Catholic communion some forty to sixty years ago, many persons charged with preaching the word were beginning to recover their biblical and patristic heritage. They tried to make it enliven the sacramental heritage they had never lost. Bible readings had always been part of these sacramental rites. The problem was not that Bible passages were read in Latin before they were read in English; the problem went deeper.

The Bible was being preached in a catechetical spirit, which, translated, means in the spirit of dogmatic (or systematic) and moral (or ethical) theology. In early efforts to preach liturgically, that is, biblically, in the oldest tradition, homilies (the patristic term, "homily," was already in use at the time) were verbal tapestries. They were woven from the text of the entrance song, perhaps the psalm verse recited at the preparation of the gifts, and the verse sung or said after communion. The text of the unchanging canon (or eucharistic prayer) and phrases from the *oratio, secreta* and *postcommunio* were also interwoven.

To change the figure of speech, all these served as minor spotlights trained on the centerpiece, the axis of epistle and gospel. It is hard to convey how exhilarating this style of preaching was to congregations overly familiar with the warmhearted pieties of friars, canons and clerks regular which had prevailed in the parish pulpit since well before Trent. People who belonged to parishes staffed by Benedictine monks or clergy influenced by monks got a rude shock as they left those sheltering arms for a larger world. They had been raised on liturgical preaching, often not knowing the term, and learned with sadness that there was something else abroad that went by the name of preaching.

Superior to the general run of preaching as this pastiche of texts from the mass and divine office was, it proved most effective with that 10 percent of worshipers who followed the service with a missal in hand. These were the favored ones. They were generally the educated, though as the council came on, missal use was spreading to the devout of every class. Still, the preaching described here was a kind of tour de force. The Bible texts were not so much penetrated as juxtaposed or concatenated. They all had a place in a rite that had grown like a wild weed from the time of Charlemagne onward. The texts were carefully selected and then laid end to end by those who preached "liturgically." It was a marvel but a limited marvel.

A second aspect of liturgical preaching in that not-too-distant age was the laying bare of how things had once been in the worship of the west and how they had arrived at their present form. The eucharistic rite itself was explained, the "mass of the presanctified" (the Good Friday service at which only the presider communicated), the baptismal rite, the rite of last anointing *(extrema unctio)*. Provided they were not an unvarnished repetition of Adrian Fortescue or Edmund Bishop, such lessons in liturgical history were immensely valuable to the congregations. Better favored were the people whose preachers possessed the volumes of Gueranger or Parsch, or popularizations thereof. It was history.

It was interesting history. But a further step had to be taken to make it serve the word of God. Some preachers knew how to take the step, and some did not. But, oh, the difference it made in those years to be exposed to even a little of this rich fare: an account of where the church had been and — despite a vast overlay of allegorical symbolisms and an obscure tongue — still was. The family history of a centuries-old worshiping communion was intensely interesting to many of its members.

Continuity with the biblical community

Liturgical preaching takes place within a rite. It is itself a ritual act. The various symbolic steps in the rite should be self-explanatory. Brief directions for participation — to be given by someone other than the presider — may be needed occasionally but not explanations. The ritual deed should be comprehensible immediately on being performed. And the preached word that is an extension of the word of God is the informing spirit of that deed.

How does the preached word act as that soul or spirit? Liturgical preaching is an act carried on from within the Bible, that is, in a worshiping community that sees itself as contemporaneous with everything reported there in the life of Israel and the apostolic church. The life of this assembly and the lives of those long-dead believers is the same life, for this is the same people.

An awareness of this dimension on the part of preachers speaking in a worship context will be conveyed only if they are possessed of this understanding. What this comes to is not unrelenting archaic speech: the use of a Bible translation done many years ago. Neither is it a constant storytelling: all the adventures of the patriarchs, prophets and apostles reiterated. It is a matter of situating both homilist and hearers in a faith life that is not timeless but set in time, the time called now.

Adam and Eve, Cain and Abel become the worshipers' contemporaries. Abraham, that noble old desert sheik, is a familiar figure to them. David's weakness and Solomon's folly, Isaiah's boldness and Jeremiah's heroism, Simon Peter's complexity and Nathaniel's simplicity are as second nature to liturgical preachers. They do not, of course, take a biblical narrative and spin it out for twenty minutes, trying to make it "relevant." Rather, they make deft reference to this and that statement, scene or story from the sacred page, supplying both text and context in swift strokes. An hour may be needed to craft one paragraph of that kind of biblical preaching. The time must be taken for the words to have their full impact; it is well worth the while.

Contemporary congregations, it may be objected, do not know the Bible. That is quite true; they must learn it from their preachers. Inundating hearers with quotations is next to useless, for they soon realize either that the full weight of biblical authority is being lowered onto their shoulders or that the homilist, in order to win a hearing, is constantly saying, "As you may remember from the Bible," when in fact they remember very little. The burden is rendered even heavier. How then can worshipers be made to feel at home in this immense body of literature they almost never encounter outside the worship situation?

They can learn it from the homilist who opens the scriptures to them regularly. That requires considerably more of preachers than exhortations to Christian living based on the Sunday or weekday readings. It means getting inside those readings. As the pericopes proposed find a place within their biblical books, their period in Israel's history or their decade in primitive Christian history, so they must be laid bare.

A free-floating prophetic charge or a disciplinary proposal from, let's say, a Deutero-Pauline epistle is next to useless. Whatever the text, it cries out for context. What made Zephaniah indulge in this outcry which, admittedly, will only be encountered publicly once in three years? What is the perspective of Lukan thought that makes Luke tell a parable of Jesus differently from Mark? What is there in a Pauline letter that survives the ages while some of the polemic that immediately engaged him can be profitably disregarded?

No little ingenuity and a lot of hard study are required to place the proclaimed biblical words in the setting that first elicited them. If the attempt is not made regularly, the words become so many oracular utterances that do not bite into consciousness. How can contemporaries be expected to take seriously a word that applies to them if no effort is made to show how it affected those to whom it was first addressed? The insistence that this is "the word of the Lord" will not do. People need to know why a particular passage is being read and expounded in their hearing now. Nothing does this quite so well as showing the sense these texts made to their first hearers.

The saving grace in all this is that the Bible, the very spine of liturgical preaching, is interested in every aspect of human life. If it were only concerned with something called religion, or even faith, it could be meaningless to modern ears. The scriptures of Jews and Christians, mercifully, are books about family life and neighborhoods, economics and politics, the noblest self-effacement and the meanest self-promotion. In a word, they touch on every mood and tense of the human psyche, corporate and individual.

Throughout these books, in their concern with sin and saintliness, there runs the thread of God's pursuit of us humans. Our God is forever the hound of heaven sniffing out an elusive prey. Since the frightened quarry is made up of both preachers and preached to, it is a comfort to all to be able to follow the chase as if it were happening to others. That psychic distance is helpful. And then the truth dawns. Through that cloud of unpronounceable names and frequently unmemorable events, it is ourselves the Deuteronomist or the chronicler is getting at. The evangelists do not much care if the event happened to Levi or Zacchaeus or Matthew. They are after larger game than the often hazy figures who populate the Gospels. They wish to reach their own contemporaries and through them all of us.

Anecdotes calculated to attract and hold attention have their place in liturgical preaching. But preaching that employs them is never an alternation between the ancient and the modern, the newly introduced and the familiar. Everything in a good homily is contemporary for the worshiper, whether it is a tale out of the ninth century B.C.E. or a reference to a television commercial. The rubric for all biblical preaching will always be, "This is your life." Is its purpose, then, to recommend a course of action to hearers, something they can "take away with them" and apply at the appropriate time? For the long term, that is an admirable goal, but it could characterize much effective preaching that is not liturgical.

Liturgical preaching strives to convince hearers of their solidarity in faith — or tragically, unfaith — with the people of the Bible. It does so in order to move them to action within the framework of this service of worship. Choices in the spirit of the gospel may come later, but for now, the word is spoken as part of an immediate deed.

If the eucharist is the setting, the assembly must be invited to participate in the mystery of redemption in the symbol in which they are engaged at that moment. If infants or adults are to be baptized at the conclusion of this homily, or a couple joined for life, or servants of the gospel sent on mission, or a Christian buried, if Mary is to be crowned as queen of heaven, or the safety of migrant workers implored in a bitter strike or, yes, an ambulance dedicated, the word must lead to the act. For liturgy is act. It is a state of mind and heart called faith, acted out with the whole body in a human company, seeking a grace effect in symbol. This often happens in the midst of a grimy and not especially "religious" life. Strike that. It *is* life — in a perfect continuum with anything else deserving of that name.

34

David's Song in Our Land

DON E. SALIERS

Rediscovery of the psalms as central to the prayer of the gathered assembly is one of the most fascinating and notable features of the liturgical renewal in our time. The revival of interest in musical settings and the exploration of varieties of styles of psalm singing is nothing less than a renaissance, a rebirth of language and song within and among the Christian churches. Where there is a liturgy workshop, there is necessarily a session for cantors and choirs and people singing the psalms.

This revolution in psalmody and psalm singing has affected nearly every major Christian church tradition in this country during the past decade. Spurred on most notably by the liturgical reforms of the Second Vatican Council, the phenomenon is also part of our culture's search for a more adequate liturgical expression of biblical faith. The work of Joseph Gelineau, the contributions of various monastic communities such as the Benedictines of St. Meinrad's, the restoration of the sung daily prayer emerging from the work at Notre Dame, the simple but sturdy psalm tones and pointed texts in the *Lutheran Book of Worship*, the pilot project of ICEL, the setting of versified psalms from the older Scottish and Genevan Psalters to American hymn tunes, and the individual work of many talented younger composers — all of these are the surfacing of enormous energy born out of the search for a renewed and renewing Christian liturgy.

Such creativity and ferment require both theological and pastoral assessment and practical explanation. How is the language of the psalms the language of the human heart? How does the singing of psalms provide a living way of hearing and responding to God's word? What does this rebirth mean for the formation of faith and the responsibilities of pastors, musicians and other liturgical ministers? These and other questions that emerge from pastoral experience form the background of these reflections.

From *Liturgy: With Lyre and Harp* 3, no. 3

A language of the heart

We begin with the basics. The psalms are songs, prayers meant for singing in the context of communal worship. Their language is the language of human experience at full stretch before God. Sometimes the psalms open doxology to the rhythm of ecstasy; sometimes they open yearning and grief to the pitch of desolation. But whether in the seasons of God's presence or in the experiences of God's absence, they are always a language of dialogue and encounter with God's word.

From the very origins of Christian worship, the psalms were oriented to the rhythms of the day and the night, to the week with its focus on Sunday and to the year with its great feasts and seasons of the gospel. In this sense the psalms are the sung access to Christian time, to seasons that bear the configuration of God's mighty works and the narrative of Christ's person and work. From the beginning the church realized that if the psalms truly possess us, they will offer us God in Christ; they will express Christ's liturgy and our life with him over time.

Scripture speaks and tells forth creation, precept, prophecy, holy history, human suffering, guilt and reconciliation, salvation and the hope for the consummation of all things. This emotional range of life is the power and the way God speaks through the psalms. They sing of all these matters. David's songs link us with the whole sweep of biblical history. And as David is the prototype of Jesus Christ, according to Christian tradition and the biblical witness, Christ also prays the psalms and leads us in praying them. The Psalter constitutes the prayerbook of God's people from generation to generation.

Here in the Book of Psalms, which the church rightly calls a "school of prayer," we find and experience anew the ongoing liturgy of call and response between Israel and the Lord God. In every age the psalms provide models and images of authentic faith and honest prayer. This is why we cannot domesticate the psalms — musically or liturgically. Always we must allow them to speak in their full expressive range. At the same time, the Christian community confesses that Jesus Christ leads us in prayer to God, the Holy One of Israel whom he calls "Abba." In the liturgical use of the psalms the Christian assembly discovers the person and work of Jesus to be the archetypal antiphon before and after every psalm. This gives special focus to their human range. Christ teaches us to pray and leads us in prayer, sometimes crying out a psalm with terrifying presence as in Psalm 22 in the Good Friday liturgy.

The psalms have played a crucial role in the faith experience of God's people through the centuries. They contain and express the entire emotional range of life before God. Whenever the discipline of Christian spirituality is revitalized, Christians return to the psalms to taste their humanity and to learn the depths of God's presence once again. God, the very God who is enthroned upon the praises of Israel, is in these prayers but never contained by them — no more than God is contained in temples made by human hands. As Roland Murphy puts it:

It may be said that the Lord is never more present than when [The Lord] is absent. The cry of the wounded psalmist ... testifies to the divine absence.... [Yet] Even in those psalms which end on a despairing note (Pss 39, 88) there is a sense of active presence of God.[1]

In his brief classic *Psalms: The Prayer Book of the Bible,* Dietrich Bonhoeffer asks, Who prays the psalms? He speaks of them as the prayer of our humanity assumed by Jesus who comes with us before God. But we cannot grasp this until we understand that David and all of Jewish scripture with him also pray the psalms. Christ prays and we pray — in our own time and place — with them. We, "the entire community in which alone the vast richness of the Psalter can be prayed but also ... every individual insofar as he (or she) participates in Christ and his community and prays their prayer."[2] Together in common humanity before God, we enter a wondrous and demanding school of prayer.

The psalms are such a school only because they are so integral a part of the liturgy. A profound aspect of all worship, and particularly of liturgical worship, is its ability to form and express us in the fundamental experiences that relate us to God. The systole and diastole, the breathing out and the breathing in of God's manifold word to us is at the very heart of the continuing liturgical prayer of the church — in the daily offices, the structures of the church's calendar and lectionary, the cycle of saints, the rites of initiation, the pastoral offices and the eucharistic celebrations of proclamation and sacrament. The psalms permeate all these, especially the daily prayer and the eucharistic celebrations. Any adequate rediscovery of the psalms as sung prayer must take seriously their role in the whole economy of Christian worship.

What are we formed in and what do we express when the psalms become integral to the prayer of the whole community? Precisely the whole range of reality we taste and see and hear in the themes, images, emotions and passions that the psalms teach and portray.

> The Lord is my shepherd, I shall not want.
>
> Out of the depths I cry to you, O Lord.
>
> You wrap yourself with light as with a cloak,
> and spread out the heavens like a curtain.
>
> Let us shout for joy to the Rock of our salvation.
>
> As the deer longs for the water-brooks,
> so longs my soul for you, O God.
>
> Raise a song and sound the timbrel,
> the merry harp and the lyre.

On and on the images and the emotions flow. They express praise, joy, sorrow, yearning, anxiety, hope, certainty and jubilation. The very form of these Hebrew poems calls us to participate in the reality they express. For this reason the psalms are filled to overflowing with the word that addresses and touches human existence in its deepest reality. The poetry of the psalms is paradoxical; they are at once universal and particular. They describe the real experiences of desert wilderness, exile, human enmity and vengeance, pilgrimage, ascent, rest and festival joy. It is no mere coincidence that the whole Psalter ends on a note of exultation. It invites everything that has life and breath, to praise God.

From these first considerations three points emerge: (1) the psalms are the language of the human heart at full stretch before God; (2) they are integral to the church's prayer, season upon season and throughout the ages; and (3) the psalms provide an ever-fresh place of encounter between God and God's people, a crucible of faith experience. Let us examine each point in turn.

The psalms take us into the deepest parts of our humanity by calling us toward God. Praise is there and joyful thanksgiving: these are primary experiential patterns in the liturgical use of the psalms. But the praise of God and the blessing of the holy name serve as a center for the real experience of living in a beautiful, terrifying and often difficult world of suffering. This is why the language of the heart has such range in these songs of faith. As Roland Murphy observes:

> This was a faith that was totally expressive. Shouts of enthusiasm, directions given by a master of ceremonies, oracles from the Lord, counseling and encouraging words from temple personnel, the outcry of the aggrieved, the serenity of sincere worship — all these pass before us in the Psalter.[3]

One clear implication for our contemporary liturgical use of the psalms emerges from this. We must continue to search for adequate musical forms and new translations of the texts so that our community's experience of and with psalmody will inform, uncover and release this emotional authenticity. At the same time we must never mistake the arousal of intense feelings for depth and range of emotion. Episodic states of feeling are not to be confused with deep emotions. The former burn off in the heat of noonday; the latter endure and are part of our emotional capacity and disposition toward God and neighbor.[4]

We may claim, then, that the language of the psalms is the language of the heart. But since the psalms are prayed both as poetry and song, they are far more than aesthetic utterances. Thomas Merton speaks of this "more than language" as the drive toward silence. The psalms, he urges, "contain within themselves the silence of high mountains and the silence of heaven."

> It is only when we stand at the bottom of the mountain that it is hard for us to distinguish the language of the Psalter from the tongues of this earth: for Christ must still perforce travel among us as a pilgrim disguised in our own tattered garments. The Psalter only truly begins to speak and sing within us when we have been led by God and lifted up by Him and have ascended into its silences.[5]

Such an experience of the psalms is not restricted to monks and nuns or mystics, or other artists of religious virtuosity. We ordinary believers, struggling with faith and doubt, life, suffering, death and resurrection, may find in the recovery of the psalms in liturgical and devotional prayer just such a language beyond the noise of our words.

A liturgical song

The second point that applies to our rediscovery of psalms today concerns their central role in the liturgy. Simply to think of the response psalm (the "gradual") as a minor event between readings misses the point, even though the way we actually sing or recite the appointed psalm may be dull and routinized! We must begin again to use the psalms in catechetical structures, beginning with preparation for baptism, confirmation, marriage, funerals and reconciliation.

Most parishes have had little formation in the psalms as prayer and even less instruction in the range of musical settings requisite to an adequate prayer repertoire. The responsorial psalm appointed for the Sunday liturgy can show a far greater range of styles of singing (antiphonal, responsorial, psalm-tone, through-composed, hymnic) and a more ample range of musical settings by which to reflect seasonal and thematic differentiations. But we must go on to consider entrance psalms, communion psalms and choral anthems based on psalm texts, along with versified psalms in the congregational hymns. These, together with the morning and evening prayer in households and in the parish celebrations, constitute a primary dimension of the whole body of prayer throughout the seasons of the church year and in all the seasons of our lives.

Proper training in the general and seasonal psalms appointed in the lectionary—indeed, in the whole body of texts drawn from the Psalter—involves learning their scriptural and historical contexts as well. For the psalms not only form and express fundamental images and experiences; they also link our liturgy with the life experiences of Israel. They join Israel's particular pilgrimage, exile, prophetic call, its seasons of feast and famine, fear of enemies and triumphs of victory, with our own. Above all, in anguished laments and festival hymns, in thanksgiving, instructional and processional songs, the psalms speak of the presence of God.

In this regard we should not force a christological interpretation of the psalms but respect the continuity of our experience with that of ancient Israel, whether it be suffering or praise. These texts carry such possible experience from age to age. The very wide emotional range of the psalms may speak more powerfully to us than some contemporary texts. Nor should we settle for a merely comfortable devotional reading that would refer the psalms solely to our interior life of piety. Rather, the way of lament and praise itself proclaims the identity of Jesus as one who lived in solidarity with the humanity expressed in the psalms. In continuity with the history of all God's people, in extremity and in shalom, he also sang the psalms of David.

Living with the psalms along their full emotional range and with all their accumulated history means learning to bring our own lives to these songs. Images forged in the biblical experience of God's people take us more deeply into our own places of encounter with God. Participation in the story of creation, fall, covenant, redemption and hope for God's shalom takes time to unfold. This time is invited and enabled by the psalms, which often take us places we do not wish to go — into the desert, into solidarity with the oppressed and abandoned, into the fear of the Lord that is the beginning of wisdom and into luminous expanses of doxology and blessings. The psalms, once entered into by the community at worship over the cycles of time, seep into the very marrow of our bones. This is what the New Testament writers refer to in passages such as Colossians 3:16: "Let the word of Christ dwell in you richly; teach and admonish one another in all wisdom; and with gratitude in your hearts sing psalms, hymns and spiritual songs to God."

All this is but a beginning. The psalms are the language of the heart. They articulate the passional life before God; they are integral, even indispensable to the church's prayer season upon season. They provide a well-spring, an ever-fresh place of encounter between God and our lives, a crucible of faith experience wherein the word becomes flesh. In the final analysis, the psalms assist us in our journey into God and into our own humanity — they are the call of the gospel and our response to it in life and the church's prayer.

The treasury of psalmody now being recovered permeates the whole liturgical economy. Reforms across a wide ecumenical spectrum have shown us that what the early church practiced, what the monastic communities preserved and what all subsequent reformers wish to recover is this treasury: the psalms as the church's common prayer book. The enthusiastic reception the nonliturgical churches have given to the musical settings of Gelineau, David Isele, Christopher Willcock, Michael Joncas and Howard Hughes among others is impressive. The so-called Free Church traditions receive these new developments as scriptural song, but in some cases their delight in the musical forms of the psalms also leads them to new levels of liturgical awareness. For the explicitly liturgical traditions, the psalms promise more than we have yet explored. As Massey Shepherd says in *The Psalms in Christian Worship:*

> Thus in the liturgical churches today the Psalms come back into their own but not in restrictive texts or ways of rendition. Whether sung or said, they may be rendered in unison by the choir or the people, or in responsive methods in various combinations of cantors, choirs, people, or alternate groupings of choirs and people.[6]

Extended musical forms, such as harmonized antiphons, more complex musical textures for cantors, choirs and people, and instrumental elaborations, are needed to reflect the whole range of psalmody in prayer. Once again more serious musicians are attracted to write music for the church's worship, despite the discipline required by the primacy of the text. These are welcome developments, for it is the recovery of biblical song that enables the liturgy to become once more the sung prayer of the whole people of God. The most striking feature of the renaissance of psalmody in the Sunday liturgy and the daily offices is the accent it places upon congregational participation.

The challenge now before us is to bring all people into living contact with the psalms in the liturgy and in their lives so that Christian spirituality may be deepened and the church's prayer made more responsive to God's word and the treasury of tradition. In so doing, if our musical forms are adequate, the psalms will not only invite us into God's presence but will also direct us to a more mature encounter with God in contemporary existence.

A remarkable new possibility has dawned: a genuine ecumenical sharing of psalm traditions in which we may appreciate and appropriate one another's sense and sensibility with these songs. Thus we can experience plainsong in its more recently adapted forms in English (at Gethsemani or St. Meinrad's, for example) alongside the older Gregorian Latin modes; Gelineau psalmody alongside harmonized chants emerging from the Anglican tradition; hymnic versions in the lineage of the Scottish and Genevan Psalters (but now often set to early American hymn tunes as in the style of Henry Brian Hays, O.S.B.) alongside the twentieth-century harmonized antiphon; and the elaborations of simple psalm tones again. With the restoration of this plenitude of song comes the hope that all who are baptized into Christ will begin to understand that we sing one song and have one hope in Jesus Christ our Lord. "Come, let us sing unto the Lord" with "everything that breathes." Let the whole world be filled with the praises of our God and Savior.

Notes

1. Roland E. Murphy, "The Faith of the Psalmist," *Interpretation* 36, no. 3 (July 1980): 233.

2. Dietrich Bonhoeffer, *Psalms: The Prayer Book of the Bible* (Minneapolis: Augsburg Publishing House, 1970), 21.

3. Murphy, "The Faith of the Psalmist," 229.

4. For further exploration of this point, see D. E. Saliers, *The Soul in Paraphrase: Prayer and the Religious Affections* (New York: Seabury Press, 1980).

5. Thomas Merton, *Bread in The Wilderness* (Collegeville, Minn.: Liturgical Press, 1971), 113.

6. Massey H. Shepherd, Jr., *The Psalms in Christian Worship*, (Minneapolis: Augsburg Publishing House; Collegeville, Minn.: Liturgical Press, 1976), 79.

35

Hymnody and Liturgy

JOHN T. FESPERMAN

"A song in praise of God," as a general definition of the hymn, goes back at least to Augustine (353–430 C.E.), though devotion, contrition and thanksgiving are among other subjects deemed appropriate for hymn texts. Corporate participation in hymn singing encourages unanimity of intent and action, much as kneeling does for prayer or standing for a psalm. While hymn singing is central to worship in the free churches, this essay focuses on the use of hymns in parishes observing the traditional eucharistic liturgy and the orders for daily office. This grouping includes Lutherans, Anglicans and Roman Catholics — for whom hymn singing may be a relatively recent innovation — as well as parishes from other polities. The word "corporate," as used here, does not exclude references to the individual but suggests that hymn texts should be appropriate for congregational use and not limited to isolated or private concerns.

Music "appropriate for congregational singing" consists not only of a tune but also of a harmonization. The tune must be a fine melody that stays in the range of approximately an octave to accommodate the limited vocal ranges of average singers; rhythmically, the tune must avoid boredom yet be sufficiently uncomplicated so as to be easily learned by a congregation. The harmonization should be in four parts, with vocal lines interesting for choral singing and playable on the organ. (More complicated "accompaniments" can be invented by the accomplished player, but they should not preclude part singing by a choir or confuse the congregation; and they cannot turn a poor hymn into a fine one.) However simple this may sound, one has only to look at the subtle qualities of a masterpiece, such as Luther's "A Mighty Fortress" or Vaughan Williams's "For all the Saints," to discern the delicate balances that must be struck if a great hymn is to be the outcome. A convincing match of tune and text requires musical and poetic skills of a high order.

From *Liturgy: Glad Shouts and Songs* 9, no. 1.

The people's music

Although hymns constitute only one form of congregational participation in the liturgy, they have been "the people's music" at least since the time of Luther, who not only wrote hymn texts and music himself but also solicited the help of musicians, poets and theologians. "I place music next to theology and give it highest praise," he says in his *Tischreden.*

Evelyn Underhill also emphasizes the importance of artistic communication when she speaks of the ritual of worship as "an action and an experience which transcend the logical levels of the mind, and demand an artistic rather than an intellectual form of expression," and when she later observes that "it is in hymns above all that we hear the accents of the people's worship."[1]

Despite early puritanical objections to music in general, hymns became extremely important in the free churches and in the more liturgical ones. *The United Methodist Hymnal* (1989) notes in its preface that "next to the Bible, our hymnals have been our most formative resource." The reprinting in the new hymnal of John Wesley's "Directions for Singing" (delivered in 1761) is confirmation of the long-standing primacy of hymn singing among Methodists. Such listings as that of the "Consultation on Ecumenical Hymnody" attest that hymnody flourishes in different liturgical contexts. New hymnals, including *The United Methodist Hymnal* (1989), the Episcopal *Hymnal* (1982), *Worship: A Hymnal and Service Book for Roman Catholics* (3rd edition, 1986), the *Lutheran Book of Worship* (1978) and the *Presbyterian Hymnal* (1990) continue to be published, and the musical, poetic and theological quality of the hymns they contain is rising.

Hymnody for an Easter people

Lionel Dakers has this to say about the proper basis for using music and the other arts in corporate worship:

> [M]usic is used in Church because an Easter people simply cannot do justice to their experience without it, and indeed, without all the other arts as well.

If that sounds unbelievably theological or a bit pious, I would defend it on two counts. First, it roots the reason for music in an *abiding experience,* and therefore the question is no longer primarily what we can afford, or what we happen to like or understand but what does this experience produce. Second, it unravels quite a number of thorny problems about standards and suitability, taste and the rest. For when the controlling factor *is the experience of the Resurrection,* our task will be to match the art we use with the experience. What is tawdry, second-rate and inappropriate will be shown up because it is inadequate to express Easter joy and faith, and unworthy of what it is we are celebrating.[2]

These powerful words clear the air for a discussion of hymnody and its function in the liturgy. When the standard is the mystery of the resurrection, arguments for "what we happen to like or understand" or for the "tawdry, second-rate and inappropriate" fall by their own weight. So do the objections of the Philistine, whom Robertson Davies defines as "someone who is content to live in a wholly unexplored world."[3] The necessary exploration is not for novelty or variety but for that which is genuine and ineffable.

When Davies speaks of the Philistine or Dakers of the "second-rate and inappropriate," they know as artists whereof they speak. Even people of prayer often yearn to find an easier way than the best way, and original sin is just as insidious in liturgy and hymnody as in other areas of corporate life. Humankind's frailties make it difficult to keep the mystery of the resurrection and the standards it enjoins at the center of corporate worship.

Artists: people of vocation

The resurrection implies the incarnation, the word made flesh. Christians believe that God is and was among us, so that the incarnation continues to occur in the lives and works of human beings. God working through humans gives us the Christian concept of vocation: being called to a certain work. The distinction between "sacred" and "secular" work is dismantled; all good work is sacramental, whether specifically related to liturgy or not.

As Dakers notes, there is a distinction between what is appropriate and what is not, yet this entails no value judgment on the intrinsic worth of anything created by God or humans. That the organ is well suited to supporting congregational singing, for example, does not make it a holier or more sacred instrument than any other. Creators of music for liturgy have a very specialized task but one no holier than the creation of music for an opera or symphony. What matters most is the quality of the work.

When hymns are used within established liturgical traditions, both clergy and musicians exercise the vocation of teachers. In addition to having ample competence and patience, they must be very clear about what is fundamental to worship and what is merely based on custom, preference or even ignorance. The lofty guideline suggested here for "people of vocation" must be practically applied in the choosing of hymns for weekly or daily worship.

The ideal must be held up for all to see; if compromises are necessary, they should be identified as such rather than being glossed over or confused with the optimum. Musicians and clergy who are truly engaged in a search for the excellent are more likely to find it. They can be true teachers, sharing their findings with their congregations. With good will, competence and persistence on the part of all, communities can make slow but rewarding progress.

Enhancing the liturgy

Since hymns are meant to heighten and intensify the liturgy, no hymn can be inserted without considering its effect on the rest of the service. An undiscriminating literalism dictates that the text of the hymn specifically reflect the day's lessons or collects. Many preachers insist that the hymn must have something to do with the homily's theme. This insistence often results in the selection of an inferior piece that neither enhances the liturgical season nor fulfills other functions of sung texts in the liturgy.

If the integrity of the hymn is of real importance, deeper and more subtle qualities must be taken into consideration. If a good hymn is found that also reinforces the lectionary or homily, so much the better; but one that only makes a surface connection will move the congregation less than a fine hymn that is related to the season or supports the great truths of faith.

Unless liturgy is broadly understood as the work of the assembly, lay participation in planning and worship will be superficial. A key area of lay participation is the work of the serious artist. Understandably, artists feel unwelcome in communities where their vocations are undervalued or ignored. Here, even staff musicians tend to be viewed solely as functionaries. This devaluing of the arts, especially music, in liturgical parishes is likely to be a signal that the liturgy itself is not taken very seriously. That is a frightening prospect, one that requires patient and subtle remedies on the part of both clergy and musicians.

Liturgical and musical integrity

Ralph Vaughan Williams, musical editor of the *English Hymnal,* made a clear and brief case for the quality of hymns in the preface of that work:

> The usual argument in favor of bad music is that the fine tunes are doubtless "musically correct" but that the people want "something simple." Now the expression "musically correct" has no meaning; the only "correct" music is that which is beautiful and noble. As for simplicity, what could be simpler than st. anne or the old hundredth, and what could be finer? It is indeed a moral rather than a musical issue.

Vaughan Williams charges the musician with a moral task: to present only what is "beautiful and noble." To do less is to betray the trust placed by the congregation in the teacher. This presumes not only that the teacher will always recognize the "beautiful and noble" but that the teacher also has the trust of the "students." Ideally, the musician or artist comes from within the local community and practices the artistic vocation as one of the community's own. Even this, of course, does not imply infallibility. As Linda Clark has written, "Mistakes are permitted; indolence is not."[4]

Erik Routley has written of the awesome responsibility of the musician or artist:

> A trained musician will be able to distinguish good music from bad music — even when he argues heatedly with another trained musician about where the boundary runs. But the nonspecialist has no equipment for doing that. So, what is carelessly or unscrupulously offered to him will go straight into his affections, bypassing the intellect.[5]

Routley uses the example of Plato's "philosopher king" to develop the contrast between the responsible and the irresponsible teacher. Plato describes the philosopher king as going out into the light, seeing the real things and then coming back to interpret them.[6] If the supposed teacher does not return and interpret, he or she is behaving as a snob or an elitist who is unconcerned that others stumble.

Ann B. Ulanov, speaking to seminary graduates about their vocation, singled out two ways of "denying God":

> To please people and do what they want so they will like us. This is the way of sentimentality.... At the opposite end of the spectrum, we deny God by fixing a rigid formula.... Then we coerce our neighbors to conform to our scheme. This is the way of power.[7]

For the musician to be faithful to his or her vocation, neither the way of sentimentality nor the way of power is viable. What is required is the way of integrity: the presentation of what is "beautiful and noble." Yet to stand consistently for such integrity is no easy task. When a congregation is faced with a new text and tune, perhaps in a style new to it, there may be resistance. This can be countered only by the teacher's patient persistence and conviction that with repetition, what is genuine will be recognized and appropriated. When presented alongside the second-rate, masterpieces will assert themselves.

Integrating cultural contexts

Present ecumenical trends in worship are borne out in the diverse sources of hymns in the new hymnals. Although masterpieces may be mixed with the second-rate, a gratifyingly large number of excellent hymns exist in most of the recently published hymnals. The range includes early plainsong tunes and texts, Lutheran chorales, psalm tunes from the French, Genevan and Scottish psalters, eighteenth-century English hymns (some with texts by the Wesleys), hymns of folk origin and twentieth century works.

The hymns are also diverse in the eras from which they derive; thus the new hymnals also reinforce the continuity of Christian worship over the generations. The singing of a great text or tune that has inspired Christians for generations in widely differing times and places has an effect on corporate worship unlike any other.

The importance of non-Western and "ethnic" sources is increasingly acknowledged, and significant efforts are being made to include some of them in new publications. Much more work is needed, however, to find appropriate ways to integrate such sources into traditional liturgical worship without impugning the integrity of either the music or the liturgy.

Deciding what musical and poetic styles are suitable for use in a given corporate context often presents a dilemma. The difficulty can result from differences in ethnicity or simply from differences in the era of the hymn's origin. In the recent *United Methodist Hymnal,* for example, Thomas A. Dorsey's "Precious Lord, take my hand" faces the page containing Vaughan Williams's "Down Ampney," whose text is a translation of the fifteenth-century poem "Come down, O Love divine." The musical differences are, of course, vast. More daunting is the cultural difference between the two texts and tunes. Most sobering of all is the question of how or whether these diverse styles can be liturgically related.

Serious stylistic and liturgical problems are involved in achieving an ecumenical music of integrity that unities characteristics from different ethnic, regional or theological traditions. Solutions are probably best sought in light of conditions within a single parish — not an easy matter, given the diversity of many congregations. It seems reasonable to attempt some mixing of styles for congregations in which a demonstrated need exists, rather than legislating such changes for all.

A high degree of sincerity and stylistic sophistication is required to produce liturgy of integrity, especially when traditions other than those of Western Europe are combined. For hymns of traditional or nontraditional origin, innate quality must be the chief point of discernment; if that quality is lacking, other considerations should not normally override the decision to exclude the song. Unless great care is taken, the result can only be synthetic and unconvincing — in short, bad liturgy. Nevertheless, the attempts at integrating various cultures and styles deserve more serious consideration than has so far been given them by musicians and clergy.

The sources and examples listed here only scratch the surface of a vast reservoir of splendid hymnody, giving a tiny sample from various eras of Christian congregational song. They testify to the activity of the Holy Spirit through the vocations of artists from the beginning of Christendom onward. Deo gratias!

Notes

1. Evelyn Underhill, *Worship* (1937; reprint ed., New York: Crossroad, 1989), II:2 and VI:1.

2. Lionel Dakers, *The World of Church Music* (Croydon, England: The Royal School of Church Music, 1986), 21.

3. Robertson Davies, *The Lyre of Orpheus* (New York: Viking Press, 1988).

4. Linda Clark, "Aesthetic Value in Church Music," in *Liturgy: The Song of all Creation* (Washington, D.C.: Liturgical Conference, 1987), 53.

5. Erik Routley, *Divine Formula* (Princeton, N.J.: Prestige Press, 1986).

6. Plato, *Republic,* Book VII.

7. Ann B. Ulanov, *Anglican Theological Review* 71, no. 2 (Spring 1989).

36

Gospel Music and Afro-American Worship

IRENE V. JACKSON-BROWN

Music is performed in Afro-American worship to invite our participation in the healing and saving drama of the liturgy; black music engages the whole community and moves people from crucifixion to resurrection. To sing black liturgical music is to know truly the faith our songs affirm. "There [really] is," as we sing, "a balm in Gilead, to make the wounded whole."

Black liturgical music is the music of the black folk church that forms the context in which Afro-Americans worship in culturally black ways. The texts and rhythms of Afro-American liturgical music — spirituals, gospels, hymns — express the experiences of Afro-American people. Black people hear their own stories in these songs. In order to recognize black expressions within a given worship event, one has to know something of the black experience: "If you don't know what it looks like, you won't know it when you see it."

The liturgical experience of Blacks has been largely ignored or dismissed. Indeed, in 1910 scholars could write that the Negro's worship was "simple." "He has not the appreciation of elaborate rituals...of services consisting of forms and ceremonies." Unfortunately, such naive and racist attitudes still prevail. To counter them, I will clarify the distinctiveness of black worship, focusing on its music.

Black cultural norms

Cultural norms shape musical sounds and performance practices. Certain norms, behaviors and concepts are intrinsic to black expressive culture. Subtle African traits are often preserved in black performance practice.

From *Liturgy: Glad Shouts and Songs* 9, no. 1.

Black music — wherever it is found and whether it is or is not liturgical — expresses the communal nature of the black experience. It edifies the family of God by placing the individual within the community. Solo singing in African or Afro-American culture is rare. In an African context, group singing is the norm. In the Afro-American spiritual, "Lord I want to be a Christian in my heart, in my heart," the "I" is really the collective "we."

Black music is meant to be sung or played or danced by everyone. It binds all who walk the same existential path. When missionaries in mid-eighteenth-century New York wrote that "Blacks often meet in the evenings on a regular basis for instruction in the singing of psalm tunes," it is likely that the psalm tunes in and of themselves were not the motive for the enthusiastic singing. Rather, black people have always found singing a way to communal expression and social cohesion, a fact that is well documented in cross-cultural studies of Blacks in religious and secular settings.

A central African experience noted by the Ghanaian ethnomusicologist J. H. Nketia is the "metronomic sense." Howard University instructor Evelyn White, an eminent choral conductor, frequently stresses the importance of articulating the "underlying pulse" when performing spirituals. As a student, I did not recognize that performance practice as African. Yet it is precisely that characteristic — the "metronomic sense" — that distinguishes a white performance of spirituals from one in the black tradition.

Another cultural norm in black expressive culture is movement. Or as Janheinz Jahn describes it: "The difference between European rhythmic conception and African is the fact that Europeans perceive rhythm by hearing, while Africans perceive rhythm by movement."[1] A video of the enthronement of Archbishop Desmond Tutu shows him dancing while a choir of Blacks sings. The white choir at the enthronement remained motionless; the black choir swayed in the black tradition.

In the black aesthetic, time is suspended. Black music goes on and on; ritual in the black tradition goes on and on. I recently visited an Episcopal parish in New Haven, Connecticut, served by a priest from the West Indies. The service was much longer than its white counterpart; each element — the singing, preaching and the passing of the peace — was of long duration. This flow is not accidental; it is the black aesthetic in full operation.

In his study of new-world Blacks, the anthropologist Melville Herkovits maintains that the intangible concept of time held by Blacks is an African retention. He says that "approximations of time, rather than punctuality, characterize black culture." In the black community, time is negotiated freely.

Closely related to the concept of time in black expressive culture is the notion of musical pitch. Like time, pitch is approximate. Singers, particularly gospel singers, manipulate pitch as they manipulate time, adding all kinds of ornamentation to the vocal line. Varying from the exact time or pitch, stretching a song, singing "between the cracks of the piano," are practices embedded in black expressive culture as it shapes the musical sound and performance.

Cueing is another culturally determined behavior. In a musical performance, cueing is the leader's way of signaling to others what will happen next, when the end is approaching or when a new song is to begin. In Afro-American gospel music, the organist, pianist or sometimes the soloist, who may also be the preacher, controls the liturgy. Through rhythmic, melodic or harmonic formulas, an organist can signal the point at which the Spirit is manifest.

Cueing is of great importance for the proper continuity and impact of the worship service. Cueing underscores the responsorial, or call-and-response format, of black worship. The cueing system itself makes it difficult to blend gospel music with other liturgical traditions. An example of this difficulty occurred during a recent annual meeting of the Union of Black Episcopalians, at which the music for one mass was provided by a local black gospel choir. The organist did not understand the cues in the Episcopal tradition, and the Episcopal priest did not understand gospel cues. The liturgy was awkward, and many departed feeling that gospel music "doesn't work" in the Episcopal Church.

Yet it was not the music — the sound — that was unacceptable; it was the missed performance cues that made the blending of the music into the liturgy unacceptable. In the Episcopal tradition, the priest "controls" the liturgy, not the organist and choir as in the black folk church. Gospel music can have a place in the liturgies of the Episcopal and other mainline churches, but the creation of a successful blend demands that we find a way to accommodate these traditions. The peculiar extramusical behaviors of black expressive culture, including improvisation, repetition, dance, dialogue, movement, song and drama, must be understood and appreciated. A "translation" must occur, taking into account idiomatic expressions and, above all, the cueing system.

Afro-American gospel music

Afro-American gospel music is a specific genre of the celebration of the black religious experience. Gospel, the music of the black folk church, is an urban musical genre that began in the 1920s, emerging primarily from the worship patterns of black Pentecostal and holiness groups. At first, the new religious music was rejected in black independent churches, but by 1940 gospel had revolutionized the music there as well.

Gospel is an eclectic tradition. It welds the jubilee, the spiritual, hymnody and the blues, using an essentially black aesthetic. Textual phrases from hymns, spirituals and the Bible are refashioned into gospel lyrics. Unlike spirituals, which have a communal origin and develop entirely in an oral tradition, gospel songs can be credited to an author and composer. Yet gospel is also deeply rooted in an oral folk or vernacular tradition. A gospel presentation varies from performance to performance by a process referred to as "communal re-creation" or "the making of variants." In gospel music, the score is only a blueprint for performance.

Besides being a tradition or genre, gospel is also a vocal and instrumental style. Because all black music traditions share common musical characteristics (for example, the use of certain scales, harmonies, rhythmic patterns and performance practices), the casual listener or "outsider" often finds it difficult to distinguish between the blues, gospel, spirituals or the popular contemporary idiom known as "soul music." Yet there are certain scales, vocal mannerisms, rhythmic and melodic formulas, instrumentation and performance practices that are distinctively "gospel." Thus one can sing the spiritual "Swing Low, Sweet Chariot" in a gospel style, or the nineteenth-century hymn "Amazing Grace" can be performed gospel style.

The history of gospel

A sketch of the historical development of the genre dispels the notion that the gospel tradition and the spiritual tradition are identical.

Before the introduction of hymn singing in the early eighteenth-century colonies, congregational music consisted of the "lining-out" of psalms. A precentor or song leader would sing one or two lines of a psalm and the congregation would then sing the same melodic line but with elaboration. Hymns were taught to Blacks by the process of lining-out. The affinity between lining-out and the African practice of call and response probably accounts for how Blacks learned and adopted European hymns with ease.

As the practice persisted, a style called "surge-singing" developed. Surge-singing of psalms merged with the melismatic vocal style that characterized the "field holler" of slaves, an example of musical syncretism resulting in an Afro-American folk song style. "Lining-out," the call-and-response pattern and the highly melismatic vocal style persist in gospel.

The Great Awakening (1725–65), a name given to a series of religious revivals among Protestants in the colonies, fostered changes in the existing musical practices in the churches. One change was an improvement in the quality of congregational singing, with hymns replacing psalms. The hymns of Isaac Watts, introduced in the colonies at this time, were especially popular among Blacks, as evidenced by their preponderance in gospel repertoire.

The atmosphere surrounding the Second Great Awakening (1797–1805) called for a kind of music that reflected the zeal of the camp meeting, which was characterized by fervent preaching, praying and singing. In camp meetings, Blacks and Whites shared and borrowed various musical practices. Black participants made their presence felt by their singing and performance practices. The "shout," a religious activity first observed in slave quarters and still present today in black churches, was a distinctive feature of worship in the camp meetings. The new songs created by the camp-meeting phenomenon were called "spiritual songs" as distinguished from the literary hymn.

About the same time that the Second Great Awakening was occurring in the south, black independent congregations were emerging in the north. Richard Allen organized the first independent church and in 1801 published a hymnal for the exclusive use of his congregation. Allen made certain modifications in the hymn texts, a majority of which were by Watts and Wesley. In her book *The Music of Black Americans,* Eileen Southern suggests that the purpose of these alterations was to make the words and phrases more meaningful to Allen's coworshipers.[2]

According to Southern, the tunes in Allen's collection derive from several sources. Some were from other hymnals, some were folk tunes, and some were probably original compositions. Allen's hymnal contained many songs that were, or would become, popular among Blacks. These hymns became source material for the growing body of Afro-American religious songs, thus indirectly shaping the gospel tradition.

Until the early nineteenth century, Blacks were concentrated in southern rural areas. By 1865, extensive migration to urban centers had begun. At the same time, two white men active in evangelistic endeavors began to influence American folk hymnody: Ira D. Sankey and Dwight L. Moody rejuvenated the revival spirit through Sankey's singing and Moody's preaching. Sankey's hymns became popular among Blacks and also influenced the gospel repertoire.

The post–Civil War period also fostered another musical tradition that combined black melodic elements with European harmonic practices, resulting in the highly stylized arrangement of spirituals popularized by the Fisk Jubilee Singers and continued today by the concert choirs of black universities. This cultivated tradition, which I call the "concert spiritual tradition," is distinct from the black folk or vernacular spiritual tradition that also flourished during this time.

By the first two decades of the twentieth century, more Blacks than ever were faced with a new challenge: the city. Gospel emerged from the need for a religious musical expression that would be responsive to the needs of Blacks in this new setting. As an urban musical form, gospel is a response to the impact of the city on former country folk; as such, gospel is also a folk genre for expressing white religious experience.

The history of gospel per se, then, begins in the 1920s, in the cities, with the rise of black Pentecostal and holiness churches. It was among the holiness denominations that the free expression of religious and musical behavior common to rural southern Blacks began to assert itself and undergo further development in an urban setting. The holiness and Pentecostal groups went beyond the rhythmic elements of hand-clapping and foot-stomping to introduce the use of drums, tambourines and horns into the church service.

Qualities of the gospel genre

The broad characteristics of gospel include the use of the responsorial format; the use of percussion and percussive techniques; emphasis on short musical phrases, units or motifs; repetition; syncopation and polymeters; and communal participation. In addition to sound, the "gospel event" includes dance, ritual and drama. The musical characteristics of Afro-American gospel are largely present in West African traditional music; Africanisms are found to be quite persistent in new world religious rituals.

The aforementioned characteristics are present in all aspects of the gospel event. For example, the responsorial format can occur in several ways: between the soloist and the choir (often an overlapping call-and-response pattern); between the organ and the piano; between the preacher and the congregation; or between the preacher and the organ or piano. Sometimes the call is a verbal behavior, while the response is a motor behavior; for example, a phrase sung by the choir could be answered by hand-clapping, foot-stomping or dance. An instrumental call by organ or piano could evoke a motor response such as "the shout." As we can see from those few examples of the responsorial format, gospel is without doubt a multidimensional presentation — music, song, dance, drama.

Another broad characteristic of gospel is the use of syncopation and polymeters; for example, the clapping that accompanies gospel singing is always on the off-or secondary beat. A communicant may sing in one meter while stomping feet in another and swaying the body in yet another. This rhythmic complexity reminds us again of Jahn's explanation, quoted earlier, concerning the different ways we can conceive of rhythm, either by hearing (the European way) or by movement (as Africans do).

The gospel sound-ideal involves a bias toward loud dynamics, abrupt shifts and careful, subtle manipulation of vocal and instrumental timbres. It also prefers musical textures that embody percussive sounds which increase the ratio of sounds of indefinite pitch to sounds of definite pitch. The gospel aesthetic involves a filling up of space, both musical and physical. Musical space is filled with hand-clapping, foot-stomping, tambourines, drums, vocal exclamations between lines of text, song, organ and piano; it has no silence. Physical space is consumed by the swaying of the choir, the preacher's movements (particularly in chanted portions of the delivery) and shouting. During the gospel performance, movement is perpetual.

The music makers

Communal participation is everywhere a distinctive feature of black worship. Cohesion in the black folk church is usually very strong, and church members are expected to participate musically. Everyone is involved in the music making, but three groups of music makers can be identified: core, supportive and marginal. The three designations are determined by proximity to the "sacred space" or pulpit as well as by the music makers' visibility.

Nearest to, sometimes even within, the sacred space are the "core" music makers, who typically include a pianist, an organist and a singing group designated as "choir" or "chorus." A "choir" sings anthems, hymns or concert arrangements of spirituals; a "chorus" performs gospel. Also included in the core class are the soloists and choir director. The final member of the core group is the preacher whose musical contributions cannot be overlooked, since at the high point of the sermon he or she may break into chantlike delivery or song.

Members of the "core group" have one major function: to encourage the Spirit. They achieve this through vocal and instrumental repetition, and emphasis on rhythm and percussive devices. The organ and piano are used percussively—the piano supporting the organ and the organ controlling the entire liturgy. The organist must be a masterful "timer." Certain tempos, rhythmic and harmonic patterns are manipulated by the organist as the liturgy heightens to the point where shouting begins. Since the organist and pianist are generally within the "sacred inner space" or the exclusive and protected space in which the most sacred activities occur, the keyboard instruments are ritually bound, sacred entities.

The "supportive group" of music makers consists of drummers, horn players and guitarists. Supportive music makers are also generally within the sacred inner space. It is possible to belong to the core and supportive groups simultaneously—as, for example, when a chorus member plays a tambourine.

The third group of music makers are designated as "marginal" because they do not bear the major responsibility for making music in the ritual, though they are expected to participate. Membership in this group fluctuates. A worshiper only becomes a member of this class by shouting or — when moved to lead a song or provide rhythmic accompaniment — by playing instruments, hand-clapping, foot-stomping or singing along with the chorus.

The primary indication of successful gospel worship is the manifestation of the Spirit. This is why solos, for instance, are not necessarily performed by the most outstanding singers. Nevertheless, membership in the core class normally does require some musical talent and specialization.

A "good" chorus or choir director must have a powerful voice. S/he must also be able to indicate through a configuration of body movements what is desired from the singers rhythmically and in the way of nuance. In the African aesthetic, a director's conducting gestures are angular and percussive, unlike gestures in the European style that tend to be circular and lyrical.

A gospel keyboardist must be able to play by ear; hymnals and sheet music are not generally used. A "good" keyboardist must be able to accompany any song spontaneously introduced, providing at the appropriate moment the right embellishments, dynamics and rhythms. The keyboardist must have rapport with the preacher; often the organ and piano aid the preacher's timing in chanted portions of the sermon. Pianists and organists usually do not shout; rather, being in the Spirit is signaled through rhythmic formulas immediately communicating that the keyboardist has "gotten happy" or is "in the Spirit."

The vitality of black music

Afro-American liturgical music is music of an Easter people. It is joyful, moving. It is music that is inherently communal, that binds people together. Black music is *living*. It is, like the liturgy itself, the worship of the living body of Christ.

Black music exclaims God's care. It is music that moves people, that stirs and undergirds the entire community. Paraphrasing theologian James Cone, Harold Dean Trulear writes: "It is not possible to encounter the spirit of black music and not be moved." Joy comes through this liturgical music, as "people are raised to new life in Christ in vicarious resurrection [through song texts] which rehearse the crucifixion-resurrection motif."[3]

Notes

1. Janheinz Jahn, *Muntu: An Outline of the New African Culture* (New York: Grove Press, 1961).

2. Eileen Southern, *The Music of Black Americans: A History* (New York: W. W. Norton, 1971).

3. Harold Dean Trulear, "The Sacramentality of Preaching," in *Liturgy: Central Symbols* (Washington, D.C.: Liturgical Conference, 1987), 21.

37

The Praise of Ordinary People

David G. Buttrick

Liturgical language is public language, the ordinary common language of a people who have no special "sacred" vocabulary. Just as the early Christians spoke, so they scribbled in ordinary, or *koine*, Greek, and the liturgy they gave us, though formal and celebrative, uses a mode of ordinary, public language. All liturgy embodies tradition and echoes the gospel; nevertheless, it is shaped by a common vocabulary, the words shared by a people. Now ordinary words may be used in an extraordinary activity, namely, praise of God, but because Christian community is a society within societies, the language of liturgy is drawn from a social repertoire. By analogy, liturgical language is incarnational.

In some bright eras language has soared, skipping about in a poetry of transcendence, because the social language was alive with metaphors of faith. In other ages liturgical language has been leaden, even prosaic, because the public language was strangely demystified. So, whatever else it is, liturgical language is human social language, though stretched and heightened and sometimes on the verge of song, it is still emphatically human.[1]

At the same time, Christian liturgical language flows from a definite scriptural tradition. In liturgy, we sing psalms, we read lections, we speak verses from the Bible; we delight in all kinds of scriptural allusion. It is no accident, therefore, that scriptural language influences liturgical style. Liturgy and scripture are drawn together not by any strict biblical compulsion, but because scripture recounts the story from which the church has sprung, the same story that provides the structure and drama of liturgical action. We worship in response to divine disclosure; liturgy also remembers and gives praise. Thus, scripture, as crystallized moments of revelation, lives in the ordinary language of the liturgy.

If liturgical language is ordinary, however, it is also mysterious, and it can be difficult to construct. Putting it all together is a theological task. In both eastern and western traditions, liturgy has taught the substance of faith in every generation.[2] Groups that develop liturgical texts are frequently caught up in theological

From *Liturgy: Language and Metaphor* 4, no. 4.

controversy as well as theological compromise. From the briefest three-line collect to the awesome unfolding of a eucharistic prayer, liturgical language always reflects a "knowledge of God" that rests on some kind of theological understanding. In one sense liturgical language is expressive; it is the voice of a faith community speaking out of new life in the Spirit. Nevertheless, because the language of liturgy is public language, it can easily acquire from the culture fads, slogans and social attitudes alien to the gospel. Theology assesses liturgical language so that our words in worship will rightly reflect the glory of God in Christ Jesus. Liturgy is a theological event.

Language forms

The language of liturgy also has a structure. All human conversation employs conventional patterns of speech; fairy tales begin with "Once upon a time..."; formal invitations follow a fixed wording, e.g., "Mr. and Mrs. John Doe request the presence of...." Christians also use forms drawn from social custom for speaking to God. The eucharistic prayer has a basic structure, as do litanies and other types of prayer.[3] Forms are not arbitrary. Forms emerge from the natural rhetoric of the social world as it is pressed into theological service. Forms cannot be "made up" indiscriminately or patched together according to whim. Rather, ancient forms display deep theological wisdom.

Perhaps the most familiar prayer form is the collect which, deriving from the Jewish *"Shemone 'Esreh,"* has been a standard component of Christian worship for centuries.[4]

The design of the collect is brief. It consists of an address, followed by a descriptive clause or clauses; a petition followed by subordinate clauses; and a conclusion.

> Mighty God,
> you split the seas and set your children free from slavery.
> Liberate us from every bondage,
> so that free for love we may serve our neighbors
> in your name;
> through Jesus Christ the Lord.

The form of the collect is profoundly sane. The address includes an adjective that signals an attribute of God: "Mighty." The descriptive clause that follows is frequently an appeal to revelation (either drawn from scripture or brought to mind by tradition); in this instance, the appeal is to the story of the children of Israel delivered from Egypt. In light of the descriptive clause, we comprehend the prayer's address, "Mighty." The petition that follows, "Liberate us..." is related to both address and descriptive clause, for only as we recall God's past faithfulness can we dare pray in the present. The final clause beginning "so that..." points to our fulfillment of God's good purpose. Thus the collect spans past, present and future.

Traditionally, most collects end with a phrase such as, "Through Jesus Christ," a powerful theological affirmation. We pray from faith in Jesus Christ, who embodies God-with-us; through Jesus Christ, who as high priest brings our intercessions before God; and in the Spirit of Christ with us, for as Paul remarks to the Romans, the Spirit prays in our prayers.[5] Liturgical form is not rigid and in no way prevents a free outpouring of our hearts; liturgical form helps us to pray, so that prayers may be both natural to human speaking and appropriate to the God we worship.

One of the strange features of liturgical form is its combination of referential language with direct address. In liturgical prayer we talk *about* God and *to* God. A prayer may begin by recalling God's goodness to us and then, abruptly, give thanks to God directly. Worshipers are sometimes troubled by the combined language; they feel most peculiar talking to God about God. But the tradition is theologically wise. Christian worship lives between memory and hope. We would not dare speak to God now if we do not remember God's past faithfulness. All through the psalms and in much biblical discourse, Israel first recites God's mighty deeds and then, in trust renewed, prays for the future. Without the recalling of God to common memory, we might pray to some amorphous nothing, "O x to the *nth!*" All Christian prayer rests on *anamnesis*.

Metaphors and models

Beneath liturgical language lie deep theological mysteries. As we two-legged creatures cannot comprehend the full glory of God, we are bound, if we are to speak of God at all, to use the language of analogy; "God is like a mighty river," for example. Liturgy often employs analogy and speaks from "models" native to faith. Metaphors for God are all products of human experience. Though they may refer to God, they also cast light on our lives. When we use a parental image and speak of God as "Mother" or "Father," we also comprehend humanity as God's children. In ages past we picked up an image from Isaiah and referred to God as "King" and indirectly viewed ourselves as human subjects.

Biblical metaphors for God are many and have always figured in liturgical texts. But for metaphors to function effectively, they must bridge the mystery of God and our common lives, and some biblical images are no longer as useful as they once were. The "slave" image is biblical, but it is less than useful in societies that view slavery as abhorrent. The marvelous thing about a people's journey in faith through the ages is that, as language changes, not to mention social customs, new metaphors emerge that probe the mystery of God and deepen the self-understanding of God's people.

As Aquinas noted, however, the language of analogy may not be used uncritically. When we use analogy in liturgy, we add stature to the term: "O God, your love is greater than the measure of our minds"; or we simply acknowledge our lack of preparation: "you live beyond our knowing, your ways are robed in mystery." Liturgical language is often paradoxical, pushing past simple analogy with a "more than" or a "not like," lest analogy domesticate God or give rise to idolatry. At times, liturgical language will even set one analogy against another: "you capture us with a silent word, you overwhelm us with your love." The effect of putting "power" words together with "silent" and "love" is to suggest that God cannot be defined in terms of dreams of dominance. Recent theological work that explores analogy, metaphor and "models" for God casts much light on the "poetry" of liturgical language.[6]

Lately, concern has arisen over sexist language in liturgy, the overuse of paternal imagery, male genetics and, of course, masculine personal pronouns.[7] The objections are deep-seated, for liturgy does intend to serve all God's people, a major percentage of whom are women. The problem is further complicated by the fact that liturgy draws from scriptural translation, and many recent versions are sexist. It will not do to argue that because English is our common language, we must tolerate "sexist" usage in the liturgy. To so argue would be to elevate a human norm, linguistic usage, above issues of theological concern. While liturgy does employ a public language, it employs such language with theological discipline in the praise of God. Liturgy uses language to display the "new humanity" in which there is "neither Jew nor Greek, neither slave nor free, neither male nor female, for all are one in Christ Jesus."[8]

Liturgy can and must find ways to praise God by drawing on both feminine and masculine imagery. Surely liturgy is not designed to endorse a paternal society in or outside church but to liberate the children of God. Admittedly the English language may be less helpful than languages that retain reference to gender. The French use of "le" and "la" names a gendered world from which to draw metaphors. More than most tongues, genderless English leaves us with pronouns and role models. Even in English, however, liturgical texts can be phrased to avoid the male generic and stereotyped paternal "models," while at the same time drawing on the feminine images in scripture and the church's devotional history. God's great salvation may well embrace sexuality, but it cannot conceivably perpetuate "sexism."[9]

Liturgical metaphor and transcendence

What of liturgical style? Many of the liturgical texts produced in the recent past have been labeled "bland"; lacking the poetry of transcendence, they appear "secular" and sadly prosaic. The complaint is worth considering. Liturgy is rhetorical in that it borrows speech patterns from a social repertoire; it is poetic as it ventures with theological courage to employ metaphors. The rhetorical character of liturgy defers to our humanness, while the poetry in liturgy dances near the "edges of language" and seeks to speak of the God whose name cannot be spoken.[10] If liturgy is too rhetorical it can become mere conversation, a language of unfaith; but a liturgy too poetic can evaporate in air too thin to support a more visceral humanity. The Western liturgical tradition is slightly more rhetorical and thus is more objective and socially binding. The Eastern tradition, given to more elaborate metaphor, evokes a heightened sense of mystery but may be more subjective.

The problem of transcendent language is not simple. Metaphors in liturgy can be strained and strangely "arty" if they do not relate to the faith of common Christian people. Right now the English language is passing through a time of rapid change. During the first half of our century the language was shrinking in size, becoming more abstract and less metaphorical. Since about the time of Vatican II, the language has been expanding, finding new terms, flashing new metaphors, gaining life at the cost of stability.[11] Liturgies written during the '60s drew on a fairly impoverished language, a secular, matter-of-fact language. Although language may be in the process of renewal, metaphors of transcendence are not yet common stock. Meanwhile, we have in our liturgical texts a language that speaks simply and offers basic metaphors — light, darkness, birth and death. Simplicity is no small achievement. With a simple, common language, people can worship together and faith increases. Straining for a poetry of transcendence before it is socially generated will only produce an unnatural, inflated language that will not well serve people of faith. Our present task is to wait like children for a time when God's word may animate our words once more.

Simplicity, poetry and praise

Good liturgical style is simple and, in its simplicity, useful to God's people. So liturgy employs short words, strong verbs and nouns, and brief phrases designed to fit common corporate speech patterns. Liturgy shuns polysyllabic words (such as "polysyllabic") and technical jargon not yet within a common conversational vocabulary: terms drawn from psychological, business or academic communities.[12] The child of five has a fine vocabulary of about 5,000 words (about the size of the New Testament vocabulary). This basic vocabulary is in us all. With it we name the world, live our lives and understand ourselves. Through the centuries, such common vocabulary has provided liturgical language. We may revel in Latinate words that sonorously rumble — incarnation, exaltation, glorification — but "child-words," the vocabulary of parable and psalm, sing more sweetly in worship.

The great virtue of the simple, common vocabulary is concreteness; it can name the things we see and touch and cast into metaphor. Liturgical prayer shuns both abstract concept and elaborate euphemism. We will pray for people in hospital rooms, not in "beds of pain," a phrase we seldom use in common speech. We will pray for the children who reach out empty hands for bread, but we will have difficulty with "those who suffer deprivation." If our prayers become too full of human imagery, of course, we can end up talking more about ourselves than to God. So while good liturgical language is simple and concrete, it is still governed by purpose: it is for speaking to God.

Liturgical language skirts the fringes of poetic diction. Liturgical style employs subtle rhythmics to speed or slow spoken phrases, plays with the evocative sounds of words, uses repetition, cadence, alliteration, internal vowel rhymes, which, while natural to human speech patterns, also relate to deep affective levels within the self. Writing liturgy is also a technical theological work. Use of poetic devices is not primarily an expressive striving for effect but rather an offering of our words to God. Liturgy is not casual conversation but a dialogue with God. Because faith addresses God in liturgy, ordinary language must "stretch" to voice our awe in the presence of the Holy. The devices that liturgical writers employ must be used modestly and with unusual discipline lest they call attention to themselves and disrupt the focus of corporate worship.

Liturgical language is a language of recollection and response. It is not a language of immediate religious experience. Scholars who have studied forms of religious experience remark on mystic silences or ecstatic utterance, not to mention fixed "mantra" words and types of glossolalia. Liturgical language does not attempt to serve up some immediate dazzle of God; rather liturgy is a response to God's remembered goodness, gratitude for God's presence to faith, and petition in view of the future God has promised. Liturgical language, therefore, strives to be useful rather than conceited, truthful rather than elaborate. Liturgical writing at best is not so much a high art as a form of neighbor love and a modest service of God.

Notes

1. For literature on liturgical language, see Daniel B. Stevick, *Language in Worship* (New York: Seabury Press, 1970); also David G. Buttrick, "On Liturgical Language," *Reformed Liturgy and Music* 15, no. 2 (Spring 1981): 74–82.

2. For discussion, see Gwen K. Neville and John H. Westerhoff, *Learning through Liturgy* (New York: Seabury Press, 1979).

3. See James F. White, "Function and Form of the Eucharistic Prayer," *Reformed Liturgy and Music* 16, no. 1 (Winter 1982): 18–21; also, see texts in R. Jasper and G. Cuming, *Prayers of the Eucharist* (New York: Oxford University Press, 1980).

4. The collect can be rearranged or written loosely. For a classic essay on this topic, see John Wallace Sutter, Jr., *The Book of English Collects* (New York: Harper and Bros., 1940), xv–lii.

5. Rom 8:26–27.

6. For an examination of social metaphors, see G. Lakoff and M. Johnson, *Metaphors We Live By* (Chicago: University of Chicago Press, 1980). Catholic theologians have studied religious metaphor: David Burrell, *Analogy and Philosophical Language* (Yale University Press, 1973) and David Tracy, *The Analogical Imagination: Christian Theology and the Culture of Pluralism* (New York: Crossroad, 1981). For Protestant studies, see Sallie McFague, *Metaphorical Theology* (Philadelphia: Fortress Press, 1982), Ian Ramsey, *Models and Mystery* (New York: Oxford University Press, 1964), *Religious Language* (New York: Macmillan, 1967), *Models for Divine Activity* (London: SCM Press, 1973), and especially Paul Ricoeur, *The Rule of Metaphor* (University of Toronto Press, 1970).

7. The Presbyterian Church's *Worshipbook* is an unfortunate example, although its liturgical texts were eventually rewritten in response to feminist concern; for texts see the special issue of *Reformed Liturgy and Music* (Fall 1974).

8. Gal 3:28.

9. For a sensitive discussion of the "sexism" issue plus bibliographic help, see Keith Watkins, *Faithful and Fair* (Nashville: Abingdon Press, 1981).

10. The "edges of language" is a phrase borrowed from Paul van Buren, *The Edges of Language* (New York: Macmillan, 1972).

11. See my essay, "Renewal of Worship — A Source of Unity?," *Ecumenism, The Spirit, and Worship,* ed. L. Swidler (Pittsburgh: Duquesne University Press, 1967), 215–36.

12. For amusing if terrifying examples of cant, see Arthur Herzog, *The B. S. Factor* (Baltimore: Penguin Books, 1974).

38

The Names and Images of God

J. FRANK HENDERSON

Only in our generation have Christians begun to reflect seriously on how they name and describe God in liturgical prayer. Names and predominant metaphors referring to God have remained remarkably constant throughout Christian history; when small changes have occurred, they do not seem to have been based on conscious reflection or explicit criteria.

In the twentieth century, however, changes have been occurring in the images of God in liturgical prayer. Some have been small and others major, some deliberate and others quite unconscious; the new liturgical books of the several churches have varied considerably in this regard. Independently, serious challenges have arisen to some of our language about God, both traditional and modern. Sometimes the two movements of change and challenge run together; at other times they collide, but always they lead us to hard questions: Who is the God whom we address in our liturgical prayer? How should we name this God, and what metaphors should we associate with the divine names? What do these names and images mean to us, and how do the invocations of our prayers function within the prayer-texts as a whole? Are our ways of naming and imaging God in liturgical prayer satisfactory today? Although many partial answers have been offered, much more thought needs to be given to this area of concern.

Recognizing the problem

These questions apply to all of liturgical prayer, but they come into sharpest focus in the addresses or invocations of prayers, and these will be the starting point of this discussion.

Liturgical prayers may be divided into several distinct categories with respect to names and images of God. One category includes the Lord's Prayer, the sign of the cross, creeds, blessings and doxologies. All of these prayers contain ex-

From *Liturgy: Language and Metaphor* 4, no. 4.

plicit trinitarian formulas. They are relatively resistant to change, though they have not escaped some criticism. These prayers will not be mentioned further.

A second group of prayers consists of collects, which until recently have been characterized by a very sparse use of the divine name "Father." In these collects, "Lord" is the most common name for the divine, followed by "God."

A third and final category includes the many prefaces and eucharistic prayers in which "Father" has been a predominant divine name. In these prayers, major metaphors are traditionally associated with the divine name, whether "God," "Lord" or "Father." Such metaphors include "almighty," "eternal" and, less frequently, "merciful."

Major changes have occurred in the invocations of the collects, prefaces and eucharistic prayers in the modern liturgical books in most churches. The present Roman Catholic texts in English may be taken as examples. Very briefly, three types of changes have been made in the traditional language about God. First, the use of the divine name "Father" in the invocations of collects has greatly increased. Second, the range of metaphors used in the same invocations has also very much increased, although the newer language tends to be found in less frequently used texts. Third, greater variation is observed in the invocations of the prefaces and eucharistic prayers; whereas "Father" is still predominant, it is no longer the sole divine name used.

Traditional and modern invocations of liturgical prayers may be questioned or criticized on a number of grounds. Several problems arise because the range of names and images, even in the modern texts, is quite small.

First, the invocations have become poor prayer; many are pious clichés, conventional "throat-clearing" phrases that have little impact and no longer function as real faith statements. Also, the language used for these invocations tends to be more conceptual than affective; for example, the tradition that almost automatically attaches "almighty" to "God" without concern for any meaning this might convey.

Second, some of the metaphors come from a very different age and culture than our own. They may contain social and political implications with which we are no longer comfortable or relate to experiences of God that are not always contemporary. Many such images have their origin in Roman and Byzantine court language and emphasize lordship and power.

Third, the view of God that is drawn from the invocations is quite limited; "almighty," "eternal" and to a lesser extent, "merciful" are by far the most common images. In addition, some features of our invocation language express views of God that simply are not acceptable, at least to some segments of the contemporary church.

Fourth, invocation language is often not taken very seriously. In translations one divine name or metaphor is interchanged with another at will. In the English translation of the modern Roman Catholic Sacramentary, for example, "Deus" and "Dominus" have been rendered as "Father" more than 500 times. Position, rhythm and euphony often are more important than content in determining which divine name and metaphors are used; commentaries rarely speak about the invocations or explain their varied formulations.

Fifth, and related to the above, there usually is little relationship between the invocation and the remainder of the prayer-text; the "story" told by the body of the prayer is often preceded by divine names and metaphors that are inappropriate.

Seeking appropriate language

How are these concerns regarding liturgical language about God to be approached? The contemporary conversation about liturgical language and religious language in general originates in several different quarters and exhibits diverse concerns. Philosophers, systematic theologians, theoreticians of language, anthropologists and sociologists, biblical specialists and literary critics as well as liturgists are involved — and each from a particular point of view.

The blending of these diverse approaches to liturgical language and language about God is still in process; some would say still in its infancy. Some of the questions that need to be addressed are formulated here from a liturgical viewpoint.

What kind (or kinds) of language is appropriate, if we consider liturgy to be prayer that is (a) ritual in nature; (b) communal rather than private; and (c) a religious experience for the participants?

As ritual prayer, liturgy is something people do and do repetitively (at greater or lesser intervals); its most basic mode of communication is nonverbal, though verbal language is also used. Ritual prayer proclaims the foundational myths and symbols of the community; thus, liturgy is always celebrative. In addition, ritual prayer is of more than one type. There are different kinds of ritual structures and several individual rites, and ritual prayers vary in form and type of content.

Because it is communal prayer, liturgy is most often spoken aloud or sung. It has some degree of formality (that may vary depending on the circumstances), and it comes out of and leads back to daily life and other religious experiences. Liturgy is the prayer of a community of believers and disciples, the prayer of a community with a history. It should be inclusive in nature, the prayer of all the members.

Although it is communal in nature, liturgy is also a religious experience. It speaks to individuals-in-community. Liturgy invokes the whole person; it is transformative, relational and very powerful. Thus, liturgy has God as its origin, focus and end. Liturgical prayer expresses, interprets, shapes and intensifies our understanding and experience of the Holy One. It also expresses the interrelationships among God, humankind, church and creation. Christian liturgy shapes a world view through, in and with Jesus Christ and in the power of the Holy Spirit.

What, then, are some of the questions regarding language that are raised by the preceding considerations?

If liturgical language is communal, then we must ask what distinguishes communal prayer from private prayer; formal prayer from informal prayer; and oral or sung prayer from prayer that is read silently. How is an appropriate balance to be achieved that respects tradition and responds to contemporary need? How is the good news to be effectively proclaimed in liturgical prayer? What language is so inclusive as to be real prayer for all who worship?

Much of the contemporary conversation regarding language about God arises out of philosophical and basic theological interests. Therefore, it is necessary to ask what distinguishes the language of believers addressed to God from the language of philosophy and reflective theology about God.

What language is appropriate for the religious experience of persons with both cognitive and affective needs? What makes a language powerful, evocative and transformative so that it elicits responses marked by feelings as well as thoughts, by intuitive reactions as well as logic? What kind of language is aesthetically acceptable?

What are the characteristics of language that accompanies the more fundamental nonverbal communication of ritual? What kind of language helps to convey the foundational myths of the community, so that they become stories that we can turn to again and again for further enrichment?

What languages are appropriate for the different liturgical structures, individual rites and distinct prayer genres?

What kind of language is least idolatrous in addressing God? What language is most effective in evoking and intensifying the experience of God.

The most promising approaches to many of these questions seem to lie in greater appreciation and more effective use of the language of storytelling, drama, rhetoric and poetry. In addition, contemporary discussions on the nature of metaphor and images are most helpful.

The major obstacles to better liturgical language also seem apparent, though this is perhaps more controversial. One obstacle is an unwillingness to allow liturgical language to be properly liturgical and to distance itself from the language of reflective theology. Literalism is another serious problem: the refusal or inability to accept story as story, metaphor as metaphor. Certainly many problems have arisen because liturgical language that once was intended and accepted as metaphor later was understood in a more literal manner. Whether these hurdles can be overcome remains to be seen; the task will not be easy.

Initial guidelines

How might these considerations and concerns be applied to the specific need to name and image God in the invocations of our liturgical prayers? Perhaps the following will serve as initial guidelines in a search for answers.

First, language to or about God must avoid any threat of idolatry. Though no human speech really is adequate in this regard, we should use language that least distorts, narrows or hampers our appreciation, understanding, experience and relationship with God.

Second, a wide range of metaphors should be used in our prayer invocations. These may be taken from both the biblical and postbiblical traditions; our storehouse of images has barely been explored.

Third, the names and metaphors used in liturgical prayer should be in touch not only with our tradition but also with our contemporary experiences of God, which may have shifted significantly from those of former times. At the present some nonverbal aspects of the liturgical renewal express these new experiences better than verbal language does.

Fourth, the names and images used should be such as to resist, if not exclude, literalism. This depends in part on the vocabulary used and in part on the way it is used. Current discussions on the use of "broken" images are helpful here. In this connection we need to discern whether older names and images that have been distorted by literal interpretations should be discarded or whether they can or should be reused in ways in which their original force can be appreciated once again.

Fifth, the invocations should be effective and engaging faith statements, capable of seizing the attention of heart and mind.

Sixth, the invocation should be a real and meaningful part of the story told by the prayer-text as a whole.

How, then, shall the invocations of liturgical prayers be composed? I suggest that the body of the prayer be written first, with due consideration for its liturgical context and function, rite, season and literary form. Next, the composer will consider who the God is that this particular prayer — this one story — addresses, and what our experience is of this God in liturgy and in daily life.

Such a meditation will lead to decision. One of the traditional divine names will appear as more appropriate than the others for this prayer, or perhaps some image (for example, the creator) should be used in place of such a name. One or more metaphors can then be chosen to relate to the story of the prayer, to the particular divine name chosen and to the particular experience of God that it relates. The greatest creativity should be used in finding appropriate images.

After the prayer has been written, the invocation that results and its connection with the body of the prayer will be criticized from a literary point of view. When a set of prayers is under consideration, the entire collection should be examined as a whole to insure that God is appropriately portrayed and the community story is faithfully presented.

In the end we simply have to accept that our language of faith is now in crisis, that our solutions quite likely are only temporary and provisional. We will stumble on our journey to a better liturgical language, however, if we do not seriously attend to our language for God, especially in the invocations of our prayers.

39

The Rite of Sprinkling
as an Invitation to Worship

MARGARET MARY KELLEHER

Similar origins, common meanings and values draw people together in communities. The members of a community share an identity, which is continually reinforced and reappropriated each time the group convenes to act together for the common good. The group that does not meet disintegrates; hence, the rituals surrounding births, deaths and holidays are important occasions for recognizing and strengthening families, organizations and other cultural groups. A document from the church of the third century reveals an awareness of the significance of gathering for the continued life of the group. It exhorts people to assemble faithfully lest the church be deprived and the Body scattered by their staying away (*Didascalia*, chap. 13).

Our shared identity as members of the body of Christ enables us to come together to celebrate the eucharist, to pray together, and to express and constitute ourselves as a church. Together we are a community of persons who share the same Spirit, the Spirit who animated and directed Jesus through his life and ministry, his death and resurrection. In our gatherings we call to mind Jesus' own transformation from death to new life in the power of the Spirit and we ourselves participate in that transformation. Thus we proclaim our hope for the complete transformation of ourselves and all creation. We come together to remember; that is our reason to hope and our mission as church. If we as a church lose our memory, we will also have lost our identity.

Role of ritual in the community

One of the major functions of ritual is to keep memory alive by communicating the values and meanings that bind a group together. The symbolic actions or

From *Liturgy: Rites of Gathering and Sending Forth* 1, no. 4.

objects used within a ritual are carriers of value and meaning. Victor Turner calls these ritual symbols multivocal because they are capable of carrying a number of meanings.[1]

Some of the meanings carried by ritual symbols are sensory and evoke feelings; some are cognitive and express the ideas and norms of the group. In a properly working ritual, the ritual symbols are alive, and there is a field of interaction between these two types of meaning. The feelings stimulated by the sensory meanings can be transferred to the cognitive or normative meanings. This brings new life to ideas and visions — to the meaning of the symbols. Persons participating in the ritual appropriate these meanings and act accordingly. The ritual effects a re-presentation to the group of its foundational meanings and values by engaging people affectively in those meanings. In the ritual, in other words, they remember and renew their identity as a community.

Every time the church gathers to celebrate a ritual, if it is celebrated effectively, those present recognize and recommit themselves to the meanings around which they have been gathered. There are, however, many factors that might inhibit this sense of a shared identity in a living church. The social and cultural context, the needs of the community and the faith of the persons present must be considered as well as the ritual itself. Above all, attention must be directed to the way in which the ritual is performed so that its symbols may be brought to life and its potential made effective for the life of the community.

The gathering of the assembly

The purposes of the introductory rites are to make the assembled people a unified community and to prepare them properly to listen to God's word and celebrate the eucharist. But these are impossible tasks unless something already unifies the community — some bond that can be made explicit. These rites must evoke a common memory and remind the people assembled of who they are as a community.

The church is an assembly gathered by the word of God and animated by the Spirit. The same Spirit whereby God anointed Jesus at his baptism has been given to each of us, and, although there may be many immediate reasons for gathering as a church, it is ultimately the communion of life we share through baptism that brings us together as a community to celebrate the eucharist.

The practice of infant baptism makes it impossible for many Christians to recall their baptism. Many come to church to celebrate a socialization process rather than to celebrate a personal conversion experience. Others remember a conversion experience, but it was many years after and unrelated to baptism. The introductory rites evoke the memory of baptism only among those who were baptized as adults. The ritual task in relation to other persons is more complicated. The meaning of their baptism must be disclosed and an invitation extended to them to continue it in their lives.

Rite of blessing and sprinkling holy water

The first appendix of the present sacramentary (Roman rite) includes a "Rite of Blessing and Sprinkling Holy Water," which may be used as an alternate to the standard introductory rites for masses celebrated on Sundays or Saturday evening. The practice is not a new one in the church. The rite of sprinkling the congregation before mass has been traced as far back as the eighth century, and rituals for the blessing of water were performed as early as the sixth century.[2]

This rite can be an effective means for gathering the community around a common identity. It opens with a greeting and invitation to prayer that is also an invitation to let the water remind one of baptism. Water is naturally a multivocal symbol capable of carrying and communicating many meanings. It is essential for life; it destroys, purifies, cleanses and refreshes. Within Christianity, this multiplicity of meanings is condensed in baptism. Christians have been born again of water and the Spirit; they have passed through the waters of death with Jesus into new life; and, cleansed by flowing water, they have been given a new heart and a new Spirit. Christians are led to the refreshing waters of life over and over again by the shepherd whose flock they are.

When a multivocal symbol is used within a ritual its meaning is specified by its position in relation to the other elements in the ritual field. The prayers and songs and gestures accompanying the use of water in the rite of sprinkling play a major role in drawing out one or more of the meanings associated with baptism. For example, the psalm most commonly associated with this rite in the past was Psalm 51, especially the words: "Take hyssop and sprinkle me, that I may be clean; wash me, that I may become whiter than snow." This obviously emphasizes the cleansing properties of water and suggests that after we have been washed clean in the healing waters we can come to the table of the Lord. Unfortunately for hundreds of years, our spirituality was greatly impoverished because only this meaning, of purification and cleansing, was reflected in our traditions, to the exclusion of the others. Although this is the traditional understanding, it is not the only possibility.

The elements in the rite are the invitation to prayer, the blessing of the water and the sprinkling of all those present while an appropriate song is sung. This can lead immediately into the opening prayer, unless the Gloria is to be said or sung. These elements form a unit in themselves but one that is part of the total eucharistic ritual. The peak moment in the small unit, the action of the sprinkling, should be related to the climactic moment of the total ritual, the action of sharing the bread and the cup. Then the identity of the group as church, the body of Christ sharing the one Spirit, is reinforced.

The intensity of meaning builds when all of the elements in the rite of blessing and sprinkling are directed to the communication of one or another of the meanings of baptism. Instead of the purifying aspect of water we may wish to stress its life-giving aspect; it is the water of life, the living spring of which we all partake and which makes us one. The first of the blessings suggested in the rite communicates this idea and the careful choice of an appropriate song will reinforce the meaning.

Planning the rite

If meaning is to be effectively communicated in a ritual, a dynamic interaction must occur between its sensory and cognitive components. The symbols used must engage persons affectively. Thus in the case of a water rite, attention must be given to visual and tactile dimensions of meaning, to the way in which people see and feel the water. Carefully managed, water will communicate its natural properties: its ability to refresh, quicken, cleanse and purify. It is in its natural state that water is a carrier for those meanings associated with it in the Christian tradition of baptism. Water placed in a small opaque container where it cannot be seen has little if any ability to signify meaning. On the other hand, placing the water in a large, clear glass bowl offers a sensory stimulus to the gathering that can lead to a variety of associations when the prayers of blessing are said. It also provides a focus of attention. This ritual action of sprinkling was chosen for the same reason. It allows for the touching of each individual with the blessed water.[3]

Every ritual action is subordinate to a goal, which must be kept in mind by those in charge of planning and executing the ritual. The goal of the blessing and sprinkling is to gather the congregation in the memory and meaning of baptism in order that they may be aware of the oneness they already have in the Lord as they begin the celebration of the eucharist. The actions, prayers and gestures of the ritual proclaim this meaning and invite those gathered to participate in it. The degree and extent of that participation results ultimately from the freedom of those present, but it is important that the invitation be carefully and graciously extended.

The following illustrations of the rite of blessing and sprinkling have been used successfully, but it is critical that planners attend to the context or social field within which the rite occurs. What works in one situation may be a disaster in another. Consequently, these are offered not as patterns to be copied but as ideas to stimulate further creativity.

Texts for the rite

This first celebration of the rite of sprinkling symbolized that the new life received by all in the living waters of baptism is still available to all who seek it. Before the door leading into the chapel a large glass bowl filled with water was set on a table. Its base was surrounded by green branches and it was placed in such a way that it caught the sunlight coming through the window. Standing next to the table with the water was a lighted candle on a stand. Participants gathered in the reception area outside the chapel. The president of the assembly and a lay minister positioned themselves next to the bowl to begin the rite.

1. The Rite of Sprinkling: an invitation to worship

A member of the congregation says the invitatory:

In these past days we have been discovering the living streams which flow deep within us.

We gather here to celebrate the eucharist because we believe that the source of that living stream is the same Spirit which led Jesus through the valley of death in glory.

Let us remember and seek once again his Spirit by which we were made one in the waters of baptism.

President of the assembly blesses the water:

> God our Father,
> Your gift of water
> brings life and freshness to the earth;
> it washes away our sins and brings us eternal life.
> We ask you now to bless this water
> and to give us your protection on this day
> which you have made your own.
> Renew the living spring of your life within us
> and protect us in Spirit and body,
> that we may be free from sin
> and come into your presence
> to receive your gift of salvation.
> We ask this through Christ our Lord. Amen.
>
> (from the Sacramentary)

After the blessing of the water, the president and another participant dip their hands in the water and touch one another's mouth. As the members of the gathering proceed into the chapel they pass the water, pausing momentarily to be blest by the president and lay minister who dip their hands into the water and touch the participants lightly on the lips, or make the sign of the cross on their foreheads. During this action all sing.

COME TO THE WATER

> O let all who thirst, let them come to the water.
> O let all who have nothing, let them come to the Lord:
>   without money, without price.
> Why should you pay the price except for the Lord?
> And let all who seek, let them come to the water.
> And let all who have nothing, let them come to the Lord:
>   without money, without strife.
> Why should you spend your life, except for the Lord?

After the procession, the bowl and candle are placed in front of the altar. The opening prayer of the mass follows, leading into the liturgy of the word.

At the invitation to communion, the president recalls the opening rite, announcing that we now share in the bread and cup of life because we have received the waters of life. A poem from John of the Cross, which also relates the eternal spring to the living bread of the eucharist, can be used as a postcommunion reading.

> Song of the Soul that Rejoices in
>   Knowing God through Faith
> That eternal spring is hidden,
> For I know well where it has its rise,
>   Although it is night.
> I do not know its origin, for it hasn't one,
> But I know that every origin has come from it.
>   Although it is night.
> I know that nothing else is so beautiful,
> And that the heavens and the earth drink there
>   Although it is night.
> I know well that it is bottomless
> And that no one is able to cross it
>   Although it is night.
> Its clarity is never darkened,
> And I know that every light has come from it
>   Although it is night.
> I know that its streams are so brimming
> They water the lands of hell, the heavens, and earth,
>   Although it is night.
> I know well the stream that flows from this spring
> Is mighty in compass and power,
> Although it is night.
> I know that the stream proceeding from these two
> Is preceded by neither of them,
>   Although it is night.
> This eternal spring is hidden
> In this living bread for our life's sake
>   Although it is night.
> It is here to call to creatures: and they
> Are filled with this water, although in darkness,
>   Because it is night.
> This living spring which I long for,
> I see in this bread of life,
>   Although it is night.

> (From *The Collected Words of St. John of the Cross*,
> trans. Kieran Kavanaugh, O.C.D., and
> Otilio Rodriguez, O.C.D. [Washington, D.C.:
> ICS Publications, 1973]).

In a variation of this first rite, the second emphasizes the water of baptism as a cleansing and purifying agent. The bowl and candle are placed as before, but after the people have gathered in the chapel, the ministers come to the water and bless it, using the second blessing from the sacramentary.

2. The Rite of Sprinkling: a purification

> Lord God almighty,
> creator of all life,
> of body and soul
> we ask you to bless this water:
> as we use it in faith
> forgive our sins
> and save us from all illness
> and the power of evil.
> Lord,
> in your mercy,
> give us living water,
> always springing up as a fountain of salvation:
> free us, body and soul, from every danger,
> and admit us to your presence
> in purity of heart.
> Grant this through Christ our Lord. Amen.

As cantors and congregation alternate the verses of Psalm 51 (the Gelineau version has an antiphon), the ministers walk among the congregation sprinkling all with water, using the green branches to do so. The opening prayer of the mass follows and the liturgy of the word.

Although the emphasis in this article has been primarily on the use of sprinkling as an introductory rite, a third variation could occur during a eucharist that includes a liturgy of infant baptism. The focus of the rite is after the baptism and before the anointing. (This rite could easily be adapted for use during an adult baptism.) Such a ritual can be particularly effective in engaging the congregation and creating in them a sense of themselves as church. The child and its parents and godparents are met in the foyer by the minister, who is accompanied by two persons from the regular Sunday congregation. The minister signs the child with the sign of the cross, welcoming the infant in the name of the church, and the two people do likewise in the name of the local church. The parents and godparents first, then all in the congregation are invited to recall their own baptism and to receive from one another the sign of the cross.

When it is time for the baptism, the same two representatives of the congregation approach the font with the minister and family. After the baptism and before the anointing, they fill glass bowls with water from the font and join the minister who sprinkles the people, while processing up and down the aisle. The congregation sings the Deiss hymn "There Is One Lord."

Final reflections

There is much potential in the "Rite of Blessing and Sprinkling Holy Water," if it is used carefully and if attention is given to all the symbolic objects, actions and persons involved. The association of the symbol of the cross, for example, with the symbol of the water communicates another meaning of baptism; that we have died with Jesus into a new life and that we as a church are gathered under the sign of the cross. The use of a variety of ministers communicates the fact that all who are baptized are members of and responsible for the life of the church.

To signify, the water should always be visible and inviting and available for people to touch again or to take home with them if they wish. Moreover, the meaning of the rite within the larger celebration must be clear. It is not meant to be an action that dominates but one that leads the gathering to the table of the Lord.

If it achieves its purpose, it will help the people gathered at the eucharist to remember who they are and why they come to the same table. Then they may be able to understand and appropriate the truth of Augustine's statement to the newly baptized:

> If then you are the Body of Christ and his members, it is your sacrament that reposes on the altar of the Lord. It is your sacrament which you receive. You answer "Amen" to what you yourself are and in answering you are enrolled. You answer "Amen" to the word "The Body of Christ." Be, then, a member of the Body of Christ to verify your "Amen." . . . Be what you see and receive what you are (Sermon 272).

Notes

1. Victor Turner, *Dramas, Fields, and Metaphors* (Ithaca, N.Y.: Cornell University Press, 1974). See also his "Forms of Symbolic Action: Introduction," in *Forms of Symbolic Action* (Seattle: University of Washington Press, 1969), and "Symbolic Studies," in the *Annual Review of Anthropology (1975)*. I rely on Turner's theory for much of the present article.

2. An early blessing of water can be found in the *Gelasian Sacramentary*, Reg. 316, ed. L. C. Mohlberg (Rome, 1966), 75, and a description of a ritual for the blessing and use of lustral water, in 76. For commentary, see A. Chavasse, *Le Sacramentaire Gelasien* (Tournai: Desclée, 1958), 50–56.

3. Joseph Jungmann, S.J., *The Mass of the Roman Rite* (New York: Benziger, 1951).

Part IV

There Is No East or West

"To love the world as God loves the world is to embrace it as it is and run with it, straining towards salvation."

—Rachel Reeder in *Liturgy: The Art of Celebration*

40

Culture, Counterculture and the Word

Michael Warren

The conjunction of catechesis and liturgy brings great problems and great opportunities. Two stories, one a modern-day parable, the other an exemplary tale, graphically illustrate this.

The first story has to do with the Nazi-era exploits of one Oskar Schindler, a German mechanical engineer born into a Roman Catholic family in a corner of what is now East Germany. Much to the distress of his devout mother, Schindler, even as a youth, was a negligent Catholic. His biographer, Thomas Keneally, writes, "If he spends a part of some June morning at Mass, he does not bring back to the villa [his home] much of a sense of sin.[1]

Schindler became a notorious womanizer, a drinker of almost legendary capacity, a lover of fast cars and motorcycles, a wheeler-dealer. At one time he had, in addition to his prayerful Roman Catholic wife, a German mistress, a Polish secretary with whom he had a long affair, and so many casual liaisons that nobody could number them. He drank only the best, and he drank a lot of it, though somehow he always managed to keep his wits through frequent late-night carousings.

The good Samaritan

Yet this Schindler, a fallen-away Catholic and sexual profligate, risked his life many times over to protect the lives of the Polish and Central European Jews who worked in the munitions factories he managed as part of the Nazi war effort. He told so many lies and pulled so many strings to save the thousand or so Jews who worked for him that he was three times jailed by the Gestapo. He could easily have been killed for using his factories as a sort of Noah's ark. Each

From *Liturgy: The Church and Culture* 6, no. 1.

time he escaped death but only by bribing his way with large sums of money, jewels and goods.

Near the end of the war, in a last, desperate and ultimately successful effort to preserve the workers' lives for a few more months, he moved his factory from Cracow to a more remote area in the village of Brinnlitz, not far from where the Czech, German and Polish borders meet. Since Schindler himself had been born near the area, it is likely that many Roman Catholics, and certainly many Christians, lived there. Yet these people used what little political power they had to oppose the Jews. When the first group of Jewish workers arrived, they were met with graffiti exhorting Schindler to "Keep the Jews out of Brinnlitz!"

As a Roman Catholic, I could not read this part of Keneally's book without wondering about the worship life of these people — Christians whose ill hospitality would deny these condemned Jewish workers not just a place to stay but their very lives. Were some of these anti-Semites devout? Did they engage in Marian devotions? Did any regularly spend hours in prayer before the blessed sacrament? Did some of them attend daily mass in the village church at Brinnlitz?

These questions arise from the irony that the one in this tale closest to Jesus' way of life is the womanizing, nonworshiping Oskar Schindler, who risked his life to stand in solidarity with others. This is the man for whom the life of every single victim was priceless. Schindler's story confronts us with basic questions about what it means to be religious and to follow Jesus in our day. Like the parables of the New Testament, this story turns religion upside down. When we are overexposed to the story of the good Samaritan and dulled to the ironies of simple goodness, we need to find such a neighbor again in the face of Oskar Schindler.

The word as subversive

The second story began when I met a Maryknoll missioner who had been hounded out of Guatemala by death threats. For years, Daniel Jensen had trained peasant catechists in a remote area of the country near the Mexican border. Before he left the country, three hundred of his catechists had been murdered by government death squads.[2] His story shocked me. I could not stop thinking about it.

A few weeks later, I attended a lecture in which a woman from Nicaragua showed slides of camps in her country for Guatemalan refugees. She casually remarked that in one camp there were only women and children because the men, who were catechists, had all been killed.

At that comment, something clicked. Suddenly I caught a glimpse of the catechist as a dangerous and subversive person. In Latin America, a catechist is a *delegado de la palabra*, a "representative of the word." And it is obvious, at least to those in Guatemala, that this "word" is dangerous and upsetting. The word that the catechists represent is a transforming word; it calls people to do justice on a daily basis and to replace unjust systems with a society in keeping with God's kingdom. The simple man or woman who translates this word into ordinary speech becomes so threatening to the status quo that he or she must be eliminated, murdered.

In that moment of insight, I did not forget that in most parishes in the United States, the catechist is the most predictable and the safest of persons. There is little to fear from the catechist's ministry or message. Aimed predominantly at children and rarely dealing with questions of justice, the catechist's word tends to foster predictable and correct behavior.

These two stories harbor some of the profound questions liturgists and catechists must face now and in the future. We are all in danger of trivializing our liturgical and catechetical concerns. There is a lingering possibility that liturgists may become preoccupied with the worship act or event and forget that its context is the life of a group of persons who do or do not embody gospel values in deeds, not just in words. We could be aesthetically astute in our latter-day village churches of Brinnlitz, while ignoring matters of greater moment. Parish catechetical leaders can become the technicians of sacramental preparation and ritualization, focused behaviorally if not theoretically on programs for children, while avoiding the deeper questions of the lived faith of the community. Such a catechesis has little relationship to the dangerous message of the Guatemalan martyrs.

Liturgy and life

In contemporary liturgical writing, the slogan "Liturgical action is an embodiment of the community's life" is a recurrent theme. I began to come to terms with the radical implications of this slogan several years ago when I was asked to address the question, "Can the liturgy speak to teens?"[3]

It did not take long for me to realize that the question was wrong-headed. The liturgy is not some sort of message, nor is it a communications system. It does not speak to, it speaks from. Liturgy is expressive human activity, a symbolic expression of the life of a particular group of people. It does for the life of the group what sharing a meal does for married couples. Eating together embodies more than personal nourishment; it embodies a way of being together. In the same way, the liturgy is more than personal devotion. It is the assembly's way of life.

Several liturgical scholars have worked on this theme. Geoffrey Wainwright's *Doxology* has helped us see that liturgical practice embodies an entire stance toward God.[4] Worship is as much a key theological source as are doctrinal statements. At a more popular level, Robert Hovda has also examined the relationship between culture and worship.[5] He alerts us to the danger in a worship practice that embodies a dominant culture instead of confronting it. A community's consciousness can be so dominated by cultural presuppositions that even in worship those presuppositions have more meaning and power for us than our commitment to Jesus' way. Hovda writes, for example,

> "Cultural adaptation" is a two-edged sword in the liturgical life of the churches. If it means that liturgy is the work of a concrete faith community in a particular time and place and therefore that it cannot be celebrated except in the context and out of the stuff of that church's life and experience, it is simply a requisite of true public worship. If, however, it should become, by some jaded process in the corporate psyche of the local church, an excuse for capitulating to inimical aspects of the culture of the time and place, then it is devilish indeed. Then it becomes an excuse for avoiding the gospel call to reconcile, to liberate and unify the human family, to witness to and work for the reign of God.[6]

Liturgy embodies the life of a group of people. The dominant culture finds its way into this life just as sand on a windy day at the beach gets into everything, including your sandwich.

More attention needs to be given to this problem in liturgical and catechetical studies. Its oversight is especially glaring, however, in catechetical circles. For the last twenty years, for example, the youth-retreat movement has been presenting to youth, pretty much unchallenged, a middle-class Jesus. This Jesus of comfort represents God's personal love for the individual youth; he is the assuager of adolescent anxieties, the giver of the Jesus hug. The Jesus who confronted social and political structures, and paid for it with his life is notably absent. Such an approach reflects the catechetical message that the Jesus who exposed injustice in his day, the Jesus who is dangerous like the Guatemalan catechists, is dismissible, while the Jesus of the personal hug is indispensable. In this catechesis, the man for others has been transformed into the man for us.

A new spirituality

Catechists and liturgists can find common ground in examining how our catechetical or liturgical programs embody cultural presuppositions. To give a hint of the work before us, let me cite Robert Coles's description of worship among the middle and upper classes. In the churches of the privileged classes, he writes,

> There is more order [than in the churches of the poor], but order of a different kind, more self-regard in the way in which one worships. *Attention* is paid, and in a certain way: to what one sees and what one hears and what one reads, yes, but also, significantly, to oneself. You enter the churches of the privileged full of yourself. You are well-dressed, pleased to be in a place where you are treated well, with great respect and personal attention, and where there will be — and this is important — no surprises. The format is fixed, and the words and music are modulated, no extremes either from church or from those who are at worship. Without having been told, you understand that if anything happens to you of a spiritual nature, you are to keep it to yourself. Just as there are certain words used in certain ways in rural services, these privileged places of worship have theirs, and time moves along here in a measured (but pleasant) fashion. By contrast [with the worship of the

poor] there are no unplanned stops at this word, no responses or outbreaks to that
moment of sound; in these places of worship there are no abrupt moves forward or
doubling back, either in response to the minister or those at worship. As I said, the
privileged ones do not like to be surprised; they have not come to be confronted or
to be put into situations where they are not in control.[7]

Even beyond Coles's assertions, I have reached the conclusion that the
most serious question affecting those in pastoral ministry is the question of
spirituality. Liturgists and catechists face an enormous dilemma: how to help
middle-class and upper-class Christians find a gospel-centered spirituality that
will affect their lifestyle.[8]

This task is made difficult by the massive and adverse cultural forces affecting
us today. They override the effects of an hour's dalliance before the altar or in
some catechetical program. Our society is now dominated by hundreds of thousands of well-trained, highly paid, clever and technically proficient orchestrators
of attention, whose task is to make sure we only pay attention to those matters
that help their employers.[9] Our world is characterized by a wild proliferation
of verbal, graphic and sound images, which can be printed or electronically re-
produced in great quantities. Those who control the way the world is named, it
has been said, control consciousness. Today we must add that those who control
the images by which we interpret the world control consciousness from an even
deeper level.[10]

In a world where so many forces vie for our attention, the crisis of the human
spirit has become the crisis of knowing what matters are worth our attention.
Our spirits are defined by our attention. Pay attention to trivial matters as a way
of life, and one's life becomes characterized by trivia. Pay attention to commercial imagery concocted to bring endlessly before consciousness the next set of
products to purchase, and one's spirit becomes preoccupied with having and con-
suming; even one's speech becomes littered with commercial imagery. One may
eventually approach worship or catechesis as a commercial product, evaluated by
whether it does or does not satisfy, enlarge or comfort the self.

This is an enormous problem for persons who wish to direct attention to
Jesus' imagery of compassion and mutuality across cultural barriers. We may
know that worship involves refocusing attention and that catechesis is a sort
of attention therapy. Still, our catechists inhabit the land of commercially concocted imagery, as do our presiders and other liturgical ministers.[11] To compound
the problem, we ourselves also dwell in that land, and we tend to dwell there not
as if it were the place of our exile or of our wandering passage but as if it were
the land of milk and honey.

The positive side of this problem is that it joins us, catechists and liturgists,
in a common task. Since the religious meanings in ritual can be easily over-
ridden or dominated by cultural presuppositions, liturgists cannot counter the
power of high-tech inculturation by themselves. Nor can catechists by themselves successfully counter this problem, as the current attempts at a catechesis
of peace are showing us. The only decisive counterforce to the cultural pres-

sures of our time may be the power of whole communities struggling together toward an appropriate spirituality characterized by a transformed way of paying attention. These communities will be formed with the collaboration of liturgists and catechists. In the period of Christian origins, liturgy and catechesis were siblings, but like many siblings they have tended to drift apart with time. If we are to assist communities in becoming credible gospel witnesses, we will have to re-establish their proper close bonds.

The power of images

I cannot set forth here a complete program for the closer collaboration of liturgists and catechists. I do want to suggest, however, that an important first step in an image-dominated culture is to become more aware of images and how they work.[12] Certain kinds of images provide the lenses through which we view reality. As with any kind of lens, we can easily forget that we are seeing through it.

The cultural image of woman, for example, is a lens that shapes perception, behavior and social structures.[13] This "image" goes beyond the image of any particular woman, and even beyond the specific knowledge a person has of anatomy, physiology, psychology or history. The lens image of woman, in fact, precedes such specific kinds of knowledge. The image selects the aspects of knowledge we choose to pay attention to and arranges them into a pattern. In this sense, the image of woman has with it a whole train of associations and expectations that are preconscious and closely tied to feelings.

I find two very different images of woman in the college-age men I meet. These young men are continually evaluating the womanliness of the women they meet according to criteria latent in their lens images. For some, a woman is a coy, dependent, not overbright individual with a particular "look," usually a look corresponding to fashion and anatomical calculations. Such a woman does not readily disagree with a man, is apt to smile a lot in his presence, and takes special pleasure in his sense of humor, that is, she laughs at his jokes. Others have a different image: a woman is a self-directed adult, compassionate, reflective, possibly witty, but in general, able to meet other adults of either sex on an equal footing. She is not better than men, nor is she worse. These images are more than simple personality preferences; they are lens images that select and arrange the significance of what one sees and experiences.

Underlying these lens images are even more basic images. Gibson Winter calls them comprehensive metaphors, which function almost the way the eye does as the primal lens through which we see.[14] If we take the lens image for granted because we are too busy seeing through it, the lens of the eye is taken for granted in an even more fundamental way. Comprehensive metaphors, then, furnish coherence to our world and impose a fundamental pattern on all our experience.

Images of domination

The image of domination and subordination is a comprehensive metaphor that characterizes the consciousness of many in our society, yet it is profoundly at odds with the message of Jesus.[15] This metaphor or mind set tends to break personal and social reality into two categories: superior and inferior. It also contains the notion that the inferior are rightfully under the control or domination of the superior.

The domination-subordination metaphor subsumes a variety of dichotomies. One is the winners-losers dichotomy. In victory, one group proves superiority and affirms how right it is to dominate the beaten, defeated or simply unequal group. The winner-loser dichotomy divides the superior from the inferior but also the stronger from the weaker. It may be difficult, for example, to convince a young man who unconsciously uses this metaphor that although women's physical strength is of a different sort than men's, women are not necessarily poorer athletes. In the universe interpreted through the domination-subordination metaphor, stronger means superior and dominant.

These dichotomies, superior-inferior, winner-loser, stronger-weaker, find their way into everyday language. In popular speech, certain individuals are named "losers" and others "winners." Winners are those who successfully dominate; they are the ones on top. Popular speech also enshrines a range of expressions about being ahead or getting ahead or getting the advantage, as in a race. When we speak of the "arms race," images from the playing field are transformed to address the political arena.[16] Another popular word that derives from domination-subordination thinking is "clout," which combines the imagery of the baseball bat with that of the prehistoric club.

The imagery that emerges from this comprehensive metaphor is clearly at odds with the gospel. Think of the word "one" as it is used in two very different celebrations. In sports, the word "one" usually means number one, the victors, those who have dominated their inferiors. The winners of a contest prance around and shout ecstatically, "We're number one!" In the eucharistic liturgy, however, the word "one" signifies the human unity of those joined by the Spirit of Jesus. Here "one" means communion and unity.

Once one sees the metaphor or examines the lens as a lens, a fundamental shift takes place in one's consciousness. Once we are aware, for example, of the metaphor implied in saying that women cannot preside in the assembly, no amount of theological sleight of hand can prevent us from realizing that we have ritualized a cultural pattern of male domination.

Countercultural catechesis

This brings us back to the heart of our problem. We "church people" operate out of the same culturally conditioned mind set as everyone else in our society. The primary conclusion from my study of how images and metaphors function in our society and how easily they can co-opt the network of meanings we call our tradition is that catechists and liturgists need to explore more consciously the power-laden metaphors proclaimed in our catechesis and dramatized in our worship.[17] We can too easily sidestep the radical, culture-questioning images and substitute slicker, more readily acceptable ones.

For instance, a highly appropriate but easily overlooked metaphor for Christian experience in our time may be "exile." How can we live in a nation having a first-strike policy that would kill millions of people in other lands without feeling like exiles, at least in the sense that the psychological and spiritual landscape is quite foreign to us? Yet we often develop our catechesis of faith story and faith journey in ways that exclude any sense of exile, while justifying individualistic progress toward greater religious self-actualization.[18] To use another example, the potentially powerful imagery of "the people of God" is often reduced to family imagery. The stress, then, is on warmth and intimacy, on private relationships rather than public witness.[19] These shifts reduce catechesis and worship to a middle-class ambience and take the edge off the gospel message.

Liberation theologians have begun to re-examine Christian imagery with an eye to posing it as a counter-imagery to that of the dominant culture. Their writings will aid us in our ministry to remove cultural cataracts. Middle-class persons seeking to redirect their spirituality need to think, however, not so much of liberation but of resistance.[20] In our day, Christian spirituality involves moving away from patterns of compliance and toward patterns of resistance.

When our communities come to adopt a public stance of solidarity with victims, then we will know we are moving again as a people in response to God's will. We will be in good company with others who similarly established such solidarity with victims. Leading the way will be Jesus whom we call Lord; and there, in the joyful throng among a horde of others, will be one Oskar Schindler.

Notes

1. Thomas Keneally, *Schindler's List* (New York: Penguin, 1983), 33.

2. Daniel Jensen, M.M., worked in the Department of Huehuetenango, which comprises the diocese of the same name. He left Guatemala in 1981, but the murders, which began in 1978, continue to the present. For background and corroboration, see Allan Nairn, "The Guns of Guatemala," *New Republic*, April 11, 1983, 17–21, and Gordon L. Bowen, "No Roadblocks to Death," *Commonweal* 111, no. 12 (June 15, 1984): 361–64.

3. See "Can the Liturgy Speak to Today's Teenagers?" in *Resources for Youth Ministry*, ed. Michael Warren (New York: Paulist Press, 1978), 225–36.

4. Geoffrey Wainwright, *Doxology: The Praise of God in Worship, Doctrine, and Life* (New York: Oxford University Press, 1980).

5. I have in mind especially his columns for *Worship:* nos. 1, 2 and 3, (1984).

6. Robert W. Hovda, "The Amen Corner," *Worship* 58, no.3 (1984): 251.

7. Robert Coles and George Abbott White, "The Religion of the Privileged Ones," *Cross Currents* 31, no. 1 (1981): 1–14; esp. 7.

8. Much more work needs to be done along the lines of Matthew Lamb, "Christian

Spirituality and Social Justice," *Horizons* 10, no. 1 (1983): 32–49; and Joe Holland, "The Spiritual Crisis of Modern Culture" (Washington, D.C.: Center of Concern, 1983). I find concern for lifestyle to be the central issue in Regis Duffy, *Real Presence* (San Francisco: Harper & Row, 1982); Matthew Lamb, *Solidarity with Victims* (New York: Crossroad, 1982); John F. Kavanaugh, *Following Christ in a Consumer Society* (Maryknoll, N.Y.: Orbis Books, 1982).

9. For a useful overview of this problem, see Stuart Ewen and Elizabeth Ewen, *Channels of Desire: Mass Images and the Shaping of American Consciousness* (New York: McGraw-Hill, 1982).

10. See Barbara Goldsmith, "The Meaning of Celebrity," *New York Times Magazine* (December 4, 1983): 75ff.; Kennedy Fraser, "The Fashionable Mind," *New Yorker* (March 13, 1978): 87ff.

11. John H. McKenna shows that liturgy need not contravene popular culture in "Liturgy: Toward Liberation or Oppression," *Worship* 56, no. 4 (1982): 291–308. See also A. Pieris, "Spirituality in a Liberation Perspective," *East Asian Pastoral Review* 20, no. 2 (1983): 139–50, esp. 140–41.

12. A valuable work on this question is Gibson Winter, *Liberating Creation* (New York: Crossroad, 1981).

13. Here, I am following Charles Davis, "Religion and the Sense of the Sacred," *CTSA Proceedings* 31 (1976): 87–105, esp. 87–91.

14. Winter, *Liberating Creation,* 1–28.

15. This metaphor is explored in Lamb, "Christian Spirituality and Social Justice." See also "Domination-Subordination," in Jean Baker Miller, *Toward a New Psychology of Women* (Boston: Beacon Press, 1976), 3–12.

16. See George Orwell's treatment of this transformation in his brief essay, "The Sporting Spirit," in *Selected Writings* (London: Heinemann, 1947), 159–62.

17. See Mark Searle, "Liturgy as Metaphor," *Worship* 55, no. 2 (1981): 98–120.

18. See Gregory Baum's critique of the journey image as middle-class in "Theology Questions Psychiatry," *Ecumenist* 20, no. 4 (May–June 1982): 55–59; and Gustavo Gutiérrez's use of the exile metaphor in *We Drink from Our Own Wells* (Maryknoll, N.Y.: Orbis Books, 1984).

19. See Parker Palmer, *The Company of Strangers* (New York: Crossroad, 1983); and Robert N. Bellah, "Religion and Power in America Today," *Commonweal* (December 3, 1982): 650–55.

20. Two useful sources for further reflection on resistance are "Toward a Theology of Resistance," in *Thomas Merton: The Nonviolent Alternative,* ed. Gordon Zahn (New York: Farrar, Straus & Giroux, 1980), 186–92; and Dorothee Soelle, "Resistance: Toward a First World Theology," *Christianity and Crisis* 39, no. 23 (July 1979): 178–82.

41

A Furore Normanorum, Libera Nos Domine

JAMES NOTEBAART

Thus another invective was added to the litany of the saints in the British Isles during the eleventh century, repeating a pattern that has occurred throughout the history of Christianity, as outsiders and their religious perspectives were judged. Such a pattern is not what you would call ecumenism!

When we speak about pastoral ecumenism and the initiatives that develop between churches, we often focus on social projects: food shelves, clothing closets, loaves and fishes. Our kitchens are ecumenical, but often our sanctuaries are not. Among fellow Christians, how hospitable is our table? Among those outside the borders of the Christian faith, how hospitable is our welcome? When we are talking about Christian ecumenism, we need to focus on how we create the boundaries of acceptance among us. But the same holds true for those outside the Christian faith. Will we, like the inhabitants of the British Isles, resort to the invective "From the fury of the Normans, Lord deliver us" to designate those whom we do not know?

On a recent Sunday an Episcopal congregation, a United Church of Christ community, a Christian gay community and a Roman Catholic mission gathered for eucharistic worship. In the most ancient sense of concelebration, we yielded the table to one of our members for eucharistic leadership. I recall the second-century *quartodeciman* controversy and the argument about the date of Easter in Rome. Anecitus, Bishop of Rome, yielded the Roman altar to Polycarp of Smyrna. Though the differences were deeply rooted in praxis, communion was shared as the outsider raised his hands over the gifts.

Among the four churches of our "communion," we find a bond that transcends denomination because we belong to a single cultural group. Our churches meet together each month because of our cultural commonality. Our communities often feel alone and oppressed in the dominant society. By the social

From *Liturgy: No East or West* 11, no. 3.

standards of our country, we are outsiders, the very group Victor Turner in his anthropology would describe as liminal. But therein lies our power: community exists at the edges. The bond that unites us is a perspective, a rhythm of life that is ancient.

This cultural bond creates a new set of relationships that I would not have expected. Ironically we have a growing bond with the "pagans," a bond that is stronger than with some Christian groups. That bond is created by our sense of what life is all about. That is why I asked at the beginning: How do we set the boundaries of acceptance? Never in my life would I have thought that the "pagans" and the Christians would rise up in prayer together, but that too happens as we mark the memorial of our dead or special gifts to our community. The Christian communities are always invited to participate in the indigenous religious ceremonies.

Sovereignty for our Sunday

I am reminded from my own classical background of Constantine's edict of March 21, 321, in which he called people of all persuasions to mark the day of the sun with a proper votive by gathering in an open field or in small groups. We, the Christians, rapidly read the edict as a proclamation of sovereignty for the Christian Sunday. We quickly labeled those who lived outside the village as *pagani* — "the peasants" — those on the heath as "heathens" and those in the forests as "savages" (from *silvatus* through the old French). Our very terminology set up a negative polarity that diminished the outsider and the outsider's religious faith; we did not think about what each group could contribute to the other. Our praxis, like that of Boniface destroying the sacred tree of the Teutonic peoples and Patrick changing the megaliths into crosses, was to destroy what we defined as non-Christian. We grounded our response to the outside based on the polity and doctrine of the Christian faith. We knew from our own doctrinal base what was Christian; Christianity came wrapped in a European cloak. Anything that wasn't in harmony was suppressed in the process of evangelization, a logical starting place that did not always bear the right kind of fruit but created an adversarial relationship rather than a partnership, resulting in a kind of cultural schizophrenia.

This antagonism, almost imperialism, has marked many of our 2,000 years. We have set fire to houses of prayer, Christian and non-Christian alike. Jacob Marcus's book *The Jew in Medieval Europe* tells the story of the nobleman Emico, who with a band of crusaders raided the Jewish communities in Speier, Mainz and Cologne in May 1096. Solomon bar Samson recounts the deaths of thousands of Jews, poignantly describing the anguish of one mother, Rachel, daughter of Rabbi Isaac ben Asher, who saw her four children dragged from the fearsome hiding place to die in front of each other. The death of William of Norwich in 1173 and the burning of the houses of prayer echo the same infamy. We have called the outsiders Arians, Albigensians, Huguenots, Jews or

Anabaptists. John Huss, Mazakute, Black Elk, Joan of Arc, Anne Frank, Rachel ba Isaac, Nestorius and Arius are the names of theological "losers" in the battle for orthopraxy. They came from within the fold and outside it; they were people of dignity and substance, concerned with the faith and its living expression.

The "pagans" of old

How do we critically evaluate this legacy of the Christian faith? What is Christian, and by what criteria do we judge its truth? These are the parameters of an ancient debate whose processes were defined by councils and synods. Orthopraxy (right living), Orthodoxy (right praise) and orthopistis (right belief) are important; they guide us in the tradition of a living Christian faith. But when we look at the first generation of Christians, though there was clearly a social mix, they were the "underdogs" who had little political power. They were the very people whom the Roman society accused of being godless because they grounded their faith in praxis and weren't adherents to the classical religious tradition of Rome. Has the process reversed itself? In other words, are we so much a part of the classical (albeit our own) religious tradition that praxis has fallen to the wayside? Are we living what we believe?

Today, with a growing Asian population and a newly recognized religious freedom of the North American Indians (1978), we need to ask the questions of acceptance and community anew. Now factored into the equation must be the contribution offered by the "outsiders," i.e., those who are not Christian, to the sustained life of faith. This potential oneness with outsiders is wider than personal comfort and acceptance, more penetrating than political solidarity, deeper than a common social vision. It has to do with faith and the ability to listen to the voice of God, who has spoken in other cultures with the same resonance that we hear in the Christian communion. This idea flies in the face of nineteenth-century missionary activities, yet it is part of the fabric of our world of belief today.

When we dig deep into the core act of our worship, we learn that we've always defined it as the worship Christ gives to the Father. It is a response to God, what God has asked of creation, the body of Christ giving praise to God. If we agree with the maxim that God is the end of our prayer, then the parameters of acceptance are stretched in a way that embraces other faiths, not merely other Christian communities.

There are mixed feelings about the official *Christian* ecumenical dialogue. Ministry, orders, church polity, theological diversity, the structures of worship, approaches to scriptural interpretation, even a common lectionary, have been primary focuses. Accords and covenants have been signed among the Christian churches, indicating progress from the stone-throwing days when children were told to pass by the "other people's" church buildings and never to look in the front doors.

But it appears that cultural diversity has grown faster than Christian ecumenism. There are different issues today than in the classical days of ecumenical dialogue; namely, the renaming of God, claiming the feminine, the indigenous religious beliefs that stretch across our continent in the American Indian peoples and the immigrant faiths from Asia and the Pacific Islands. To some these are threatening issues that belong outside the common structures of dialogue, but having been raised, these issues will not go away. Always part of the struggle are the central questions: Is the faith somehow watered down by diversity? What are we giving up to embrace diverse opinion? What are the principles that still keep us "theologically sound"?

The four communities that gathered on that recent Sunday are Christian American Indians from four tribes, the Ojibwey, the Dakota-Lakota and the Winnebego. We are proud of the religious heritage and the spiritual legacy of our ancestors. We know that some of our ceremonies date back five thousand years. Archaeology has proved this dating, for example, in the case of the plains people's use of the sweat lodge, an unbroken religious tradition that harmonizes with the Christian faith and deepens certain aspects of its spirituality, especially its sense of the goodness of all creation. How far do the doors open to embrace these expressions of faith? These are the "pagans" of old, yet how different it is when we put a name to them. Pagans? Hardly! See, the lines of definition are changing.

Does diversity weaken or strengthen?

The Roman Catholic church over the past three decades has begun to widen its language when it refers to other cultures and their religious expression. It has done this in part by widening the accepted definition of culture. Previously, the model for judging all other cultures was the European expression of the Greco-Roman world view; this accepted "norm" served as the control for evaluating the worthiness of other cultures. Today the Roman church uses the plural term "cultures" and accepts the innate validity underlying them as the premise of evangelization. Such a change in attitude was seen in Paul VI's trips to Africa (his talk in Uganda on the occasion of the canonization of the Uganda martyrs, for example; see also the Encyclical "Evangelization in the Modern World"). We see it in early official documents, such as "Gaudium et Spes" and "Sacrosanctum Concilium" of the Second Vatican Council. Indigenization is a respected term, as are inculturation and adaptation. The terms come through the works of Anscar J. Chupungco, John Waliggo and others. This change in approach represents the church's attitude to other continents. The model has widened. But what does it say within the confines of our own continent, which is filled with diverse world views and expressions of religious faith?

Two positions are apparently developing: one suggests that diversity will weaken the Christian creed, code and cult — it will confuse things and make us syncretistic; the other recognizes the difficulty of convergence but acknowledges the advantage of diversity because it contributes to a richer texture of the lived faith. So what happens when the "pagans" and the Christians sit down at table? Do we follow the adage "Don't feed pearls to swine"? or the words "Come to me all who labor and are heavy burdened, and I will give you rest"? What happens when we struggle with images that are foreign to our own cultural understanding and religious tradition? Can we endure the tension that the dialogue entails?

Obviously the steps we take in this new form of ecumenism will be testing a whole arena of dialogue. Can we yield the presidency of the table in spite of our differences, as Anecitus did for Polycarp? Can we convene with a world that is non-Christian, for the sake of the faith and the life of the world?

If we are looking for models, I believe the starting place is with the stories of the people themselves. They will tell us where the points of convergence lie, focusing on issues that are central to their life. From there, a pattern of hospitality and true communion develops. I will give you several instances in which the cooperation between the traditional faiths and the Christian people yielded the fruit of mutual respect. That respect is grounded in the courage to yield to the prayer of the other cultures.

Memorial of Wounded Knee

On December 29, 1890, there was a military riot in South Dakota that left 120 wounded men and 230 women and children dying in the bitter cold of a snow-storm. It began when the Seventh U.S. Cavalry invited Chief Sitanka (Big Foot) of the Minniconjou, the Cheyenne River Sioux, to live near the fort for protection and food. The winter was beginning to set in, and Sitanka's band trekked 250 miles from Cherry Creek to Wounded Knee Creek and set up their tepees near the fort on December 27, where they surrendered. Once there, the cavalry realized that the Sioux had weapons and that their proximity to the fort was a threat. The military ordered that all weapons be turned in. They then made a search of the tepees and confiscated all cooking knives, axes and even tent staves. As the soldiers were going through the camp, a young deaf boy, Black Coyote, held his new Winchester high as a sign that the weapon was of great value to him but that he was surrendering it. Misinterpreting the gesture, the soldiers opened fire on the assembled people. The women, men and children fled for safety near the creek bank. The firing continued until only fifty people survived. That night the wounded and dead were loaded onto wagons to be taken to Pine Ridge, but a blizzard developed and the soldiers forced the survivors to stay in the wagons without blankets.

On the sixth day after Christmas the bodies of the dead were carried into the Episcopal Church at Pine Ridge with all the Christmas greenery and garlands and a banner across the pulpit that read: "Peace on earth, good will to men."

The outrage at this brutal massacre continues; the survivors' families retain the memories. To mark the 100th anniversary of the massacre, the Lakota people of our metropolitan community held a twenty-four-hour fast before a sa-cred fire that was lighted at the time the shooting began and extinguished when the last victim was found. During the fast Christians and traditional people alike gathered to remember and to mourn. We tied tobacco ties (prayers) for those who died; we sang traditional honor songs to the drum; we read the names of the dead from a list compiled in 1920 from the remembrances of the survivors. At the end of the fast we ate together, preparing first a spirit plate, a symbol of solidarity with the dead.

Black Elk, the spiritual leader of the Lakota nation, talked about the event in the early decades of this century:

> I did not know then how much was ended. When I look back now from the high hill of my old age, I can see the butchered women and children all along the crooked gulch as plain as when I saw them with younger eyes. And I can see that something else died there in the bloody mud and was buried in the blizzard. A people's dream died there.

The Mankato Execution

In December 26, 1863, President Lincoln, whose grandfather was killed by Indians, commuted the sentences of nearly 300 Dakota Indians charged with insurrection. In order to show the Indian people that such behavior was unacceptable, however, Lincoln had thirty-eight Indians hanged at Mankato, Minnesota, the largest single execution in United States history. The rebellion was instigated by Congress when it broke agreements for land purchase made with the Dakotas. Hoksila Duta, the Chief, had negotiated with the federal government over the purchase of the southern part of Minnesota. Treaties were signed agreeing to a fair price for tens of thousands of acres. After the agreement, however, Congress halved the payment without negotiation. A series of expanding claims by the government followed, thus reducing further the Indian land. At each step the Indian people were relocated farther south, until a strip only five miles wide remained near Saint Peter, Minnesota. Finally, the Congress incorporated even this strip, ordering the Indian people removed entirely from their hereditary land in Minnesota and sending them to a more arid location in the South Dakota territories. Hoksila Duta gathered a band of warriors to protest this injustice; in the ensuing battles, he and his band were captured. The execution of the thirty-eight took place the day after Christmas.

Many of the Indians climbed the scaffold holding hands and singing a Christian hymn, "Many and Great, O God are your works, Maker of earth and sky." When the spectators heard the song, sung in Dakota, they thought it was a war cry and, fearing a revolt, sped up the execution. The words of the hymn's last stanza are: "Grant now to us communion with you, O star-abiding one; come now to us and dwell with us; with you are found the gifts of life. Bless us with life that has no end, eternal life with you" *(Worship,* 3rd. ed., #503).

Following the execution, Hoksila Duta's corpse was dragged naked through the streets as people placed firecrackers into his body. Later his remains became part of a museum display; he was finally given burial within the past five

years, when his grandson sought court help to gain the body's release. Each year
traditional people and Christians gather for a sweat-lodge ceremony on December 26; thirty-eight rocks are placed in the sacred fire to remember the day of
execution.

Quincentennial covenants

In 1991 a consortium of various cultures gathered to discuss how to mark the
anniversary of Columbus. We came from Viet Nam, Cambodia, Japan and
America; the Americans were African Americans, European and Latin Americans, and indigenous peoples of our continent. For a year we talked about
reconciliation and forgiveness: How could we use this time as an opportunity
for cultures to live out a vision of the way society should be? We felt the need to
face each other and say: "We repent of the cultural imperialism that has marked
our humanity." One woman, a Cambodian, went back to Cambodia to confront
the Khmer Rouge who killed her family. In that meeting she forgave the soldiers
who had done this. After years of grief she wept, but so did the soldiers. During the year our group went to the Phat An Temple for a Buddhist ceremony
of repentance. We also gathered at a Dakota reservation to perform the Wiping
of Tears ceremony, where the pain that marks people's lives is swept from their
bodies by an eagle-feather fan and gathered into the center, placing all the grief
before God. That pain is then bundled in a tobacco tie and offered back to God.
At the end of the ceremony the group decided to send the cloth containing the
pain to Europe. It was brought by a delegation to a meeting of Moral Rearma-
ment in Cohe, Switzerland. When the story of our ceremony was told at the
conference, the participants representing the indigenous people of India asked
to take the cloth back to India with them because they too felt the need to add
to it their people's sorrow. After a ceremony in India, the cloth was cremated to
allow for new freedom.

In America, on the following Ash Wednesday, a group of European Christians responded to the Wiping of Tears with a ceremony of ashes and cleansing
water at an Indian reservation. Since then we have marked the Wiping of Tears
here in the midst of the urban community that has its own unique pain. This
year the cloth was presented to me. I am the keeper of the people's pain for the
next twelve months. It is the focus of my personal prayer, a trust that the Indian
people have placed on me.

Those are a few brief examples of how dialogue has developed among the
traditional faith of the Indian people and the Christians. It is a multicultural
dialogue, and we have yielded to each other to allow the power of the ceremony
to penetrate our hearts. Our Wiping of Tears committee, as it is now called,
has made a ten-year commitment to forgive each other the pain we have caused
and to acknowledge the history that has kept us apart. We will do this in a
ceremonial way that respects each other's religious belief. Who knows where we
will be at the end of this ten-year covenant?

42

Native American Liturgy

JOHN S. HASCALL

Religious ceremony and worship of the one God have always been the way of the people native to these islands called the Americas. Native Americans conceive of God as "the One who had no beginning and who created all that is." We have never sought to limit this "Great Spirit" in any way, and certainly not by adding to God our human limitations or the limits of gender. In our linguistic treatment of the concept of God, there is no limiting article. As native people, we know and experience God in our relationships with all things. We experience life and God's influence in all creation. God always has worked and always will work with all creation for the good of all.

Native religious ceremonies grew out of our relationships with God, our brothers and sisters and all creation. Native dances represent our relationships with the animals, the seasons and our own emotions relating to God, creation or each other; likewise, the objects we use in our sacred ceremonies come from the earth around us. The ceremonies themselves — feasts of the pueblo or village, the coming-out ceremony of the young girl reaching puberty, the vision quest of a young man coming into adult life, the killing of the first deer, the coming of each season, planting or harvesting, feasts of the elders, death, marriage, sickness and healing — are centered around the circle of life. The sacred circle teaches us that we are all related to one another; our lives are interdependent and shared: human, animal, vegetable and mineral. We are one creation as the God who created us is one, though called by many names. Among our many tribes God is "Spirit," "Power," "Creator," "Mystery"; yet it is one God who created this life and is personally involved in our relationships.

Native life is lived in 450 different tribes. I am Ojibwa (Chippewa); therefore, I speak as a Chippewa when I describe the way we celebrate our seasonal feasts. In the last ten years, I have been on the road visiting and praying with many of our tribes throughout this continent. I have experienced the ceremonies and celebrations of many different native cultures. Each time I pray with the

From *Liturgy: Central Symbols* 7, no. 1.

different tribes, I pray as an Ojibwa spiritual leader, and not as a Cheyenne, a Crow, a Pueblo, or other native American.

I mention this to point out the difficulty of trying to create a liturgical ceremony that is appropriate for every tribe. A ceremony must be sensitive to the needs and aspirations of individual tribes. The more particularity we express, the more we strengthen ourselves and those around us, thus creating a stronger community. In this article, I hope to treat the general background of our native American "liturgical" way of life.

Our way of prayer

We look to our elders to teach us the different ceremonies of our people. Our elders, in turn, learned the ceremonies from their elders. The prayers they spoke and the actions they performed are rituals passed down by oral tradition. Native prayer comes from the heart of the one who prays, each in his or her own way. Such prayer expresses the fullness of heart of all the grandmothers and grandfathers who have gone before us. Its content consists of all that the individual, village, season and occasion conjures in the person who is praying. Yet the person prays on behalf of all the people who have requested prayer. Communal prayer is not the custom for many of our tribes. Rather, our songs, often sung by one person or group of singers, draw on the riches of the centuries; they hand on the good and the suffering our people have endured throughout the ages.

The main instruments of song and prayer are the drum, the flute, the rattle, the voice itself. Among the northern tribes that I know best, there are many songs that express the people's petitions. Long teaching songs, of more recent origin, came from the missionaries who tried to teach us church doctrine and Bible stories in the form of song. Our native songs are basically words of praise. The drummers and singers chant their prayer to the creator on behalf of the people. The drum echoes the heartbeat of all creation. As we dance with the drum, we are united with creation and each other.

Among the different tribes I have visited, I have heard beautiful songs based on the chants of the people. I have heard the songs of the Crow tribe of Montana and experienced the dance and songs of the Pueblo people of the southwest. At a Pueblo feast, celebrated in union with a church feast, the people dance the traditional deer dance, the buffalo dance, the corn dance, the eagle dance or any other dance appropriate for the season or occasion. The drum, dance and song are central to our worship.

The water rite

All the symbols of our worship are natural gifts — like the gift of water. We begin many of our eucharistic celebrations with a water rite to remind us of our baptism and our life within the community. We seek to restore harmony in our relationships with God, each other and the world. Coming to the water for healing, we restore our relationships and renew the harmonious community into which we were baptized. For native people, water is the basis of life.

We learn the value of water when we fast three or four days on the mountain, in the forest or in some other sacred place. For many tribes this means we refrain from all water and food for four days. Our purpose in fasting is to create harmony in the world and within ourselves. As we pray in the fast, we pray that all people of the earth, all nations and cultures, may be strengthened. This has been the way of our people long before we heard or knew of other nations.

The opening rites of the eucharist can take many forms; a basic one used by many of our people is a prayer in the four directions, which we call the grandfathers, a name that comes from our great respect for our elders as teachers and people of prayer. Grandfather is also a name we give respectfully to God. In this rite we look to God as creator as we experience God's great love reflected in each of the four directions of creation.

Such a water rite, used by itself or as a preliminary to the eucharist, begins with the blessing of the water. After the blessing, a bowl of water is set in each of the four directions of the place at the ceremonial grounds. As each person approaches one of the four bowls, s/he prays for the people.

First, the water to the east is pointed in the direction of the sunrise, which represents newness of life and resurrection. As we approach the water in this direction we pray for the young people, the children, the unborn. We pray that the young may be protected from all harm and evil as they grow and that they may be healed from all hurts. The water is poured into our hands. We touch our eyes, ears, nose, mouth, all our senses and body with the blessed water; then we drink it. This ceremony strengthens and heals us spiritually, emotionally and physically. It reminds us of our baptism and our relationship with God, others and ourselves. Some of us pour water on mother earth, who gives us life in the gift of water. Likewise in the sweat lodge we pour water on the hot stones and pray that our people may be strong.

Second, we approach the bowl to the south. The southern direction reminds us of woman's beauty and her life-giving role. My people use the gift or medicine of cedar for this rite. Cedar, which is also used in blessing the water, is the medicine of the woman. The woman prepares the cedar by picking it at certain times of the year.

In the form of oil (pressed from the cedar berries), cedar is also used in healing ceremonies. As the south wind comes in the spring and throughout the summer, it brings new growth and life to the foods and medicines of our people. The woman gives life to our people and is thus highly respected. We pray for a deeper respect for woman in our lives, for the healing of woman and the healing of the world in respect of woman. Again to the south we strengthen ourselves, our five senses, and drink of the healing water for all people.

Third, we approach the bowl of water to the west. In the west we see the reflection of God's love for us. The thunderbirds bring water and new life to mother earth in rain and storm. This water is blessed with sage, the medicine of travel. When we drink it, we recall our journey in life and the relationships that have broken along the way. We constantly need to be strengthened and healed. In this direction we recall the eucharist and its meaning for our life as a native and Catholic people. The eucharist is our food, Jesus, who empowers us for life's journey. As we pray for healing, we recall the many ways that we need healing in the world. We remember the people who are drug- and alcohol-addicted or dependent, whose lives are broken or who suffer drought, famine, prejudice or discrimination; we remember all human suffering in the world, and we intercede for all the people. Again we bless ourselves and drink the water of healing.

Fourth and finally, to the north, the medicine of tobacco is used to bless the water. Tobacco, which is common to most tribes, is the medicine for prayer offerings to God. As we drink water to the north we thank God for all our medicines. We pray for the living elders and those who have passed on. We pray for their healing in mind, body and spirit. We pray that they may continue to teach and pray for us and that we may have a deeper respect for elders through-out the world. To the north we also pray for all spiritual leaders, all medicine people of all nations and cultures, that we may always walk in harmony. We pray that all may come to know God — and Jesus — as the center of all culture and life. We then pray for all Ways of prayer: the Midewiwin (Ojibwa), the Long House (Iroquois), the Sun Dance (Plains), the Kiva (Southwest) and the Native American Church (that is, the whole church). We pray in thanks-giving for mother earth and all of creation. Finally we give thanks to God for being God: Father, Son and Holy Spirit. We pray also for all we may have forgotten.

Alternative forms

The form of this water ritual varies from tribe to tribe. Tribes that do not have water use corn pollen. Or this rite may take the form of a "smudge" blessing, in which sweetgrass, greasewood, sage, cedar or tobacco is burned on hot coals. The smoke is brought to the people or fanned over them with an eagle feather or ceremonial fan. In the same way that the water is used in the water ceremony, the smoke is brought to us. We, in turn, "smudge" our senses and body.

The one who performs this blessing may differ from tribe to tribe. The ritual may be led by a spiritual leader, priest or deacon, medicine person or elder or by a governor or other person of prayer. In the tribal way of life people are chosen for specific roles in the tribe, such as blessing, teaching or performing different ceremonies.

In all these ways, the liturgy of native Americans mirrors the ways of our culture. In effect, as native Christians, our sacramental life must reflect our native ways so that we can grow to wholeness as a people of God to help build the body of Christ. As I go among the different tribes, I go to draw forth the

Christ who has always been with our people. My prayer is that we native Catholic people will continue to grow in greater harmony with our creator, with others, with the world and with ourselves through the many gifts we have been given as native people.

43

Black Worship in a Small Town

Melva Costen

Summer days in the piedmont section of South Carolina seemed extremely hot and humid during the '40s. Perhaps the Smoky Mountain chain just northwest of us blocked some of the breeze. Or perhaps it was the excitement of those summer months when family and extended family gatherings were frequent. Year-round communal involvement was an undergirding and solidifying factor in the life of the Blacks in our small town nicknamed "Holy City," but the summer gatherings were extended in very special ways.

Our town's real name was Due West, South Carolina. For many years it did not even appear on the map. This never really mattered since anyone going there already knew how to get there. Others merely stumbled upon the sleepy little town. If they qualified racially — that is, if they were white — they might stay long enough to finish Erskine College and Seminary. Most visitors came only to see relatives or to seek directions to Abbeville (the closest town listed on the map). Then they left. The small black population exited by rite of passage as teenagers en route to secondary boarding schools and colleges or to find jobs in the north. A few returned to work as teachers and otherwise help "lift up" the community.

No one is exactly sure how the town acquired the name "Holy City." According to the oral tradition, the people were particularly concerned that the Lord's day be celebrated in appropriate solemnity. They demanded, therefore, that the Southern Railroad line be rerouted and its tracks removed. Even the animals of Due West seemed to refrain from normal sound production on Sunday: no crowing roosters, cackling hens or mooing cows!

Baptism day

This particular Sunday in June was the day for baptism in two of the four black churches in the town. The occasion called for an extended celebration.

From *Liturgy: The Church and Culture* 6, no. 1.

300

The Presbyterians started promptly at 11:00 a.m., with the crowd of extended family members already in place by 10:45. Even with all the windows opened and hand-fans from the local funeral home fluttering, there was only a slight breeze in the church. Like the womb of the mothers from which the two infant baptismal candidates had emerged, the waiting church was pregnant with spirit and excitement, ready to embrace and nurture the ever-growing young membership.

Few of the faces were unfamiliar to us children, even though many of those present belonged to other denominations in the community. Cousins and aunts and uncles had come all the way from New York, Detroit and Chicago. Families drove in from miles around to participate in this momentous event; they stayed until the benediction, then drove more miles to attend worship services in their own churches. In fact, most of those in attendance at the morning baptisms continued on to the afternoon baptismal service at the local Baptist church, and then to the evening service with the African Methodist Episcopal (AME) congregation.

The morning baptismal candidates were baptized at the font. The afternoon candidates would be believers, old enough to make their own profession of faith; they would be immersed in the creek. All were related either by blood, marriage or communal adoption, and all belonged to the beloved community. Everyone was concerned to be present, to participate, support and subsequently to nurture the newly baptized members of Christ's body. No one was concerned that the theology of baptism differed among the particular denominations.

The community as a whole took seriously its commitment to support each member of the body, not only on Sunday but throughout the week for the rest of their lives. There were no lines of demarcation between secular and sacred, between Sunday and Monday, for a people who had been relegated to the margin of society even in their "Holy City." The black community experienced diversity rather than difference, wholeness rather than division, support rather than separation. They lived in a special kind of love-flow initiated by God in Jesus Christ.

This was our introduction to *leitourgia* — liturgy, the work and service of the people. Of course, no one identified our communal action by this Greek term, and today we would probably call it *harambee,* a Swahili term that means "working or pulling together." But in those days, there was no need to describe it; we just lived as a matter of fact in extended communal and familial relationships.

A look at this day of baptism in a small black southern community helps focus the liturgical experience of an Afro-American people. We had the experience long before we were aware of the words *leitourgia* and *oikomene,* liturgy and ecumenism. Similarly, the younger members of the community were not aware of the close similarity of these experiences with those of our African ancestors. Like the Africans, we lived without modern conveniences that might have put us in touch with the broader world community and, like them, we came to know brokenness and bloodshed as a means of bonded love.

The water of freedom

From a child's-eye view, the children outnumbered the adults that morning in the Presbyterian church. It would have been impossible to exclude children from worship in black communities. African people experience children as vital and viable members of the community. They are not only expected to be there but to be well behaved in the "special presence" of the Almighty.

Images of water, new life, drowning and new birth flowed from the minister's well-prepared sermon. The children were not clear about the "convenient" (actually "prevenient") grace that had already been given the infants. The adults seemed to understand, for they all responded with "Amen." There were no printed bulletins available, yet everyone knew exactly what to do to move the families toward the font. There were scripture readings, prayers, much singing and a sermon by the visiting minister — the same preacher had baptized my mother, me and many others among those gathered. He was like the African *griot*, a person especially gifted in "telling the story" and recalling for the community the history of Blacks from Africa to America. His words were exciting and meaningful even for the children:

> We recall on this day with the Hebrew children their passage through the waters of the sea. And before them... can't you just see Noah as he looked out his narrow window at the blazing sun reflecting on the waters that covered the earth? What a sight it must have been! Like at creation, water everywhere.... I can hear the sounds of our people as they sang about the deep river and how they longed to cross over into campground — new life for an enslaved people!

Amidst the fervent "Amens" of the people, the minister connected these early experiences with contemporary events:

> I can hear the cries of our parents and grandparents as they prayed for rain to quench the thirst of the dry land on which we walk everyday.... Can't you see Elder Jones as he walked down to the spring this morning to get the water for this baptism — the water we drink and the water through which we pass?

In the tradition of the community, preachers made biblical imagery meaningful and powerful by connecting it with the history of the black people past and present. The minister, a college and seminary graduate, combined academic education with the reality of these particular people, helping to affirm their "somebodiness."

The water symbolism made a particular impression on me that June morning. The elder brought the clear, fresh water into the sanctuary in a pail, then carefully poured it into the improvised font so that it splashed and resounded over the small sanctuary. As the pouring continued, the minister led the congregation in singing "Take me to the water, take me to the water... to be baptized." The parents of the infants brought them forward, followed by grandparents and godparents. With the increasing momentum of the singing, a few siblings began to cry in a desire to join their parents at the font. As the crying and singing ceased, silence prevailed. All eyes and ears focused forward as the minister asked a lot of questions. There were responses of "I do" and congregational jubilation as one infant was startled and awakened.

Then the minister asked the congregation to stand, and he reminded us all of our joint responsibility for the Christian nurture of the infants: our new relations. He spoke especially to the children. Pretty soon we would have to hold these little ones' hands and walk with them down the dusty path to the church. We were bigger, so we would protect them from danger. We had to help them "grow up." There were so many things they could not do, especially in town. If a child got caught drinking from the wrong water fountain, he would be whipped; if a child used the wrong (but cleaner) rest room, she would get a week of punishment at home. And a child would be whipped for walking alone near the woods, for people sometimes disappeared — we heard they were lynched in some places. Just as we had been carefully nurtured by the community, we were big enough now to help these babies grow up, not only to be good Christians but to stay alive.

The sound of the water splashing as it was sprinkled over the babies' heads brought us back into the reality of the moment: "In the name of the Father, and of the Son, and of the Holy Ghost..." The people sang and clapped to the rhythm of "Amen, amen" as the families returned to their seats.

Community of life

Since there were other baptisms scheduled later that day, the community agreed to start the communal meal on the grounds of the Baptist church. This facilitated preparations for afternoon worship and baptism at the church near the creek. The final service for the day would be held in the evening at the AME church, with the entire community continuing in worship.

The meal was not a traditional Lord's Supper celebration, but a "table" gathering much like the *palava* in African traditions. Everyone brought covered dishes and baskets of food with plenty of lemonade. Certain teen-aged children were designated to fan the flies and gnats. There were games and songs led by young and old in turn, and time for the elders to share their stories in historical sequence as they had for generations in Africa. This was the time to hear and transmit our history and culture, the stories that were already told in every home. New people in the community shared these and their own stories. All the adults present handed around the newly baptized infants and bestowed special blessings on them. Religious leaders in the community were acknowledged, dates for subsequent meetings were identified, and plans for the August revivals were announced.

In the afternoon songs from the spiritual tradition were recalled, reshaped and taught in the light of contemporary events. No one needed books for this portion of the day, since even the children learned all songs by heart. "Kum Ba Yah" and "Ev'ry time I Feel the Spirit" signaled the call to worship for the afternoon

Baptist service. In the lively spirit of black Baptists, a devotional and testimo-
nial period was first in the order of service. The preacher preached a lengthy
sermon with the rhythm of the "call and response involvement" providing the
momentum for shouting and holy dancing. After a prayer for the candidates for
baptism, the church sang its way to the nearby creek, led by all the ministers.

Ten candidates for baptism, attired in white, stood nervously by the creek.
The minister, assisted by the deacon, asked questions of the candidates and immersed them in the water "In the name of the Father, the Son, and the Holy
Ghost" — the same words used in all the churches. Three of the baptizands were
my schoolmates, so we all rushed over to welcome them after they were dried
and attired in new white outfits. At one point there was shouting among the
congregation, triggered, it seems, by the rejoicing of one of the candidates. It
was as if we had all been baptized in death, burial and new resurrection. Hand
in hand with the newly baptized, we walked or ran to the AME church for
evening service.

Natural ecumenism

With the exception of communicant classes and Sunday school where we
learned the doctrine of the church in catechism and creed, we received little explanation about the meaning of worship. Somehow the entire community knew
without instruction. The celebration of the Lord's Supper took place at least
monthly on the same day in all the different denominations, so this time was
shared only if one visited away from one's own church, which was a rarity.

In a town this small, AMEs, Baptists, Pentecostals and Presbyterians never
asked a lot of questions about theology and methodology. We lived out our
baptisms as a community, bound together by the love of God and each other.
With frequent marriages across denominational lines, there was a lot of merging
and blending of worship styles. The most observable effect was the freedom
that allowed Presbyterians to respond aloud to the preacher and shout if the
Spirit so dictated, just like the Methodists, Baptists and Pentecostals. Few of us
realized that Presbyterians all over the world did not become so involved; none
of us really cared.

Modes of worship in black congregations in small communities most often reflect communal rather than denominational distinctions. A denominational
ethos may be evident, but there is usually a unifying link, a racial bond, a constant reminder of the uniqueness of this particular people living as a marginal
portion of the larger society. The connecting link is an expression of the African
culture operative in a new environment. It is, after all, out of the African familial
understanding that the framework for Afro-American Christianity developed.
Joseph Washington's observation applies to this and other small towns:

> Born in slavery, weaned in segregation and reared in discrimination, the religion of
> the Negro [sic] folk was chosen to bear the roles of protest and relief. Thus the

uniqueness of black religion is the racial bond which seeks to risk its life for the elusive but ultimate goal of freedom and equality by means of protest and action.[1]

Many years removed from the early days of slavery, Blacks in southern towns did not dwell on the injustices of segregation and oppression; instead, they took the more positive approach of community bonding. Black Presbyterians, for instance, although faithful to a larger institution based on a reformed understanding, expressed their adherence to this understanding in terms of the local communal context. Their worship was contextualized rather than denominationalized. Although the order of worship contained the appropriate reform elements and the minister was college and seminary educated, the manner and mode of black Presbyterian worship continued to reflect local demographics, historical lifestyles and the experience of marginality.[2]

In addition to these communal days of baptism, the denominations in Due West worshiped together during the traditional August revivals. The first week was led by the Presbyterians, the second by the Pentecostals, the third by the Baptists and the last two weeks, most often, by the AMEs. August days were spent at work, but August nights were for the community. People from the community who had moved north or who were away earning extra money for college returned for the homecoming activities that preceded each week of revival. The entire community participated in all the events. It was especially important to welcome relatives home and to greet new children and other new members of the family.

At one special gathering, everyone brought baskets of fresh vegetables to one of the churchyards and spread them out, along with clothes and housewares. After a meal of roasted meats, marshmallows and freshly prepared salads and desserts, everybody sang. At dusk one of the religious leaders began the song "Steal Away," and as we sang, each family gathered vegetables and other items from the tables before "stealing away" into the night. What great joy this mutual sharing created in every home. Here was a significant way to understand *leitourgia* and ecumenism as true koinonia and diakonia!

In spirit and truth

The focus of black worship in the early days was praise and glory to almighty God, and the people's response was their growth in the spirit and in the knowledge of God. The nurturing element of the liturgy included Sunday school, youth and adult organizations, and especially the public schools. Teachers and other community leaders took their responsibilities seriously as part of their Christian commitment. In these small towns, most of the teachers, even those in Sunday school, were "normal school" or college graduates.

The strong emphasis on education began in the home and was later continued by missionaries from the north. The older members of the community remember the influx of Presbyterian missionaries in the latter part of the nineteenth century. They first held classes in the church sanctuary, to teach all ages the "three Rs."

In educational activity as in life, the community maintained its African roots. Without written records to document dates, the older people remembered and orally recited the important events in the community's life. They even recalled all the names of the schoolteachers, in proper sequence.

I remember an elder telling us about the first schoolhouse, which was built "just before the big rain." Wells in the community had begun to dry up and farmlands were parched, so the "big rain" was a visible sign of hope. After the rain people gathered in the new school building — the only space large enough to accommodate the entire community — with their McGuffey Readers and Bibles. They spent their first day of "school" praying in praise and gratitude for the refreshing and nourishing rain.

Throughout my childhood, public school was unashamedly an extended expression of the liturgy. In many instances, classroom teachers were also Sunday school teachers and youth leaders, so the Christian mode of teaching continued. Since there was only one school, this was an opportunity for interdenominational interaction. We often shared news of Sunday services, the preacher's message and the "height of the Spirit" in school.

Each day began with an assembly of the entire school enthusiastically singing the Negro National Anthem, "Lift Ev'ry Voice and Sing" by James Weldon Johnson. The principal, affectionately known as "Prof," led the singing from a piano. We learned at least one other hymn each week, memorizing all the words. As the secular and sacred were seen as one entity, school singing was a continuation of the liturgy of the community in prayer, praise, song and interpretation. This, after all, was what we had all agreed on at each baptism.

Academic studies from grade one through high school were combined with spiritual formation and growth. Just as our lives and religion embraced each other during the Sunday liturgy (for example, in the mode of delivery and the response of the people in celebration and dance), so our "day school" provided a liturgical environment. From Monday through Friday, the "hermeneutical principle" was continually applied as scripture was lived out in a new context.

Lift up your heads

At family meals and later at family prayer, the trinitarian dimension of communal nurture was evident. First, you are God's child, sent through the mother and father; the goodness of God should be present in all that you do. Next, you are part of the beloved community, therefore your behavior is not only your own but a reflection of your whole group — especially of your immediate family; and, finally, you are an individual who should always "lift up your head" and be the best possible person.

Each of these three dimensions is a characteristic mark of Christian character, but they are also basic to African character and tradition. They emphasize the importance of the community to the individual and vice versa. An individual is nothing without the community, which includes both the living and the "living dead," with God at the center of the entire family. The often-repeated adage from the African traditions holds true: "I am because you are; you are because I am; we are nothing without each other."

Participation in plays, operettas, oratorical contests, creative writing contests and piano recitals always had this focus: "Lift up your heads, and the community will also be lifted closer to God." Instead of having to write over and over, "I will not throw spitballs," the children of this community wrote: "I am somebody and I will lift up my head." The nurturing adults of this community knew that the punishable act was most often a denial of the appropriate opinion of oneself.

All students were encouraged to look forward to college with an acknowledgement of their need to help nurture others. With many children living with their grandparents, there was a special commitment to immediate cousins and siblings. Education was revered as the way to overcome oppression and marginality. One could not attain this alone but only with the support of the entire community.

Liturgy and politics

In Afro-American communities, politics, like education, is part of the liturgical continuum. The emergence and continuation of black denominations and black congregations are major indications of a "politicum sacramentum." Blacks easily appropriate the histories of the independent black church movement, from the first black congregation on record, a Baptist church organized in 1758 in Mecklenburg, Virginia, to and beyond the historic actions of Richard Allen and Absolom Jones in 1787.[3] Before officially organizing independent churches and separate congregations for Blacks in other denominations, Allen and Jones established the Free African Society. The major objective of this and other models was to provide not only for religious needs but for social services, mutual aid and solidarity among peoples of African descent in America. Unlike other ethnic groups coming to America and establishing immigrant organizations, the Free African Societies added out of necessity "the protest and resistance against prejudice" which they faced in the new world.

Some of the unrecorded liturgical experiences of life have depth and meaning as well as political overtones. In addition to their baptismal names, children were often given a "working-life" name when they were old enough to understand its meaning. The names assigned in this small town were names of black women and men who had made or were making significant contributions to the "extended family" of all Blacks. Persons with the leadership of Nat Turner and Denmark Vesey were still needed to avert the dangers of new forms of slavery. During school assemblies, students were encouraged to "lift up their heads" as they received the names of Harriet Tubman, Mordecai Johnson, Marian Anderson, Benjamin Mays, Lucy Laney, Charles Drew, George Washington Carver and others. The life story of each famous person was equally well known not only by the assigned "bearer" but by the whole community as well. The community, then, assumed the responsibility of helping the name bearer work toward similar levels of fulfillment.

My assigned name was Mary MacLeod Bethune. She had been born nearby in South Carolina and became an educator who also established a school (Bethune-Cookman College, Daytona Beach, Florida). With this assignment, the community pointed me toward a career in education. Years later this encouragement reached a peak when I met the real Mary Bethune face to face on the campus founded by her.

The worship environment provided an arena for persons in the community to become political leaders both within local and national church structures and in the community. From the early days of protest, Blacks recognized their lack of access to positions of power within the structure of the larger Christian community. Even where Blacks outnumbered others in the total membership, they often had fewer opportunities to preach and hold office. In independent churches and small congregations within larger structures, positions of leadership were more readily available. Women are a large percentage of church membership, yet they have been denied certain positions of power throughout history. Many small communities, however, have included women in positions of strong leadership.

Life in black communities, while not as church-centered as in previous years, flows holistically as a religious phenomenon. In the days of the civil rights movement the end-of-service benediction was often followed by an opening prayer announcing the beginning of the political rally and NAACP meeting; the congregation simply remained in its place. Under the leadership of Martin Luther King, Jr., demonstrations began with prayer and were permeated with song. The liturgy continued. Ecumenism was not so much discussed as it was acted out in experience. Such is the meaning of liturgy in action.

Notes

1. Joseph R. Washington, Jr., *Black Religion* (Boston: Beacon Press, 1964), 33.
2. Melva Wilson Costen, "A Study of Worship and Music Styles in Black Presbyterian Congregations," conducted at the Interdenominational Theological Center, 1980–82.
3. Gayraud S. Wilmore, *Black Religion and Black Radicalism*, 2nd ed. (Maryknoll, N.Y.: Orbis Books, 1983). This is an excellent and concise interpretation of the religious history of the Afro-American people; see especially chapter 4, "The Black Freedom Church Movement," 74–98.

44

Hispanic Liturgy as Prophecy

Dominga M. Zapata

Liturgy in the abstract does not exist, and yet it is "our life, our very spirit," as Cardinal Bernardin once wrote in a pastoral letter:

> When we let the liturgy shape us ... then we shall find what it is "to put on Christ." [But] ... participation in liturgy does not exhaust our duties as Christians. We shall be judged for attending to justice and giving witness to the truth, for hungry people fed and prisoners visited. Liturgy itself does not do these things. Yet good liturgy makes us a people whose hearts are set on such deeds.[1]

Nevertheless, Christians often act as if liturgy could be separated from life. We find the application of general and abstract definitions, and rubrics to any and all pastoral situations a more comfortable task than creating new, lively expressions. As liturgy drifts away from life, it also ceases to bear the fruit of concrete acts of charity and justice. Inculturation challenges this kind of pastoral practice, for it demands that liturgy rediscover the sources of its nourishment in the actual life experience of Christians. In the United States today, Hispanics place this challenge before the larger church in a special way, innately refusing to let Christian life and religious expression drift too far apart. If the church does not listen to their prophetic voice, Hispanics will continue to drift away from liturgy and even from the church.

Inculturation and evangelization

All the recent documents of the Roman church speak of the interrelationship between culture and the mission of the church. The God proclaimed and worshiped by the church is a God present and active in history, in the human situation. Only in the context of a particular time and place is it possible to speak of salvation. It is necessary, therefore, to understand the meaning of inculturation in its relation to the church's central mission of evangelization.

From *Liturgy: The Church and Culture* 6, no. 1.

Inculturation is the incarnation of Christian life and of the Christian message in a particular cultural context in such a way that this experience not only finds expression through elements proper to the culture in question but becomes a principle that animates, directs and unifies the culture, transforming it and remaking it so as to bring about a new creation.

The church continues the mission of Christ through the evangelization of all cultures. The church recognizes the seeds of Christ's presence in every culture as well as the need to enrich it through the message of the gospel. History may show how the effectiveness of the church's mission was limited by imposing a cultural expression on all and by not recognizing the seeds already present in each culture.

Vatican II opened new horizons for the church to be present as evangelizer as well as being evangelized in every culture. Our God is a God always in relationship with the life of the people. The culture of a people becomes the "locus" through which they live their faith in an incarnated God. "He became like unto us in all things, except sin."[2]

Evangelization, then, takes place in the heart of culture. The missionaries who came from Spain to Latin America brought the Christian faith to a people who already had a deeply religious culture. Some missionaries made efforts to include existing cultural expressions in Christian practice, but in most cases either church or people refused them.

This initial failure of dialogue between the existing culture and the new faith may have contributed to the syncretism present to this day in Hispanic Catholicism. Since culture and religion were inseparable in the life of the people, they found ways to unite them apart from official sanction. The fruits of this union are evident in the words of the Hispanic bishops of the United States: "Hispanic Catholicism is an outstanding example of how the Gospel can permeate a culture to its very roots."[3]

Thus inculturation has always been part of the religious history of the Hispanics. Both indigenous religion and African religion mark this history. In our pastoral work with Hispanics, this double cultural dimension must not be ignored. While our common heritage now is Catholicism, the expression of this heritage is not homogeneous. Hispanics with a *mestizaje* of indigenous Native Americans and Spaniards do not hold the same core religious expressions as those of a *mestizaje* of Africans and Spaniards. The root mystery of the first is creation, while the root mystery of the second is movement. This diversity, however, is not a threat to unity. Hispanic culture is inclusive; it negates neither the African nor the Native American reality; rather, the Hispanic culture is both, together in complementarity.

The *convivencia* of Hispanics as a *pueblo* in the United States also provides for an expansion of the core religious expressions. Those who have ministered in a mixed Hispanic community know the capacity of such communities to move from the mystery found in creation to the mystery found in movement as they celebrate religious festivals.

The relationship between inculturation and evangelization can also present pastoral challenges. It can create a fusion of culture and religion. The lack of adequate religious formation may prevent the people from seeing the difference between cultural religious practices such as spiritism and practices based on the gospel. When symbols such as holy water and candles are taken from the official liturgy of the church and used in popular religious practice, they obtain different meanings by the context in which they are used. Though they always retain a sacred significance, distortions may become established.

Popular religion

For the great majority of Hispanics, direct evangelization takes place solely through liturgical gatherings. Thus the topic of inculturation in the liturgy has great pastoral relevance. Yet as long as Hispanics do not experience liturgical celebrations as expressions of their life and culture, they will participate in them only from deep tradition or obligation. At the same time, they will continue to celebrate their lively faith through popular religiosity.

Unfortunately, many liturgical celebrations in Hispanic communities seem to reflect the fulfillment of prescribed rubrics more than they manifest and touch the life of the people now. Popular religiosity, on the other hand, draws life from the concrete situation of the people. It provides for the expression of real feelings, such as powerlessness in the face of a crisis or the willingness to sacrifice anything for the life of a loved one. People seem to know what saint to go to, what ritual to use, how to reach out to other members of the community for spiritual help; at crisis moments, the Hispanic is able to reach out to God in a culturally understood form.

To sum up, inculturation is alive in popular religiosity, but the same cannot be said for the liturgical life of Hispanics. Guitars, *sarapes* and Spanish language are not enough. The core of inculturation is the mutuality between what is and what the community is called to be. The liturgy must not only celebrate what the community is living; it must also point to the source of the community's hope and meaning.

The need for community

To get at the basic issues for Hispanic liturgy we must consider: Why do Hispanics come to liturgy? What events or feelings do they need to celebrate? These questions probe the motive and essential content of liturgy.

A great number of Hispanics go to liturgy every week, I think, because of a deep social need to be with people of their own culture in an atmosphere familiar to them. The alienation experienced by the poor, the refugee, the undocumented and the immigrant makes the social need even stronger. Few Hispanics consciously think of the Sunday liturgy as an obligation. People travel from one end of the city to the other to celebrate where they feel most at home.

They need to celebrate a sense of belonging, community, identity and life. For most, the Sunday celebration is the lift and the strength to live the rest of the week with some sense of meaning and without being absorbed by alienation. This is what Hispanics seek from the church. Thus they bring a great gift for the making of a truly liturgical celebration: their own deep desire and need to be there.

Ministers must find a way to transform this gift of the people into liturgical experience. The first requirement is that the Sunday liturgical celebration be inculturated with the concrete reality lived by the Hispanics. Ministers must not succumb to the impression that because Hispanics continue to attend mass in significant numbers, to baptize their children and to get married in the church, the primary motivating force for these religious activities is faith, pure and simple. Yet we must not fail to recognize the seed of faith that is present in this experience. We must discover to what extent the liturgy in itself is meant to celebrate the desire and need to be together and to find meaning in such gatherings.

Pastoral implications

Liturgy as such was not a theme of the third Encuentro (a national gathering of Hispanic clergy and lay leaders that organized for the purpose of implementing the National Hispanic Plan of the National Conference of Catholic Bishops). There are no direct references to liturgy in its pastoral implications and commitments, yet the essence of liturgy is strongly affirmed. Hispanics desire an evangelizing, missionary church that witnesses to the justice of the gospel through its life. They seek a church incarnated in the life they live day by day.

The church they seek would celebrate all liturgical events in the context of the people. Given all that has been discussed, there are definite pastoral steps to be taken. Ministers must learn that welcoming is as important a role as taking up the collection. Time to visit before and after must become an integral part of the celebration. Homilies marked by less scholarly exegesis and more interpretation of God's movements in life and the obstacles to these movements presented by society are a genuine need.

How can Hispanics experience a deeper response to their need for community through the liturgy? If we do not reach the core of the human experience in the celebration of faith, that experience may seek expression in other ways. Research indicates that Hispanics join various Protestant denominations because of the welcoming and homey atmosphere they find in small churches. Likewise, if membership in secular social clubs and activities can meet their social needs, then church participation may suffer.

The Constitution on the Sacred Liturgy (#10) defines the liturgy as the climax and source of all life and action in the church. Hispanics need to experience the liturgy as integrated with the rest of life. Because of the lack of ongoing evangelization, Hispanics may see the sacraments as entities in themselves. They marry sacramentally, baptize the baby, send the child to preparation classes for communion, confession and confirmation, but may not make connections between these rituals and the things that really concern them in daily life.

We need liturgies that precede and lead to a commitment in life. Inculturation in the liturgy is not limited to the already given elements of a culture, but it must also include the here and now situation. We cannot celebrate as if every Sunday is Easter when most of the people are living the reality of Good Friday. Homilies and songs must address the reality of oppression and the hope of liberation in relationship to the actual people in the congregation.

If liturgy is the life of the believing community, each community must be able to celebrate that life in the way it finds significant. Liturgical expressions must be both true to life and capable of transforming culture. They cannot simply follow the rubrics; liturgy must also include enough time to celebrate well, to touch the emotions and to be intuitive. Each local context challenges our pastoral practice to expand and modify itself in response to a unique life. Inculturation is the incarnation of faith, the realization of the reign of God in a living community.

A prophetic liturgy

The Latin American bishops at Medellín wrote, "The liturgical celebration crowns and implies a commitment to the human situation, to development and human promotion."[4] A truly enculturated liturgical celebration must embrace the totality of life, create social consciousness, denounce concrete sinful situations, and exhort the faithful to participate in the struggle for justice.

> Love for the poorest and least helped is the criterion for adoration of God, because of the right of the poor to participate with dignity in human existence. The danger of worship is evident when it collaborates in the construction of an unjust social power; when it justifies it and even sacralizes it.[5]

The situation of the poor demands a prophetic liturgy that is never satisfied with abstract ritual. The ritual of a prophetic liturgy comes from lived experience and sends the assembly forward in a commitment to transformation. Only such liturgy is pleasing to the Lord (Prov 21:3), for it makes the poor agents of their own history of salvation.

Thus does the liturgy become the fullness of the paschal mystery in the life of Hispanics. Christ in the liturgy becomes the voice interceding before God for the profound desires of the people. The social need to come together and struggle against oppression can be transformed into the sacramental experience of an encounter with the God of our salvation who gathers us in communion until Christ returns to bring us totally to God. When commitment is manifest beyond the ritual, the celebration has credibility in the community, and liturgy in itself becomes a liberating, transforming and evangelizing experience for the Hispanic.

Notes

1. Joseph Cardinal Bernardin, *Our Communion, Our Peace, Our Promise*, A Pastoral Letter on the Liturgy (Chicago: Liturgy Training Publications, 1984), 4–5.

2. *Studies in the International Apostolate of the Jesuits* 8 (June 1979): 2.

3. United States Roman Catholic Bishops' Pastoral Letter, *Hispanic Presence: Challenge and Commitment*, December 12, 1983 (Washington, D.C.: United States Catholic Conference, 1984), #5.

4. *The Church in the Present-Day Transformation of Latin America in the Light of the Council*, Medellín Conclusions (Bogota, Colombia: CELAM, 1971), #4.

5. Casiano Floristán, course notes, Hispanic Institute, Mundelein College, Chicago, 1979.

45

Wholeness and Holiness among the Campesinos

Richard Allen Bower

Christians know that the incarnation celebrates the connection between the sacred and the profane. But how do we, in simple terms, weave the life of faith into the day-to-day times and places of our lives? Most of us are aware of a separation between the spiritual and the material, and few know how to give expression to the weaving.

Recently during one of my weekly visits to Monte Claro, a rural community in the mountains near Arraijan, Panama, where I work among campesinos, I visited an older woman named Señora Mariana, who, like other women in this community, presides over an extended family of brothers, sons, daughters and their families, some grandchildren and a few temporary members of the household. Her husband died, and she is the glue that holds the family together, a role exercised with remarkable gentleness amid hardship, poverty and rebellious behavior. She is obviously respected and loved.

I arrived at Mariana's house a few minutes within the scheduled time. I have learned to be more relaxed about clock timing. Here in rural Panama there is another kind of time, a time more like the biblical *kairos* — a time when things are ready. It is a kind of within-an-hour-or-two-of-schedule time. On climbing the small hill to her palm-thatched house, I saw that almost the entire family, about ten people, were sitting and waiting. Apparently this was not to be a casual visit.

After a generous round of welcomes, the Señora told me how happy she was for my visit. "*¡Nunca nos ha visitado el Señor Cura!* The priest has never visited us." Glowing with pride, she also betrayed a bit of anxiety. Her older brother Pepito was often drunk in the afternoons, but today he blessed us with his presence and sobriety. "*Buenas tardes, hermano,*" I greeted him. "*¿Que tal?* How are you?" He shrugged his shoulders in a kind of greeting. "*Aquí,* Here, okay."

From *Liturgy: In Daily Life* 7, no. 3.

I went around the hardened-dirt patio greeting people, taking their arms in the local style. Children had been washed and dressed. Pepito was sober. Anna (about thirteen) stood at the edge, a shy and embarrassed teenager. An old man, who I learned later was another of Mariana's brothers, sat quietly alone. At first he didn't respond at all. Later, when I had penetrated the barrier of his deafness, he wouldn't stop talking.

Señora Mariana's house, a compound of small ranchos made of bamboo and palm branches, was rather neat and tidy. In one rancho people sleep. One is for cooking. The *sala* (living room) is the open space where we sat, with just enough roof to shield us from sun or rain. Chickens live in another one; and still other ranchos are for family members who need more privacy, or from whom the rest of the family, perhaps, want some distance.

Conversation began quickly, several people often talking at the same time. Personal stories were told: where they had come from, how long they had been in Monte Claro, and their current problems. I was struck by how ready this family was to talk. Usually very timid and reserved, near strangers were pouring out years of words and memories. I knew they were confiding in God or the church. As priest I was a symbol; simply as myself, I would not have elicited such a flow of confession. Almost everything was spoken. Family problems. Pregnancies (*"Juanita está embarazada, ¿No?"*). Feuds. The corn and rice just planted. The chicken project down the hill. Community politics. Illnesses. Children and education. Weather. The new Episcopal congregation in Monte Claro. My family. On and on.

The usual coffee was brought to me, a special kind grown on local hills. For me, black and without sugar, they had learned. No sugar? Strange padre! Later we were also served *chicha* or *chichemi,* a treat made of ground corn, water, powdered milk and some dark cane sugar.

The blessing

The formal gathering had broken down into a more relaxed conversation. We all loosened up a bit. When the time came to go, about two hours into the visit, I offered to bless the family. By then I knew exactly how much we needed blessing.

The Señora quickly disappeared and came back with a pan of water for me to bless. I thanked God for water, remembering how deeply and richly it touches our lives: water is for crops and food, for coffee and *chicha,* for cleansing and healing, for baptism and knowing God's love. Señora Mariana's family also needed protection from water: water swells the streams to dangerous proportions and brings seasons of disease, months of hard living for those who live on Panama's clay hillsides exposed to the storms. We prayed too for clear, drinkable safe water which this community has yet to obtain.

We tried to name the whole. We gave thanks for water and asked that it be our friend, not our foe. We blessed it so it would better remind us of God's presence and love, helping us to find God in what is given and taken away, in wet times and dry.

Mariana led me around her yard, rancho by rancho, place by place. I blessed and she sprinkled, until all that we had talked about during the last two hours was wet with her blessed water. I had meant to do a fairly limited "religious" thing in my prayer: to remind us that God had been with us in that patio and would stay near.

But she reminded me and the others that her entire thirsty world was God's arena. Just as our conversation had been catholic in scope, so her pan of holy water was sprinkled universally over her whole world. Dripping with holiness, this harsh and lovely world was blessed — the ugly with the beautiful, the gentle with the hostile, the fearful with the hopeful, beds, chickens, pots and pans, children, pregnant women, deaf old men, plans and discouragements, meanness and love were wet with her blessing, woven together now with a deeper recognition of God's presence and care. Nothing was left unbaptized that afternoon, nothing left outside the boundaries of God's interest. All the world was holy.

The search for wholeness

In naming the relationship between the sacred and the profane as one of struggle, I am pointing to the fragmentation that is so much a part of a pluralistic, post-Christian world, as we know it in the West. Its causes are legion and related to such things as the emergence of the subject-object controversies in postenlightenment philosophy and the alienation between labor, management, production and tools in the industrial and postindustrial economies. They have to do with the rise of individualism peculiar to the modern Western experience; with specializations and high technology in the workplace where our tools have lost their "conviviality," their capacity to be understood or fixed by those who use them. These fragmentations result from deep and abiding pluralisms in culture, politics and religion.

In many places there is no longer a clear, understandable connection between birth, family, labor, political life, religion, play, rites of passage and death. These radical experiences have been compartmentalized into a house divided, with many important rooms but few passageways connecting them. Many progressive, liberating movements of human culture in the past 200 years have also led to deeper divisions, to heightened fragmentation in the experience and understanding of our reality.

The "holy" has to do with seeing things in their harmony or wholeness. As people of faith we experience our lives and world in relation to God, the one who unifies and integrates life — "the one in whom we live and move and have our being." We do not put the holy into the mundane so much as we learn to wait and watch more carefully, discovering and participating in what is already there. But like a spinning planet in a solar system whose gravitational pull has lost its power, religion as we experience it is racing off to somewhere more and more disconnected from the rest of life, less and less able to integrate, to reveal meaning and value and the sense of awe and wonder in it all.

As Christians, though, we tell a different story — one about a creator God, the source and ground of all that is. If there is meaning, integration and value in the universe, it is because creation has God as its source. Christians speak of the presence of God woven into the fabric of life. The biblical God is not aloof or disinterested but engaged in creation, human life; we speak of this involvement in terms of passion and love, energies that long for unity and wholeness.

This belief in a creative, indwelling God is also rooted in an appreciation of creation's unknowability, unfathomability. God is knowable but transcends our full understanding. So too our universe can be known, but only as a reality soaked in mystery. At times when our clarity fails us, we can only stand before life and weep or praise, trusting it will all hold together because it rests in God. The world fills us with awe. Its meaning and coherence are not known objectively or logically but intuitively, in the way lovers find joy and wonder in a reality they trust but cannot explain.

I think my friend Señora Mariana has this intuition, an ability to grasp the holy in her life's fragmentedness. She knows it is all related and that each part of it participates in the same brokenness and redemption. So she sprinkles everything with the same water, gathering it together as her world of concern, as well as God's.

A sacramental vision

What then are we who do not live in Mariana's world to do? We must deal with a world more divided and less integrated, one that resists and is sometimes embarrassed by our attempts to bless it or to find blessing in it. How do we help one another to recognize and live a reality of wholeness, so that what happens on Sunday connects with the rest of the week and what happens during the week is renewed and integrated through our worship on the Lord's day?

The sacramental understanding of things provides a key to unlock some of the doors between our separated rooms. Sacramental signs, especially the traditional signs of baptism and eucharist, are meant to indicate the true nature of reality. We set apart or bless places, words, actions and material and call them "holy," not to drive a deeper wedge between the sacred and the profane but to ensure that amid life's loneliness and fragmentation, there are faithful reminders of its true integrity.

The bread and cup we bless on the altar remind us of what is or will be true about all bread and wine, all creation, all life and labor. Offered to God, these symbols become bearers of the life and presence of Jesus. In this bread and wine Christ's presence represents the integration and holiness that is promised for all reality. Through his redemptive love, "the earth shall be filled with the glory and presence of God as the waters cover the sea." The church, God's people set apart for holiness, is also a sacrament. We are not set apart to divide the human community but to bear witness to the truth of the whole of humanity. The church is an image of the world as it will be when it is healed and restored through God's love. Christians are not holy in contrast to others but only as faithful reminders of God's intent for all humankind. Our "being set apart" is vocational: to be salt, light and leaven in the tasteless darkness of all that is fragmented and broken.

Story, symbol and rhythm

Three aspects of human life make possible the integration of the whole: story, symbol and the rhythm of time, the heart of the language of faith, which helps us to discover and participate in what is holy. Each of these three energies can be threatened by the momentum and fragmentation of modern life. But it does no good to condemn modernity and long for some distant, simpler past. Our task is to rediscover holiness in, with and under the life given to us.

Story is one element that unifies the human experience. Christian faith is rooted in the shared narrative of the people. We are a community that experiences God's love and guidance, sometimes losing sight of its meaning but knowing again and again the renewal of grace and forgiveness. Families and cultures alienated from their stories are usually people lost and confused. Christians unclear about the sacred story are unclear about their own identity and purpose in history. Stories are unifying meaning-bearers, seeking to reveal the truth about God and the human community. They help us to feel less alone, "surrounded by a great cloud of witnesses." In the connections made between our story and the "old story," our lives of faith find integration and meaning.

The second element necessary to recover the holy in the world is renewed appreciation of symbols. If the story helps us not to be alone, symbols give us a community language. Symbols integrate life and connect meaning with meaning, experience with experience.

Some symbols are deep and almost timeless: water, light, darkness, wind, sacrifice, silence; others must be discovered in each age. Today especially we need adequate symbols to connect individual meaning and worth with the vastness and interdependence of the collective human family. Clan and nationalistic symbols no longer serve us very well. We also need symbols to help integrate the complex intricacies of modern technology with the quality of human life. What kinds of symbols can help us unite the two realities of "may" and "ought" in genetic research, for example? Modern technology far outstrips our sophistication as people capable of ethical choices. Presently we have few if any symbols or language to begin the necessary dialogue between the realms of science and technology and ethics and values.

The third element enabling the recognition of the holy in the profane concerns time and rhythm, elements necessary to the discovery of the "sacred" in life. Religion has always seen the need for ritual and prayer. Both require time and seasons as well as a kind of rhythm that helps us to see and experience life more profoundly in its variations. Modern life, however, offers protection from these experiences. We have so little time. And when it is there, as in times of sickness, we hardly know what to do with it. Even the ritual time of the Sunday assembly, when extended past an hour, is wearisome to many.

Modern life in developed urban settings protects us from the power of the usual rhythms — from light and dark, summer and winter, birth and death. We are often artificially sheltered from the immediacy and power of these natural rhythms by electricity, heat and air conditioning.

Discovering and living the sacred within the mundane require a different kind and value of time than we in our impatience and need to achieve can give ourselves. As in human love, though, so in human spirituality: patient, carefully cultivated times and rhythms are needed. We should try to recover extended time, "unproductive" time: time to let go and time to receive; time to be and time to do; time to listen and time to speak; time to wait and time to move on.

Mariana's lessons

In Monte Claro, Mariana taught me a number of things about faith, especially about finding holiness within life. Though she may not put it this way, she is accomplished in the language of love. She values and longs for unity in her life. She knows how important it is to remember, and in remembering, to share with those who will listen. She knows that what is impatient and hurried cannot serve her well. And especially in her life, harsh in poverty but rich in other ways, she knows the importance of attending to connections. Like one who meets her lover at the end of the day, she wants to know everything, wants to be part of everything. She wants all the world to matter to God as much as to herself. Simply, but not naively, she is committed to a God of wholeness.

Therefore Mariana is unafraid to look for God in the rain and mud, in the birth of grandchildren, in her brother's sickness, in the dangers of rural storms, in the struggles for justice in her small community, in loneliness and in her childlike delight in a starry night. She knows about sin and brokenness. She knows, too, the dream of a love stronger than death; a love holy, whole and boundless; a healing love richer and deeper than all her wounds. She trusts in God's love, for herself and her family, and finds God's presence in them all. And so she continues to sprinkle water all about.

46

A New Relationship: Guidelines for Intertraditional Worship

Susan J. White

Like other important trends in modern theology and practice, the religious en-terprise we call "ecumenism" has undergone significant change over the years. Though the history of that change has yet to be written in full,[1] our own twentieth-century experience testifies to the fact that shifts in the ecumeni-cal agenda have instigated new responses and approaches to the basic tasks of Christian unity and interfaith dialogue. For those of us who live in the world of the Decade of Evangelism, the world of the Malines Conversations of the 1920s seems alien and strange. And yet the sense of urgency remains, drawing us onward toward mutual understanding and tolerance.

For liturgists, who have often assumed leadership roles in the ecumenical movement, keeping abreast of current thinking in this area can be daunting. The progress of interdenominational and interfaith conversations is not always even and is often marked by roadblocks, detours and wrong turns along the way. The Anglican-Roman Catholic dialogue and the Orthodox-Lutheran dialogue, for example, move at different speeds, attend to different theological issues and arrive at different results; even in more comprehensive bodies such as the World Council of Churches (WCC), debates in the various areas of concern are difficult to monitor.

Yet despite the divergences and discontinuities, one liturgical presupposition has dominated the work of both the World Council of Churches and its re-gional and local counterparts; namely, that because of the strong links between liturgy and theology (often expressed by the Latin tag "lex orandi, lex credendi"), theological consensus and liturgical uniformity will always go together. In other

From *Liturgy: Practicing Ecumenism* 10, no. 1.

words, once we reach full agreement in doctrinal matters, a unity in worship forms will automatically follow. And conversely, by forging agreement on prayer forms, we are increasing the possibility of agreement on doctrinal matters.

For this reason, no rationale for the rites that have come to be called the "Lima liturgies" (1982)[2] was seen to be necessary, nor was one offered in the official texts. In 1979 the WCC subcommittee on Renewal and Congregational Life had recommended "the preparation of one or more liturgical structures that accord with the consensus already achieved." Following this, it was simply taken for granted that the rites that arose out of the Lima meeting three years later were the proper end of the ecumenical process: a common form of worship among those of diverse denominational allegiances. Indeed, the subtitle of the volume of historical essays that accompanied the liturgical texts was "Ecumenical Convergence in Celebration,"[3] and the rites themselves were described as "giving liturgical expression to ... emerging doctrinal agreement."

Taking differences seriously

But something of a sea change has begun to be felt in ecumenical circles in the years since Lima, and a revised model for ecumenical relations has begun to emerge. In preparations for the Decade of Evangelism and in the concomitant interest in the work of missiologists and those concerned with interfaith dialogue, ecumenists have begun to suggest that perhaps we had plunged too quickly into the search for doctrinal consensus, without having taken our religious differences seriously enough (or rejoiced in them fully enough) before doing so. A renewed appreciation of religious pluralism and an emphasis on such concepts as "identity," "relationship" and "encounter" are nourishing an ecumenical climate in which the search for consensus is seen only as one by-product of a mutual respect for and understanding of the various forms of religious expression. The idea that we must first try to enter as fully as possible into the experience of others and to engage with them in genuine dialogue has deep christological roots. As missiologist Kenneth Cracknell puts it:

> [What is needed is] a way of seeing that what [we] believe about Jesus opens doors rather than shuts them, pulls down barriers between people rather than builds them higher, and sets us free to enter into marvelous new relationships with just that sense of expectation and yet with just as much vulnerability as Jesus himself demonstrated when he walked the paths of Galilee and Samaria, and the streets of Jerusalem.[4]

Though Cracknell is speaking here of interfaith dialogue, the same principles of openness and vulnerability are being applied to conversations among Christian denominations as well. Out of this development has arisen a renewed demand on Christian ecumenists to explore the various forms of religious expression, not for the purpose of reaching a quick consensus but to ensure that the richness of God's revelation might be apprehended by large numbers of us.

Implications for liturgists

Apparently this shift in ecumenical sensibilities makes similar demands on those of us involved in liturgical ecumenism. Indeed, liturgists were among the first to see some of the difficulties inherent in the consensus model of ecumenism as we moved deeper into ecumenical relations. On one hand, we discovered that even where similarities already existed in worship practice, deep theological differences could — and often did — lie hidden underneath. (The Presbyterian understanding of the role of the words of institution in the Lord's Supper, for example, is vastly different from that of Roman Catholics, even though for the most part the actual words have been the same.) On the other hand, we also saw that even as Christians of various denominations began to move self-consciously from variety to unity in worship, those underlying theological, ideological and functional differences seemed not to diminish significantly. In other words, we found that the principle of "lex orandi, lex credendi" had its limitations in practice. And finally, complaints about the weaknesses of "lowest common denominator" worship were increasingly laid at the feet of liturgists.

Perceptive appreciation for liturgical diversity has various implications for liturgists involved in ecumenical relations. First, it implies an obligation to avoid embracing a false liturgical ecumenism based on a superficial assessment of similarities *and* differences in worship and doctrine. Second, and perhaps more importantly, it implies a willingness to enter into the worship of Christians and those of other faiths with openness and the vulnerability that that involves.[5]

A host of questions now arise. Can we put aside our own particular liturgical agenda long enough to worship with Christians of other denominations and people of other faiths without the element of prejudice? Can we allow the worship of others to speak to us freely and with an independent voice? Are we willing to look, listen and enter into a liturgical world different from our own with due respect for its integrity and value? And are we able to move into genuine dialogue, in which each liturgical voice is truly heard?

If the answer to those questions is yes, then the question that follows is equally important: "How do we go about the venture?" The following guidelines are offered as a partial answer to that question, a first step in the process of growing in our appreciation of liturgical pluralism.

These guidelines are not only intended for professional liturgists but for all Christians who assume the role of outsiders attempting to penetrate the mysteries of the worship of other believers. These guides are for the Baptist who is invited to the wedding or Bar Mitzvah of a friend in a synagogue, the Roman Catholic who attends the funeral of a relative in a United Methodist church, the Episcopalian present at the baptism of a Pentecostalist coworker. Because these suggestions must be adaptable to a variety of situations, they are quite general in approach but offer specific examples for the sake of clarity.

Eight steps toward understanding

1. *Learn to appreciate the world view of which worship is a part.* Entering into worship involves more than simply entering into a specific set of rites and ceremonies. It involves entering into a world bounded by scriptures (of various kinds) and by their interpretation; class, race and culture; theological and doctrinal presuppositions; and historically significant persons and places.

The first step, then, in appreciating a particular liturgical tradition is to gain some knowledge of its underlying structures. Know something about the Book of Mormon before attending services with members of the Church of Jesus Christ of Latter-Day Saints; find out about the hymns of Charles Wesley and discover the work of John Calvin before worshiping at United Methodist or Presbyterian services. The same regard needs to be shown for understanding the worship of other faith traditions; for example, read at least some of the Qur'an before you go to a mosque.

Cultural structures can be equally significant, if somewhat harder to pin down. What is the role of women in the community, and how is it reflected in worship? How does a history of poverty, family breakdown or unemployment affect the liturgical life of a local church? Are there worship elements that are rooted in the community's ethnic identity, and how central are they to the proclamation of the gospel? Who are the local heroes of the faith? The present-day guardians of tradition?

The rationale for asking questions of this kind rests on the traditional dictum: "The liturgy is not the texts." Years ago I worshiped in an Episcopal church, an affluent, white congregation in a suburb of Boston. We had a pastoral link with a Haitian congregation in the inner city and on occasion would gather for worship at one or the other of our churches. Surprisingly, even though we were both using *The Book of Common Prayer*, 1979, and uttering the same words (Rite II Eucharist), the liturgy was entirely different in the two places. That difference suggests what we refer to as liturgical "style" which, while hard to quantify, is one reality that renders texts and ceremonies meaningful. Indeed, the recognition that worship happens in an economic, social, historical, theological, racial and cultural context is indispensable to the work of liturgical ecumenism.

2. *Learn the names of things.* In liturgy as in other worlds, naming things correctly is a first step toward understanding things correctly. Our ability to enter into others' worship depends in large part on our ability to identify liturgical participants, objects and actions without making immediate analogical reference to our own liturgical experience. Accurate naming not only helps us to disengage from our liturgical presuppositions but also lowers our chances of offending those with whom we wish to pray.

The problem of accurate naming is further complicated by the fact that certain terms can be fluid even within denominations and faith traditions. (Some Episcopalians, for example, happily call their clergy "priests" and address them as "Father," while others strongly denounce this practice.)

Whatever the difficulties, taking the first steps toward understanding is crucial; perhaps the first step for worship observers is to presume that we do not know the names of anything! What are the leaders of the community called? What are the parts of the building called? What are the names of objects and actions, times and seasons? What does this or that image represent? How does the congregation refer to itself? We can easily underestimate the theological importance of these questions, but by doing so we underestimate the power of naming as a way to shape religious consciousness.

3. *Find an interpreter.* Anthropologists tell us that a "native informant" is one of their most valuable tools; so with liturgists and others engaging in ecumenical exploration. Often, in the first instance, a friend will invite you to join in his or her worship and will serve as an interpreter of the proceedings. Many communities are alert to the presence of newcomers and will go out of their way to ensure that someone join you for worship, should you come alone. In most cases, however, you can easily ask the person sitting next to you for advice and information. (Be sensitive, though, to that person's own need for space to pray.)

You might choose to make contact with the community before you attend a worship service by speaking with the leader and discovering something about the community's ethos and liturgical practice. In some cases that step is essential, since not all places of worship are open to outsiders. Temples of the Church of Jesus Christ of Latter-Day Saints (Mormons) and Exclusive Brethren congregations never admit nonbelievers, and many mosques and Hindu temples have special regulations for women who wish to attend. In any case, consult your informant before and after the service if possible; if you make a friend in this way, you will be furthering intertraditional relations in another way.[6]

4. *Learn to observe and listen.* Even with the help of a reliable informant, basic observation skills are indispensable to understanding the worship of other religious traditions. Learning to detach ourselves from our own theological and liturgical presuppositions is a necessary first step toward useful observation; asking the right questions is essential. If there is anything about "lex orandi, lex credendi" that is valid, it is that people *do* express their operative theology in and through their worship. By close observation and by attempting to abandon theological and liturgical bias, we can uncover perspectives on God and the world, human beings and the nature of the community, that might resist detection by other means.

Who plays what roles in the community? Where are the sacred spaces? Are certain objects or people treated as holy? Of how much value is silence? Where do people sit? Is worship a place where emotions — or only thoughts — can be expressed? Can one find the entrance to the building without being an "insider"? How do children worship? What do people wear? Some of these questions may seem extraneous to ordinary liturgical method, but in determining the liturgical ethos and theological ground of a tradition no detail is insignificant.

Keep in mind that objective observation does not necessarily exclude active participation in worship. Feel free to tap your feet to the music, pray spontaneously, clap your hands, receive communion if you can. This may be the only way to answer the most important questions of all: Why are people here? What does it feel like to be a member of this particular worshiping community?

5. *Abide by the conventions.* Some practices are simply part of religious "good manners," even though they may have deep historical or theological roots. These conventions may be most apparent when you enter a place of worship outside your own faith. A man attending an Orthodox or Conservative synagogue will be asked to wear a yarmulke (*kippah*) to cover his head as a sign of respect for God.[7] Before entering a mosque you will be expected to take off your shoes. At a Hindu festival meal you may be expected to eat with your right hand.

Here again, observation skills are essential, as is having a friendly interpreter. Does one kneel at communion or stand? Does one sit for prayer? Does the Peace involve a handshake, an embrace, or merely words exchanged responsively between leader and congregation? Does the congregation join in the "Amen" at the end of a prayer? Most of these conventions do not reflect significant religious or ritual meaning, but their observance will help to make you and those with whom you worship feel more comfortable.

6. *Respect the practices reserved for "insiders."* Clearly, there are some liturgical words, postures and observances that only faithful adherents to a religious tradition are admitted to. Among Christians, the eucharist is such an action, and different denominations mark the boundaries of participation in the breaking of bread in different ways. Sometimes a note in the service sheet will say, "all baptized Christians are welcome to join in the Lord's Supper," but often there is no way of telling whether the "table is fenced" (closed to outsiders) or not. Here again, having an informant or talking beforehand to a leader of the community is invaluable.

There are analogous practices in other religious traditions. Among Jews, for example, the wearing of the tallith (the prayer shawl) and the tefillin (the binding, containing the commandments, which is wrapped around the head and forearm) has ritual significance and is forbidden to outsiders. Some traditions ask that outsiders sit in specially designated sections of the building, thus exhibiting a measure of control over your behavior. Though "blending in" is more difficult in these circumstances, you may find that customs of this kind provide a certain sense of security.

7. *Expect surprises.* If you are paying close attention to the proceedings, surprises will be an inevitable part of worshiping with people of another religious tradition. You may find grape juice instead of wine as you approach the holy table; you may even see someone dressed as a clown standing in the pulpit. Parts of very familiar prayers may be omitted. (The doxological embolism on the Lord's Prayer can be a source of particular difficulty.) The service may go on for three hours; the homilist may preach for forty-five minutes or five. You may be asked to stand and introduce yourself, to give a testimony, to commit yourself to Jesus. If you can enter into worship taking nothing for granted, you will very likely be better able to enjoy the surprises rather than be alarmed by them.

In Pentecostal churches the element of surprise is almost built into the worship; the Holy Spirit moves where it will and the participants are wholly open to its guidance. Speaking in tongues, the simultaneous voicing of individuals' prayers, kneeling for prayer but facing the back of the pew, spontaneous outbreaking of praise, song or witness, all characterize Pentecostal worship. The same focus on the work of the Holy Spirit in worship is found in the Quaker Meeting, and while we usually think of silence as the normal mode of Quaker worship, some unexpected things can happen when the Spirit moves people to speak.

8. *Reflect theologically on your experience.* The problem of hermeneutics consists in taking what you have seen and heard, felt and understood, as you have worshiped in a tradition not your own and trying to make theological sense out of it. The enterprise is about asking specifically *theological* questions of the liturgy. Who is God for the people who worship in this way? How does this God operate? What does the action say about the nature of the human person and the created order, about revelation and salvation? In word, symbol and gesture — implicitly or explicitly — the cultic answers to these questions are being expressed.

Two words of caution are appropriate here, however. First, one should use a variety of liturgical data to approach a given theological question. You may ask, for example, "What is the role of the sacraments in this community of faith?" and you may then observe that communion is celebrated only once every three months as justification for the view that the sacraments are relatively insignificant. But then you overhear someone beside you saying, "There certainly is a good crowd today. Of course there always is when it's Communion Sunday." And suddenly you are aware of evidence of a deep reverence for the sacrament. You look at people's faces as they sit waiting for the bread and wine to be passed to them, and you hear the words of the hymn being sung; you realize that your interpretation of the infrequency of communion as a sign of disinterest is a sign of something else entirely. Once again, no detail is insignificant to the reading of theology out of the liturgical event.

A second *caveat* is also necessary. No single, local instance of a particular worship tradition gives enough evidence on which to base a theology of the whole tradition. You may have encountered an utterly eccentric example of a ritual form, or you may be attending worship on a day when particular theological motifs are emphasized. Even within a single tradition, there can be substantial liturgical and theological variety, which makes any overall judgment very risky. The differences between Anglo-Catholics and Protestant Episcopalians, Orthodox Jews and Reformed Jews, Nazarenes and United Methodists, can be enormous (often wider than the differences between denominations or traditions). Check out your perceptions and conclusions against other, nonliturgical sources and with people on the inside. Worship observation and theological reflection are only parts of a larger theological enterprise in which ecumenists, liturgists, sociologists, theologians, historians and the interpreters of sacred texts all play a part.

Rejoicing together in Christ's life

There is clearly a place for interdenominational worship in the world of ecumenical relations. Christians from various traditions will always want to find ways of rejoicing together in their common life in Christ, and Christians and those of other faiths will naturally seek times and occasions to express their mutual trust in a God who loves and redeems all humankind. But without an appreciation of the existing richness and diversity of liturgical prayer, we are likely to think that our own patch of ground is a liturgical Garden of Eden and that those outside simply need to be drawn in. The diversity of worship forms is eloquent testimony to the diversity of human responses to God, of human needs and aspirations, of ways of seeking the truth. And to understand and celebrate that diversity is a gift that liturgists and ecumenists can share with one another as we enter into new relationships and find new possibilities in acceptance and love.

Notes

1. See Ruth Rouse and Stephen Neill, *A History of the Ecumenical Movement, 1517–1948* (London: SPCK, 1954); and Norman Goodall, *The Ecumenical Movement* (New York: Oxford University Press, 1961).

2. The eucharistic liturgy was used first in Lima, Peru, at the plenary session of the Faith and Order Commission on January 15, 1982.

3. Max Thurian and Geoffrey Wainwright, eds., *Baptism and Eucharist: Ecumenical Convergence in Celebration* (Geneva: World Council of Churches, 1983).

4. Kenneth Cracknell, *Towards a New Relationship: Christians and People of Other Faith* (London: Epworth Press, 1986). I am indebted to this book for many insights in this regard and thank the author for permission to adapt the title for the present article.

5. A third and equally important obligation is placed on scholars of the history and theology of worship in terms of taking liturgical pluralism seriously and viewing it positively. This development is occurring in some quarters, notably in the recent book *Protestant Worship: Traditions in Transition* by J. F. White (Louisville: Westminster/John Knox Press, 1989).

6. One of the four principles of dialogue, derived from WCC material on interreligious issues, is the following: "Dialogue begins when people meet each other." Kenneth Cracknell expands on this in the work cited above, 114ff.

7. Helpful advice for the non-Jewish participant in a synagogue service can be found in Rabbi Hayim Halevy Donin, *To Pray as a Jew: A Guide to the Prayer Book and the Synagogue Service* (New York: Basic Books, 1980).

Biblical Index

General Index